Listening to the Logos

STUDIES IN RHETORIC/COMMUNICATION
Thomas W. Benson, Series Editor

LISTENING *to the* LOGOS

*Speech and the
Coming of Wisdom
in Ancient Greece*

CHRISTOPHER LYLE JOHNSTONE

THE UNIVERSITY OF SOUTH CAROLINA PRESS

© 2009 University of South Carolina

Published by the University of South Carolina Press
Columbia, South Carolina 29208

www.sc.edu/uscpress

Manufactured in the United States of America

18 17 16 15 14 13 12 11 10 09   10 9 8 7 6 5 4 3 2 1

Library of Congress Cataloging-in-Publication Data
Johnstone, Christopher Lyle, 1947–
  Listening to the logos : speech and the coming of wisdom in ancient
Greece / Christopher Lyle Johnstone.
      p. cm. — (Studies in rhetoric/communication)
  Includes bibliographical references and index.
  ISBN 978-1-57003-854-9 (cloth : alk. paper)
  1. Logos (Philosophy) 2. Philosophy, Ancient. 3. Rhetoric, Ancient. I. Title.
  B187.L6J635 2009
  180—dc22
                          2009021900

This book was printed on Glatfelter Natures, a recycled paper with 30 percent postconsumer
waste content.

To my maternal grandfather, Robert I. Plomert, who encouraged me to ask questions. He was the wisest person I ever knew in real life.

Man is conscious of a universal soul within or behind his individual life, wherein as in a firmament, the nature of Justice, Truth, Love, Freedom, arise and shine. This universal soul he calls Reason: it is not mine, or thine, or his, but we are its property. . . .
Ralph Waldo Emerson, "Nature"

Contents

Series Editor's Preface

In *Listening to the Logos: Speech and the Coming of Wisdom in Ancient Greece,* Christopher Lyle Johnstone explores how the ancient Greeks thought about the connections between wisdom and speech. He finds not a unified idea of how these connections can or should develop but a consistent inquiry into the issues of speech, language, dialogue, and argument on the one hand and the pursuit of wisdom on the other. Are these separate, perhaps even competing or incompatible, disciplines and practices, or interacting principles, or resources for one another?

Johnstone focuses on the Greek world in the period 620–322 B.C.E., when, according to his account, understandings of the world that had been grounded largely in myth were joined rapidly by new rational, naturalistic, and philosophical modes. The three centuries studied in this work saw the interacting development of what came to be called philosophy and rhetoric. Johnstone's book is not so much a history of early Greek philosophy or early Greek rhetoric as a synthetic account of the emerging and enduring sense of the connections between speech and wisdom from early Greek thought to the flowering of systematic rhetorical and philosophical thought.

Johnstone traces the complex relations among language and thought as variously understood in Homer, Hesiod, Heraclitus, Parmenides, Empedocles, Protagoras, Gorgias, Socrates, Plato, Isocrates, and Aristotle. At the same time, Johnstone draws widely on generations of scholarship that inform our understandings of these issues and thinkers.

Johnstone provides an appreciation of the achievements of fourth-century B.C.E. Greek rhetorical and philosophical thought without, however, losing his simultaneous appreciation of the earlier modes of thought and expression from which they emerged. *Listening to the Logos* is the fruit of one scholar-teacher's lifetime of study and reflection and a book to which scholars and students of rhetoric may turn for instruction and refreshment.

THOMAS W. BENSON

Acknowledgments

The author is grateful for permission to use previously published material from the following sources: "Sophistical Wisdom: *Politikê Aretê* and 'Logosophia,'" *Philosophy and Rhetoric* 39, no. 4 (2006): 265–89, © 2006 by the Pennsylvania State University, by permission of the Penn State University Press, University Park; "'Speech Is a Powerful Lord': Speech, Sound, and Enchantment in Greek Oratorical Performance," *Advances in the History of Rhetoric* 8 (2005): 1–20, © 2005 by the American Society for the History of Rhetoric, by permission of the American Society for the History of Rhetoric; "Eros, Logos, and Sophia in Plato: Philosophical Conversation, Spiritual Lovemaking, and Dialogic Ethics," in *Communication Ethics: Between Cosmopolitanism and Provinciality*, edited by Kathleen Glenister Roberts and Ronald C. Arnett (New York: Peter Lang, 2008), 155–86, © 2008 by Peter Lang Publishing, Inc., used by permission of Peter Lang Publishing.

Research for this book commenced during a 1986–87 sabbatical leave supported by the Pennsylvania State University and by Dennis Gouran, then head of the Department of Speech Communication. I am also grateful to the Classics Faculty Library at Cambridge University for granting me visiting-scholar status during the summer of 1986 and to the American School of Classical Studies at Athens, Greece, for my appointment as senior associate member in 1987 and again in 1991, 1997, 2002, and 2007. I am especially appreciative to Richard Leo Enos, Edward Schiappa, and Janet Atwill, all of whom read early versions of several chapters and provided encouraging and helpful feedback. Stephen Browne, Thomas Benson, and Michael Hogan provided useful guidance in the later stages of the project. Bill Rawlins read and provided very helpful comments about my discussion of Plato and engaged me in "loving conversation" about key ideas in it. I also want to acknowledge Michael Hyde, who once asked me, "Why study the Greeks?" In a way, this book is my answer to his question.

Over the years when I was studying the materials on which I draw here, I taught both graduate and undergraduate courses that focused on one or another set of these texts. Discussions and debates with the students in those courses were important sources of insight into the ideas I write about in this book. I cannot name them all here, but among those who deserve my acknowledgment and gratitude are George Elder, Pat Gehrke, Gina Ercolini, David Tell, and David Dzikowski. Thank you for taking these texts, questions, and ideas seriously. I am also indebted to two reviewers for the University of South Carolina Press, whose comments, suggestions, and encouraging responses to the manuscripts were instructive and affirming. The second reader in particular and James Denton, acquisitions editor at the press, provided valuable guidance and exhibited great patience. Finally, I owe more than words can ever express to my soul mate and life partner, Patty, for never losing faith in me and this project.

Prologue

Early in my career I published three essays (1980, 1981, 1983) that, in examining how ethical standards for communication might be devised, focus on connections between speech and wisdom—between oral expression, *sophia*, and *phronêsis*. In the first of these essays I conclude from a synthetic reading of the *Nicomachean Ethics*, the *Rhetoric*, and the *Politics* that Aristotle conceived rhetoric as an exercise of *phronêsis* or practical wisdom and of the latter as fundamentally rhetorical. Following a trajectory set by Aristotle's notion (*Nic. Eth.* 1.7) that the (morally) good or happy life for a human being lies in the fulfillment of his/her proper "function" or "work" (*ergon*), the second essay sets out explicitly to situate guidelines for ethical speech in a commitment to the "realization" of our fundamental nature as human beings. The third essay examines the implications for a rhetorical ethics of John Dewey's moral theory and his conception of communication, and it points toward a contemporary conception of practical wisdom.

A point of departure for the present work comes from a passage in the second essay, where I consider the ethical implications of our species designation, Homo sapiens, understood as "the wise human" (as distinct from "the upright-walking human," *Homo erectus*, and "the adaptable human," *Homo habilis*): "A humanistic ethic that embraces [this conception] of human nature will commit its adherents to the pursuit of wisdom, for in this pursuit lies the fulfillment of human being" (Johnstone 1981, 180). In the remainder of the paragraph I sketch a conception of wisdom that informed my thinking at that time. "Human wisdom," I write, "involves a kind of knowing, as is indicated by the significance of *sapience*. Wisdom is both a grasping of 'the way things are'—of the patterns and regularities in human experience and of how these fit into the *kosmos*—and an appreciation of the truths thus grasped. . . . It is generated by apprehensions of the truths of human nature, by one's realization or understanding of how humanness 'fits into' the nature of things."

I am particularly interested in the relationship between wisdom and speech—between what Aristotle termed "the most finished form of knowledge" and the instrumentalities of language. What *is* wisdom, and how is it acquired? Can it be communicated or taught to others? What is the role of speech, language, dialogue, argument—that is, of *logos*—in its attainment? If the pursuit of wisdom is taken as the highest moral end of human conduct, what are the implications for how language ought to be used in the conduct of everyday life? How, more particularly, can the resources of rhetoric be employed in the quest for wisdom? These are some general questions that animate the present inquiry.

Narrower questions concentrate on events in a relatively small area of the eastern Mediterranean during the brief span of three centuries—roughly from 620 to 322 B.C.E.—when understanding of the world expanded from a purely mythopoetic view to include a naturalistic/cosmological/philosophical orientation. During the intellectual movement from *mythos* to a philosophic/scientific outlook, how did meanings of *sophia* evolve? As emergent explanations for natural phenomena shifted causality from the actions of deities to the operation in nature of a "rational principle," what occurred in the relationship between wisdom and "the divine" (*to theion*)? What was the role of *logos* in the emergence and substance of a cosmological/scientific/philosophic worldview? What was distinctive about the form and content of this worldview?

I begin with an awareness and appreciation of the fact that something profoundly important happened in the Greek world during the archaic and classical eras. A flowering of human intelligence, poetic imagination, and cultural expression occurred that is unrivaled in the West for its originality and enduring impact. In our own time science and art, education and academic inquiry, government and politics, athletics and entertainment all bear the stamp of Greek ideas and values. Preserved in the written record of that ancient flowering are insights and understandings that may be as important and useful now as they were then.

The discussion proceeds chronologically, beginning with the mythopoetic tradition embodied in the epic verse of Homer and Hesiod, progressing through the emergence of a naturalistic worldview disclosed in the writings of the Presocratic thinkers, to the humanistic turn of Socrates and the Sophists, and culminating in the letters and orations of Isocrates, the dialogues of Plato, and the treatises of Aristotle, in whom the insights and methodologies of the earliest Greek thinkers find their fullest and most systematic expression. The central terms to be traced through the course of this development are *logos* and *sophia*, but other significant terms include *mythos, kosmos, archê, nous, physis, theion*, and *phronêsis*. Through an examination of the changing meanings of and relationships among such terms, I reconstruct (to the extent possible) the understandings and insights that constituted the *sophia* of the earliest Western thinkers and seek finally to illuminate the ways in which *logos* functions in the coming of wisdom. This focus highlights the nexus of philosophy and rhetoric in a way that illuminates the origins and early development of these ideas and the relations between them.

ONE

The Greek Stones Speak

Toward an Archaeology of Consciousness

We shall not cease from exploration
And the end of all our exploring
Will be to arrive where we started
And know the place for the first time.

T. S. Eliot, *Four Quartets*

The relationship between wisdom and utterance, reflected at times in more specific connections between philosophy and rhetoric, has been a focus of intellectual interest in the West since at least the time of Heraclitus of Ephesus (ca. 500 B.C.E.). Parmenides, Empedocles, Protagoras, Gorgias, Socrates, Plato, Isocrates, Aristotle, Cicero, Quintilian, Augustine, Bacon, Vico—all have been concerned, either directly or indirectly, with the links between speech or eloquence and what they take to be the highest form of knowledge. Recent scholarship has pursued this relationship along several related lines of inquiry, though sometimes obliquely. Some investigators have examined the role of speech in the creation of all human knowledge.[1] Others have concentrated more particularly on the role of rhetoric in the creation and exercise of wisdom.[2] In an effort to illuminate the ancient foundations of these connections, several scholars have lately studied the link between language and thought in Greek philosophy and rhetoric.[3]

This book synthesizes these lines of inquiry. I examine the relationship between speech and wisdom—between *logos* and *sophia*—in early Greek thought both to illuminate Greek conceptions of wisdom and to clarify the role of the word—especially the spoken word—in its acquisition and exercise. Changes in the idea of wisdom from the mythopoetic tradition of Homer and Hesiod to its systematic elaboration in the works of Plato and Aristotle arise from certain social and linguistic developments that are foregrounded in order to illuminate the contexts in which new ways of thinking and using language emerged and were refined. The appearance of literacy and prose composition during the archaic period, the expansion of trade along the Ionian coast during the seventh and sixth centuries B.C.E., the formation of the polis and the growing importance of public debate in Greek political life, the elaboration of a philosophical vocabulary and syntax by the Presocratics, the suzerainty of Athens over the Aegean city-states following the Persian Wars, the Sophists' challenge to established custom and to the new philosophical doctrines, the challenges and excesses of democracy in Athens during the late fifth and the fourth centuries—all influenced intellectual developments throughout this brief period in Western history.

These tracings are by no means a comprehensive history of or a commentary on Greek speculative thought. A number of such studies have been produced, beginning perhaps with Aristotle and continuing throughout the Western intellectual tradition. Rather, I follow the career of an idea, wisdom, from its roots in the mythic mind to its systematic articulation by the most prodigious intellect the Greek world produced. Similarly I am not reconstructing the historical development of rhetorical theory in ancient Greece.[4] Instead, I examine the intellectual, conceptual, and linguistic milieu in which Greek rhetorical theory emerged, and I illuminate the ideas and terms with which the speaker's art had to deal from the outset: wisdom, truth, knowledge, belief, prudence, justice, reason. These concepts have a history that predates that of rhetoric, and we can appreciate the development and substance of Greek rhetorical theory more fully by understanding that history. However one conceives such fourth-century ideas as rhetoric, poetics, and dialectic, the association of speech and wisdom in the earliest Greek texts—whether rhetorical, poetical, or philosophical—is present from the outset and persists throughout the intellectual tradition of the archaic and classical periods. Indeed Aristotle's distinction between rhetorical proof and scientific demonstration mirrors his distinction between practical and speculative wisdom. The grounds for these classifications can be grasped fully only when we see how speech and wisdom are related in the tradition upon which he drew.

Several important conclusions emerge from these inquiries. Greek conceptions of wisdom evolved over time, from the identification of *sophia* with the poet's skill and early belief in the mantic powers of the priest, the soothsayer, and the oracle to the Platonic/Aristotelian idea of *sophia* as speculative knowledge of fundamental cosmic principles. This evolution was neither wholly linear nor progressive. Nonetheless certain key elements persist or recur, and there are loci of coherence in the account. Moreover the idea of wisdom generally (though not always) included some sense of divine knowledge, and the relationships among *to theion* (divinity), *physis* (nature), and *o kosmos* (the world-order) are central to wisdom in many of its incarnations. Indeed "rational cosmology" and natural philosophy retained important links to myth

and poetic language, and the "transition from *mythos* to *logos*" (as it is sometimes expressed) signaled not so much a break with the past as the emergence
of a new form of consciousness that coexisted with and was infused by a
mythopoetic mind set as old as humanity itself. Greek views of wisdom also
included a practical, moral dimension wherein knowledge of the divine or universal realm had important implications for practical decision and thus for
personal conduct. Wisdom, consequently, came to comprehend both *sophia*
(speculative or cosmological knowledge) and *phronêsis* (practical sagacity or
prudence). Hence the ontological and moral realms at some points converge.

The oral use of language figures centrally in the acquisition and exercise of
wisdom, though the invention of alphabetic writing in the eighth century
B.C.E. made an essential contribution. From the tales of epic poets and conversations among the Ionian nature philosophers to the speeches of the Sophists
and the dialectical exchanges of the Socratics, it was the spoken word that
most directly inspired, awakened, or deepened the insights and understandings that are comprehended under the idea of wisdom. The philosophical or
"wisdom-creative" efficacy of speech can be understood in terms of both content and form, and the substantive and formal characteristics of such speech
can be identified and their operation explained. One Hellenic conception
of wisdom features the cosmic principle of balance/proportion/equilibrium/
reciprocity—the *logos* according to which all things come to pass—and the
ability to live in harmony with this principle. This principle, "which steers all
things through all," is disclosed in natural events and processes, in human
intelligence, and in speech. Another conception emphasizes the limits of
human knowledge and our reliance on perception in determining how to live.
This is the conceptual milieu in which the speaker's art—the principles of
rhetoric—first appeared during the fifth century B.C.E. and in which the relationship between rhetoric and philosophy developed. Understanding this
milieu enables us to grasp and appreciate the ideas and terms that shaped the
art and its connections with philosophical speculation.

My overarching goals here are to disclose, to the extent possible, the major
insights of these ancient thinkers, to make accessible whatever wisdom they
themselves—by their own accounts—may have possessed, and to discern the
role and functions of reasoned speech in the attainment and exercise of this
wisdom. The emergence of naturalistic accounts of the origins and operations
of the world and their competition with mythopoetic explanations took place
over several centuries, beginning with the Ionians and culminating during the
classical era in the writings of Aristotle. Moreover, even as intellectuals inquired
into the material origins and natural workings of the world around them, the
concept of the *divine* was not so much displaced as it was transformed.[5] The
real intellectual revolution in Greece was not so much a shift from *theos* (god)

to *physis* (nature) as a shift from a supernatural to a naturalistic understanding of divinity and the causes of world events. What emerges from the record of this shift is that, rather than being ruled by immortal, anthropomorphic beings who exist outside nature, the world-process is governed by an indwelling rational principle that is at once natural and divine.

This ancient wisdom both initiated the scientific quest in which we are still engaged for the *archê* or origin of the universe and anticipated some of the insights this quest has yielded. Recent books herald, as Stephen Toulmin puts it, a "return to cosmology." Beginning perhaps with Carl Sagan's immensely popular *Cosmos* (1980), the scientific search for ultimate truths in the universe has entered the popular consciousness and excited the popular imagination. Toulmin's own foray into the territory—*The Return to Cosmology: Postmodern Science and the Theology of Nature* (1982)—reveals a spirit remarkably close to what we find in early Greek cosmological speculations. Likewise, such volumes as Timothy Ferris's *Coming of Age in the Milky Way* (1988), Stephen Hawking's *A Brief History of Time: From the Big Bang to Black Holes* (1988), Dennis Overbye's *Lonely Hearts of the Cosmos: The Story of the Scientific Quest for the Secret of the Universe* (1991), and Lee Smolin's *The Life of the Cosmos* (1997) show contemporary cosmological inquiry to be working out ideas and testing theories that have their roots in the thinking of Thales, Anaximander, Heraclitus, Empedocles, and Democritus, among others. The ancient search for universal wisdom beckons us still.

A culture's ways of accounting for its own existence and for its experience of the world—its creation myths and stories, its theogonies and cosmogonies, its philosophies and cosmologies—articulate various ways of relating to the world and of dwelling in it. These "ways" are embodied in artifacts as diverse as painted or carved images, religious rituals and objects, preserved stories and tales, metaphysical doctrines, and cosmological theories. Each discloses a sense of *being-in-the-world* that is rooted in convictions about the essential character of the world and our place in it.[6] There is an architecture in consciousness, a structure or framework in terms of which one comes to understand one's experiences. My aim in examining some of the artifacts that manifest mythopoetic and naturalistic ways of seeing the world is to illuminate the forms of consciousness they express and the relationships between these.

The artifacts to be examined here, of course, are texts rather than stones, structures, tools, or coins, but they are embedded in their historical and cultural milieu as surely as any bronze weapon or painted potsherd is.[7] By examining certain features of this milieu we can make probabilistic determinations of how these artifacts functioned in their contexts—of what they *meant*, of the purposes and thoughts they embodied, and of the forms of consciousness they bespoke. From analysis of intrinsic and contextual clues in the artifacts, informed efforts can be made at reconstructing a social history. Such reconstructions are always in some degree speculative or conjectural, and the legitimacy of any particular reconstruction rests finally on how persuasively it accounts for the evidence discovered. In other words, the reconstruction of social history from archaeological evidence is fundamentally rhetorical, and competing reconstructions compel adherence only within the limits of probability. Again within probabilistic limits, alternative reconstructions—competing "readings" of the evidence—can impose equivalent claims on our adherence, so that often several possible readings must be considered as having equal legitimacy. This is especially so when the evidence is incomplete and/or ambiguous.[8]

My reading of texts representing the Greek wisdom-tradition proceeds in this spirit. The very notion of seeking through textual analysis to retrieve and reconstruct ancient ideas strikes some scholars as being problematic, if not impossible (Poulakos 1990). Nonetheless, the distinction between "historical reconstruction" and "contemporary appropriation" can be useful in contrasting different approaches to reading and interpretation.[9] Even granting that "any statement we make about the past is anchored in the present, [and] that the past-as-it-was is [ultimately] irretrievable" (Poulakos 1990, 221; also see Segal 1984–85), there is a difference between treating a thinker "as within *our own* philosophical framework" and seeking to reconstruct "how the [ancient] author and his or her contemporaries [might have] understood the text."[10] The former aims at appropriating the terms of earlier writers in constructing contemporary ideas and illuminating contemporary problems. The latter aims, like the work of the archaeologist and the historian, at using the available evidence to speculate about what might have existed or occurred long ago and to determine the relative probabilities of competing reconstructions of past ideas, events, and conditions.

So it is with our texts. Some readings are more readily sustained by the evidence than others, or multiple readings claim our consideration simultaneously.[11] Accordingly my readings aim at recovering to the extent possible the insights the authors themselves sought to express and, more generally, the forms of consciousness or modes of awareness that disclose themselves in different ways of accounting for the world. Such recovery is based on determining, within the writers' own intellectual and linguistic contexts, what ideas can be associated with certain terms and phrases and then discerning which interpretations are more compelling than others (Schiappa 2003, 32–33). Moreover we must recognize that multiple "correct" interpretations are possible for a given text inasmuch as writers can and do exploit the ambiguities of certain terms with a view to expressing multiple meanings.[12]

The interpretation of Greek texts is inevitably problematic, but we can sometimes distinguish between more and less likely readings by recognizing the centrality in Greek philosophical and protoscientific writing of *metaphorical expression* and of *analogical thinking*. Ricoeur (1977) insists that the downward movement of analysis—the archaeological investigation of texts—must be complemented by an upward movement of interpretation, an "ascending dialectic" through which the metaphorical meanings of a text are illuminated and its ontological implications discerned. This approach is particularly appropriate when texts exhibit emerging metaphorical expressions in the development of a philosophical vocabulary. In his account of Presocratic thought, Havelock emphasizes that the language of philosophical inquiry and argument did not come ready-made to those who charted the path from a mythopoetic to a naturalistic consciousness. "From the standpoint of a sophisticated philosophical language, such as was available to Aristotle, what was lacking was a set of commonplace but abstract terms which by their interrelations could describe the physical world conceptually. . . . The history of early philosophy is usually written under the assumption that this kind of vocabulary was already available to the first Greek thinkers. The evidence of their own language is that it was not. They had to initiate the process of inventing it" (1983, 14).[13]

One of Havelock's examples of such "linguistic invention" is the word *kosmos*, employed by Plato (*Gorgias* 508A) and other classical thinkers to denote the "ordered world" or "universe" but perhaps introduced with this meaning by Heraclitus. "It was doubtfully put forth by the Milesians, but this [DK 30] is the first fully attested entry of the term into philosophical language. It has been borrowed from the epic vocabulary, in particular from previous application to the orderly array of an army controlled by its 'orderer' (*cosmêtôr*); but it is now 'stretched,' so to speak, . . . to cover a whole world or universe or physical system, and to identify it as such" (Havelock 1983, 24; also see Kahn 1960, 193).

A key to understanding the development of abstract philosophical language as it appears in Plato and Aristotle is to recognize that earlier conceptual advances necessitated the metaphorical use of older terms to express novel ideas.[14] Thus thought precedes and instigates the development of terminology precisely because there are ideas—not yet formed into concepts—for the expression of which no terms exist. The Presocratics' task of "stretching" the language is performed through the figurative use of such archaic terms as *genesis, logos, physis, kosmos, theos,* and *archê* to express new ways of perceiving the causes of events and the relations among them. In this sense, much philosophical and scientific language even now is metaphorical. We can understand this language and its implications fully only when we read its archaic significance into it by considering the root metaphors of key terms—only, for instance, insofar as we read into the term "generate" the wholly organic process of pro-creation and birth, of "bringing forth"; or into "physics" (as a study of nature) the idea of organic growth and natural change. Thus do the seeds of new ways of thinking about the world precede expression, and the resources of language are extended and augmented metaphorically precisely because people have ideas for which there are no words.

This may seem to be at odds with what Havelock implies when he states, "As is the level of language, so is the level of consciousness" (1983, 16). One implication of this statement—and one reading of Havelock's thesis—is that advances in thinking and conceptualization cannot precede linguistic advances. Because the "linguistic task of the Presocratics" was to invent a vocabulary and syntax necessary for constructing abstract philosophical con-cepts, these men could not themselves have achieved levels of abstraction that were accessible to later thinkers, who could exploit the possibilities of these linguistic advances. However, Havelock also notes Parmenides' awareness of "the need for a new level of consciousness to achieve the new language. . . . The Presocratics all search variously for terms by which to identify this kind of consciousness. They are seeking to isolate what we might describe as an act of cognition or intellection, directed toward grasping conceptual abstractions rather than narrating and describing events" (27). This suggests that these thinkers *already had in mind* some new ideas about the origins and workings of the world, and that they "stretched" existing terms and developed a new syn-tax precisely in order to give expression to these ideas.

It is just this sort of linguistic evolution that made speculative, positivist thought possible. Something happens when we examine the world through the prism of language. When an archaic term is used in a novel sense—that is, metaphorically rather than literally—the mind can extend and elaborate con-cepts through the process of playing out the implications of the terminology (Ricoeur 1977, 216ff.). As one considers and reflects on a certain term and experiments with meanings, implications, and constructs, one both stretches the way in which the term can be used and has new and more elaborate ways of understanding things. What this means for the interpretation of ancient philosophical and protophilosophical texts is that, in seeking to illuminate an author's ideas when he employed a given term or expression, we should con-sider the senses suggested by a metaphorical/analogical reading. This seems especially fitting when we recognize that conceptions of wisdom accompany-ing the emergent cosmological consciousness manifest a radically new way of understanding the world. Perhaps more fully than any other verbal technique, metaphorical expression reveals the form of consciousness, the world vision, behind any naturalistic account of the "way of things."

The principal evidence for a mythopoetic consciousness lies in the poems of Homer and Hesiod, in the Homeric Hymns, and in ancient drama, wherein the characters and actions of the gods are portrayed and their impact on world events and human experience is described.[15] Examining the earliest of these sources—that is, Homer's *Iliad* and *Odyssey* and Hesiod's *Theogony* and *Works and Days*—permits us to reconstruct the worldview that manifested itself in Greek mythology and religious practice and that was disclosed in later poetry and drama.

The case of the Presocratic thinkers is more troublesome. Their earliest writings are preserved only in fragmentary quotations and in references and accounts of later philosophers, commentators, and compendiasts whose own intellectual agendas and conceptions often shaped their interpretations and restatements of older writings.[16] Likewise, though such later sources as Plutarch, Sextus, Clement, and Diogenes Laertius are considered reliable, even here it is problematic to conclude that what we have are the ipsissima verba of the ancient authors. In many instances we will find close paraphrases rather than actual quotations. This makes the task of reconstruction difficult, and one must exercise great caution in attributing thoughts and ideas to these authors. For all this caution, however, Kirk, Raven, and Schofield conclude that "it is legitimate to feel complete confidence in our understanding of a Presocratic thinker . . . when the Aristotelian or Theophrastean interpretation . . . is confirmed by relevant and well-authenticated extracts from the philosopher himself" (1983, 6). For my part, I am cognizant of potential problems posed by the state of the evidence, and I argue for my interpretations with whatever level of confidence seems warranted.

What has been said regarding the sources for Presocratic texts also holds for the writings of the older Sophists. What remains of these writings is often fragmentary, and they come to us principally via quotations, paraphrases, commentaries, and imitations in the works of later authors. As with the Presocratic thinkers, the sometimes-fragmentary texts concerning the fifth-century Sophists are collected in Diels and Kranz, which for the purposes of this study is considered the authoritative source of such fragments. My reading of sophistical texts proceeds in the same cautious spirit with which I approach the earlier thinkers.

Something must be said, at least preliminarily, about "the Socratic problem." One cannot examine the development of a Greek conception of wisdom without considering what Socrates had to say about it. The "problem," of course, is that Socrates apparently did not commit to writing what he thought or said. Any conclusions about Socratic speech and thought will be qualified by unresolved questions of authorship, but even with this caveat we can infer some things about his sense of wisdom and the role of speech in its attainment. We have some diversity of sources upon whom to draw: Aristophanes, Xenophon, Plato, and Aristotle, plus an important entry in Diogenes Laertius.[17] From such diversity we can perform a kind of "triangulation," comparing various accounts of specific features of Socratic talk and, where there are consistencies, inferring with some degree of confidence that we are seeing an authentic portrait.[18] Moreover, even granting that personal motives and viewpoints might distort any single source, each has a legitimate tale to tell about Socrates as a person and as a thinker, and from any one of them might come a singular piece of information that contributes credibly to the composite portrait. These matters will be considered more fully in chapter 4.

So the sources—the "stones on the ground"—are sometimes problematic, but still they can yield information that will allow us to draw reasonable inferences about the thoughts behind the words and to reconstruct histories of some important ideas. Perhaps, if we just listen, we can hear what these "stones" have to say.

TWO

Singing the Muses' Song

Myth, Wisdom, and Speech

I begin my song with the Helikonian Muses;
they have made Helikon, the great god-haunted mountain, their domain;
their soft feet move in the dance that rings the violet-dark spring and the altar of
   mighty Zeus.
. . . On Helikon's peak they join hands in lovely dances and their pounding feet
   awaken desire.
From there they set out and, veiled in mist, glide through the night
and raise enchanting voices to exalt aegis-bearing Zeus and queenly Hera,
   the Lady of Argo who walks in golden sandals;
gray-eyed Athena, daughter of aegis-bearing Zeus,
and Phoibos Apollon and arrow-shooting Artemis.
They exalt Poseidon, holder and shaker of the earth,
stately Themis and Aphrodite of the fluttering eyelids,
and gold-wreathed Hebe and fair Dione.
And then they turn their song to Eos, Helios, and bright Selene,
to Leto, Iapetos, and sinuous-minded Kronos, to Gaia, great Okeanos, and
   black Night,
and to the holy race of the other deathless gods.
It was they who taught Hesiod beautiful song as he tended his sheep
at the foothills of god-haunted Helikon.

Hesiod, Theogony 1–23

The visions of wisdom bequeathed to us by ancient Greeks find their fullest
expression in classical thought, but they originate in the vision of the seer, the
revelation of the oracle, and the verse of the poet, whose utterances are products of the psychic state of *entheos*, "full of the god" or "inspired."[1] The
prophetic powers of the seer spring from a knowledge that is greater than
human. The song of the *rhapsôdos* is inspired by his Muse, who gives him
words to speak. The wisdom of the seer, the oracle, the priestess, and the poet

is divine, sacred. It comes not from the human soul but from the gods. It concerns what is wholly other, beyond the ken of normal experience. The *sophos* (f. *sophê*) sees, hears, and experiences things that are not present to ordinary folk. He or she stands in direct contact with divine beings, communicates with gods and spirits. Through the prophecies of the seer, the diviner, and the oracle, through the verse of the poet, through the song of the rhapsode, such divine wisdom is made accessible to others. Thus do the traditional myths become sources of inspiration to the nonpoet: the speech of mythopoesis and prophecy is the language of divine wisdom.

Walker (2000) observes that "rhetoric" as an art of epideictic argumentation and persuasion "*derives originally from the poetic tradition* and . . . extends, in 'applied' versions of itself, to the practical discourses of public and private life" (viii, italics in original). One might likewise propose that "philosophy," as it came to be known, derives originally from the mythic tradition in which oral poetry is the voice of wisdom. In order to understand rhetoric and its relationship to philosophy in the fourth century, we should start with the mythopoetic tradition from which it derives. Likewise, to recover whatever wisdom may be preserved in the writings of Thales, Anaximander, Xenophanes, Pythagoras, and Heraclitus, for example, and later in the works of Plato and Aristotle, we must begin by understanding the mythopoetic consciousness from which these writings emerged and from which, in significant ways, they ultimately departed. Connections between rhetoric and philosophy in the classical era have their roots in the magical powers of poetic speech to carry ordinary listeners into the realm of the immortals and to give them a share, however diluted, in divine wisdom. Particularly important in the poet's ability to open his listeners to divine wisdom is the power of speech itself—the potency of the *oral* word—to move the soul. The link between persuasion and orality is explicitly recognized in Gorgias's fifth-century pronouncement that "speech is a powerful lord" (*Helen*, DK 82 B 11.8), but it derives from the psychological potency of oral poetry.

Mythology—defined now as the study of myths and their meanings—has a rich and complex history. As objects of anthropological, literary, sociological, psychological, and philosophical scrutiny, myths from various cultures have yielded insight into these cultures' senses of themselves as well as into a number of transcultural themes. We can study myth "as a means to learn what happened in the prehistoric past, to interpret history, to understand religious concepts, to probe the secret mind of an individual or a tribe, to determine the universals in human thinking."[2] My present interest embraces all these perspectives. A mythopoetic consciousness is not specific to a given culture or even to a particular era; rather, it is a way of being and thinking rooted in a worldview in which all events—natural, social, and personal—are manifestations of divine power(s). The fundamental beliefs that constitute such a worldview see in such powers the origins of things and the causes of events. By examining specific myths in terms of their content, forms, and language we can discern how members of a particular culture understood the workings of the world and their place in it. We can see, in short, how their myths gave meaning to experience. Myths, as expressions of social beliefs about the origins and significance of events, are a portal into the very heart of a society, into its "secret mind."

The root of myth is mystery. To a self-conscious, observant creature—one who perceives a distinction between things that can be controlled and things that are beyond controlling, one who views events with intellectual curiosity—the world around us is at once familiar and bewildering. Things change, and they stay the same. The sun rises every morning and sets every evening, but not in precisely the same place. As time passes, the points on the horizon where sunrise and sunset occur shift to the south, linger there for a time, and then migrate north again. What makes it happen so? Sometimes there is much rain; sometimes it is hot and dry. Why? Sometimes the meadow by the river is full of grazing animals and the hunting is good; other times no game is seen for months. Sometimes the river is alive with fish and many can be caught; at other times there are few. Why do these things happen as they do? Sometimes a person falls into the sleep from which there is no awakening, and what is left behind becomes dirt and bones. When this happens, where has she gone? Who has taken her? Will she need her body where she is? Will she need tools? Food? Clothing? Where have our people come from? Who are the ancestors of our ancestors? How have we come to be in this land?

Such perplexities are the mother of myth: they compel the mind to seek an explanation, an accounting. Michalopoulos writes:

> folklore and myth are primitive man's earliest articulate expression of his bewilderment and awe as he is confronted by the overwhelming forces of Nature, which he is unable to predict, to control, or to understand. . . . For a very long time during the early period of his evolution, he is baffled and often terrified by Nature's violent or disquieting phenomena, such as thunder and lightening, storms, hurricanes, earthquakes, floods, volcanic eruptions, or by the eerie rustling of leaves in the darkness of the forest, or by the majestic progress of sun, moon, and stars across the vast dome of the skies. These are all deep mysteries, and mystery fills the primitive soul with fear. In order to remove fear, the savage endeavors to placate the unknown powers which cause it. Since he knows nothing of nature, his untutored imagination creates . . . divinities as numerous and as varied as the phenomena they appear to produce. (1966, 13–14)[3]

A people's mythology provides first of all just such an explanation of why things happen as they do and of how the world came to be as it is, with us in it. Myth is a way of giving order to the variety and variability in what happens around us and of apprehending the causes behind events.[4] In its primal meaning *mythos* comprehends the idea of telling a story, of presenting a narrative that enables a people—a tribe, a clan, a culture—to make sense of the mysterious.[5] It is a "saying," an "utterance" that satisfies the uniquely human desire to grasp what is behind the events of daily experience, to know the beginnings of things. Myth, says Eliade, "has no other function than to reveal *how something came into being . . .* how worlds are born and what happened afterward" (1977, 16).

As a way of making sense of things, myth is distinctive in how it answers the question, "why?" In general, the answer of myth is, "because some very powerful beings, who have dominion over the heavens and the earth and the seas, and who make things happen through their own wills and acts, have made it so." As Eliade puts it, "Myth tells how, through the deeds of Supernatural Beings, a reality came into existence, be it the whole of reality, the Cosmos, or only a fragment of reality—an island, a species of plant, a particular kind of human behavior, an institution. Myth, then, is always an account of a 'creation'; it relates how something was produced, began to *be*. . . . The actors in myths are Supernatural Beings" (1963, 5–6).[6] Thus do the seasons change through the actions of gods; thus does the rain come, or not; thus is the harvest rich, or not; thus is the hunt successful, or not. What is distinctive about myth is that it locates what Aristotle would later term the "efficient" causes of events in the actions of superhuman beings—powerful, sometimes terrible, usually immortal. The objects and events that hold sway over human experience—sun and moon, thunder and rain, fire and water, earth and sky, war and peace, pestilence and death—are perceived either as embodying such beings or as manifesting their power. Each being has its own character; each has a sphere over which it has dominion; each must be propitiated in its own way.

Myth also provides an account of social origins, an explanation of how a particular *ethnos* came into being. It answers not only the question, why? but also the question, whence? Where have *we* come from—our people, our tribe, our clan? Eliade writes, "Myth teaches ancient man the primordial 'stories' that have constituted him existentially. . . . Just as modern man considers himself to be constituted by History, the man of the archaic societies declares that he is the result of a certain number of mythical events. . . . Events that took place *in mythical times* . . . therefore make up a *sacred history* because the actors in the drama are not men but Supernatural Beings. In addition, while a modern man, though regarding himself as the result of the course of Universal

History, does not feel obliged to know the whole of it, the man of the archaic societies is not only obliged to remember mythical history but also to *re-enact* a large part of it periodically" (1963, 12–13). Thus arise creation myths and accounts of ethnogenesis. Here is the origin of ritual and rite—the symbolic reenactment of the sacred history through which a people has been constituted. In all such myths and accounts, however, it is the actions of supernatural beings that underlie the origins of the world and of the people whose account it is. Myth, as an explanation, is a way of giving meaning to the existence and history of the group.

Myth also explains how the individual and the social group "fit into" the order of things. It provides a moral ground for action; it has normative force. Myth "expresses, enhances and codifies belief; it safeguards and enforces morality; it vouches for the efficiency of ritual and contains practical rules for the guidance of men, . . . [it provides] a pragmatic charter of primitive faith and moral wisdom," says Malinowski (1954, 101; also see Eliade 1963, 9). Learning the myths of one's people constitutes the most ancient form of education, the means of passing from one generation to the next the fundamental truths that give meaning to the world and to the group's existence within it and that provide practical guidance in the quest for survival. Leakey and Lewin note that "perhaps the single most important behavioral adaptation of *Homo sapiens* is the passage from generation to generation of the elements of culture, the folk knowledge of the means of survival. Part of that cultural passage is the profoundly felt urge to understand the world. A people's mythology is its means of coping with that urge, for mythology is a body of explanation, an embodiment of the Truth" (1992, 306).

Against this general understanding of myth, we can consider the sociocultural and psychological significance of Greek tales of gods and heroes. Thence we can reconstruct the ontological outlook of those for whom these tales have spiritual and historical validity. The early Greeks, like all ancient peoples, confronted a world that was complex, occasionally beneficent, often threatening, always full of mystery, with unseen powers revealing themselves in every facet of human experience (Dickinson 1958, 2–12). The Greeks, no less than we, were moved by the characteristically human impulse to *explain* the world in an effort to find order in it and ultimately to exercise some control over it. Their myths embody their attempt to provide an account of the powers and forces that hold sway over world events and human experience.[7] From a mythopoetic perspective, the world and our experience of it are explainable not in terms of universal, abstract natural principles, and it is not knowable in a rational, positivistic manner. Rather, for Greeks of the Homeric age and before, the world is explainable in terms of the sexual unions, genealogical histories, petty jealousies, and titanic struggles of supernatural beings; and it was graspable by means of a poetic narrative that portrayed these unions, genealogies, and struggles grandly, dramatically, and anthropomorphically.[8]

The Greek myths of the last half of the second millennium B.C.E., though they incorporate elements drawn from older traditions, have a distinctively Hellenic form.[9] These tales—as they have come to us through the poems of Homer and Hesiod, through the Homeric Hymns and lyric poetry of the archaic era, through the plays of the tragedians and the sculptures that adorned temples from the fifth century on, and as they are evident in cult activity (including festivals, rituals, and worship at sacred sites)—were composed by epic poets and by the bards (*aoidoi*) who wandered during the Dark Ages (ca. 1100–750 B.C.E.) from hamlet to hamlet singing stories of long-dead warrior-heroes and of the gods whose impulses and plots were played out on the world stage.[10] Incorporating elements of older mythological traditions and embellishing the ancient tales with their own inventions, these storytellers recounted the deeds of Bronze Age kings and nobles in a great war. They described fantastic adventures that some of these fighters experienced during their long voyage home. They related the tales of gods and goddesses whose own conflicts, intrigues, seductions, conquests, and rivalries were manifested in storms at sea, conflagrations in great citadels, and anger in the hearts of comrades-in-arms. These are the tales, told and retold over centuries, that constituted the oral literature of Dark Age Greece, set down in the eighth century by Homer and the writers of the Homeric Hymns, and systematized by Hesiod (Hooper 1978, 55–62).

The tales of gods and heroes rendered by Homer are woven into the larger narratives that relate his principal subjects in the *Iliad* and the *Odyssey:* the climactic weeks of the long war of attrition between Greeks and Trojans, and the ten-year journey by way of which some of the victors in that war returned home. Neither poem presents a coherent account of the history of the gods themselves, so one's sense of this history is fragmented. Nonetheless, the tales of gods and goddesses—led by vanity, jealousy, lust, anger, and other very human emotions to intervene in human affairs and to shape our thoughts and actions—provide supernatural explanations for all events. As Guthrie observes, myth sees causes "in terms of a clash of living, personal wills . . . , the wrath of a god, the jealousy of a goddess" (1953, 5). Pomeroy et al. write that "in their totality, the gods, nature spirits, and abstractions represent the whole of being. The diversity of the supernatural realm offered the Greeks a satisfactory way of ordering and explaining the baffling complexity of human experience, from the vast mysterious universe of stars and planets, to the benign and hostile world of nature, to the confusing inner world of the human psyche. . . . The complex intersection of the eternal divine and ephemeral mortality lay at the base of all later Greek philosophical and scientific speculation about the order and structure of the universe and the human condition" (1999, 64–65).

This is precisely the picture painted by Homer. The opening of the *Iliad* finds the Greek camp suffering a "fatal plague [that] swept through the army—men were dying" (1.10).[11] The cause? Apollo was roused to anger by Agamemnon, who affronted Apollo's priest Chryses in seeking to ransom his daughter, Chryseis. When he heard Chryses' prayer and learned of Agamemnon's arrogance, Apollo, a god of healing, sent a plague with his feathered shafts. "Down he strode from Olympus' peaks, storming at heart with his bow and hooded quiver. . . . First he went for the mules and circling dogs but then, launching a piercing shaft at the men themselves, he cut them down in droves—and the corpse-fires burned on, night and day, no end in sight" (1.45–52). For nine days the god's arrows fell on the camp. On the tenth day Achilles, prince of the Myrmidons and greatest of the Greek warriors, called a conference among the Greeks to discuss the matter. Why? Because "the impulse seized him, sent by white-armed Hera grieving to see Achaean fighters drop and die" (1.55–56). From the very outset, then, the gods are at work in what has befallen the Greek host. In the plague that visits the camp, in the very thoughts and dreams that enter the men's minds, the power of the gods and their acute interest in human affairs are made manifest. Moreover the Greeks cannot win the war without their help, as is clear from Chryses' invocation on the Greeks' behalf: "May the gods who hold the halls of Olympus give you Priam's city to plunder, then safe passage home" (1.18–19).

The expedition itself is the result of divine intrusion into human affairs: Helen's affection for and abduction by Paris are consequences of the jealousy-inspired manipulations of Aphrodite, Athena, and Hera. Throughout the final months of the conflict, direct intervention by these goddesses—as well as by Zeus, Apollo, Ares, and other Olympians—steers the ebb and flow of the fighting. Indeed, in most cases decisive actions by such mortals as Achilles and Agamemnon, Paris and Hector are the direct result of divine intercession. An especially vivid instance of this occurs when Achilles, angry with his erstwhile ally Agamemnon and of two minds about whether he should draw his sword and "slay the son of Atreus," begins to take his weapon from its sheath and is then guided in the matter by Hera, acting through Athena: "As his racing spirit veered back and forth, just as he drew his huge blade from its sheath, down from the vaulting heavens swept Athena, the white-armed goddess Hera sped her down" (1.193–95). Appearing to Achilles alone and pulling him by his hair, Athena induces him to put the sword away and to take his retribution instead in a denunciation of Agamemnon. Achilles obeys the goddess, not because of a promise of great wealth but because "if a man obeys the gods they're quick to hear his prayers" (221–22).

What is particularly interesting about this episode is the picture it paints of the act of choosing. The contest is not between two elements of Achilles' own *psychê* but between his own *thymos* (his passion or anger) and the *logos* of the goddess. Thus does the locus of self-control lie outside the self, and thus is divine action a factor in all human decision. Jaynes observes that "there is . . . no concept of will or word for it [in the *Iliad*], the concept developing curiously late in Greek thought. Thus, Iliadic men have no will of their own and certainly no notion of free will" (1976, 70). A little later he notes that "the characters of the Iliad do not sit down and think out what to do. They have no conscious minds such as we say we have, and certainly no introspections. It is impossible for us with our subjectivity to appreciate what it was like. . . . The beginnings of action are not in conscious plans, reasons, and motives; they are in the actions and speeches of gods" (72). The immortals are ever present among us.

Later Agamemnon's decision to "take the city of Priam that very day" was inspired by a dream sent by Zeus to deceive the Achaean king (2.1–40). Why would Zeus seek to deceive Agamemnon and thus to lead him into military disaster? Because he was implored by Thetis, Achilles' mother and herself an immortal, to "grant the Trojans victory after victory till the Achaean armies pay my dear son back, building higher the honor he deserves" (1.500–510). So it goes throughout the *Iliad*. Again and again gods and goddesses guide spears and arrows to their marks, or they shield their favorites from harm by hiding them in mists or darkness or by sheltering them in their shining robes. Aphrodite causes a helmet strap to break just as Menelaus is about to catch Paris and pull him to the ground (3.369–76). As the Trojans throw themselves into battle against the Achaean fortifications, Zeus "bewitches" or "spellbinds" (*thelge*) the minds of the Greeks when "from Ida's summits a sudden howling gale . . . whipped a dust storm hard against their ships" (12.251–53). Thus do the deities direct the tide of battle. As Snell writes, "In Homer every new turn of events is engineered by the gods. . . . Two dramas are acted out simultaneously, the one on a higher stage, among the gods, and the other here on earth. Everything that happens down below is determined by the transactions of the gods with one another. For human initiative has no source of its own. Whatever is planned and executed is the plan and deed of the gods" (1982, 29–30).[12]

Homer's epics and the later Homeric Hymns disclose a world in which natural events, and often human thoughts and actions, are the products of supernatural agency. Some of these agents have physical manifestations in the realm of nature: Zeus throws lightening, rattles the sky with his thunder, and waters crops with rain; Poseidon is Earth Shaker and the storm at sea; Demeter is the very grain that nourishes the folk, she "bestows rich fruit," and her withdrawal from the world brings winter's desolation.[13] To the mythopoetic mind, everything in the world manifests divine, supernatural beings whose own desires and choices bring about the events to which humans must respond and adapt; so, too, with human actions and institutions. The Homeric divinities hold sway over all spheres of human experience and influence all facets of human life, including individual choice and action. As Snell observes, "Homer's man does not yet regard himself as the source of his own decisions; that development is reserved for tragedy. When the Homeric hero, after duly weighing his alternatives, comes to a final conclusion, he feels that his course is shaped by the gods" (1982, 20).[14]

This way of seeing the world also permeates Hesiod's *Theogony*, the first known account of the origins and subsequent history of the gods, and to a lesser extent his *Works and Days*.[15] The first poem is an epic narrative of births and lines of descent—and of the couplings, rivalries, and conflicts of the superhuman beings whose actions are behind virtually everything that happens: the primeval deities Chaos and Gaia, Tartaros and Eros; Okeanos, Kronos, Rhea, Themis, and the other Titans; the Furies and the Muses; and ultimately the Olympians. At the same time, the poem describes the events that culminated in the preeminence of Zeus among the gods and of how he brought justice, law, and order to the world. Thus does the poem provide both an account of origins and a sacred history of the divine powers by which the world is ruled. Beyond this it imposes a systematic structure on the earlier myths by presenting a divine genealogy, and it provides a foundation for moral order by sanctioning Zeus's rise to supremacy.

The poem opens with an invocation to the Muses (lines 1–115), but the theogonic/cosmogonic process begins with the appearance of the first beings: "Chaos was born first and after her came Gaia the broad-breasted, . . . and then misty Tartaros in the depth of broad-pathed earth and Eros, the fairest of the deathless gods" (116–20).[16] With the birth from Gaia of Ouranos begins the lineage of Zeus (126), and from the incestuous union between Gaia and Ouranos are born the Titans, of whom Kronos is the last (137). Following a section of the poem relating the castration of Ouranos by his son Kronos and the subsequent birth of Aphrodite and the progeny of Night (154–413), the poem introduces the first Olympian generation (Hestia, Demeter, Hera, Hades, Zeus) and the deception and overthrow of Kronos (453–506). The remainder of the poem is dominated by Zeus, as he deals with various challenges and threats to his supremacy, first from Prometheus (507–616), then from the Titans (617–819), and finally from Typhoeus (820–69). The poem closes with a genealogical narrative dealing primarily with the progeny of Zeus and the other Olympians.

The gods of the *Theogony* are the gods of Homer: powerful, contentious, jealous, and deathless. They are "the holy gods to whom death never comes"

(105), the "gods who never die" (407). They are those upon whom humankind depends for all that makes life livable, "the givers of blessings" (111). They are subject to passion and rage. Kronos was "a most fearful child who hated his mighty father [Ouranos]" (138), and in the end, "all these awesome children born of Ouranos and Gaia hated their own father from the day they were born" (155). They could be capricious in granting favors to mortals; their help is given when it pleases them to give it:

> Even now, when a mortal propitiates the gods and, following custom, sac-rifices well-chosen victims, he invokes Hekate, and *if she receives his prayers with favor,* then honor goes to him . . . and he is given blessings. . . . She can greatly aid a man—*if this is her wish.* In trials her seat is at the side of illustrious kings, and in assemblies the man she favors gains distinction. And when men arm themselves for man-destroying battle, the goddess always stands beside those she prefers and gladly grants them victory and glory. . . . To horsemen, too, *when she wishes,* she is a noble helper and to those working out on the stormy and gray sea. . . . with ease this glorious goddess grants a great catch of fish and with ease, *if that is her wish,* she makes it vanish." (416–43; italics added)

Hesiod's other great poem, *Works and Days,* expresses a similar outlook. An epic in form if not in subject matter, the poem is simultaneously an exhortation to live a just life according to the dictates of Zeus, a recounting of the Five Ages of Man that provides a *mythos* to explain the origins of the human race, and a collection of practical instructions concerning agriculture—when to plant and when to reap, how to select the best wood for making a plow, and so on. The poem is addressed not only to the Boeotian farmer but to all who care to improve their lot through righteousness and hard work.

According to Hesiod, the present wretchedness of the human condition—his own "race of iron" is beset by "toil and pain" and must work continuously to eke out the means of survival—resulted from Zeus's wrath. "I wish," Hesiod writes, "I were not counted among the fifth race of men, but rather had died before, or been born after it. This is the race of iron. Neither day nor night will give them rest as they waste away with toil and pain. Growing cares will be given them by the gods, and their lot will be a blend of good and bad. Zeus will destroy this race of mortals" (174–80).[17] The Iron Age in Hesiod's chronology was preceded by the races of Gold, Silver, Bronze, and Heroes (110–73), some of the last of whom Zeus settled—"unburdened by cares"—in the Islands of the Blessed, where "three times a year the barley-giving land brings forth full grain sweet as honey."

Humankind has been punished by Zeus, says Hesiod, for the deviousness of Prometheus, who cheated the god at a sacrifice and stole fire from heaven

and gave it to mortals. The punishment took two forms: "the gods keep liveli-
hood hidden from men" (42); and woman (in the person of Pandora) was
created as the bearer of all the evils to which humans are now subject—toil,
famine, sorrow, quarrel, and a whole host of physical and mental ailments
(58–106). It is only through justice and fair dealings—and thus through obedience to the will of Zeus—that humans might escape the scourge:

> Those who give straight verdicts and follow justice, both when fellow citi-
> zens and [when] strangers are on trial, live in a city that blossoms, a city that
> prospers. Then youth-nurturing peace comes over the land, and Zeus who
> sees afar does not decree for them the pains of war. Men whose justice is
> straight know neither hunger nor ruin, but amid feasts enjoy the yield of
> their labors. For them the earth brings forth a rich harvest; and for them
> the top of an oak teems with acorn and the middle with bees. Fleecy sheep
> are weighed down with wool, and women bear children who resemble their
> fathers. There is an abundance of blessings. . . . But far-seeing Zeus, son
> of Kronos, is the judge of wanton wrongdoers who plot deeds of harsh-
> ness. Many times one man's wickedness ruins a whole city, if such a man
> breaks the law and turns his mind to recklessness. Then the son of Kronos
> sends a great bane from the sky, hunger and plague, and the people waste
> away. . . . Zeus the Olympian, the son of Kronos, . . . punishes wrong by
> wiping out large armies, walls, and ships at sea. Kings, give this verdict no
> little thought, for the immortals are ever present among men. (225–49; see
> Atwill 1998, 103–7)

Much of what Hesiod wrote in both poems was shaped by existing myth.
As in the poems of Homer, so also for Hesiod such fundamental entities as
Earth (*Gaia*), Sky (*Ouranos*), and Sea (*Pontos*) were not dead elements but living gods. Positive and negative forces such as Justice (*Dikê*) and Peace (*Eirênê*),
both daughters of Zeus, and their opposites are not social conditions or
abstract forces but individual divinities who act and react within well-defined
areas of jurisdiction. As Dickinson puts the matter, "Nature has become a company of spirits; every cave and fountain is haunted by a nymph; in the ocean
dwell the Nereids, in the mountain the Oread, the Dryad in the wood. . . . Thus
conceived, the world has become less terrible because more familiar" (1958,
3–4).

What is the form of consciousness expressed in these poems and in the
Homeric epics? The mythopoetic mind sees the world as being in some measure unpredictable and as ultimately uncontrollable. "The gods of Homer . . . ,
both in their relations to one another and in the governance of their particular spheres, do not act according to stable ordinances; and as these divinities
are the only effective agents or causes of activity in the world, the universe is

operated without regularity" (Scoon 1928, 9). We sacrifice and pray to the gods in order to win their favor—for battle, for marriage, for births and deaths, for fair winds and good crops, for protection against enemies. Sometimes our prayers are answered because the gods are pleased and bestow their blessings upon us. Other times they are not pleased, and events go against us. The best we can do is perform the proper rituals, sacrifice, and pray. We cannot know how the gods will respond. This way of being-in-the-world is also marked by a sense of the divine as omnipresent and omniscient: in the streams and trees of the countryside, in the wind and sea, in the fire of the hearth, in the bounty of the land, *the immortals are ever present among men*.[18] Moreover "the gods know all things" (*Od.* 4.379).[19] A mythopoetic consciousness sees in everything that happens the work of divine personalities, whose caprices, contests, and couplings have created the history in which human beings are swept up.

To a mythopoetic mind, then, every event has divine meaning. In the *Iliad* (2.311–19), for example, Odysseus tells of the "great portent" in the "miraculous" appearance of a serpent that swallowed nine sparrows. Calchas, a seer, told the Achaians the meaning of this omen: "we will fight in Troy that many years and then, then in the tenth we'll take her broad streets." Thus reassured by Odysseus's report of the event, the Achaians were persuaded to resist their impulse to return home and subsequently to press their attack on Troy. As Homer tells the tale, they were successful. Such is the importance of divine signs or omens. Likewise, natural objects and occurrences are sacred and thus are worthy of reverence, for the proper attitude toward the divine is one of awe and supplication. "A mortal," as Hesiod puts it, "propitiates the gods and, following custom, sacrifices well-chosen victims" (*Th.* 416–17). Thence derives the ubiquity of ritual in Greek life, for if everything that happens manifests the powers and preferences of the immortals, then every human enterprise and event—the prosecution of a war, the founding of a city, the deliberations of an assembly or council, the birth of a child, the burial of a parent, the sowing of seeds, and the harvesting of grain—must be accompanied by the proper rituals so that the gods will bestow their blessings.[20]

What is perhaps most fundamental to a mythopoetic consciousness is that the myths in which one believes *constitute* the world in which one lives. "The myth," Eliade writes, "is regarded as a sacred story, and hence a 'true history,' because it always deals with *realities*. The cosmogonic myth is 'true' because the existence of the World is there to prove it" (1963, 6).[21] For one whose sense of the world is thus constituted, myth is a "living reality," as Malinowski tells us. "The myth in a primitive society, i.e. in its original living form, is not a mere tale told but a reality lived. . . . These stories are not kept alive by vain curiosity, neither as tales that have been invented nor again as tales that are true. For the natives on the contrary they are the assertion of an original, greater, and more important reality through which the present life, fate, and work of mankind are governed, and the knowledge of which provides men on the one hand with motives for ritual and moral acts, on the other with directions for their performance" (1954, 99).[22] For the Greeks of the Dark Age and the early archaic period, then, tales about gods and goddesses, heroes and kings, comprised an etiology of the world of human experience. Accordingly, to a mind conditioned by such a way of accounting for things, the world is infused with the presence of the divine, and it inspires reverence and wonder.

This form of consciousness expresses itself most conspicuously in the speech of the epic poet, whose vision of such truths is articulated in divinely inspired, vividly particular verbal imagery that is taken to represent literally the events it portrays. The language of Greek myth is dramatic, rhythmic, and repetitive. An oral society, Havelock and others have argued, must preserve its sacred account of origins and history through speech that is easily remembered. Thus mythic language "must tell stories rather than relate facts. . . . For the oral memory accommodates language which describes the acts of persons and the happening of events, but is unfriendly to abstracted and conceptual speech" (1983, 13).[23] Mythic speech cannot explain the world in terms of general principles and abstract ideas, nor can it be a mere record of names and events. Rather, it must embed these names and events in a fabric of action, a dramatic narrative that relates origins and causes in terms of the concrete acts of actual *beings*—gods and heroes, Titans and Olympians, giants and Amazons, centaurs and monsters, kings and queens. Ong writes, "The original oral epic derives from and registers an oral noetic economy, in which knowledge was conceived, stored, recalled, and circulated largely through narratives about 'heavy' or heroic figures. Heroic figures, as Havelock's work suggests, are typical not simply of epic as such, but of oral cultures as such" (1977, 191).

The language of myth must also be friendly to the ear and appeal to one's auditory appetites. It must have cadences, rhythms, inflections, and sound combinations that both aid retention and engage the listener's imagination and emotions. Some contend that, for an oral culture to preserve its own sacred history, the tale *must* be cast in the form of poetry. "Preservation in prose," Havelock argues, "was impossible. The only possible verbal technology available to guarantee the preservation and fixity of transmission [from one generation to the next] was that of the rhythmic word organised cunningly in verbal and metrical patterns which were unique enough to retain their shape" (1963, 42–43).[24] Likewise, Ong maintains:

> to store and retrieve its knowledge, an oral culture must think in heavily patterned forms facilitating recall—antitheses, epithets, assertive rhythms, proverbs, and other formulas of many sorts. Without these, in a purely oral

culture thinking is impossible, for, without writing, unless one's articulated thoughts occur in heavy mnemonic patterns they cannot be retained or retrieved. . . . In a completely oral noetic economy, thought which does not consist in memorable patterns is in effect nonthought: you can normally never get it back again. Not merely poetry, but serious discourse of all sorts in such a culture is thus of necessity formulaic—mythology, jurisprudence (consisting of maxims, proverbs, and other sayings and formulas), administrative directives, and the rest. (1977, 191)[25]

Whatever its role in retention and retrieval, oral poetry does more than assist memory. Through its rhythms and cadences, its repetitions and crescendos, its sounds and silences, the spoken poem also draws the listener into itself. It engages the imagination and permits one to lose oneself in the vibrations and variations of the human voice. Orality is particularly important here. The voice is a powerful instrument, and the recitation of epic verse—chanted, almost sung—has an incantational, mesmerizing, even hypnotic quality.[26] Listening to spoken poetry invites not an objective consideration of the matter rendered but an emotional identification with and aesthetic participation in that matter. Vernant writes that "this functional difference between speech and writing has a direct bearing on the position of myth. If the tendency of the spoken word is to give pleasure, this is because it affects the listener in the manner of an incantation. Through its metrical form, its rhythm, its consonances, its musicality, and the gestures or the dances that sometimes accompany it, oral narration stimulates its public to an affective communion with the dramatic actions recounted in the story. This magic quality of speech . . . is considered by the Greeks to be one of the specific qualities of *muthos* as opposed to *logos*. . . . [It is] an operation involving *mimêsis* or emotional participation (*sumpatheia*) on the part of the audience" (1980, 206–7). Accordingly, listening to the epic poem makes one a vicarious player in the drama as it unfolds. There is no objective perception of the poem as a "work of art." There is only the experience of communion, through the sound and sense of the recitation, with the gods and heroes who are one's forebears and who constitute the ground of one's very being (see Havelock 1963, 45–47). Thus the poetic performance can occasion a moment of epiphany: the realm of the immortals is made palpable, and the listener senses the divine.

Several scholars have recently argued that the fourth-century art of rhetoric is rooted in the oral, mythopoetic tradition that Homer and Hesiod formalized in their written poems. Walker, for instance, claims that "what comes to be called the art of rhetoric, *technê rhêtorikê*, in fact originates not from the pragmatic discourse of the fifth-to-fourth-century *rhêtôr* but from an expansion of the poetic/epideictic realm" (2000, 18). He argues that Hesiod's

"Hymn to the Muses" at the beginning of the *Theogony*—and archaic poetry generally—embodies a "'pretheoretical' discursive practice—preceding the emergence of 'rhetoric' and 'poetics' as systematic, disciplinary discourses" (x). Kirby also examines Hesiod's two great poems as instances of "pre-conceptual rhetoric" (1992, 35). Hesiod "considers the poet a kind of rhetor . . . because poetics is, so to say, a species of the genus rhetoric" (54).[27] The persuasive potency of the poems derives especially from their *orality*—from the power of the spoken word to enchant and entrance listeners, and thus to open them to the divinely inspired insights portrayed in the epic poems. Segal notes that words "have an immediate, almost physical impact" upon the psyche (1962, 105). Though he appears to emphasize the *visual* causes of this impact (106–7, 114–15), Segal illuminates the connection between the persuasive impact of speech (*peitho*) and the delight or enjoyment (*terpsis*) that is aroused by the sensory impact of the spoken word. "Successful persuasion," he writes, "works through the aesthetic process of *terpsis* and the emotions connected with it. . . . The fully effective impact of *peitho* involves the emotional participation of the audience, which is made possible and takes place through the aesthetic pleasure of *terpsis*" (122). Significantly, Segal attributes the psychological power of speech to the acoustical qualities of the spoken word, particularly to its quasi-musical features (127). The connections between persuasion and the aural impact of speech emphasized in the fifth century by Gorgias and others have their foundations in the poems of Homer, Hesiod, and their predecessors in the rhapsodic tradition.

The structure of the epic myth-poem, too, is distinctive. An "accounting" rather than an exposition or argument, *mythos* takes a dramatistic, narratival form where the account is punctuated by emotional crescendos—moments of death and salvation, despair and victory—that are the inevitable outcomes of divine acts. Deeds divine and human beget their consequences, and under the pervasive influence of the immortals men and women meet their fates. As with the sounds and rhythms of recitation, so also do the structural features of the epic tale invite emotional involvement and psychological submission rather than objective scrutiny and critical appraisal. Vernant notes that "because it is possible, when reading a text, to turn back and analyze it critically, the operation of reading presupposes a quite different attitude of mind—both more detached and at the same time more demanding—from that involved in listening to spoken discourse. The Greeks themselves were fully aware of this; they contrasted on the one hand the charm that speech must deploy to hold its listeners under its spell and, on the other, the somewhat austere but more rigorous gravity of writing" (1980, 206). To yield to the story, and thereby to encounter the beings upon whose moods and designs one's whole existence depends, is to dwell in mythopoesis.[28]

Histories of Greek thought sometimes describe the "transition from *mythos* to *logos*" as a movement from nonrational or irrational modes of thought (the mythic) to modes that feature "reason" as a foundational principle. Guthrie, for example, writes of "the development . . . from a mythopoetic to a rational view of the world" (1953, 5). Vernant, citing such scholars as Burnet and Snell, describes a view in which "rational thought" is distinguished from *mythos:* "In this view the birth of philosophy . . . was seen as the beginning of scientific thought—or one might even say, [of] 'thought' itself. In the Milesian school *logos* was for the first time freed from myth, just as scales fall from the eyes of a blind man; it was not so much a change in intellectual attitude, a mental mutation, as a single decisive and definitive revelation: the discovery of the mind. . . . The arrival of the *logos* is thus held to have introduced a radical discontinuity into history" (1983, 343). "Reason" and "rationality" are vexed terms here, and to distinguish between a mythopoetic and a "rational" worldview is to beg the question, what is "rationality"? As Hatab and others have pointed out, "a strict separation between myth and logic is ultimately untenable. There is a logic in myth, namely a coherence within which the world is organized and understood and through which the form of whole societies and sets of practices can be defined, guided, supported, and transmitted" (1990, 29).[29]

The logic of *mythos* is the logic of narration as a communicative form. Narration, as Fisher has argued, invokes its own form of rationality, one rooted in humans' responsiveness to *narrative probability* or *coherence* and of *narrative fidelity:* "Narrative *coherence* refers to the formal features of a story conceived as a discrete sequence of thought and/or action in life or literature . . . ; that is, it concerns whether the story coheres or 'hangs together,' whether or not a story is free of contradictions. Narrative *fidelity* concerns the 'truth qualities' of a story, the degree to which it accords with the logic of good reasons: the soundness of its reasoning and the value of its values" (1987, 88). Consequently, insofar as they provided consistent, coherent explanations for the events of life, and to the extent that they comported with the practical experience of their auditors and thus "made sense," the Greek myths provided a structure within which practical decisions could be made and explained. The "reason" of *mythos* lies in the regularities one discerns across the mythic tales regarding what the gods favor and in the explanatory power of the myths to account for one's experience of the world—for floods and earthquakes, growth and decay, conflict and tranquility, plenitude and privation.

One could behave "rationally" if behaving in accordance with accepted understandings of divine preferences. One would be "foolish" or "irrational" to act with disregard for the gods or in opposition to their wills. This is the essence of hubris, as with the "insolence of Agamemnon" (*Il.*1.203) in his treatment of Achilles, Chryses, and ultimately Apollo. On the other hand, piety and prudence were virtually the same thing. The "good counsel" given by Odysseus in the Achaeans' debate over whether or not to continue the war hinges finally on obeying a portent from Zeus (2.283). In any case, we must recognize that the "transition" from myth to philosophy was not so much from the irrational to the rational as from one form of "reasonableness" to another, significantly different form.

What of wisdom in all this? The terms later used by Aristotle to signify two forms of wisdom—*sophia* or speculative wisdom, and *phronêsis* or practical wisdom—do not have these meanings in Homer and Hesiod. The seeds of later significations can nonetheless be detected in the way these terms are deployed by the poets. For Homer, the wise person displays *sophiê* in his/her skill at his/her craft (for example, at *Il.*15.412). Being *sophos* suggests being accomplished at one's art, and thus the term can be used to describe the poet's skill. Hesiod (*Works* 649) echoes this sense when he uses a form of *sophizô* to indicate the activity of giving instruction in the skill of seamanship: "I will teach you the rules that govern the sea." In Pindar, writing in the early fifth century B.C.E., *sophos, sophia, sophistês,* and *sophisma* especially denote skill mated with the power of expressing it well.[30] In its origins, then, *sophia* suggests a kind of active knowledge or competence that is linked specifically with the practice of a *technê*, an art or craft. Aristotle acknowledges this archaic use (*Ethics* 1141a) when he writes that "the term Wisdom (*tên sophian*) is employed in the arts to denote those men who are the most perfect masters of their art, for instance, it is applied to Pheidias as a sculptor and to Polycleitus as a statuary. In this use then Wisdom merely signifies artistic excellence." As the term is "stretched" by writers after Homer and Hesiod, it comes to denote skill in matters of living generally, and so the Seven Sages are called *sophistai* by Theognis and Herodotus.[31] Lloyd notes that "from the seventh century onwards, many different kinds of leaders gained a reputation for *Sophia* in general. They included seers, holy men, [and] wonder-workers. . . . [Such men] were consulted in crises or disasters, plagues or pollutions" (1987, 84).

The term *phronêsis* and its cognates (*phroneô, phronimos, phrontis,* and so on) are rooted in *phrên* and *phrenos*, which in the *Iliad* (for example, at 10.10, 16.481) denotes the "breast" or "midriff" (literally the diaphragm) in which the heart—the seat of the passions and of thought—is enclosed. Thus it comes secondarily to mean "mind," "wits," "thought," "understanding," and "intellectual activity" as opposed to "physical prowess." In the *Iliad* (6.79), for example, Murray translates the term *phroneein* as "counsel": "in every undertaking ye are the best both in war and in counsel" (Homer 1924; also 15.724). Thus *phron-* comes to be associated with reflecting, thinking something out, devising or contriving how a thing is to be done. These associations eventually suggest being thoughtful, prudent, or wise about practical matters.

Although these two terms—*sophia* and *phronêsis*—have their roots in mythopoetic language and are ultimately "stretched" to express classical conceptions of wisdom, they do not tell us much about how wisdom may have been viewed by the Homeric mind. Consequently we must look elsewhere to discern a mythopoetic conception of wisdom that anticipates later developments. In general, wisdom is understood as the highest and most perfect form of knowledge. It turns out that the gods alone possess such knowledge. Zeus, preeminent among the gods (for "his power is greatest of all," *Il.* 2.116) and described by a variety of epithets (for example, Thunderer, Cloud-Gatherer, Invincible), is also known in Homer as *mêtieta*, "allwise" or "the god of good counsel."[32] Similarly Hesiod refers to "Zeus the counselor" (*Th.* 457) and recurringly to "Zeus, whose counsels never perish" (for example, at *Th.* 545, 550, 561). According to Hesiod (*Th.* 886–900), Zeus, after marrying Metis— "a mate wiser than all gods and mortal men"—swallows her, thus incorporating her wisdom into himself "that she might advise him in matters good and bad." The god is thence able to rule with justice.

By his second wife, "radiant Themis," Zeus fathered "Lawfulness and Justice and blooming Peace, . . . and also the Fates, . . . [who] give mortals their share of good and evil" (*Th.* 901–7). Zeus, all-seeing and all-wise, knows what takes place on the earth among men, for "the eye of Zeus sees all, notices all" (*Works* 267); and so he metes out justice in proper measure. He blesses those "whose justice is straight" and punishes "wanton wrongdoers who plot deeds of harshness" (*Works* 230–39), for "this is the law Zeus laid down for men" (276). Even as he dispenses justice, however, "Zeus feels sympathy and is grieved for man, but he acts in accordance with what is ordained" (Burkert 1985, 129). The god knows what must become of everyone, for he knows what has been allotted to each by Fate. As Priam says to the assembled Trojan and Achaean men-at-arms prior to the fight between Menelaus and Paris, "home I go to windy Ilium, straight home now. This is more than I can bear, I tell you—to watch my son do battle with Menelaus loved by the War-god [Ares], right before my eyes. Zeus knows, no doubt, and every immortal too, which fighter is doomed to end all this in death" (*Il.* 3.305–9).

This prescience is at the heart of divine wisdom, and it is what enables Zeus to be a giver of "good counsel." Foreknowledge of what has been ordained is what humans seek when they consult prophets and diviners, soothsayers and oracles. Above all, this is what makes the gods wise beyond what mere mortals can attain. Additionally, just as Zeus sees both present and future, he judges human conduct by the standard of justice. Zeus is "Lawgiver," and the law he gives is Justice (*Dikê*). This is an especially important idea, and it reverberates through Greek thought for centuries to come. To the mythopoetic mind *Dikê* is a divinity, and human understanding of justice rests on knowing what is pleasing and displeasing to the gods. Zeus's Justice, however, rests on a principle of proportion: we are blessed by the gods in proportion to the goodness of our actions, and we are punished in measures befitting our transgressions. This is the pattern that recurs throughout Homer and Hesiod, and it anticipates a central tenet of the naturalistic worldview that both emerged and departed from the mythopoetic tradition.

Human wisdom is derivative. It comes from the gods, who alone can apprehend true justice, who alone can know what the Fates have ordained, and who alone can give "counsel that never fails." "Sing to me now," Homer implores, "you Muses who hold the halls of Olympus! You are goddesses, you are everywhere, you know all things—all we hear is the distant ring of glory, we know nothing" (*Il.* 2.489–91). The "wisdom" of the wisest people—the poet, the oracle, the seer, the soothsayer—consists in being able to recount the histories and genealogies of the gods, in apprehending what is pleasing to them, and in discerning from divine signs which human endeavors they might favor (Burkert 1985; Cornford 1952). All such knowledge comes from the gods themselves through inspiration, revelation, or omens and portents. "I begin my song with the Helikonian Muses," Hesiod tells us. "They have made Helikon, the great god-haunted mountain, their domain. . . . It was they who taught Hesiod beautiful song as he tended his sheep at the foothills of god-haunted Helikon" (*Th.* 1–23). As Burkert observes, "The oral singer is dependent on his goddess, the Muse, who sends him happy inspiration from moment to moment" (1985, 111). Likewise, oracles received their wisdom directly from the gods and were thence empowered to predict the future in ecstatic moments of transcendence induced by psychoactive vapors, wine, or frenzied dancing.[33] Thus was the divine will disclosed directly to mortals through revelation: what the gods favored or foresaw was shown to those who had been chosen to receive this insight. "The experience may rest on natural disposition, acquired technique, or the influence of drugs, but at all events, the individual sees, hears, and experiences things which are not present for others; he stands in direct contact with a higher being and communicates with ghosts and spirits. . . . It is said that a god seizes or carries a person, that he holds him in his power, *katechei*, which gives in translation the term *possessio*, possession" (Burkert 1985, 109–10).

The will of the gods was disclosed indirectly in omens, signs, and portents, whence comes the wisdom of the soothsayer, the seer, the diviner. Signs come from the gods, and through these signs the gods give direction and guidance to humans, though usually in cryptic form. The seer or mantis is a prototype of the wise person, one whose knowledge comes from the ability to interpret divine omens.[34] The seer reads the signs—ranging from the entrails of sacrificial animals to such natural events as eclipses and thunderstorms—and tries to determine what they reveal about the gods' wishes. The seer thus provides guidance in practical affairs and decisions. In the *Iliad*, for instance, Calchas was "the clearest by far of all the seers. . . . He knew all things that are, all things that are past and all that are to come, the seer who had led the Argive ships to Troy with the second sight that god Apollo gave him" (1.69–72). Still, neither the oracle nor the seer knows what the gods know; that is, they do not know for themselves what is just and unjust nor what is ordained by the Fates. They "know" only what the gods permit them to see, and even then portents can be misread.

Ordinary folk could acquire some measure of divine wisdom—some understanding of what would be pleasing to the gods and thus of what ought to be done—through knowing the divine origins of things and their sacred meanings. Such knowledge, moreover, comes in part through intimacy with the myths themselves. Eliade writes that "for the man of the archaic societies . . . what happened *ab origine* can be repeated by the power of rites. For him, then, the essential thing is to know the myths. It is essential not only because the myths provide him with an explanation of the World and his own mode of being in the World, but above all because, by recollecting the myths, by re-enacting them, he is able to repeat what the Gods, the Heroes, or the Ancestors did *ab origine*. To know the myths is to learn the secret of the origin of things. In other words, one learns not only how things came into existence but also where to find them and how to make them reappear when they disappear" (1963, 13–14).[35] To know the myths is to know which divinities have jurisdiction over what places and what sorts of activities, and thus what rites are appropriate to a given setting or occasion.[36] Likewise, apprehending the personal characters of the gods permits one to understand what actions will be pleasing and displeasing to each. Burkert observes that "the Greek gods are persons, not abstractions, ideas or concepts. . . . An individual personality appears that has its own plastic being. This cannot be defined, but it can be known, and such knowledge can bring joy, help, and salvation" (1985, 182–83). To grasp the character of a particular god or goddess is to know how to worship and propitiate the divinity in the proper ways. Such knowledge is a kind of "practical wisdom," a know-how concerning the proper conduct of daily affairs. Moreover it is a wisdom to which the common person—one with no oracular, poetic, or soothsaying powers—can have access, and it originates in knowledge of the sacred tales.[37]

Thence comes also a kind of moral knowledge, insofar as actions the gods find pleasing or displeasing are modeled in the behavior of the mythic protagonists: Achilles' loyalty to Patroclus and his courage in battle; the arrogance of Agamemnon in his treatment of Chryses and thus toward Apollo, whose priest Chryses was. By learning the poems of Homer, Greek youths learned the value of courage, loyalty, honor, and, above all, piety, for these please the gods and can win their favor. Thus did one also come to understand the consequences of hubris and impiety, for these anger the gods and invite their wrath.

Only against this background can we appreciate the transformation in the idea of wisdom that was to come about through the supplantation for some of myth by natural philosophy, of theogony by cosmology, as ways of understanding the origins and causes of things. A mythopoetic consciousness sees in world events the work of the supernatural. Hence the world is full of magic and wonder. Because the gods govern such things as weather and growth, birth and death, and because they interject themselves into the course of events when it suits them to do so, to the mythopoetic mind the world is ultimately unpredictable and uncontrollable. Insofar as human beings can affect what happens around and to them, they can do so only through soliciting and winning the favor of the gods. This requires insight into divine ways and wills. Such insight—a limited wisdom derived from the true wisdom of the gods—comes directly to the oracle and the poet through revelation and inspiration, indirectly to the seer and the diviner through omens, and to the common person through the rituals and myths. In all cases, nonetheless, such wisdom as humans are capable of is rooted in knowledge of the divine.

What can mortals do to augment their own, derivative wisdom? Can such human wisdom be passed from one person to another? The answers to such questions are complex. Human wisdom, as a gift from the gods, is to some extent dependent upon being *chosen*. Like the gift of divine grace in some Christian traditions, so too the gifts of prophecy, divination, and poetry result from the dispositions and preferences of the gods. There is nothing one can do to increase the likelihood of being chosen. Indeed, to some extent it is an accident of birth. "From time immemorial," writes Burkert, "this task [of interpreting divine signs] has been performed by a highly esteemed specialist, the seer, *mantis*, a prototype of the wise man. This gift is handed down from generation to generation. Not only did mythology create genealogical connections between the legendary seers—Mopsos as grandson of Teiresias—but even historical seers would trace themselves back to some figure such as Melampus" (1985, 112).

On the other hand, there were certain religious practices, always associated with cult worship, that "opened" one to divine revelation. The Eleusinian mysteries, the Dionysian frenzy, the practices of the Orphic groups—all sought to break down barriers between immortal and mortal realms so that mere mortals would be open to such gifts of insight as the gods might choose to bestow.[38] To hear the words of the poet, moreover, was to experience indirectly the divine inspiration behind the poet's own *sophia* or word skill, and thus to be given access to some measure of divine knowledge. Though the poet could not make another wise through the communication of insight, the poem could serve as an aperture through which the listener might glimpse the divine realm and experience a kind of communion with the gods. Such "wisdom" comes at thirdhand, to be sure, but it is the only kind of wisdom to which most mortals might aspire.

The mythopoetic mind set did not disappear from Greek culture with the advent of positivistic, protoscientific thought. As Guthrie notes, "the mythical mentality did not die a sudden death" (1953, 6).[39] It was preserved and exercised in daily religious practice, in communal religious festivals and other observances, in the tradition of Homeric poetry, in Greek drama, and in persuasive speech. The persistence and pervasiveness of the traditional worldview, indeed, is expressed clearly in Xenophon's fourth-century account of Hermogenes' speech at *The Dinner Party* (4.47):

> Well, it's quite plain that both Greeks and non-Greeks believe that the gods know everything that is and will be; at any rate, all States and all peoples inquire of the gods by means of divination what they ought and ought not to do. Next, it's also clear that we believe they can do us both good and harm; at least, everyone asks the gods to avert what is evil and grant what is good. Well, these omniscient and omnipotent gods are such good friends to me that, because of their concern for me, I am never beyond their notice night or day, wherever I am bound and whatever I intend to do. And because of their foreknowledge, they indicate to me the result of every action, sending me messages by utterances, dreams and omens to tell me what I ought to do and what I ought not; and when I obey these, I am never sorry for it, but when I have sometimes disobeyed in the past, I have been punished for it. (1990, 248)

With the postulation by Thales, Anaximander, Heraclitus, and others of an indwelling, universal, originative substance or principle (an *archê*) that underlies all that happens, a new form of rationality, a new conception of divinity, and new ideas of wisdom emerged in Greek thought. In some ways the history of the Western world has been marked ever since by a competition between this outlook and vestiges of the mythopoetic mind set as the latter has been preserved in and transformed by Christianity. The historical conflict between "science" and "religion," as between "reason" and "faith," has its roots in the discontinuities between naturalistic and mythopoetic ways of seeing the world.

In Greek societies some perceived this new way of looking at things as a threat to established religious tradition, and it was rejected, even attacked, as being impious (witness the trials of Anaxagoras and Socrates). In other instances it invited atheism or agnosticism (as with Xenophanes and Protagoras). Arrayed between these two poles were a great many Greeks—simultaneously intrigued by and suspicious of the new "philosophy" but not ready to give up their religious convictions or their daily pieties. Even Socrates, for all his "rationalism," hearkened to omens and divine signs and invoked the gods in his daily speech. Old and new ways of seeing the world coexisted, intermingled in parts and in parts at odds with one another. What is certain is that, beginning early in the sixth century B.C.E. along the western coast of Asia Minor, there emerged a way of understanding and being-in-the-world that in some respects constituted a radical departure from the mythopoetic mind set that preceded it.

Connections between wisdom and speech in the mythopoetic tradition shaped the evolution of these two ideas in Greek society for centuries to come. While it would be anachronistic to speak of "philosophy" and "rhetoric" at this point, we can see that the pursuit of wisdom aimed finally at being "touched" by a god, and wise speech is *entheos logos*—filled with the divine. True wisdom is the wisdom of the gods; human wisdom is an imperfect apprehension of the gods' will. What the gods decide comes to pass, so understanding their wishes gives the human being some measure of prophetic power, a limited capacity to foresee the future. This power of foresight is the essence of mythopoetic wisdom. It equips one to answer the most important of questions: What will happen? What should be done? To the extent that one can plumb the mind of a god, one can know these things.

Speech—oral *logos*—is central in the mythopoetic vision of *sophia*. While the highest human wisdom comes directly from the gods, it is speech—in the form of poetry—that disseminates wisdom among those lacking the divine vision. The inspired words of the poet, heard in all their aural sensuousness, can inspire the listener. As one hears the sounds of metrical, aesthetically pleasing speech, one can enter a state of *entheos* and "breathe in" the divine mind as it is disclosed in the *mythos* of the poem. Speech, indeed, can be a "powerful lord." If the poet is "touched by a god," the hearer can be given glimpses of what the poet has apprehended and so can participate in the poet's vision, if only at a distance.

Thus are wisdom and speech intermingled in Greek thought from the very beginning. The gods, indeed, speak to the common folk through the poet and oracle, whose words are wisdom speaking.

THREE

Physis, Kosmos, Logos

Presocratic Thought and the Emergence of Nature-Consciousness

Wisdom is one [thing]: knowing the plan by which
all things are steered through all.

Heraclitus (DK 41)

Some years ago I went with my wife and younger son to visit Penn's Cave, a
central Pennsylvania limestone cavern that can be examined only by boat
because the stream that formed it still runs through it, creating a lake for its
entire length. We toured the cavern under the direction of a professional guide
who controlled the boat and explained the cave's geological and social history
(it figures in a local legend that allegedly derives from Native American folk-
lore). In the course of his account, our guide noted that the numerous stalag-
mites and stalactites in the cave grow at a rate of about an inch per century,
and using this rate, along with the size of the largest formations, it has been
determined that the cavern itself is some thirty million years old. As soon as
the guide had made this statement, one of the boat's passengers spoke up, suggesting as an "alternative explanation" that "God created this cavern in its
present form just a few thousand years ago." These two accounts of the cave's
formation reflect very different worldviews: one in which what we see in the
world is the result of natural, law-governed processes that unfold in regular,
predictable ways; and another in which the world we know is the product of
supernatural action, wherein the behavior of a divine being (or beings) is the
ultimate cause of the "works" that others attribute to nature.

The contrast between these two worldviews captures quite accurately a key
difference between a mythopoetic mind set and a new way of looking at the
world that emerged in Greece during the seventh and sixth centuries B.C.E.
Beginning with the Ionian thinkers—Thales, Anaximander, Anaximenes, Xenophanes, and Heraclitus are those whose words have come down to us—a conceptual and linguistic revolution occurred that constituted what Kuhn (1970)

has termed a "paradigm shift." The conceptual shift here was not from one scientific paradigm to another—for example, from a geocentric to a heliocentric model of planetary motion. Rather, it was from a supernaturalistic to a naturalistic world-paradigm. This conceptual revolution was furthered by Greek thinkers working in colonies in Sicily and southern Italy. Pythagoras, Parmenides, Zeno, Empedocles, and Philolaus refined, extended, or augmented the naturalistic cosmologies they inherited from their Ionian forebears. With Anaxagoras, Melissus, and the Atomists such speculation returned to Ionia, yielding more-sophisticated explanations for natural events. These conceptual changes were accompanied by linguistic developments no less dramatic in their impact. Indeed, the two processes were acutely interrelated, with conceptual changes both instigating and growing out of several important advances in the use of language: the invention of alphabetic writing, the appearance of prose composition, the emergence of a philosophical vocabulary and syntax, and the deployment of argument as a method of collective, public decision making and of intellectual speculation.

The implications of these changes were profound for the idea of wisdom and the role of speech in its acquisition and exercise. Though wisdom continued its association with a kind of "divine" knowledge, the objective of this knowledge was no longer to understand what pleases the gods, and wisdom was no longer gained through inspiration coming through wine, trances, and the rapture of hearing the epics. Instead, human wisdom was conceived as grasping the cosmic "plan" or "principle" according to which all things come to pass, and its attainment was seen in part as springing from human discourse and interaction. As an apprehension of cosmic principles that direct the flow of world events, the wisdom of the first "nature philosophers" discloses a foundation for regularity and predictability in these events. This makes possible the arguments from probability that later became a key feature of rhetoric and a staple of persuasive discourse in the assembly and in court. The Presocratics, accordingly, provided a necessary condition for rhetorical theorizing and practice in the classical era.

The "transition from myth to reason"—from mythopoetic to naturalistic ways of understanding the world—was neither sudden nor linear nor final.[1] Even with the advent of positivistic thinking among the intelligentsia of such Ionian towns as Miletos and Ephesos, most people held to traditional beliefs and practices.[2] The Ionian thinkers had their feet planted in "two worlds, the mythical and the rational, both at once" (Guthrie 1953, 6), as shown both by the language they employed in the service of naturalistic explanation and by the fundamental concepts upon which the new cosmologies were based.[3] Moreover the shift from a supernaturalistic to a naturalistic cosmology brought about not so much a movement from *theos* to *physis* as a transformation of the concept of divinity itself. This idea is altered by a process of abstraction through which it is stripped of its associations with supernatural, anthropomorphic beings who are not bound by any "laws" of nature, and it is subjected to the rigors of positivistic analysis. What remains are universal qualities of divinity retained after mythic, anthropomorphic features are taken away—timelessness, omnipresence, and omnipotence. Vernant comments that "the Milesian elements may not be mythical figures such as *Gaia*, but nor are they concrete realities such as earth. They are eternally active powers, *both divine and natural at the same time*. What is new, conceptually, is that these powers are strictly defined and conceived in abstract terms: they are limited to producing a definite physical effect, and this effect is a general, abstract quality" (1983, 348; my emphasis). Later he adds, "The birth of philosophy thus seems connected with two major transformations of thought. The first is the emergence of positivist thought that excludes all forms of the supernatural and rejects the implicit assimilation, in myth, of physical phenomena with divine agents; the second is the development of abstract thought that strips reality of the power of change that myth had ascribed to it" (351).

What were the conditions—social, political, economic, intellectual—that incubated the seeds of Western scientific and philosophical thought? One such factor is the infusion into Greek thought of non-Greek cosmogonies, myths, ideas, and customs. It is no coincidence that new ways of explaining world events first emerged in Ionia, the eastern frontier of the Greek world. Before the turn of the first millennium B.C.E., Mycenaean outposts in Rhodes and Cyprus, and at Miletos on the west coast of the Anatolian peninsula, had contacts with Asiatic and Middle Eastern cultures.[4] By the eighth century Miletos was already a flourishing trade center. During the so-called "Age of Colonization" (ca. 750–550 B.C.E.), this prosperous town occupied an intersection of trade routes between the Aegean and the western Mediterranean, on the one hand, and the ancient civilizations of the Near East—the Hittites, Phoenicians, Babylonians, Egyptians, and Persians—on the other. Hooper notes, "In this city of contrasts and diversities, a crossroads for east and west, the strange was a commonplace and the new only incidental. If there were to be a startling breakthrough in man's thinking, a shift toward rationalism, Miletos was the place for it" (1978, 126).[5] Exposure to a wide variety of mythic traditions and to alternative ways of understanding the origins and operation of world-processes invited at least a few inquiring minds to question and finally to reject the Homeric and Hesiodic accounts. In their place, these thinkers constructed explanations rooted in natural rather than supernatural causes. Thales' purported prediction of an eclipse in 585 B.C.E. (Herodotus 1.74), for example, may have been a product of his study of Babylonian astronomical observations from the preceding 150 years. For him, such predictability was a key to seeing world events as products of natural regularities rather than of divine acts. Hooper observes that "when he correctly predicted the eclipse, . . . it was for him a starting point toward new knowledge, not merely confirmation of an old belief in omens. To him the eclipse was a natural event about which a curious man might wonder and perhaps learn more. To the Babylonian priests it was a message from the gods" (1978, 127).[6] The importation of information and ideas from the diverse civilizations of Asia and Africa created in Miletos especially, and among Ionian communities generally, a rich intellectual culture by which a few extraordinary minds would be nourished and thence would beget new ways of looking at things.

Among the most significant of such imports was the Phoenician system of writing (Herodotus 5.58). Though there is some controversy about when the Phoenician alphabet entered Greek society, it is generally agreed that its use had become fairly widespread by the end of the eighth century B.C.E.[7] The impact of this innovation cannot be overestimated. In addition to recording the traditional myths when the epic poems of Homer and Hesiod were written down, the invention of Greek writing also made possible an entirely new orientation toward these myths and toward their account of the origins and causes of things. Havelock notes that the emergence of natural philosophy occurs at the cusp between the oral and the literate traditions precisely because the written word induces a form of consciousness rooted in a distinction between the knower and the known, between subject and object (1963, chap. 11).[8] With writing, speech acquires the status of object—it exists independently of the speaker. It survives and thus transcends the moment of utterance and hearing. Oral speech survives only in the personal memories of speaker and hearer. Indeed, if Havelock's view is correct, it is precisely the mnemonic utility of rhythmic speech that explains the supposed necessity in oral cultures of poetry as "preserved communication." In any event, oral utterance is transitory, and the recollection of a *mythos* serves merely to keep alive a people's mythic accounts of their own origins and history. Surviving only in memory and recitation, such utterance has no independent presence, no existence except in the voice of the rhapsode and in the memory of the hearer.

When such accounts are written down, however, they acquire an objective status outside the consciousness of poet and auditor. Since writing obviates the need for memorization, the mind can regard a written account in a way altogether different from how the oral poem must be regarded. Rather than being preoccupied, as the oral mind must be, with the immediate enjoyment and preservation of the tale, the literate mind is free to regard it objectively and, finally, *critically.* "Because it is possible," Vernant writes, "when reading a text, to turn back and analyze it critically, the operation of reading presupposes a quite different attitude of mind—both more detached and at the same time more demanding—from that involved in listening to spoken discourse" (1990, 206). The invention of writing, consequently, enabled a critical assessment of traditional accounts of the origins and workings of the world, and assessment made possible the development of alternative accounts and a new mode of thinking about the world.[9] No longer universally viewed as sacred tales and divine histories (*mythoi*) to be preserved and passed on, the myths are seen now by some as accounts or explanations (*logoi*) to be examined, questioned, responded to, and even rejected. Thus emerged an orientation toward *all* accounts, traditional and contemporary, that was fundamentally *interrogatory* rather than participatory and submissive.

The emergence of the polis as a form of political organization also had an important impact on the development of a new consciousness. Indeed, civic activity in the polis stimulated the development of new ways of thinking about the world and its workings and created a new role for oral discourse in the quest for wisdom. The decline and eventual disappearance of Mycenaean civilization was followed by a general depopulation of Greek lands and by a decentralization and fragmentation of political and economic power. During the Dark Age and early archaic period (ca. 1100–600 B.C.E.), Greek political life was organized around small towns and villages that were generally ruled by local, aristocratic chieftain-kings.[10] These monarchies were later replaced by aristocracies, and aristocracies in turn by tyrannies.

What happened next depended on local conditions and experiences. In places such as Miletus, Ephesos, and Priene in Ionia, and in Athens, Megara, and Corinth on the Greek mainland, the consolidation of local hamlets under the suzerainty of a dominant city led to the emergence of a complex political structure in which residents began to identify themselves as citizens linked by a shared constitution and by their devotion to a city and its patron deities. At Athens this took place during the sixth and fifth centuries, when natives of the hamlets and villages of Attica were granted Athenian citizenship. Moreover changes in the laws and the implementation of constitutional arrangements that further broadened participation in the political process led to the emergence in various cities and towns of an "assembly of all citizens"—an *ekklêsia*— as a principal component of government.[11]

The popular assembly of the Greek polis had its roots in the *agorê* of the Homeric age: the assembly or "gathering" of the army or of the people.[12] As the action in book 2 of the *Iliad* clearly demonstrates, however, this assembly of the commons had no decision-making power. The judgment as to whether to persist in the war or to abandon it is taken by Agamemnon as a result of the message Zeus sends him in a dream. When the troops are finally brought together in the "place of gathering" (*agorê*, 2.93) they are subjected to various exhortations and harangues by several speakers—but only so that they might ultimately be stirred to action (2.100–403). This early assembly was not so much a deliberative body as it was a mob to be rallied by a leader's eloquence.

With the advent of the polis and new constitutional arrangements that brought the common people into the decision-making process, the popular assembly was transformed from Homer's rally of roused tribesmen into an arena in which proposed laws and policies were subjected to criticism, discussion, and debate. Thus did speech and public argument function as the means whereby ideas were scrutinized and appraised according to the Greek tradition of *agôn*—the contest of man against man in displays of oratorical power and virtuosity. Those that withstood such testing commanded assent (at least among the majority), while those that did not were rejected. Vernant observes that

> speech became the political tool par excellence, the key to all authority in the state, the means of commanding and dominating others. . . . Speech was no longer the ritual word, the precise formula, but open debate, discussion, argument. . . . All questions of general concern that the sovereign had to settle, and which marked out the domain of *archê* [sovereignty], were now submitted to the art of oratory and had to be resolved as the conclusion of a debate. They therefore had to be formulated as a discourse, poured into the mold of antithetical demonstrations and opposing arguments. There was a close connection, a reciprocal tie, between politics and *logos*. The art of politics became essentially the management of language. (1982, 49–50; also see Fredal 2006, 36–39)

Likewise Hawhee contends that "the role of the *agôn*, the struggle or contest, in early Greek culture cannot be overemphasized: it was the place where wars were won or lost . . . , the reason the gods and goddesses came into being, [and] the context for the emergence of philosophy and art" (2004, 15). She continues by noting that the term denotes not so much a competition aimed at winning a prize but "the contestive encounter" that occurs in the presence of a "gathering" or "assembly" of interested observers (15–16). Thus did public political debate become a kind of spectator sport.

One important consequence of the growing significance of public discussion and argument was the full exposure given to the most important aspects of social life, including intellectual inquiry into the fundamental character of the world. "We can even say," Vernant continues, "that the *polis* existed only to the extent that a *public* domain had emerged . . . : an area of common interest, as opposed to private concerns, and open practices openly arrived at, as opposed to secret procedures. . . . Knowledge, values, and mental techniques, in becoming elements of a common culture, were themselves brought to public view and submitted to criticism and controversy. . . . Now discussion, debate, polemic became the rules of the intellectual as well as [of] the political game"

(1982, 51). Popper argues that "the tradition of critical discussion" was a central factor in the early history of Greek philosophical inquiry (1970, 147–51).

Emerging political procedures nurtured in certain communities a spirit of inquiry and criticism that expressed itself in both political and intellectual realms. As the political power of the king and later the aristocracy was diffused more and more widely, questions of state were resolved more and more often in the arena of public discussion. In a sociopolitical climate where decisions concerning law and policy were reached collectively, the method of debate and the spirit of *agôn* and criticism crossed over into other areas of concern. Thus did questions of cosmogony and cosmology likewise submit to discussion and debate; and thus did the method of interrogation, critique, counterthesis, and counterargument become fundamental in understanding the world—an understanding that would lead to a new form of consciousness and a new kind of wisdom.

This intellectual innovation manifests itself first in Thales' apparent conviction that "the earth rests on water."[13] We have no direct evidence for Thales' cosmological thinking.[14] Consequently we depend on later writers' representations, most especially Aristotle's. We must be careful in what we attribute to Thales as a thinker based on the record we have. Aristotle, for instance, who was extremely cautious in ascribing opinions to him, nonetheless describes Thales as holding that water is the *archê*—the "first principle of all existing things" (*Meta.* 983b). Havelock (1983), Kahn (1960), and others have argued that it is doubtful Thales had this use of the term available to him, which raises the question as to whether he could have had such an abstract concept in mind.[15] Still, considering Havelock's views concerning the Presocratics' metaphorical "stretching" of the mythic vocabulary, we can perhaps discern a level of consciousness in Thales' account of the world.

There is ambiguity in Aristotle's representation of Thales' view. In one place (*On the Heavens* 294a) we are invited to think that Thales believed that all solid land literally floats on water, "like a log or some other such thing." In this case Thales' principal philosophical accomplishment consists in an essentially geophysical observation.[16] Elsewhere we are told that water is in some sense an originating element or foundational principle of all things. In the *Metaphysics* (983b) Aristotle says:

> most of the first philosophers thought that principles (*archas*) in the form of matter were the only principles of all things; for the original source of all existing things, that from which a thing first comes-into-being and into which it is finally destroyed, the substance persisting but changing in its qualities, this they declare is the element (*stoicheion*) and first principle (*archên*) of existing things. . . . Thales, the founder of this type of philosophy, says that it is water (and therefore declared that the earth is on water),

perhaps taking this supposition from seeing the nurture of all things to be moist, and the warm itself coming-to-be from this and living by this . . . , taking the supposition both from this and from the seeds of all things having a moist nature, water being the natural principle of moist things.

The characterization of water as an originating principle is decidedly more sophisticated than the view that the earth floats on water, and it attributes to Thales a capacity for abstract thought that may have been beyond him—but perhaps not. Guthrie observes:

> in this, our earliest account of Thales' cosmological views, they are already set forth in the abundant philosophical terminology of a later age. No early Ionian could have expressed his ideas in terms of substance and attribute (*ousia* and *pathos*), of coming-to-be in an absolute sense (*aplôs*) as opposed to relatively, or of a substratum (*hypokeimenon*) or element (*stoikeion*). These distinctions, now a part of ordinary speech, were only achieved after much strenuous logical analysis on the part of Plato and its elaboration into a technical vocabulary by Aristotle himself. Great caution is needed here, but in spite of the close interrelation between language and thought, it does not necessarily follow that what Aristotle is giving is a complete misrepresentation of the earlier views. (1962, 56)[17]

As it is, we are left only with Aristotle's account of Thales' view on this matter, and we must work with the evidence we have. Whether Thales believed that earth literally *floats on water* or even that earth somehow *comes from water* (that is, that earth is solidified out of water in some way), what is significant is that he fixed upon a natural foundation for the world, in contrast to the supernatural beings to whose actions Greek myth ascribed the origins of events. Such a view marks an important departure from a mythopoetic mind set. The fact that he located this foundation in a natural substance rather than in the realm of the supernatural amounts to a "paradigm shift" of considerable magnitude— a revolutionary change in the basic model of reality in terms of which experiences and observations are understood (Kuhn 1970, 43–91). This is the crucial first step on the path from mythopoesis to natural philosophy—and ultimately to science—as contrasting ways of understanding causality in the world and of viewing our place in it. This view rejects the supernatural account altogether and initiates the process of conceptualizing nature as an impersonal, directive force in the world. "In a word," writes Wightman, "it was Thales who first attempted to explain the variety of nature as the modifications of something *in* nature."[18]

We might suppose that Aristotle was correct in interpreting Thales as holding that water is the *archê* of things, that it is somehow the source, origin, or "material cause" of things (*Meta.* 983b). When we consider the possibility that he was engaged in some form of conceptual and linguistic experimentation, then it is not unreasonable to suppose as well that Thales could have been using the idea of water—a formless, tasteless, odorless, colorless substance that nonetheless is present "in the nurture of all things"—as an analogue for some sort of "prime matter."[19] While we must be careful to avoid anachronism here, if his thinking was at the threshold of a new conception for which no terminology yet existed, it is quite possible that Thales employed the idea of water in a somewhat analogical way—that he envisioned a common substance of all things that is somehow *like* water. In doing so, he might be taken as anticipating the subsequent quest for an abstract conception of the originating principle or universal substrate of all things, an idea for which Thales had no words. This conception would make possible the more sophisticated theses of Anaximander and later thinkers. In any case, it seems clear that he introduced an altogether novel way of looking at the structure of the world and at the origins of world events. It is for this alone that he is generally regarded as the "founder" of natural philosophy, as Aristotle described him.

Another idea attributed to Thales also bears on the development of a "new consciousness": that "all things are full of gods (*panta plêrê theôn einai*)" (Aristotle, *On the Soul* 411a). At the cusp between mythopoesis and naturalistic cosmology Thales has apparently imported into the emergent worldview a notion of divinity that has its roots in the ancient, theocentric consciousness. The natural world is somehow infused with a divine element. Again, if we take Thales' conception as an example of Havelock's metaphorical "stretching" of language, then he has used the vocabulary of myth (*theos*) to express an abstract idea—for instance, that "the whole world is somehow alive and animated" or that "all things in sum . . . [are] interpenetrated by some kind of life-principle" (Kirk, Raven, and Schofield 1983, 95, 97). Alternatively he might have intended that the natural basis of the flux and variety in world events is itself somehow timeless, unchanging. "Everlasting life is the mark of the divine, and of nothing else," writes Guthrie. "Hence Thales, though rejecting the anthropomorphic deities of popular religion, could retain its language to the extent of saying that, in a special sense, the whole world was filled with gods" (1962, 68). It is significant that the divine is somehow present even in a world where physical processes are seen to originate in natural rather than in supernatural forces. This represents a new conception of divinity, an abstract idea in which the chief distinguishing marks of the gods—their immortality, their unlimited power (their "life-force"), and that this force extends over both animate and inanimate realms—are divorced from the notion of individual, anthropomorphic deities. This naturalistic conception of the divine, incipient in Thales, emerges more fully in the writings of several later thinkers.

Thales is regarded as the first philosopher partly because he focuses on new questions. Homer was interested in explaining how the gods affected the course of physical and human events. Hesiod was concerned with the origins of the gods and the human race. In contrast, Thales was apparently interested in what the world is made of and in the mechanics of its operation. The shift is from sacred history and theogony to an empirical interest in physical phenomena. In this way Thales initiated a move away from preoccupation with the past, with what was "in the beginning," to an acute interest in the present, in the nature (the *physis*) of "what is," and in how things happen as a result of this nature's workings. This move opens the door to a new way of regarding the world around us—not as the manifestation of the acts of powerful and capricious divinities, but rather as somehow the *natural* product of regular, physical processes operating according to an indwelling *physis* (Scoon 1928, 238). Thus began the conceptual transition from *archê* as the temporal beginning of a particular thing to *archê* as the underlying substance and "first principle of [all] existing things." Thus also began the movement from a theological to a naturalistic account of the world.

The emerging nature-consciousness can be seen in Thales' intuition that the underlying substance or principle of existing things was itself *one thing* and that this unifying force exists *within nature* rather than outside it. At the same time, he seems not to have abandoned the idea of divinity even as he embraced a materialist explanation of world events. Rather, Thales may have initiated a process of transforming this idea from the particular, personal, anthropomorphic gods of mythopoesis to the abstract idea of "the divine" (*to theion*) as the timeless, impersonal, pervasive power according to which all things come to pass. The possibility of such an understanding of *theion* is at least implicit in Thales' view that "all things are full of gods." As Vlastos observes, "The unique achievement of the Presocratics as *religious* thinkers . . . lies in the fact that they, and they alone, . . . dared [to] transpose the name and function of divinity into a realm conceived as a rigorously natural order and, therefore, completely purged of miracle and magic. . . . To present the deity as wholly immanent in the order of nature and therefore [as] absolutely law-abiding was the peculiar and distinctive religious contribution of the Presocratics. . . . They took a word [*theos*] which in common speech was the hallmark of the irrational, unnatural, and unaccountable and made it the name of a power which manifests itself in the operation, not the disturbance, of intelligible law" (1970c, 119–20).[20]

Thales may have been among the first to deploy the resources of language metaphorically in service of a nonmythic account of the world. If, indeed, he intended that "water" not be understood literally but rather as an analogue for a kind of formless, plastic substance from which all things arise, then in his words we may have an example of the linguistic "stretching" that Havelock has in mind. Similarly, if the statement that "everything is full of gods" is taken metaphorically, once again we have an example of mythopoetic terminology being "stretched" to serve the purposes of abstract, naturalistic thought. If we grant Havelock's thesis (shared by Kahn, Vernant, and others) that the Greek language had not yet evolved to the level of abstraction necessary for analytical, philosophical accounts of world-processes, then perhaps it is reasonable to conclude that Thales initiated linguistic innovations whose implications were explored by such intellectual descendants as Anaximander, Anaximenes, Heraclitus, and Parmenides, among others.

Thales' speculations were advanced by his fellow Milesian Anaximander. Anaximander was called by Theophrastus the "successor and pupil" (*diadoxos kai mathêtês*), a "disciple" (*akpoatês*, literally a "hearer") and "companion" (*hetairon*) of Thales, and his "kinsman, companion, acquaintance or fellow-citizen" in the later doxographical tradition.[21] This almost offhand attribution portends an important development in the emergent Greek intellectual tradition: that instrumental in the production of a new kind of wisdom is interaction between teacher and student aiming not at the preservation of an oral *mythos* or of religious traditions and rituals but at critical investigation into the natural causes of world events and processes.

Whether or not he explicitly rejected Thales' hypothesis about the *archê*, when Anaximander offered his own account of "the principle and element of existing things," he treated the *logos* of his predecessor as a hypothesis to be scrutinized and a theory to be criticized rather than as an account to be preserved and embellished. In this way what might be described as the earliest instance of "scholarly dialogue" can be seen to figure in the production of a nonmythic understanding of natural events. Popper notes the emergence in the archaic period of a "tradition of critical discussion" and finds the origins of this tradition in Anaximander's response to Thales:

> If we look for the first signs of this new critical attitude, this new freedom of thought, we are led back to Anaximander's criticism of Thales. Here is a most striking fact: Anaximander criticizes his master and kinsman, one of the Seven Sages, the founder of the Ionian school. . . . But there is no trace in the sources of a story of dissent, of any quarrel, or of any schism. This suggests . . . that it was Thales who founded the new tradition of freedom— based upon a new relation between master and pupil—and who thus created a new type of school. . . . He seems to have been able to tolerate criticism. . . . I can hardly imagine a relationship between master and pupil in which the master merely tolerates criticism without actively encouraging it. (1970, 149)[22]

This kind of dialogue was encouraged by a number of other important developments, as we have seen, including the invention of alphabetic writing, the consequent development of prose as a form of polished artistic expression, and the emergence of the polis, with its growing emphasis on public discussion and debate as the method of civic decision making. Still, a new form of consciousness—naturalistic rather than theocentric—emerged in tandem with the development of new forms and uses of speech. It is inviting to see at work here a kind of reciprocal stimulation, each movement encouraging the growth of its counterpart.

Anaximander took the naturalistic line of speculation far beyond anything Thales had envisioned. He was apparently the first Greek to produce a written account of the workings of nature, and the surviving fragment of his writings contains the earliest credible quotation from a Greek philosophical treatise.[23] Anaximander's fragment concerning the origin and destiny of "the heavens and all the worlds in them" reveals an abstract, sophisticated conceptualization that takes us to the brink of a universe disclosed by later scientific inquiry. As it is translated from Simplicius's version of Theophrastus's writings, the fragment reads:

> Of those who say that it [the origin of things] is one, moving, and infinite, Anaximander, son of Praxiades, a Milesian, the successor and pupil of Thales, said that the principle (*archên*) and element (*stoicheion*) of existing things was the *apeiron*, being the first to introduce this name of the material principle. He says that it is neither water nor any other of the so-called elements, but some other *apeiron* nature (*physin apeiron*) from which come into being all the heavens and the worlds (*kosmoi*) in them. And the source of coming-to-be for existing things is that into which destruction, too, happens according to necessity (*kata to chreôn*); for they pay penalty and retribution to each other for their injustice according to the assessment of Time, as he describes it in these rather poetical terms.[24]

Anaximander may have been the first to use the term *archê* in a philosophical sense to refer to the origin or source of existing things.[25] This word derives from *archô* in Homer, which signifies to "lead off" or "be first" and thus to "begin" (for example, at *Od.* 5.237, *Il.* 1.495). It eventually takes on a particularly technical meaning, appearing in later philosophical writing to indicate the "first principle" or "material substratum" of existing things. Aristotle employs this term to mean a "[logically] first principle," for instance in the *Nicomachean Ethics* (1139b, 1140b) and the *Metaphysics* (981b, 982a, 983a). Such a usage represents a considerable metaphorical extension of Homer's "to lead off" (for others to follow). The passage is also notable for its explicit rejection of Thales' view that the *archê* is water or "any other of the so-called [material] elements."

It suggests a deliberate effort to critique and go beyond the views of Anaximander's teacher because it rejects the idea of a material "first principle." If this is so—if Anaximander was indeed looking for a nonmaterial *archê*—then his conceptualization represents a major step up the ladder of abstraction from where his teacher and predecessor had rested.

Perhaps his most significant contribution to the emergence of a new consciousness, and thus to a new understanding of human wisdom, is his conception of this *archê*. Anaximander, we are told, "says that it is neither water nor any of the other so-called elements but some other unbounded nature (*physin apeiron*)." The word *apeiron* may be taken to represent Anaximander's attempt at articulating an abstract philosophical concept in terms that go beyond the language of *mythos*. *Apeiron* literally means "without boundary or perimeter," and it can be taken to signify that the *archê* is spatially "unbounded," "unlimited," or "infinite." At the most literal level, then, Anaximander might be interpreted as saying that the origin or source of things is something unbounded or infinite, some "huge, inexhaustible mass, stretching away endlessly in every direction" (Kahn 1960, 233).[26] However, he may also be understood as having taken to a higher level of abstraction Thales' figurative notion of water as something "formless." To be "without perimeter" or boundary is to be without a definite form. Thus the *apeiron* may refer to a "formless" nature from which all things come (Hatab 1990, 169).

If we read *apeiron* as pushing the metaphorical power of language further still, it can signify that the origin of things is not merely "unbounded" or "limitless" in a spatial and/or temporal sense but some "indefinite" or "undefined" thing, a *physis* that is not fully expressible in language. Such a formulation resonates intriguingly with the opening verse of the almost-exactly contemporaneous *Tao Te Ching:* "The tao that can be told is not the eternal Tao. The name that can be named is not the eternal Name. The unnamable is the eternally real. Naming is the origin of all particular things. Free from desire, you realize the mystery. Caught in desire, you see only the manifestations. Yet mystery and manifestations arise from the same source. This source is called darkness. Darkness within darkness. Gateway to all understanding" (Mitchell 1988, 1). Bynner's translation introduces additional nuances: "Existence is beyond the power of words to define: Terms may be used but are none of them absolute. In the beginning of heaven and earth there were no words. Words came out of the womb of matter; and whether a man dispassionately sees to the core of life or passionately sees the surface, the core and the surface are essentially the same, words making them seem different only to express appearance. If name be needed, wonder names them both: from wonder into wonder existence opens" (1962, 25). On this reading, the *archê* of existing things would be some *undefined* and *undefinable* "nature," something beyond the power of words to express. Thus Anaximander's use of *apeiron* to describe the *archê* might provide a term for some undefinable, formless reality that gives rise to the material world we know through experience. We might also see here the earliest consideration of the relationship between language and "reality," between what can be expressed and the *physis* from which all things arise and into which they return.[27]

Another key term in Anaximander's fragment, of course, is precisely this *physis*. In its earliest attested uses the term expresses a thing's organic origin or source of growth, the indwelling force or power that causes a thing to become the kind of thing it is. Liddell and Scott list "origin" and "growth" as the first two equivalents for the term and then elaborate these as *"the natural form or constitution* of a person or thing *as the result of growth"* (1996, 1964). Likewise, Jaeger observes that *physis* "denotes quite plainly the act of *phynai*—the process of growth and emergence . . . , the origin and growth of the things we find about us. But it also includes their source of origin—that from which they have grown, and from which their growth is constantly renewed—in other words, the reality underlying the things of our experience" (1947, 20). In his study of Anaximander's fragment, Heidegger considers the term and writes that "the kind of being called *physei onta* is contrasted [by Aristotle] with that of *technê onta*. *Physei onta* is that which produces itself by arising out of itself; *technê onta* is produced by human planning and production" (1975, 15).[28] As the source of growth, *physis* is thus an *archê*, a first cause in the chain of events through which a thing comes into being. Moreover it is a cause that resides *within* the thing, rather than being imposed on it from without. In this way the term comes to signify a thing's *nature* as the indwelling source of its *genesis*, of its birth and becoming, the origin of its being as a particular *kind* of being.

This understanding of *physis* foreshadows the idea of entelechy (*entelecheia*) as Aristotle employs it (*On the Soul* 412a) to signify the indwelling potency of a thing to realize its own essence, to actualize the *"telos* contained within." Moreover, as Vlastos remarks, "Doubtless [this] concept of nature as a self-enclosed, self-regulative system is the intellectual foundation of science, and they who built it out of incredibly inadequate materials have every right to be considered the pioneers of the scientific spirit" (1970c, 96). In the case of Anaximander's statement, the idea that "the heavens and all the worlds in them" arise from and must return to some *apeiron physin* suggests that the source of change or transformation in the world is some undefinable, formless power of coming-to-be, some cosmic seed that contains within itself potentially the entire universe that we see around us. That the process of coming-to-be and destruction is described in terms of this abstract *nature*, rather than in terms of the actions of gods and goddesses, marks a definitive break with a mytho-poetic/supernaturalistic worldview.

Even so, it appears that Anaximander applied to the idea of an indeterminate or unbounded nature the chief attributes of the Homeric gods: timelessness and boundless power. "It seems not improbable that he actually called it 'divine,' and in this he was typical of the Presocratic thinkers in general" (Kirk, Raven, and Schofield 1983, 117). This reading of Anaximander arises from Aristotle's *Physics* (203b), where it is observed that "of the *apeiron* there is no beginning (*ouk estin archê*), for that would be a limit of it. Further, as it is a beginning, it is both uncreatable and indestructible. . . . That is why, as we say, there is no principle (*archê*) of *this*, but it is this which is held to be the principle of other things, and to encompass all (*periechein apanta*) and to steer all (*panta kubernan*). . . . And this is the divine (*einai to theion*); for it is 'deathless and indestructible' (*athanaton kai anôlethron*), as Anaximander says."[29] In attributing divine attributes to an "undefined nature," the source of all things, Anaximander moves us further along the path from mythopoesis to natural philosophy and toward an abstract conception of divinity.

Anaximander contributes further to a new consciousness when he invokes reciprocity or alternation between opposites as the dynamic of change or transformation, claiming that such reciprocation happens "of necessity (*kata to kreôn*) . . . according to the ordering of time (*kata tên tou chronou taxin*)." From some infinite/formless/undefinable nature the heavens and all the worlds in them are generated, and into this all things necessarily return, as is dictated by the regularity of time. Some powerful insights are disclosed here. The world-process, the process of "coming-to-be" and "destruction," unfolds according to a principle of reciprocity, equilibrium, or balance. The cosmos oscillates between two poles: the indefinite and the definite, the formless and the formed, the unnameable and the named. Moreover it does so inevitably, necessarily, *naturally*, according to its own constitution and under an arrangement prescribed by the passage of time. The "coming-to-be of existing things" out of and their "destruction" into the *apeiron* are regulated by *Justice*. These processes "pay penalty and retribution to each other for their injustice." Thus, as Kahn (1960, 66) puts it, "The universe is governed by law," and the processes of change and transformation are governed by a principle of balance, equilibrium, or symmetry.

Although Anaximander employs terminology that hearkens back to the mythopoetic worldview and his language invites a kind of anthropomorphic imaging, it is significant that no Homeric or Hesiodic Zeus serves as "law-giver." Rather, an impersonal, immaterial, universal Time (*Chronos*) governs the process. Can Anaximander be understood as grasping after the novel, profound insight that the world-process—unfolding necessarily according to a principle of reciprocity, balance, equilibrium—is finally governed by its own indwelling rule of cosmic justice: that is, by natural law? When he envisioned the *apeiron* as the source from which all worlds come and to which all return "as needs must be," the philosopher has in mind, says Cherniss, that this happens according to "the law of all nature, 'law' literally in the sense of a drastic process which continually redresses the balance [of justice] among the constituents of existence, the *apeiron* being the common fund in which all accounts are equalized. If this is to be considered in relation to theology, it must be admitted to be a complete rejection of all that was traditional in Greek religion. It is the denial that natural order can be suspended by any supernatural force of being, the denial in fact that any supernatural being can exist, and the assertion that, if the divine means anything at all, it can mean only the system of nature ordered according to infrangible law" (1970, 9–10).[30]

Anaximander envisions a universe whose fundamental logic continues to undergird the cosmological/naturalistic/scientific worldview that is generally embraced today. The processes of change we observe in the world are manifestations of a singular, undefinable, limitless, ageless, undecaying, divine Nature whose "nature" it is to give rise to the heavens and to all the worlds within them and then to take these back into itself, before once again giving rise to new heavens and worlds, all in an unending, rhythmic pulsation: the heartbeat of the universe. Moreover this pulse, this cycle of generation and destruction, unfolds through the fullness of time with regularity and balance according to the dictates of cosmic justice. This is the sense of things Anaximander bequeathed to his successors and upon which they built their cosmologies for the next two centuries. Indeed, it is the sense he has bequeathed to us.

Anaximenes, also a Milesian, is described by Diogenes Laertius as "a pupil of Anaximander."[31] His identification of *aêr* (air) as "the material principle" of the world represents a conceptual advance over Thales since, unlike water, air seems to be without weight in addition to being transparent, odorless, and so on. Moreover the coming-to-be and destruction of material objects is explained as the reciprocal condensation and rarefaction of air, which surrounds the whole cosmos. For Anaximenes, this first principle of existing things is divine.[32] Thus are the principle of reciprocity and the divinity of the *archê* more firmly embedded in the emerging nature-consciousness.

Xenophanes is credited with statements that illustrate the evolution of this idea of "divinity," distancing it from the mythopoetic image of anthropomorphic deities and moving toward a more abstract conceptualization:

> mortals consider that the gods are born, and that they have clothes and speech and bodies like their own. (B16) The Ethiopians say that their gods are snub-nosed and black, the Thracians that theirs have light blue eyes and red hair. (B15) But if cattle and horses or lions had hands, or were able to draw with their hands and do the works that men can do, horses would

draw the forms of the gods like horses, and cattle like cattle, and they would make their bodies such as they each had themselves. (B23) [Rather, there is] one god, greatest among gods and men, in no way similar to mortals either in body or in thought. (B26 + 25) Always he remains in the same place, moving not at all; nor is it fitting for him to go to different places at different times, but without toil he shakes all things by the thought of his mind. (B24) All of him sees, all thinks, and all hears.[33]

Particularly important in this passage is the idea that the "one god," unmoved and in no way similar to mortals, generates movement in the world by *thinking*. It is *mind* that permeates and moves all things. This link between mind and *archê* recurs in subsequent cosmological theories. Moreover there are clear echoes in the final sentence of the mythopoetic image of Zeus as "all-seeing" and "all-knowing," but Xenophanes' god is "in no way similar to mortals either in body or in thought." Here we see another effort to characterize a divine force in the world that is stripped of its anthropomorphic traits.

Xenophanes offers a physical explanation for natural events that once again invokes the idea of reciprocity or oscillation. As Hippolytus puts it (*Refutatio* 1.14.5), "Xenophanes thinks that a mixture of the earth with the sea is going on, and that in time the earth is dissolved by the moist. . . . All mankind is destroyed whenever the earth is carried down into the sea and becomes mud; then there is another beginning of coming-to-be, and this foundation happens for all the worlds" (Kirk, Raven, and Schofield 1983, 176–77). Moreover he advances a view of knowledge that bears directly on the emerging conception of wisdom. Following the mythopoetic tradition, if wisdom is held to be divine knowledge, then humans can never attain perfect wisdom, according to Xenophanes, for "the gods have not revealed all things to men from the beginning; but by seeking men find out better in time" (fr. 18). Consequently "no man knows, or ever will know, the truth about the gods and about everything I speak of; for even if one chanced to say the complete truth, yet oneself knows it not; but seeming is wrought over all things" (fr. 34).[34] By experiencing and observing the world around them human beings can attain opinions that "resemble truth," but we can never be certain that what we think we know is actually so. Thus human knowledge is always imperfect, and the wise person holds to beliefs tentatively rather than absolutely. Guthrie contends that Xenophanes believed humans "could have no certain knowledge at all. . . . [However,] this does not mean that all beliefs are equally probable. . . . We must not take appearances at their face value, but penetrate as near to the reality behind them as our wits will allow. When we feel that we have reached what at least resembles the truth, we must hold fast to the belief which we have won" (1962, 398).[35]

Human consciousness, as it is disclosed in the earliest protophilosophical writings, is poised on the threshold of a naturalistic cosmology and of a new conception of human wisdom. Though the term *sophia* does not appear in the extant fragments of these earliest speculative thinkers and must consequently be inferred from them, it is clear that the quest for divine knowledge has led the human mind away from the supernatural and deeply into the natural. If there is an implicit conception of *sophia* here, it centers on understanding the natural causes of coming-to-be and passing-away and on apprehending the in-dwelling principle according to which "the heavens and all the worlds within them" unfold and return to their origins in the timeless, cosmic cycle of generation and destruction. That this principle is divine—universal, all-powerful, deathless—is for these thinkers beyond question. However, they have located the divine within rather than outside of nature.

The quest for such knowledge is energized and promoted through a newly developed exercise of speech—philosophical conversation between masters and pupils in which new conceptualizations and terminologies are regarded as problematic and to be challenged, in which the range of thought is advanced through the appropriation and metaphorical extension of the mythic vocabulary, and in which the anthropomorphism and dramatic structure of myth are replaced by the use of impersonal nouns, by verbs of attribution rather than action, and by naturalistic explanations for the phenomena of experience.[36] The technique of this quest is argument and debate, and so the method of civic decision making is echoed in the method of speculative inquiry. This intimate connection between public moral judgment and theoretical investigation points to a shared ancestry for the language arts that eventually came to be conceptualized as rhetoric and philosophy, as we shall see.

What has been implicit in the earliest Ionian thinkers becomes explicit with Heraclitus of Ephesos, and in his thought the connection between wisdom and speech—between *sophia* and *logos*—emerges as central.[37] Heraclitus, like the Presocratic thinkers generally, is embedded in a transitional period of intellectual history, and in some ways he belongs to both worlds, the mythopoetic and the cosmological, at once. In the spirit of his immediate predecessors but with noticeably greater disdain, he rejects the views of both the poets and previous Ionian thinkers when he says, "Much learning does not teach understanding. For it would have taught Hesiod and Pythagoras, and also Xenophanes and Hecataeus" (DK 40), and "Homer deserves to be expelled from the competition and beaten with a staff—and Archilochus too!" (DK 42). In the surviving fragments of his writings we find evidence of yet another stage in the development of a new consciousness and a new conception of wisdom. Linkages between this conception and the operations of *logos* portend the primacy of reasoned discourse in both philosophical inquiry and the rhetorical theorizing of Plato and Aristotle.

The difficulties in translating Heraclitus's fragments are numerous and acute. "It is not even agreed that he wrote a book at all," Guthrie observes. "Such a book is indeed referred to in antiquity from Aristotle onwards, but some have guessed it to be no more than a collection of his sayings, made perhaps after his death" (1962, 406). Kirk writes that "the fragments, or many of them, have the appearance of being isolated statements, or *gnômai:* many of the connecting particles they contain belong to later sources. . . . Originally Heraclitus's utterances had been oral, and so were put into an easily memorable form [conceivably by a pupil]" (1954, 7). On the other hand, Kahn seems to be satisfied that there was a book. However, "like all Greek prose authors before Herodotus and all philosophical writings before Plato, the original text of Heraclitus is lost. We are entirely dependent upon quotations, paraphrases, and reports in later literature that happens to have survived the collapse of ancient civilization and the destruction of its papyrus libraries" (1979, 4).[38]

Problems concerning the authenticity and accuracy of particular fragments are compounded by the ambiguity and obscurity of Heraclitus's expression. As Guthrie notes, "His reputation for obscurity was practically universal throughout antiquity. He delighted in paradox and isolated aphorisms, couched in metaphorical or symbolic terms" (1962, 410). The translations provided here are informed by Heraclitus's affection for ambiguity and metaphor. Particularly in connection with the former I will employ the interrelated interpretive principles identified by Kahn (1979) as "linguistic density" and "hermeneutical generosity." The first of these refers to the recognition that "a multiplicity of ideas are expressed in a single word or phrase" (89); the second indicates that "the interpreter's task is to preserve the original richness of significance [of Heraclitus's sayings] by admitting a plurality of alternative senses—some obvious, others recondite, some superficial, others profound" (92).[39] Accordingly, in seeking to recover whatever insights might be expressed in the fragments, we must "play out" alternative readings and then synthesize these into coherent interpretations.

In place of the defective teachings of the poets and Ionian thinkers, Heraclitus offers his own views concerning the nature of wisdom, the workings of the world-process, and the means by which wisdom is to be acquired. Of the six fragments that deal explicitly with *sophia* or its variants, three are particularly germane here. In DK 50 Heraclitus tells us, "Listening not to me but to the *logos*, it is wise (*sophon estin*) to agree that all things are one." In DK 41 we are told that "the wise (*to sophon*) is one [thing], knowing the *gnômên* by which all things are steered through all."[40] In DK 112 we learn that "sound thinking (*sôphronein*) is the greatest excellence, and wisdom (*sophiê*) is to speak what is true and to act perceiving [things] according to their nature." Each of these statements will be examined, with a concentration on key terms and phrases and considering related fragments that bear on these.

It is the mark of wisdom to acknowledge that underlying the diversity in experience there is a unity, for "all things are one." Thus "day and night . . . are one" (DK 57), "the nature of every day is one and the same" (DK 106), "the way up and down is one and the same" (DK 60), and "from all things [comes] one and from one thing [come] all" (DK 10). The insight disclosed here echoes the thinking of Anaximander: generation and destruction, coming into being and passing away, the ebb and flow of the world-process—all manifest a single, indwelling reality. Indeed, "all things" reveal the *only* reality; they are the myriad embodiments of a single, existing thing. Anaximander called it "unbounded nature." Heraclitus calls it *Logos*. In his vision of the identity of opposites we encounter a profound insight into the heart of nature: all motion and change in the world, all conflict and opposition, all natural events and processes are incarnations of one underlying principle or law.[41]

In DK 41 Heraclitus tells us that to be wise is to grasp the *gnômên* by which all things are directed. *Gnômên* here can mean, among other things, "thought," "judgment," "intelligence," "purpose," or "insight." Kahn renders it "plan," in the sense of a directive, purposive intelligence or design (1979, 171).[42] Heraclitus, then, can be read as holding that wisdom is a matter of understanding the plan or design, the intelligence or purpose, "in accordance with which all things come to pass" (DK 1). This plan, moreover, is comprehended by the term *logos*, which, although it is accessible to the human mind, is not easily understood, for, "although this *logos* holds forever, men fail to comprehend [it], both before hearing it and once they have heard. Although all things come to pass in accordance with this *logos*, men are like the inexperienced when they experience such words and works as I set forth, distinguishing each [thing] according to its nature and telling how it is. Other men are oblivious of what they do awake, just as they are forgetful of what they do asleep" (DK 1).[43] The plan or purpose according to which the cosmos is unfolding, then, is this *logos*, the apprehension of which is the key to wisdom, but most people fail to grasp it. It is "common [to all things], [but] most people live as though their thinking were a private possession" (DK 2). Most live their lives in ignorance, failing to apprehend the true ground of their existence and to recognize the unity that underlies the diversity of their experience.

People should abide by the *logos* because we "must hold fast to what is shared by all, as a city holds to its law, and even more firmly. For all human laws are nourished by a divine one" (DK 114). The analogy here is illuminating. The *logos* is to the *kosmos* as the *nomos* is to the polis. Just as the law constitutes a city, making it the particular city it is and giving order to its actions and procedures, so the *logos* constitutes the *kosmos*, making the universe what it is and giving order to its processes. This *kosmos* exists as an ordered existence precisely because it is constituted by the *Logos*.[44]

Heraclitus teaches that "to the soul belongs a *logos* that increases itself" (DK 115), and that this *logos* is "so deep" that "you will not find the limits of the soul by going, even if you travel over every road" (DK 45).[45] Kahn hears in DK 45 an echo of Anaximander's *apeiron:* "the denial of limits involves an allusion to the supreme principle of cosmic structure" (1979, 128). From this allusion he infers that for Heraclitus, as for the Milesians (following Thales' dictum that "all things are full of gods"), "wherever you travel, there psyche will be." This reading resonates with the idea that "all things are one," for if this is so, then one person's *psychê* is, in actuality, merely a particular embodiment of the singular cosmic *Psychê*. Significantly, therefore, when Heraclitus went in search of the *logos*, he says, "I went in search of myself" (DK 101). The quest for wisdom takes one into oneself, for the cosmic *Logos* is continuous with the *logos* of the soul. Here is a rationale for the admonishment to "know thyself" (*gnôthi seauton*), inscribed on the Apollo temple at Delphi.

We also learn (DK 54) that the *logos* is a "hidden attunement" (*harmoniê aphanês*), superior to one that shows itself. The link between the *logos* and the idea of "harmony" recurs at DK 51: "they do not comprehend how [a thing] being brought apart is brought together with itself; it is an attunement turning back on itself, like that of the bow and the lyre." *Harmonia* literally indicates the seamless joining together of two things or the adjustment of one thing to another. However, given Heraclitus's penchant for metaphor and polysemy, it is inviting also to read into this term an image of consonance or agreement. In general, the term suggests the combining of parts into a proportioned and orderly whole. These fragments indicate that, immanent in the conflict of opposites that engenders all change or motion in the world, there is a quality of proportion and mutual adjustment in virtue of which all things fit together seamlessly.

The emphasis on the "hiddenness" of this harmony is also important. "Nature loves to hide," says Heraclitus (DK 123). The true nature of things lies beneath the surface of experience, and one must learn to "listen" *past* the immediate words of speech and to see into the depths of things in order to perceive the unity and regularity that underlie the variability in appearances. As Scoon observes, Heraclitus "seems . . . to feel that a true understanding [of the world] demands digging down beneath the surface of things to a hidden truth, which no one else had found; and that wisdom is to be gained by penetrating insights" (1928, 52). What does one discover when one penetrates beneath the surface of things? "[One] discovers that underneath all the apparent multiplicity and strife there is a hidden unity and harmony" (53; also see Kirk 1954, 227–31).

Heraclitus describes the flow of the world-process in terms of the transmutation of earth to water and water to earth, and as the kindling and dying down of the "everliving fire" of transformation (DK 31B, 30). These changes are "ordered" by the "measures" of a *logos*. The connection between *logos* and the idea of "measure" (*metron*) or "proportion" is central to the idea Heraclitus seems to have in mind here. In DK 31B the cyclical process of exchange between sea and earth is ordered by a principle of proportion: "sea pours out [from earth] in the same amount/proportion (*ton auton logon*) it was before becoming earth." Similarly, in DK 30 we are told that "the ordering (*kosmos*), the same for all, no god nor man has made, but it always was and is and will be: an everliving fire, kindled in measures (*metron*) and going out in measures." This idea of proportion, balance, or reciprocity echoes Anaximander's sense that the ebb and flow of generation and destruction are ordered by Justice, according to the order to Time.[46] Again we are reminded that what we perceive as motion and change in the world are in fact manifestations of the regular, proportionate ebb and flow of a singular reality that always was, is, and shall be.

There is some controversy over what Heraclitus had in mind when he described the cosmic process in terms of "everliving fire" (*pyr aeizôon*). In the context of such predecessors as Thales and Anaximenes, both of whom later thinkers understood as identifying the *archê* with a material substance (that is, with "water" or "air"), Heraclitus's "fire" has been viewed by some in similar terms. It is that out of which all things are made and from which all things arise. Certainly this is how he was understood by Aristotle (*Meta.* 983b–84a), Theophrastus (for example, at DK 22 A 1), and the Stoics. However, just as Thales and Anaximenes might be understood as grasping after a more abstract concept, and as employing "water" or "air" metaphorically to stand for some noncorporeal first principle, so might we understand Heraclitus's use of "fire" similarly. As Kahn remarks, "Fire has many qualities. But it is a most unlikely choice for a starting point in a literal account of the development of the world in material terms, since it is not itself a kind of matter, not a body at all, but a process of transition from one state to another, a symbol of life and death at once, the very element of paradox" (1979, 138). Among the "qualities" fire has is that it is highly energetic, unstable, dynamic. It dances, flaring up in one place and receding in another. It is an apt analogy for the idea of "pure energy" as the precursor of all matter. It would be an overstatement to say that here Heraclitus anticipates Einstein's identification of matter and energy, but the thought is nonetheless intriguing. At the very least, it is inviting to see in his "fire" a fitting metaphor for the dynamic, unstable character of the world-process, always ordered by the principle of proportion or reciprocity (see Kirk 1954, 316–23).

How do these apparently disparate thoughts about the *logos* fit together? It is precisely the ambiguity and richness of the term that allows Heraclitus—and, he might have hoped, at least some of his listeners/readers—to deploy it in exploring the world's nature and in articulating the profound insight he achieved. Moreover it is just this exploration and articulation that further enriched (or stretched) the term itself, adding layers of metaphorical and abstract meaning to its ancient core significance as "reckoning," "measure," "calculation," and "account" in the bookkeeping sense, and later as "speech," "word," "tale," and "account" in the sense of explanation or representation.

Kahn's comprehensive statement of Heraclitus's meaning captures precisely the richness fostered by the ambiguity of the term. The *logos*, he says, "is at once the discourse of Heraclitus, the nature of language itself, the structure of the psyche and the universal principle in accordance with which all things come to pass" (1979, 22). It thus becomes "a symbol for the unifying structure of the world which wisdom apprehends" (131). Kirk, Raven, and Schofield conclude that "the effect of arrangement according to a common plan or measure is that all things, although apparently plural and totally discrete, are really united in a coherent complex of which men themselves are a part, and the comprehension of which is therefore logically necessary for the adequate enactment of their own lives" (1983, 187–88). When we are invited to listen "not to me but to the *logos*," therefore, it seems clear that Heraclitus is referring to more than merely his speech.[47] He calls attention to his "account" of the world, to his "report" about the unity of all things, which is proffered as a true account, unlike those tendered by some earlier figures. However, in order for this account to be true, there must be some correlation between it and the "nature of things" of which it is an account. In order for this to be possible, there must be some inherent connection between the nature of things and the nature of language.

The use of language—that is, the meaningful deployment of sounds and markings as symbols—presupposes a certain regularity in the flow of experience, stable patterns in the flux of events. Without this patterning or regularity, nouns could have no stable referents, and thus words would have no consistent meanings from one instance of their use to another. Language or speech, viewed as *logos*, is therefore itself a manifestation of the enduring *kosmos* or world-order, where the *Logos* is the principle of that order. Thus, when Heraclitus asks us to listen not to him but to the *logos*, he is asking us to listen to his speech not as merely words he is saying but as an articulation of the underlying unity and harmonious arrangement of the universe. He is asking us to listen to the nature of things as it expresses itself through his speech. As Kahn puts the idea, "The world speaks to [people] as a kind of language they must learn to comprehend" (1979, 107). Later he adds, "The reference to a *logos* somehow independent of Heraclitus will be immediately clear if he has just spoken of the 'deep *logos*' of the soul. The thought will be: listen not to *me* but to the discourse within your soul, and it will tell you all" (130). Similarly Minar writes that "the *logos* has the double sense of meaningful human speech and the meaning which lies in things. Things speak to us, as it were" (1939, 333). Since he has been able to perceive things "according to their nature," Heraclitus has acquired *sophia*, is capable of "thinking well," and thus is speaking "what is true" (DK 112).

The relation between language and "reality" or "being" implied in this conception of *logos* is interesting and, in Heraclitus's time, unprecedented. In seeking to understand this relation for ourselves we have often dichotomized the two, and thus have created the problem of reference or correspondence that perplexes some still. In dichotomizing speech and reality, we are confronted by the problem of how speech can *represent* reality, or we are left to conclude that speech somehow *creates* reality. What Heraclitus's view suggests, however, is that the dichotomy is false: speech (*logos*) is a *manifestation* of reality (the *Logos*). In other words, reality discloses itself through language. Accordingly, to listen to the "account" is to behold an unconcealment of the cosmic *Logos*.

Unconcealment can take place only if the report is a "true account"—only if it is a genuine disclosure of the *logos* apprehended by the soul. *Psychê*, in its deepest nature, is a *logos*, and thus a genuine disclosure of the soul is at the same time a disclosure of the *Logos*. This means both that the individual soul is continuous with the ordering principle of the world and that the discursive activities of the soul are themselves realizations of this principle. To say that the *psychê* "is a *logos*" is to say that its essence is the capacity for apprehending regularity or patterns in the "flow" of experience and for perceiving the balance or proportion that permeates all that happens. Thence arises the "rationality" of the soul, and thence comes the idea of *logos* as thought, reasoning, and inward debate or deliberation.[48] "The new concept of the psyche," says Kahn, "is expressed in terms of the power of articulate speech: rationality is understood as the capacity to participate in the life of language, 'knowing how to listen and how to speak'" (1979, 107). Moreover, since this capacity is "shared" by or "common" to all people, when Heraclitus goes in search of himself, he goes in search of all of us.

The idea most commonly associated with Heraclitus is that "all things flow" (*panta rhei*), primarily as a result of Plato's paraphrase of this doctrine (*Cratylus* 402a): "Heraclitus is supposed to say that all things are in motion and nothing at rest; he compares them to the stream of a river, and says that you cannot go into the same water twice" (Jowett's translation, in Plato 1961c). This thought is expressed in several of the fragments: "As they step into the same rivers, other and still other waters flow upon them" (DK 12); "One cannot step twice into the same river, nor can one grasp any mortal substance in a stable condition, but it scatters and again gathers; it forms and dissolves, and approaches and departs" (DK 91); "Into the same rivers we step and do not step, we are and are not" (DK 49A). Of these, Kahn considers only DK 12 to be authentic (1979, 168–69, 288; see Guthrie 1962, 488–92), though Kirk (1954) views some phrases of DK 91 as presenting Heraclitus's own words (1954, 367ff.). Even so, all express a coherent insight into the implications of the belief that "all things flow." Because the world is a continually occurring process, nothing remains the same from one moment to the next. A thing never remains identical with itself, since it is always in flux. "For Heraclitus . . . there are no solid bodies. Things are not really things, they are processes, they are in flux" (Popper 1970, 141). One cannot step twice into the same river because in the next moment it is a different river. Moreover, in the next moment one is a different person, since we are part of the flow of things too. Simultaneously, however, the river *is* identical with itself: it is and is not the same river; "we are and are not."

The unifying core of these various senses of *logos* is the idea that immanent in the happenings of nature is a timeless, directive principle according to which *all* that happens takes place. The (rational) mind of the human individual can grasp the (rational) order of the cosmos through the operation of (rational) speech because all are one: psyche, speech, and cosmic order are all expressions of the universal principle that is embodied in and discloses itself through them. This principle—this universal *Logos*—is essentially a rule of "measure" (*metron*), of "harmony" or "attunement" (*harmonia*), of proportion, ratio, balance, reciprocity, equilibrium. It is this principle that unifies opposites, that leads the convergent to diverge and the divergent to converge, the consonant to become dissonant and the dissonant to become consonant, the one to become many and the many to be one, the dry to dampen and the moist to parch, death to become life and life, death—each according to the "measure" of the cosmic ordering, which is "the same for all" and which "no god nor man has made." Moreover, though no god has made it, the *Logos* is invested with the attributes of divinity: "it ever was and is and will be." The *Logos* is timeless, imperishable; it is pervasive, universal; it is all-powerful. "The *Logos* according to which everything occurs, though it still remains hidden from mankind, is the divine law itself. . . . Heraclitus's divine law is something genuinely normative. It is the highest norm of the cosmic process, and the thing which gives that process its significance and worth" (Jaeger 1947, 116). "Listening" to this principle as it discloses itself in all that happens, and thereby recognizing the fundamental unity of all things, is to be *wise;* living in accordance with this principle is living wisely.

Heraclitus envisions wisdom as a sort of heightened wakefulness, an alertness to and attunement with the rhythms of the *Logos:* "men are oblivious of what they do awake, just as they are forgetful of what they do asleep" (DK 1). People "forget where the way leads . . . and they are at odds with that with which they most constantly associate. And what they meet with every day seems strange to them. . . . We should not act and speak like men asleep" (DK 71–73). Moreover, "not comprehending, they hear like the deaf" (DK 34). If wisdom consists in "perceiving things according to their nature" (DK 112) and thus in apprehending the unity of all things, it comes as a result of "waking up" and "tuning into" the principle of proportion and reciprocity according to which all things happen. Since this principle discloses itself in every facet of our daily experience, apprehending it is simply a matter of learning to "hear" it: Listen not to *me* but to the *Logos.* Moreover, once you have heard and grasped it, you can speak truly, "distinguishing each [thing] according to its nature and telling how it is" (DK 1). Thus each of us, having heard and understood the fundamental unity of all things, can make such wisdom available to others by speaking truly. One's *sophia* is shown in being able to give an account (a *logos*) of the world that discloses this unity and that articulates the plan or intelligence that steers all things.

What might such speech be like? It will be premised on three foundational insights: all things are one; all things flow; all change is movement between opposites that is proportionate and cyclical. The speech that articulates these insights must employ the language of paradox: one steps and does not step into the same river, for the river is and is not the same, and one's self is and is not the same. "Immortals are mortal, mortals immortal, living the others' death, dead in the others' life" (DK 62); "the wise is one [thing] alone, unwilling and willing to be spoken of by the name of Zeus" (DK 32). Things are and are not what we call them, for the "is" is transitory and "becoming" is continuous. This requires the language of both/and rather than of either/or. Thus the speech of the wise must sound "obscure," if not altogether unintelligible, to those who have not yet learned to listen. This is why most people, even after they have heard wise speech, still fail to comprehend it and continue to live as if they are asleep. Given such a vision of wisdom and its verbal expression, it is little wonder that Heraclitus was not optimistic about the prospects for his teachings.

The speech of the wise will emphasize continuities among events, the unity of opposites, the reciprocal course of natural occurrences: "The same . . . : living and dead, and the waking and the sleeping, and young and old. For these transposed are those, and those transposed again are these" (DK 88). Moreover wise speech will point to the "hidden harmonies" or proportions in accordance with which the cycles of nature take place. It will articulate the sense that all things that happen are ultimately in harmony with one another, and that all movement in one direction will be compensated by its opposite.

What Heraclitus bequeathed to successors in the Greek wisdom-tradition is a deep awareness of the rational nature of the cosmos (that it is ordered by a principle of proportion) and of the ontological foundations of language (that it expresses what is fundamentally "real" in the cosmos). These insights were particularly helpful to Socrates, Plato, and Aristotle, as we shall see, and they pointed to an intimate connection between philosophical inquiry and the proper use of speech. If language manifests the rational structure of the world, then its correct use can lead the speculative thinker into that structure. This is the germ of logic—a seed that was nurtured and brought to fruition by later thinkers.

The idea that the whole universe is arranged according to a harmonious "attunement" is a central feature of teachings attributed to Pythagoras, as is the notion that a happy life is lived in concord with this cosmic attunement.[49] These teachings fell broadly into three categories: a body of mathematical and cosmological doctrines, a set of religious beliefs and "superstitions," and a set of practical prohibitions and prescriptions (Guthrie 1962, 181; Kirk, Raven, and Schofield 1983, 228–38). These teachings were originally transmitted orally in the form of *acusmata*, "things heard." The Pythagorean initiate was presumably required to commit them to memory, as a catechism of doctrine and practice. "What we may safely say," Guthrie observes, "is that for Pythagoras religious and moral motives were dominant, so that his philosophical inquiries were destined from the start to support a particular conception of the best life and [to] fulfil certain spiritual aspirations" (1962, 181).

The cosmological doctrines are of greatest importance here, since the other two sets of teachings generally followed from them.[50] Most fundamental were the beliefs that "number is real" and that "all things are number." Following this, it was held that the *tetractys*—the first four natural numbers conceived as connected in various relations—yielded the mathematical ratios according to which all of nature operates. From these four numbers one can construct the harmonic ratios of the fourth, the fifth, and the octave, which Plato identifies with the "music of the spheres" to which the heavenly bodies move.[51] The notion that numbers are real things may represent still another move toward abstraction in cosmological speculation. When they are considered as independently existing entities, divorced from the world of the senses, numbers are accessible only to the intellect. We might read this Pythagorean doctrine as presaging a conception of "reality" that invokes a purely intelligible and wholly rational realm of existence. Though it is unlikely that Pythagoras himself entertained such a conception, he may have initiated a line of thinking that culminates in Plato's idea of incorporeal Being.[52] In any event, while Heraclitus envisioned a rational universe ordered by the proportioned measures and regularities of the *Logos*, the Pythagoreans envisioned one in which these proportions are fixed and made precise by the unchanging magnitudes and exactness of numbers. The principle of proportionality embodied in the Heraclitean *Logos* acquires with Pythagoras a degree of precision that is only implicit in Ionian thought. The rationality of the cosmos originates in the invariable ordering of mathematical ratios.[53]

The premise that "all things are like (*epeoiken*) number" (Sextus Empiricus *adv. math.* 7.94) extends this last insight. All of existence is somehow akin to number. How? It might be that all things are *constituted* by numbers, by quantities. Aristotle expresses this idea at several points in the *Metaphysics* when he explicates Pythagorean number theory. For example, "the Pythagoreans . . . believe . . . that number is the essence (*ousia*) of all things" (*Meta.* 987a); "the Pythagoreans say that things exist by imitation (*mimêsis*) of numbers" (987b); "they hold that things themselves *are* numbers" (987b); "the Pythagoreans, . . . observing that many attributes of numbers apply to sensible bodies, assumed that real things are numbers; not that numbers exist separately, but that real things are composed of numbers. But why? Because the attributes of numbers are to be found in a musical scale, in the heavens, and in many other connections" (1090a).[54] Thus all things are apprehensible in terms of number. All of nature can be *quantified* and thus can be described and explained in terms of numbers and the ratios among them.[55]

It might also be held that all of nature is ordered by the logic of arithmetic and geometry, and according to the "harmonies" evoked by the sacred ratios. Recent studies of proportions in nature find that the Golden Ratio—a value that fascinated the Greeks from the time of Pythagoras onward—is a constant, appearing in the proportions of the spirals in the shell of the chambered nautilus and in the seed-head of the sunflower, among many other places (Basin 1963; Sutton 1992; Hoffer 1975). Greek architecture in the fifth century and afterward applied mathematical ratios to the proportions of monumental buildings. For instance, the Parthenon—completed in 438 B.C.E. and perhaps the best exemplar of the Doric order—is proportioned throughout according to the ratio of 9:4 and variations thereof. This ratio describes the relative proportions of the length and width of the temple, of its width and height, of the sides of the *cella* or *naos* rectangle (the room where the cult statue of the deity resided), and of the interaxial distance between columns compared to the diameter of a column measured at the top. Moreover the ratio of the length to the height of the temple is 9^2 to 4^2. These proportions were taken to be most pleasing to the eye and so were linked to the idea of beauty. In like fashion, the proportions of the *cavea* (seating area) of the amphitheater at Epidaurus, the acoustics of which have been characterized as "perfect," are described by the Golden Ratio.[56]

It is significant that the harmonic arrangement of the cosmos is expressible in terms of numerical ratios, for, once again, the rationality of the world-order is essentially mathematical. Kirk, Raven, and Schofield observe that "it is tempting to see Pythagoras as the thinker who stimulated the fascination with the idea of *harmonia* as a principle of order in things which we find in philosophers as diverse as Heraclitus, Empedocles, and Philolaus" (1983, 234). Certain properties of number give rise to important conceptual and moral considerations. Of particular importance here are the properties of oddness and evenness. If Unity is the starting point not only of number but of all things, then combining units in various configurations yields figures that are either symmetrical or asymmetrical. Given the primacy of balance and proportion in Pythagorean teachings, the symmetrical was preferred to its opposite, and so the world was divided along these lines into opposing pairs in which the symmetrical was privileged. Thus was Limit preferred to the Unlimited, the Even to the Odd, the One to the Many, the Right to the Left, the Straight to the Curved, Rest to Motion, Moderation to Excess, Order to Disorder, and so on. Guthrie writes that "for Pythagoras . . . the purification and salvation of the soul depended not merely, as in the mystery-cults, on initiation and ritual purity, but on *philosophia*; and this word, then as now, meant using the powers of reason and observation in order to gain understanding. . . . The more philosophical side of the system rests on . . . the exaltation of the related ideas of limit, moderation, and order. It was not accidental that they chose as their divine patron the god [Apollo] on whose temple were inscribed the words 'Nothing too much,' 'Observe limit,' and other precepts in the same sense" (1962, 205).[57]

Among Pythagoreans the pursuit of wisdom (*philosophia*) became a way of life, and one's apprehension of the "music of the spheres"—the concords based on the proportions of 1:2:3:4—served as the moral guide to living well. "The ethics that Pythagoras taught," Brumbaugh writes, "centered around the idea of harmony in the soul. A good soul has a proper order among its impulses and standards of value; and the aim of education is to instill a love of harmony. We become harmonious persons through appreciation of and contact with the beauties of music, the orderly abstractions of mathematics, the concrete sublime system of the stars" (1964, 41). Cornford remarks that "the human soul is not unrelated to surrounding Nature. Pythagoras taught the doctrine implied in transmigration, that there is a unity of all living things—that gods, men, and animals form one community, animated by a single principle of life" (1950, 68).[58] A life lived rightly, then, is one in which personal actions originate in a soul that is properly ordered in its several elements, attuned to the harmonious, proportionate arrangement of the universe. This idea, which

Heraclitus also embraced, is central in Greek moral thought from this point forward.

Pythagorean teachings envision a world-order based on numerical ratios or proportions, reiterating an insight first hinted at by Anaximander and extended by Heraclitus—that the *gnomê* or plan of the cosmos manifests a principle of proportion. Since numbers are "real," we encounter for the first time the idea that the universal order grows out of existences that are accessible only to the mind (Guthrie 1962, 239ff.). The abstract idea of number—indeed, the concept of "one-ness," "two-ness," and so on, as distinct from one or two *objects*— exists in a purely intellectual, changeless realm. The mathematical order, as Heraclitus might have described it, is the "same for all," was made by "no god or man," and always "was, is, and will be." It has no history or location; it is timeless, immutable, universal. In a word, it is *divine*. In views that are echoed in several Heraclitean doctrines, Pythagoras is reported to have held that the soul is immortal, that events exhibit regularity and occur in cycles, and that all living things are connected with each other. Indeed, his teachings implied that the individual soul is continuous with the divine soul of the cosmos.[59] Guthrie notes that, according to the Pythagoreans, "the breath or life of man and the breath or life of the infinite and divine Universe were essentially the same. Men were many and divided, and were mortal. But the essential part of man, his soul, was not mortal, and owed its immortality to this fact, that it was a fragment or spark of the divine soul, cut off and imprisoned in a mortal body" (1950a, 35). These ideas reverberate through the writings of Plato and, in somewhat more abstract terms, of Aristotle as well. Pythagoras saw philosophy as a way of life and held that cosmological knowledge—theoretical wisdom—has practical, moral implications. From Pythagoras and his followers came the idea that wisdom lies in grasping the mathematical relations among observable things—expressible as ratios and formulas—and that a proper life is lived in harmony with and is responsive to the proportions and harmonies of the cosmic order.

Consequences of the sixth-century expansion of the Persian Empire into western Asia Minor were the founding of Ionian colonies around the Black Sea and in Italy and the migration of people from such Ionian cities as Miletus, Samos, Colophon, and Phocaea in order to escape the turmoil. Pythagoras moved from his native Samos to Croton, in southern Italy, in the late 530s. Not long before (ca. 540 B.C.E.), Phocaeans founded a colony at Elea, on the coast of southwest Italy. It was here that the "Eleatic" thinkers extended views earlier espoused by Anaximander, Heraclitus, and other Ionians and developed novel ideas that further enriched the emerging Hellenic idea of speculative wisdom.[60]

The most important of these thinkers is Parmenides of Elea. Guthrie notes that "Presocratic philosophy is divided into two halves by the name of

Parmenides. His exceptional powers of reasoning brought speculation about the origin and constitution of the universe to a halt, and caused it to make a fresh start on different lines. . . . Philosophically Heraclitus must be regarded as pre-Parmenidean, whereas Empedocles, Anaxagoras, Leucippus and Democritus are equally certainly post-Parmenidean" (1965, 1). The other major representatives of the "school" are Zeno and Melissus. The former shows paradoxes in the ideas of plurality, divisibility, and change, while the latter defended Parmenides' conclusions against the pluralism of Empedocles and the Atomists. Parmenides' contributions to the development of Greek philosophical thought are manifold, but of particular significance for the present discussion is his bifurcation of the intelligible and the sensible realms, his privileging of the former over the latter as the "way of truth" (in contrast to the way of "seeming" or of "not being"), and his identification of the intelligible and true with what is logically possible. These views are set forth in the hexameter of Homer and Hesiod, and the poem was preserved until a relatively late date.[61]

He opens his poem proper—after a proem of thirty-two lines in which he lays claim to knowledge of a truth not attained by ordinary mortals—by distinguishing between the "path of Persuasion" and the path of impossibility: (fr. 2) "Come now and I will tell you (and you must carry my tale [*mythos*] away with you when you have heard it) the ways of inquiry that alone are to be thought of. The one, that [it] is (*estin*) and that it is impossible for [it] not to be, is the path of Persuasion (*Peithô*) (for she attends upon Truth); the other, that [it] is not and that it is necessary that [it] not be, that I declare to you is an altogether indiscernible track: for you could not know what is not—that cannot be done—nor indicate it, [fr. 3] for it is the same thing that can be thought and that can be."[62] The subject of the verb "is" (*estin*) is not explicit here. It is generally taken to be something like "what is" or "the existent."[63] Thus Parmenides might be taken to be uttering a tautology: "what is, is" or "the existent exists." Moreover it is "impossible" for what exists not to exist, while "what is not" cannot in any sense be said to "be." The tautology, however, is informative: what does it mean to say that "what exists, exists"? Whether or not he conceives "what is" as corporeal, Parmenides is exploring the implications of the meaning of the word "to be" (*einai*).[64] From this starting point he is able to argue for a conception of the world that is logically grounded in the idea of *being*. His poetic elaboration of "the way of Truth" is essentially a meditation on the nature of existence. What exists can only exist; it cannot not exist, because only what exists can be said to "be." Not-being cannot be said or thought to be, because, by the meaning of "to be," not-being cannot "be." Thus only what is exists, and only existence is possible. There can be no not-being. If the reasoning sounds circular, this was not lost on

Parmenides. In fr. 5 he states, "It is all the same to me from what point I begin, for I shall return again to the same point."[65]

Starting from the premises that what is exists and that what is not cannot exist, Parmenides reasons to the conclusion that, because what is cannot come from what is not, there is no coming-to-be. "What is" is timeless and unchanging. "It never was nor will be, since it is now, all together, one, continuous. For what birth will you seek for it? How and whence did it grow? . . . But changeless within the limits of great bonds it exists without beginning or ceasing. . . . Remaining the same and in the same place it lies on its own and thus fixed it will remain."[66] Further, there is only one existent: "what is" must, "by necessity," be singular, since plurality would require discontinuities in being. Plurality would require divisibility, and segments of "what is" would have to be separated by the nonexistent. However, the nonexistent cannot exist, so there is nothing to "segment" the existent.[67] Similarly "what is" is motionless and unchanging, for into what would it move, and how can it change into something that is not? The culmination of this line of reasoning is that there is one Reality, solid, timeless, unchanging, and perfect. It is, indeed, "like the bulk of a ball well-rounded on every side, equally balanced in every direction from the center. . . . For being equal to itself on every side, it lies uniformly within its limits."[68] Reality is a solid, perfect, unmoving sphere—the sphere of Being. This, at any rate, is the conclusion at which Parmenides arrives through a rigorous, deductive elaboration of the meaning of "to be."

What we find in this elegant argument is the first truly metaphysical speculation: a meditation on the nature of *being* as such. Parmenides may not have entertained such an abstract concept in his own mind, but this is nonetheless what his analysis is about. Moreover we find here the first truly logical philosophical argument, an argument that reasons to conclusions through the logical implications of the meaning of a term. The conclusions Parmenides reaches are implicit in the meaning of the term "being." He starts and ends with the notion of what it means "to be."

Once Parmenides' argument had been stated, it was no longer possible to make the tacit assumptions and to leave undefined the conceptions with which all earlier Presocratic speculation had operated. Natural philosophy was forced to face the logical, epistemological, and metaphysical problems of identity and difference, appearance and reality, truth and error. Subsequent efforts to provide a coherent, systematic, rational account of the cosmos proceeded through an examination of competing viewpoints in which rival theses concerning the ultimate nature of the world were subjected to the tests of deductive logic. It was this logic itself—the laws inherently governing the meaningful use of language—that determined the direction of subsequent cosmological inquiry. The nature of *words* and their proper use became the essential tool in apprehending the truths of nature, and thus in acquiring philosophic knowledge—wisdom.

Implicit in Parmenides, accordingly, we find something similar to what was explicit in Heraclitus—namely, that knowledge of the "way of Truth" comes through contemplation of the *logos*, of the "word" itself. The implication here is profound: the True and the Real are somehow "contained" or "embodied" in language, speech, and thought, and they can be apprehended directly and intuitively by the mind, for "it is the same thing that can be thought and can be" (fr. 3).[69] Additionally we see an extension of Pythagoras's view that the purely intelligible is real, taken to the more extreme notion that the ultimately real is accessible to mind alone, and consequently that the realm of sensible experience is somehow illusory. In the second and longest part of the poem, preserved only in scattered fragments, the goddess expounds "mortal opinions" in which one can place no faith. She instructs Parmenides not to be taken in by "two-headed mortals" (such as, we might infer, Heraclitus), who "are carried along, deaf and blind at once, dazed, undiscriminating hordes, who believe that to be and not to be are the same and not the same; and the path taken by them all is backward-turning."[70]

What has Parmenides brought to the emergent cosmological consciousness? He is the first thinker to consider the intrinsic meaning of the term "to be." He is the first to assert that what can be *thought* must actually exist, since one can think only of what is logically possible, and what is logically possible necessarily exists. "Being," therefore, is bound intrinsically to thought and to logic. His account of three "ways"of thinking—the "way of Persuasion and Truth," the "way of error," and a third path in which one fails to distinguish between what is and what is not—is the earliest surviving discussion of philosophical method. His rejection of the third way—that a thing can both be and not be—is the earliest surviving formulation of the law of contradiction. His idea of following the implications of a term's meanings established the method of deductive demonstration. Of fundamental importance is Parmenides' envisioning a world where "reality" is precisely what is *logically possible*. Indeed, with him the very idea of *impossibility* is new. *Being* itself suffuses and is suffused by the logic of language—by the *Logos* of *logos*. In ways that resonate with Heraclitus's insights, Parmenides conjures a world in which the *logos* of the soul—its "reason"—is the instrument by which we can grasp the *Logos* of the world, its indwelling logic. Moreover the path to such insight lies in contemplating the meanings of *logoi* themselves. Accordingly the "way of Truth" is identified with the process of reasoning or thinking. Thus is the Truth of Being accessible to the mind alone—the senses must be left behind. This dichotomization of Being and Appearance, of Reason and Sense, poses a central problem that preoccupied Greek thinkers for generations to come.

Wisdom, following this view, will consist in the immediate apprehension by reason (*logos*) or intellect (*nous*) of what is logically possible—that is, of what is implicit in the natural meanings of words. Thus will the quest for *sophia* center on the investigation of those meanings. This, of course, goes beyond what Parmenides may have envisioned, but it suggests the direction in which his thinking set the course of speculative inquiry. The practice of following the logical implications of the terms used to characterize a thing emerged as a principal feature of Greek philosophy during the fifth and fourth centuries, enshrined in what came to be known as the "dialectical method."

Empedocles, like Parmenides, contributes several key ideas that further stretch and enrich the idea of wisdom emerging from Presocratic thought. We are told that he was "an emulator and associate of Parmenides" and that "he wrote in verse *On the Nature of Things*."[71] Empedocles saw in Parmenides' work a radical epistemological challenge. He responded in a strongly Heraclitean spirit, lamenting the limited comprehension of things most people achieve through their senses but promising, according to Kirk, Raven, and Schofield, that "an intelligent use of all the sensory evidence available to mortals, aided by his own instruction, will (contrary to Parmenides' claims) make each thing clear to us."[72] Even so, the human capacity for understanding nature is limited, and so our knowledge will be incomplete: (fr. 2) "Narrow are the powers that are spread through the body, and many are the miseries that burst in, blunting thought. Men behold in their span but a little part of life, then swift to die are carried off and fly away like smoke, persuaded of one thing only, that which each has chanced on as they are driven every way: who, then, boasts that he has found the whole? (fr. 3) Come now, observe with all your powers how each thing is clear, neither holding sight in greater trust compared with hearing, nor noisy hearing above the passages of the tongue, nor withhold trust from any of the other limbs, by whatever way there is a channel to understanding, but grasp each thing in the way in which it is clear."[73] Though limited, the senses do provide "channels to understanding," insofar as the things we perceive are manifestations of underlying cosmic principles.

The world-process as Empedocles explains it—the coming-to-be and passing-away of all mortal things—is produced by the cyclical coming-together and separation of four material elements, the "roots of all things": earth, air, fire, and water. Furthermore, this cycle itself is the product of the alternating ascendance of Love (the force of fusion) and Strife (the force of dissolution, fragmentation, decomposition):

A two-fold tale I shall tell: at one time they [that is, the "four roots"] grew to be one alone out of many, at another again they grew apart to be many out of one. Double is the birth of mortal things and double their failing; for the one is brought to birth and destroyed by the coming together of all things, the other is nurtured and flies apart as they grow apart again. And these things never cease their continual interchange, now through Love (*Philotês*) all coming together into one, now again each carried apart by the hatred of Strife (*Neikos*). So insofar as they have learned to grow one from many, and again as the one grows apart grow many, thus far do they come into being and have no stable life; but insofar as they never cease their continual interchange, thus far they exist always changeless in the cycle.[74]

The objects we perceive are transitory, but the process of alternation/alteration is stable and enduring. As for Heraclitus and Anaximander, there is a timeless, immutable principle that animates and steers the flow of the material world.

The "wisdom" of Empedocles lies in several key ideas. As with Xenophanes, here too we are encouraged to recognize the limits of human knowledge. Human understanding can go far toward apprehending the workings of the world, but it will always be incomplete. Moreover the senses disclose to us what we can discern about the material world, and so they are competent sources of insight. The causes underlying events might be purely intelligible, but they are disclosed to us in their effects, and these we perceive through our senses. Though our experience of the world-process involves diversity and continuous change, the cycle itself is singular and imperishable. The cosmic cycle is immortal and thus is divine. Similarly the four roots are uncreated and indestructible, so they also are divine. Once again we find the idea of *to theion*, stripped of its mythopoetic accoutrements, occupying a central place in cosmological speculation.[75] Finally the ongoing process of alternating expansions and contractions—starting with the "divine sphere" at the center of the cosmic "vortex" and expanding outward through the action of Strife until, through the action of Love, all is pulled back to the center again, only to explode once more as Strife overcomes Love—this eternal reciprocation invokes the ideas of balance and proportion that were implicit in Anaximander and explicit in Heraclitus. Each cycle of expansion and contraction, each oscillation between unity and diversity, is but a single pulsation of the cosmos. For Empedocles as for his predecessors, wisdom can be understood as the apprehension of this divine Truth. "But come," he writes, "hear my words, for learning increases wisdom (*phrenos*). . . . I shall tell a twofold tale: at one time they grew to be one alone out of many, at another again they grew apart to be many out of one—fire and water and earth and the immense height of air, and cursed Strife apart from them, equal in every direction, and Love among them, equal in length and breadth. Her must you contemplate with your mind. . . . You must listen to the undeceitful ordering of my discourse." [76] As he states elsewhere (fr. 23, Simplicius *in Phys.* 159, 27), "the tale you hear comes from a god."

Empedocles' view of wisdom seems to have embraced both cosmological and moral interests. As Guthrie points out, "if he wished simply to restore reality to the physical world and its processes, and [to] rescue them from the Parmenidean denial of motion and plurality, then a single cause and a single process would have sufficed." That he chose to involve two forces—Love and Strife—in the cosmic cycle suggests that "for Empedocles the moral and religious order was as important as the physical, and in equal need of explanation" (1965, 182–83). Thus does Love become the unifying force both in the natural world and in the human heart, just as Strife urges both in the direction of disintegration and evil. Understanding the underlying principles at work in the ebb and flow of the cosmic process enables one to live in accordance with its rhythms, and thus to live happily: "Blessed is he who has obtained the riches of divine wisdom, and wretched is he who has a dim opinion in his thought concerning the gods" (fr. 132; trans. Guthrie, 256).

Anaxagoras, the Atomists, and the later "nature philosophers" made their own contributions to the new consciousness and to the idea of wisdom that attends it. Anaxagoras (ca. 500–428 B.C.E.) was born in Clazomenae, an Ionian coastal town a little to the north of Miletos and Ephesos. Apparently he came to Athens and began his philosophical activities around 480.[77] According to Diogenes Laertius (1.16), he wrote a single book, a work on nature in which he explicitly rejects Parmenides' conclusion that "what is" must be singular but in which he accepts the Parmenidean demand that it be unchanging—that is, "what is" cannot come into being or cease to be:

(Fr. 1) All things were together, infinite in respect of both number and smallness; for the small too was infinite. And while all things were together, none of them were plain because of their smallness; for air and aither held all things in subjection, both of them being infinite; for these are the greatest ingredients in the mixture of all things, both in number and in size.

(Fr. 4, second half) But before these things were separated off, while all things were together, there was not even any color plain; for the mixture of all things prevented it, of the moist and the dry, the hot and the cold, the bright and the dark, since there was much earth in the mixture and seeds countless in number and in no respect like one another. . . . And since this is so, we must suppose that all things were in the whole.

(Fr. 17) The Greeks are wrong to recognize coming into being and perishing; for nothing comes into being nor perishes, but is rather compounded or dissolved from things that are. So they would be right to call coming into being composition and perishing dissolution.[78]

The material world is constituted and reconstituted through the changing combinations of infinitely small particles that are, themselves, neither created nor destroyed. The changes that humans perceive in the world are the products of the natural processes of composition and decomposition through which these particles are arranged and rearranged. Anaxagoras thus articulates a doctrine that is perhaps the earliest statement of the law of physics known as the "conservation of matter," namely, that matter can be neither created nor destroyed but can only change its form.[79]

Most salient about Anaxagoras's doctrines is not that matter is uncreated and imperishable, nor even that all apparent change in the world comes about through the process of composition and dissolution. Empedocles, after all, had articulated a similar doctrine, and even Anaximenes' condensation and rarefaction of *aêr* might be construed on this model. Rather, the significance lies in the origins of this process, the source of motion in the cosmos. A theme running through Presocratic writings concerns the quest for a primary cause of things. At one level, this pursuit has sought a material substance in terms of which events can be explained—water, air, fire, earth. At another level, the search is for a more abstract principle: Anaximander's unformed, undefined "nature"; Heraclitus's *Logos;* Pythagoras's "number"; Empedocles' Love and Strife. For Anaxagoras, the material origin of the sensible world lies in the infinite array of "seeds," which combine and recombine to produce the infinite variety of substances. However, he also pursued an immaterial *archê*, an answer to the question, "why does 'body' or matter behave as it does?" Thales hints at a universal *psychê*, a living breath that suffuses all existence, an animating presence in all things. This presence, moreover, is *theios*, divine. Anaximander found his answer in the demands of cosmic Justice and ordering of Time. For Xenophanes, it is the "one god . . . , in no way similar to mortals," who moves all things by the "thought of his mind." In a further refinement of the idea, Anaxagoras finds the source of motion and change in *Nous:*

> (Fr. 12) All other things have a portion of everything, but *Nous* is infinite (*apeiron*) and self-ruled (*autokrates*), and is mixed with nothing but is all alone by itself. . . . For it is the finest of all things and the purest, it has all knowledge about everything and the greatest power; and all things having soul, both the greater and the smaller, *Nous* rules. *Nous* controlled also the whole rotation [of the primal mixture of seeds and earth], so that it began to rotate in the beginning. . . . And the things that are mingled and separated and divided off, all are known by *Nous*. And all things that were to be—those that were and those that are now and those that shall be—*Nous* arranged them all. . . . [fr. 13] And when *Nous* initiated motion, from all that was moved *Nous* was separated, and as much as *Nous* moved was all divided

off. . . . [fr. 14] But *Nous*, which always is, is assuredly even now where everything else is too.[80]

Nous is usually translated here as "Mind," but it also has the sense of "intelligence" and "thought." The use of the term is a further step toward the abstract conceptualization of an immaterial, indwelling, cosmic *archê* from which all movement and change flow. Like his predecessors, Anaxagoras may be understood as grasping after an idea for which he does not yet have a fully developed vocabulary. Kirk, Raven, and Schofield credit *Nous* with "many of the qualities of an abstract principle. . . . Anaxagoras in fact is striving, as had several of his predecessors, to imagine and describe a truly incorporeal entity. But as with them, so still with him, the only ultimate criterion of reality is extension in space. Mind, like everything else, is corporeal" (1983, 364). However, Guthrie observes that since the term "is already used of counsel or wisdom (*mêtis*) in the *Iliad*, it is hardly worth repeating the many occasions on which it is used with similar non-material subjects in classical Greek. If Anaxagoras had at last grasped the idea of non-material existence, he obviously had not the vocabulary in which to express it" (1965, 276–77).[81]

When we examine the *way* in which Mind moves all things, it is inviting to see in Anaxagoras's account a premonition of Aristotle's metaphysical doctrines. How did Mind initiate motion in the primal mixture, in which the seeds of all things were compressed at the center of the universe? We are told only that *nous* started and controlled the "whole rotation" whereby the seeds that were "mingled" in their primal state were "separated and divided off." How did Mind start the rotation? Anaxagoras does not answer this explicitly. Perhaps, like Xenophanes' "one god," Mind moves matter by its own inherent action—by the activity of thinking, *noein*. We have no evidence that Anaxagoras saw this implication of his terminology, but in the light of Xenophanes' writings it is difficult not to see in his views a similar conception at work, as well as a foreshadowing of the doctrines of later thinkers. Guthrie concludes that

> his achievement is usually summed up as twofold: the idea of Mind as the moving, ordering and ruling force in the universe, and theory of the structure of matter. The former has acquired special prominence in the light of later philosophy, especially its role in the teleological systems of Plato and Aristotle. . . . One must distinguish here, as often in the history of thought, between an idea in the mind of the man who first thought of it and its development by those who followed him. With the conception of Mind as the ultimate cause of order and regularity in the material world, and itself something separate from matter, independent and self-governing, the seed of a fully teleological view of nature has been planted. (1965, 320–21)

Nous in Anaxagoras's cosmology possesses qualities traditionally associated with the divine: it interpenetrates all things, and thus is omnipresent; it moves all things, and thus is all powerful; it knows all things, and thus is omniscient; and it "always is," uncreated and indestructible, and thus is immortal. As Guthrie concludes, "it is nowhere in the extant fragments called God, but this may be accidental and it is impossible that Anaxagoras should not have thought of it as divine (*theion*). . . . It retains a special form of control over the organic world, and seems to be identical with the *psyche* or animating principle in living things" (1965, 279).

Archelaus was an Athenian and, according to Simplicius, "the pupil of Anaxagoras with whom Socrates is said to have associated, [and he] tries to introduce something original of his own in cosmogony and other subjects, but still gives the same first principles as Anaxagoras had."[82] Scholars seem to agree that his direct contribution to philosophy is minor, but he appears to have initiated a line of speculation that would provide a bridge from Presocratic to sophistical thought, one that would become a central issue in philosophical inquiry during the latter half of the fifth century.[83] Sextus (*adv. math.* 7.14, A6) says that Archelaus pursued both the physical and ethical sides of philosophy, and Diogenes (2.16) writes that he "appears to have treated ethics, for he philosophized about laws and things fair and just." Moreover his apparent conviction that right and wrong existed not by nature but by convention foreshadowed the *physis/nomos* antithesis that was central in sophistical thinking and was a principal theme in philosophical inquiry for Socrates, Plato, and Aristotle. As Guthrie concludes, "in Archelaus we have found united the two strands of cosmogonical speculation and ethical and sociological theory" (1965, 345).

Other "nature philosophers" of the fifth century made further refinements to the doctrines of their forebears and contemporaries. Melissus of Samos (fl. ca. 444 B.C.E.), Diogenes of Apollonia (fl. ca. 440–430), and the "Atomists"— Leucippus of Miletos (fl. ca. 440–435) and Democritus of Abdera (ca. 460– ca. 400)—extended, challenged, and modified the teachings of Anaximenes, Heraclitus, Parmenides, Empedocles, and Anaxagoras, and in doing so they contributed additional insights to the emerging cosmological/natural consciousness. Melissus, though an Ionian, was an adherent of Parmenides' Eleatic logic, evidence of how completely the intellectual fruits of the Italian colonies had spread through the eastern Mediterranean world. He wrote a treatise "On Nature or on What Exists" in which he argued, by a rigorous deduction from the consequences of assuming simply that something exists, that "what is" is ungenerated and indestructible, unbounded (*apeiron*), unitary, homogeneous, unmoving, and immutable.[84] He may also have held that it is incorporeal: "If it exists, it must be one, and being one it must have no body (*sôma mê echein*).

If it had thickness, it would have parts, and would no longer be one" (fr. 9).[85] Guthrie (1965, 110–13) and Kirk, Raven, and Schofield (1983, 400–401) discuss the difficulties involved in reading this fragment and in determining the extent to which the key phrase can be understood as pointing to the idea of an abstract, immaterial reality. These authors agree that Melissus's conception must have stopped somewhere short of a Platonic or Aristotelian idea of pure form. "One of the plainest lessons of Presocratic thought," writes Guthrie, "is that the notion of incorporeal existence was not achieved by a single step, but was a gradual process" (110). If Melissus *can* be understood here as envisioning a nonmaterial "being," then he has furthered the quest for an abstract, natural *archê*. Moreover he has retained implicitly the connection with a secular divinity that has woven itself into the fabric of the new consciousness. Kirk, Raven, and Schofield conclude that "Melissus was not a great original metaphysician like Parmenides nor a brilliant exponent of paradox like Zeno. But he was inventive in argument, and his deduction of the properties of reality is in general much clearer than Parmenides'. It is his version of Eleatic doctrine to which the atomists chiefly responded and which shaped its presentation by Plato and Aristotle" (401).

Diogenes, a citizen of the Milesian colony of Apollonia on the Black Sea, made air (*aêr*) the "first element," as Anaximenes had done. However, he did so in a conception that fused Anaximenes' insight with Anaxagoras's vision of *nous* as the origin and principle of existing things. Of his writings, Simplicius gives the following account: "One must know that this Diogenes wrote a number of treatises, as he himself mentions in the *On Nature*, where he says that he has written something against the natural philosophers (whom he himself calls sophists), and a *Meteorology* (in which, he adds, he discusses the *archê*), and moreover a work *On the Nature of Man*. However, in *On Nature*, the only one of his works that has come into my hands, he sets out to demonstrate at length that in the *archê* which he posits there is much intelligence (*esti noêsis pollê*)."[86] In a surviving fragment of *On Nature*, Diogenes himself says, "It seems to me, in sum, that all existing things are created by the alteration of the same thing, and are the same thing" (fr. 2, Simplicius *in Phys.* 151, 31). The idea of a single, originative substance, of course, was a central tenet of nature-consciousness from Thales onward. Moreover a conception of the unity of all existence is as old as Heraclitus. Thus does Diogenes carry forward a key insight that is part of his intellectual inheritance. Elsewhere (fr. 5, Simplicius *in Phys.* 152, 22) he says this: "And it seems to me that that which has intelligence is what men call air, and that all men are steered (*kubernasthai*) by this and that it has power over all things. For this very thing seems to me to be a god (*theos dokei einai*) and to have reached everywhere and to dispose all things and to be in everything. And there is no single thing that does not have a share of this." Guthrie remarks that "his greatest significance lies perhaps in his explicit statement and defence of the teleological explanation of nature, which underwent such remarkable and influential developments in hands of Plato and Aristotle" (1965, 362).[87]

The Atomists of the fifth century included Leucippus and his pupil Democritus. Diogenes Laertius gives a fairly complete account of Leucippus's general principles, cosmogony, and cosmology, but in other sources the atomic theories are usually attributed either to both men together or to Democritus alone.[88] The latter, a prolific writer, followed his teacher on fundamental points. Moreover he exhibited an interest in ethical questions that apparently was not shared by Leucippus.[89] In any event, in their theorizing about the causes of motion and change in the world, about the permanent reality that underlies these changes, and about the nature of and limitations on human knowledge, we can discern a pronounced advance in sophistication over the thinking of their predecessors.

Responding to the dilemmas and paradoxes posed by the Eleatic thinkers, and to the problems of unity and plurality that remained unsolved even after Anaxagoras, Leucippus and his pupil developed the first atomic theory—an explanation of the perceived world in which all "coming into being" and "perishing" are produced by the movement of infinitely numerous, imperceptible, indivisible particles ("what is") through "void" ("what is not"). By asserting that "what is not" is just as real as "what is," these two thinkers sought to overcome the difficulties posed by the Eleatic rejection of void or nonbeing. Guthrie comments, "Atomism is the final, and most successful, attempt to rescue the reality of the physical world from the fatal effects of Eleatic logic by means of a pluralistic theory" (1965, 389).[90]

It is not their physical theories, however, that are of greatest interest here. Rather, their views concerning human knowledge and, most especially, Democritus's politico-ethical writings contribute most to emergent conceptions of wisdom. Like Xenophanes and Empedocles, who noted the limitations of human knowledge, and Parmenides, who questioned the veracity of the senses, both Leucippus and Democritus maintained that sense-perception is not an altogether reliable path to knowledge of "what is." Leucippus held the view that the objects of sense-perception exist by custom or convention (*nomos*) rather than by nature (*physis*), while Democritus developed a thorough critique of the senses: "Democritus sometimes does away with what appears to the senses, and says that none of these appears according to truth but only according to opinion: the truth in real things is that there are atoms and void. 'By convention (*nomos*) [things are] sweet,' he says, 'by convention bitter, by convention hot, by convention cold, by convention colour: but in reality atoms and void. . . . We know nothing accurately in reality, but [only] as it changes according to the bodily condition, and the constitution of those things that flow upon [the body] and impinge upon it.'"[91] In other key fragments Democritus says that we do not grasp the true nature of things (fr. 10), that humans are "separated from reality" (fr. 6), that "in reality we know nothing about anything; but each person's opinion is a reshaping" (fr. 7, after Guthrie), and that "we know nothing in reality; for truth lies in an abyss" (fr. 117). Even as he seems to discount the possibility that humans can grasp "reality," however, Democritus distinguishes between two kinds of knowing, one genuine (*gnêsia*) and the other "bastard" (*skotia*): "To the bastard belong all this group: sight, hearing, smell, taste, touch. The other [the intellect] is legitimate, and separate from that."[92] The senses are ultimately unreliable because they cannot detect the level of atomic activity.

Where the senses leave off, the powers of reason or intellect must take up the search. Knowledge of what is ultimately real—that is, wisdom—must come through a combination of sensation and reasoning. Guthrie comments that "Democritus offered a way of escape from this complete pessimism as to the possibility of knowledge. . . . Without abandoning his conviction that the truth is not in sense-impressions themselves, Democritus suggested that through them the mind might ultimately be led to it" (1965, 458–59). He adds that "the senses give us our impression of the macroscopic world, but when it is a question of understanding the microscopic (where alone reality is to be grasped), the intellect takes over" (459n1). Nonetheless, we must not view Democritus as a complete skeptic denying altogether the possibility of attaining knowledge of reality. For Democritus as for Heraclitus, truth lies in the depths. If we see only the surface, we remain unaware of the true nature of things. We are "separated from reality" by the barrier of the senses, which seem to tell us what things are but in fact give a false image. This reading clearly resonates with Heraclitus's proposed need to "listen" to the "hidden attunement" and to go beneath the surface of what the senses report.[93]

Democritus's political and ethical views deepen his conception of wisdom. Of the sixty works ascribed to him in Thrasyllus's catalog (DK 68 A 33), only eight were classified as "ethical." However, the vast majority of his surviving verbatim fragments are concerned with ethics, politics, and human conduct generally.[94] It is not surprising that Democritus evidenced a deep interest in moral topics, despite the fact that the Presocratic "nature philosophers" were primarily concerned with the mechanics of natural processes. Like Heraclitus, Pythagoras, Empedocles, and Archelaus before him, Democritus perceived a connection between the cosmological and the moral realms, and like his older contemporaries Protagoras and Socrates, he was responsive to the intellectual currents that shaped philosophical inquiry during the second half of the fifth century.

The "ethical" fragments cover a wide range of subjects—how to maintain good spirits and avoid unhappiness, the power of chance or fortune in human affairs, foolishness, child-rearing and education, pleasure and prudence, free speech and persuasion, friendship, politics, justice and the punishment of wrong-doers, and many more. Of particular interest here are things he says about wisdom, right conduct, happiness, and the power of speech. About the first, for example, Democritus says that "medicine heals diseases of the body, wisdom frees the soul from passions" (fr. 31); "neither skill nor wisdom is attainable unless one learns" (fr. 59), but "many much-learned men have no intelligence" (fr. 64). Consequently "one should practice much-sense, not much-learning" (fr. 65); "it is not time that teaches wisdom, but early training and natural endowment" (fr. 183); and finally, "to a wise person, the whole earth is open; for the native land of a good soul is the whole earth" (fr. 247).[95] From reading these fragments in the context of Democritus's views concerning truth and knowledge, it would seem that wisdom comes to one who is taught from an early age to learn through the senses how the world-process operates at the macroscopic level, and then to perceive through the intellect those underlying realities that are beyond the senses. These realities, as we have seen, are "atoms and void." To apprehend this fact and its implications is to have wisdom. In considering these ideas, one is again reminded of Heraclitus's admonition to "listen to the *Logos*" by penetrating beneath the surface appearances of events in order to apprehend the indwelling cosmic principle according to which all things happen. Wisdom comes to one who is able to "see" into or "hear" the heart of things through the powers of the mind.

For Democritus, the path to right action lies in ordering the soul according to the dictates of law and wisdom: "Those whose character is well ordered have also a well-ordered life" (fr. 61), and "well-ordered behavior consists in obedience to the law, the ruler, and the man wiser [than oneself]" (fr. 47). Characteristic of the well-ordered soul, moreover, is a disposition to desire only what is right and to desire only in moderation: "Virtue consists, not in avoiding wrong-doing, but in having no wish thereto" (fr. 62); "immoderate desire is the mark of a child, not a man" (fr. 70); "untimely pleasures produce unpleasantness" (fr. 71); "moderation multiplies pleasures, and increases pleasure" (fr. 211); and "if one oversteps the due measure, the most pleasurable things become most unpleasant" (fr. 233). The path to virtuous action, finally, lies in listening to one's own reason or intellect, to the *logos* in one's own soul, and in controlling one's desires: "Men have fashioned an image of Chance as an excuse for their own stupidity. For Chance rarely conflicts with Intelligence, and most things in life can be set in order by an intelligent sharp-sightedness" (fr. 119); and "it is hard to fight desire; but to control it is the sign of a reasonable man" (fr. 236).

A theme running through these fragments is that virtuous conduct is measured, balanced, and deliberate. Such a view resonates most conspicuously with ideas we have encountered in Heraclitus and Pythagoras, and it anticipates perspectives we will find in Socrates, Plato, and Aristotle. Fragment 191 is particularly suggestive in this regard: "Cheerfulness is created for men through moderation of enjoyment and harmoniousness of life. Things that are in excess or lacking are apt to change and cause great disturbance in the soul. Souls which are stirred by great divergences are neither stable nor cheerful. Therefore one must keep one's mind on what is attainable, and be content with what one has, paying little heed to things envied and admired, and not dwelling on them in one's mind."

According to Democritus, happiness lies in living both virtuously and wisely: "Men find happiness neither by means of the body nor through possessions, but through [moral] uprightness and wisdom" (fr. 40). Indeed, the condition of one's *soul*, not one's external circumstances, is the key to a happy life, because it brings us closer to the divine realm, the realm of "what is." "He who chooses the advantages of the soul chooses things more divine, but he who chooses those of the body, chooses things human" (fr. 37); and "it is right that men should value the soul rather than the body; for perfection of soul corrects the inferiority of the body, but physical strength without intelligence does nothing to improve the mind" (fr. 187). The link between the soul and the divine realm seems for Democritus to derive from the fact that the human individual and the universal order are intrinsically linked: "Man is a universe in miniature (*mikros kosmos*)" (fr. 34). Guthrie comments that "it is usually accepted that Democritus was the first known Greek to apply to man the term *microcosm*. . . . Man and world are built out of the same elements, atoms and void, following the same laws. Even the soul-atoms exist outside the human organism, and are breathed in along with the air" (1965, 471–72). Thus the "well-ordered soul" imitates the divine order of the cosmos, and the principles that govern human behavior reiterate those that steer natural processes.

Democritus says some things about speech and persuasion that reflect his immediate cultural milieu, as we shall see in the next chapter, and that foreshadow ideas we will encounter in Aristotle. He maintains that "in power of persuasion, reasoning is far stronger than gold" (fr. 51) and that persuasion is a more effective guide to virtue than are law and compulsion: "For the man who is prevented by law from wrongdoing will probably do wrong in secret, whereas the man who is led towards duty by persuasion will probably not do anything untoward either secretly or openly. Therefore the man who acts rightly through understanding and knowledge becomes at the same time brave and upright" (fr. 181). Democritus also holds that the speech of the wise is both truthful and succinct: "It is greed to do all the talking and not be willing to listen" (fr. 86), so "one should tell the truth, not speak at length" (fr. 225).

Democritus clearly occupies a transitional place in the unfolding of a Greek philosophical consciousness during the fifth century, and we have found in his writings both echoes of his forebears and anticipations of his successors. Indeed, his ethical writings in particular resonate closely with themes found in the thinking of his contemporaries, the older Sophists and Socrates. In any event, in Democritus we have considered the last of the Presocratic "nature philosophers" whose thoughts and writings gave rise to cosmology and naturalistic theorizing as keys to a new way of understanding and dwelling in the world, and whose ideas helped to shape a postmythic conception of wisdom.

The Presocratics initiated an intellectual revolution the effects of which reverberate into our own time. They identified *nature* itself, rather than supernatural deities, as the animating force behind/within all that happens in the world. The idea that nature is *autonomos*, a law unto itself and not governed by any external thing, is a watershed dividing the Western intellectual outlook from the realm of myth and legend. Nature as a self-contained, self-regulating system is the conceptual foundation of science. Moreover, uniquely among Mediterranean societies, these Greek thinkers dared to apply both the name and the functions of divinity to an order conceived as rigorously natural, completely purged of miracle and magic. Their distinctive theological contribution was to present divinity as immanent in the order of nature and thus as absolutely bound by natural law. The apprehension of regularity and necessity in nature was significant, for it not only gave impetus to Greek science but also made possible a new conception of human existence. On the physical side, the human being, as a part of the natural world, was now subject to its regularities, and the conditions of human existence were determined by the operation of uncreated, indestructible materials and principles rather than by the favor or displeasure of competing deities. On the psychological side, the individual was rid of interference from the gods in his/her own inner life and was therefore free to develop a sense of self-directedness within the constraints of natural processes. The move toward subjectivity and agency is an important departure from the Homeric mind, marking the origin of the Western concept of selfhood as autonomous and morally responsible. At the same time, the unity of nature means that the individual self is coextensive with the cosmos, for the human psyche has an unbounded *logos* in virtue of which we participate in and are continuous with the fundamental laws of the universe at large.

Alongside these conceptual developments, the Presocratics endowed Greek thought with new attitudes toward knowledge and language, and with linguistic tools without which later philosophical inquiry, cosmological speculation, and rhetorical theorizing would have been impossible. To approach the teachings of one's forebears as accounts to be examined, criticized, and corrected rather than as sacred tales to be preserved and passed on is to open the door on reasoned inquiry and intellectual debate as paths to truth and knowledge. It is also to focus on how language is used, on the words and syntax in terms of which naturalistic explanations are advanced. Philosophical criticism—appraising an account for its adequacy in explaining the phenomena with which it is concerned, its logical coherence, and its precision—is concerned with how language functions in particular instances, and with correcting errors through the deployment of new terminologies and linguistic devices. Principal among such devices, and one of the Presocratics' most important bequests to their intellectual heirs, were the metaphorical extension of terms such as *physis, theos, kosmos,* and *logos;* the use of the neuter noun, derived from gendered adjectives; and the use of the verb *to be* and its variants in descriptive and explanatory propositions. These linguistic innovations provided a vocabulary and syntax that enabled articulation of increasingly abstract concepts. Similarly the process of tracing out the logical implications of terms gave rise to the logical analysis of propositions and to deductive reasoning as forms of inquiry and demonstration. Moreover the abstract vocabulary developed by these thinkers made possible the expression of rhetorical concepts that we find in the writings of the Sophists, Plato, and Aristotle. Presocratic theorizing also raised important epistemological problems that occupied later Greek thinkers and that persist into our own time. To what degree can the senses be relied on as avenues to true knowledge? What is the proper role of thought, intellection, or reasoning in the acquisition of knowledge? A product of Presocratic inquiry, even if it was not a matter of consensus among these thinkers themselves, is that knowledge of the cosmos comes through a partnership of sense and thought, of perception and intellection.[96]

What is the form of consciousness to which the Presocratic worldview gives rise? In contrast to the mythopoetic mind, the Presocratics introduced and cultivated an outlook that arises from the interconnections among three ideas: *physis, kosmos,* and *logos.* It is, first, a *naturalistic* consciousness, a mode of awareness in which all that happens arises out of an animating, self-governing, universal Nature. It is precisely the intrinsic lawfulness of Nature that gives rise to the idea of an *ordered* world, a *kosmos.* For the Presocratics, the whole of existence constitutes a unified system of diverse events in which all is harmoniously regulated by a single, indwelling principle. Thus the new mind set is a *cosmological* consciousness, an awareness of Order in the universe. The ordering principle, with which all world-processes are in accord, is expressed by the term *Logos.* It is essentially a principle of proportionality, balance and equilibrium, harmony and concord, reciprocity and exchange. Thus a naturalistic/

cosmological consciousness is a *rational* consciousness. It sees the world unfolding in regular, predictable ways; as a place wherein all apparent change is the measured, cyclical transmutation of a single, fundamental reality from one phase of its being to another; as a place wherein events have not only a cause but also a reason—they can be accounted for in terms of the fixed order of Nature. We live in a rational universe. Thus can events such as eclipses be explained not as divine omens but in material terms: "The sun, the moon and all the stars," according to Anaxagoras, "are red-hot stones. . . . The moon has no light of its own but derives it from the sun. . . . Eclipses of the moon are due to its being screened by the earth . . . ; those of the sun to screening by the moon when it is new."[97] The "natural mind" is aware that stars, planets, seasons, weather, earthquakes, and other natural phenomena fit together seamlessly in a mathematically proportioned cosmos.

A naturalistic or cosmological consciousness has a cognitive architecture that represents a revolutionary departure from the Homeric mind. Its fundamental assumptions about how the world works have radically shifted the causes of events from beyond nature to deep within it. To live in the new consciousness is to inhabit a natural world wherein events possess a significant measure of predictability. It is this factor that makes argument from probability possible—for the very idea of "probability" is predicated on the fact of regularity, on the premise that similar circumstances are likely to produce similar outcomes. A cosmological worldview is also an awareness that all existence is akin. This mode of being-in-the-world, accordingly, includes a cognizance of one's own connectedness to the natural order. Presocratic thought points toward an identification of the human *psychê* with the *Psychê* or life-force of the universe.

This form of consciousness is further imbued with a sense that nature is animate and divine. For the Presocratics, all of nature is interpenetrated by a divine life-force—impersonal and law-governed, to be sure, but alive and immortal nonetheless. Positivistic thinking might have cast out all supernatural aspects of the causes behind events, but the Presocratic idea that "all things are full of *theoi*" is a naturalistic echo of the mythopoetic notion that "the immortals are ever present among men." Accordingly a naturalistic consciousness is a simultaneous awareness of the unity, the regularity, and the divinity of all that happens in the world. Just as with the mythopoetic mind set, so with the cosmological consciousness: to dwell in this is to dwell with god.

What is the wisdom that emerges from these ancient texts? For one thing, it is largely disconnected from the practical activities of political life. As we have seen particularly with Pythagoras, Empedocles, and Democritus, connections between the cosmological and the political/moral are not altogether absent, but the Presocratics' wisdom was principally concerned with how the universe works, and only secondarily with how human societies ought to be governed and how individuals should behave. The moral dimension of life is rooted in the cosmological order, and the highest wisdom lies in perceiving this order.

The new consciousness, at its core, is an awareness of the natural order at work in the world around us and in our own bodies and souls. Wisdom, in this mode of consciousness, consists in perceiving the principles of this order and apprehending the harmonies and other connections among cosmic processes. *Sophia* lies in grasping the *archai* of the world—knowing the *gnômê* (plan, intelligence, judgment) by which all is steered through all. The wisdom of the Presocratics—and an important part of their legacy to us—originates in the insight that the universe is rational, law-governed, regular, and predictable. It includes understanding that the processes of transformation and change are governed by a kind of cosmic Justice expressed in the principle of balance, proportion, and reciprocity; that human beings must live in harmony with the dictates of this Justice, whose Law is *Logos;* and that right conduct is measured, moderate, deliberate. The wise soul is "well ordered." It exhibits both an internal harmony among its elements and a harmonious relationship with the cosmic order. Thus wisdom includes the insight that all transgressions of the natural order, all violations of the principle of balance and proportion, will eventually incur "penalty and retribution . . . according to the ordinance of Time." Humans cannot violate the cosmic laws of balance and proportion without being called to account, not by Zeus or the polis but by *Physis* itself.

How is wisdom acquired? Significantly the quest for wisdom is in some respects a cooperative, communicative undertaking. Philosophical communities—the Milesians, the Pythagoreans, the Eleatics, the Atomists—developed around a particular set of teachings or theories, and a pattern of communication developed in which the views of a master—a Thales, Pythagoras, Parmenides, or Leucippus—might be criticized or challenged by his students and associates and are then extended, corrected, rejected, or transformed. The dialogical examination of various accounts of the origins and nature of the world is a process that can generate new insights, deeper understandings, and a richer wisdom. The connection between *sophia* and *logos* is intimate and profound. Most especially, the activities of discussion, debate, argument, and reasoning are implicated in the quest for new insight and knowledge. In a predisciplinary era, no distinction can be drawn between what later were labeled "poetical," "rhetorical," and "dialectical" uses of speech, but we can discern in the teachings of the Presocratics elements of language practices that developed in each of these directions. Here they are all *logos*, all "speech."

Noteworthy too is the centrality in both philosophical inquiry and political decision of *agôn*—the contest between competing perspectives, beliefs, and terms, performed in the presence of others (Fredal 2006). Neither philosophical investigation nor political decision was undertaken except in the context of the "gathering together" of people who would witness the conflict and judge the arguments of the antagonists. In the case of philosophical investigation, this gathering comprised the associates with whom thinkers such as Thales, Pythagoras, and Parmenides discoursed. In the case of political debate, the contest was witnessed by one's fellow citizens in the *agora*, assembly, or courtroom. This agonistic, competitive element plays out, as we shall see, in the teachings of both Sophists and Socratics.

The *archê* may also be apprehended through an intuitive, intellectual grasping, through attentiveness to the rhythms and regularities in experience, of an underlying, ordering principle—an intuition accessible to one who has "woken up" and who can become "attuned" to the cosmic harmonies as these are disclosed in our sensible encounters with natural events. One path to cosmological knowledge, then, can be found in our everyday experience of the world. The fundamental realities of the cosmos disclose themselves in everything that happens—in the cycle of the seasons; in the birth, growth, death, and decay of a plant or animal; in the rising of summer storms and the tranquillity of a summer evening. An account of a conversation between a Zen Buddhist monk and his master expresses this idea well: A monk approached his teacher and said, "Master, I have been studying with you for many years, and still you have not shown me the path to enlightenment." The master answered, "Do you hear the babbling of the brook? There you may enter." So it is with wisdom: the doors of perception are everywhere around us.

The cosmic harmonies can also be discerned in the words of one who, knowing that all things are one, has been able to perceive things "according to their nature" and thus who can speak "what is true." Heraclitus held that "it is wise to agree that all things are one" (DK 50). The verb *to agree* here is a translation of *homologein*, literally "to say the same as." The wise person speaks as though all things are one. Thus the speech of the wise can take the form of paradox, for things are and are not what we name them, and what appear to be opposites are actually one and the same thing. Such speech does not communicate *sophia* directly, but it can create opportunities for a wakeful soul to perceive at a deeper level than usual. As with the Zen *koan*, the paradoxical statement of Heraclitus invites the attentive listener to break through the surface of appearances and see into the heart of things. The words of the wise are apertures through which reality can be glimpsed. Again, the connection between *logos* and *sophia* is fundamental.

Insight into the heart of being can also come through rigorous, deductive reasoning that follows the logical implications of the language we use to communicate and to think. Listening not merely to the statement but to the *logos* it discloses, we can follow the chain of reasoning to truth about the nature of things. Thus the process of tracing deductive inference from the particulars of a statement to the universal principles disclosed in its premises is a pathway to insight into the cosmic *Logos* and into the nature of reality. When Parmenides, Empedocles, and Melissus reasoned from the statement "Something exists" to the conclusions at which they arrived about being, existence, or reality, they were exploiting the promise inherent in language itself: words and the deep grammatical structures of statements manifest reality, and reality can be grasped through a process of following out the logical implications of words and statements. By pursuing these implications, one is led to the point where the *archê* can be grasped.

Insight into cosmic principles and harmonies can also be attained through introspection or self-examination. Since individual *psychê* is a particular incarnation of the cosmic *Psychê*, if one follows one's own soul to its depths, one encounters the universal. *Gnôthi seauton*, "know thyself," and in doing so one will understand the nature of the world. Thus can wisdom come through apprehending the deep *logos* that lies at the foundation of one's own mental being.

In the foregoing I have aimed to synthesize from themes, motifs, and continuities running through Presocratic thinking a composite portrait of a new consciousness and new conceptions of wisdom. While important differences and disagreements can be found in the details of the various cosmologies, at a more general level there is congruence and coherence among these views. Our textual evidence discloses the emergence of a new way of seeing the world and human beings' place in it. Thenceforth these developments shaped Greek philosophical inquiry in important ways. They set the concepts and language in terms of which subsequent cosmological and moral inquiries would be carried out, and they guided the subsequent evolution of Greek conceptions of wisdom. These ideas also affected the development during the fifth century of the "speaker's art," the language-craft that came to be called "rhetoric." The relationship between "truth" and "speech," the dichotomy between "reality" and "appearance," the tension between "being" and "becoming," the distinction between "knowledge" and "opinion"—these issues arise from Presocratic doctrines, and they become fundamental in the connections and antagonisms between philosophy and rhetoric found in the teachings of the Sophists, Socrates, and their followers.

FOUR

Sophistical Wisdom, Socratic Wisdom, and the Political Life

Of all things the measure is the human—of things that are that they are,
and of things that are not that they are not.

Protagoras (DK 80 A 14)

For the human being, the unexamined life is not a proper way of life.

Socrates (Plato, *Apology* 38a)

How should one live one's life? What are the values that one should seek to
realize in one's conduct? By what moral standards should our actions be judged,
and how are these standards to be discovered? What legitimizes the laws that
govern society? Are law and morality rooted in the nature of things, or are
they merely matters of custom and convention? What forms of wisdom are
involved in making sound moral choices in one's personal and social conduct?
Such questions mark a shift in the foci of intellectual inquiry, away from the
sorts of cosmological and metaphysical questions that preoccupied Presocratic
thinkers and toward a concern with matters of praxis, politics, and morality.
This shift had some extent been anticipated in the writings of Archelaus and
Democritus, who represent a bridge between the naturalistic and cosmological speculations of the "physicists" and the ethical inquiries of Socrates and the
Sophists. During the second half of the fifth century, however, some thinkers
and teachers who appeared in the Greek world abandoned naturalistic speculation altogether, centering their investigations on moral, political, and epistemological questions instead. This shift in philosophical interest brought with
it new conceptions of wisdom that built on, enlarged, and in many ways departed from the legacy of the Presocratics.

The fifth century B.C.E. witnessed an intellectual movement toward the
human individual and the practical demands of civic and personal life. These
"First Humanists," as Guthrie (1968) has called them, realized both that the
cosmological investigations of the natural philosophers might never culminate
in "truth" and that all epistemological and ontological claims must be attenuated

by the role of the knowing subject. Consequently they concentrated instead on the nature of practical knowledge, particularly on the role of language in deciding practical, moral questions. I include in this group both the older Sophists and Socrates, although we will not find uniformity of opinion among these thinkers. Even so, several shared an interest in questions concerning moral or practical wisdom, the role of language and speech in acquiring it, and the sources of principles that can guide practical decisions, both personal and communal. The pursuit of such questions led to distinctively humanistic and practical conceptions of wisdom and to a preoccupation with *logos*—understood as speech and as reasoned argument—as the principal instrument of practical judgment. Here we find the emergence of a distinctive "art" of persuasive speech and the beginnings of the distinction between rhetoric and dialectic later articulated by Aristotle. We also find roots of the antagonisms between rhetoric and philosophy that become explicit in Plato's writings and that persist into our own time. The conflict rests on radically differing conceptions of "moral truth," "moral knowledge," and the responsible use of persuasive speech.

Since we have only fragmentary evidence for the actual writings of the Sophists, much of the available information about sophistical teachings comes from secondary sources, most particularly including Plato and Aristotle. Similarly, since Socrates apparently never wrote a book or otherwise recorded his convictions and teachings, we must depend on others, especially on Plato, Xenophon, and Aristotle, for insight into what he believed and taught. The issues associated with this dependence are considered below, but as with the Presocratics, we must be cautious in any effort at reconstructing the thinking of these figures.

We should have at least a general picture of the period in which they thrived and of the salient social, intellectual, and political conditions that engendered and shaped their thought. The older Sophists and Socrates cannot be understood or appreciated except in the context of Hellenic culture of the fifth century B.C.E., especially the culture of Athens. It was at Athens, more than anywhere else in the Greek world, that the philosophical speculations initiated by Presocratic thinkers converged and intermingled with other social and political events, so as to create the rich intellectual stew that nourished new ideas and new ways of viewing the relationship between individual, community, and nature.[1]

Several factors led to fifth-century Athens's ascendancy as the center of philosophical activity, intellectual innovation, and instruction in the speaker's art. One was the introduction of varied ideas, customs, and beliefs as a result of travelers passing through from different parts of the Mediterranean world. As with Miletos, Athens was strategically situated at the intersection of shipping routes from all quarters of this world. Cargos of timber and pitch from

Macedon and Thrace in the north; grain from the Black Sea to the northeast; wine from Chios and copper from Cyprus to the east; metals, papyrus, and perfumes from Egypt in the south; tin, silver, and iron from faraway Britain and Spain in the west; and marble from various Aegean islands—all came to Athens, both for transshipment and for local consumption. Along with their cargoes, the ships also bore merchants, sailors, and passengers who brought with them unfamiliar stories and legends, reports of strange customs and unknown divinities. Hooper comments that "by the fifth century, Athens was the largest and most prosperous city in Greece. News of her wealth and free institutions spread wide, and to her came the writers, sculptors and philosophers whose works, along with those of native citizens, have given Athens a unique place in all of human history" (1978, 133).[2] Consequently questions arose among the Athenian intelligentsia concerning the divine or natural foundations of law and custom. Once the view had gained currency that laws, customs, and conventions did not originate in the order of things (recall Heraclitus's statement in DK 114 that "all human laws are nourished by a divine one"), it was possible for new attitudes toward them to develop. These attitudes often challenged traditional thinking about the legitimacy of civil law, a challenge that was crystallized most explicitly in the antithesis between *nomos* (law, custom, convention) and *physis* (nature, reality).[3]

Another important factor in Athens's emergence as a cultural and intellectual center was the city's unrivaled power, prestige, and wealth following its victories over the Persians in the battles of Marathon (490), Salamis (480), and Plataia (479). At the beginning of the fifth century Athens was a decidedly second-tier polis. Corinth was the leading trade center of the Greek world. Sparta was by far the dominant military power, possessing a land army whose training and discipline were second to none and whose reputation for prowess in battle was unchallenged. However, following Athens's victory at Marathon in 490, which occurred without Spartan assistance, and then its naval victory at Salamis in 480 and its defeat of Persian land forces at Plataia in 479, the balance of power began to shift. Bolstered by its new prestige, Athens challenged Sparta as the dominant military power in the Greek world. In the first years after the defeat of the Persians over 150 Greek city-states joined forces in order to provide sufficient strength to repel any future Persian invasions. Athens assumed the leadership of this group, called the Delian League because its headquarters was established on the Aegean island of Delos. Hooper aptly describes the league as "an ancient N.A.T.O. The states which joined the league did so voluntarily. They contributed money, ships and manpower with which to pursue the common goals, which included keeping the Aegean free of pirates as well as Persians. Customarily the larger states sent ships and men, while the smaller states contributed only money. Policy for the league was to be decided by a synod of representatives meeting regularly on the island of Delos where a sanctuary to Apollo was especially sacred to the Ionians" (1978, 172).[4] During its first decade the league's policies were marked by a genuinely Panhellenic outlook. However, as the Persian threat receded and as member-states increasingly substituted cash payments to Athens for contributions of men and ships, Athenian self-interest came to dominate the league's actions and direction.

Among the consequences of this dominance was continued expansion of Athenian commerce and growth in the private wealth of Athenian merchants. Athens also benefited from an accumulation of public wealth as a result of its control of the Delian treasury—which, indeed, was relocated from Delos to Athens in 454, ostensibly to increase security against threats from pirates and Persians alike. One use of private wealth was support for the burgeoning dramatic and musical arts, as rich individuals provided funds needed to produce plays and to enter choral teams and other performers in various festival competitions. A principal use of the league's funds was to restore on a grand scale the buildings of the Acropolis that had been destroyed by the Persians in 480 and to augment these buildings with new temples in Athens and elsewhere in Attica. Indeed, it was the Athenians' willingness to authorize the use of tribute from subject states (which is what many members of the Delian League had, in fact, become) for a monumental local building program that led, under Pericles' leadership, to the Golden Age of Athenian culture. This vast building program brought to Athens some of the Greek world's best architects, sculptors, painters, and other artists. As a consequence of its newfound private and public wealth, Athens emerged during the middle of the fifth century as the artistic as well as the commercial center of this world.

Athens also acquired a distinctive political status as a result of its movement toward an unprecedented system of government: democracy. This development was incremental rather than abrupt, but over the course of about a century constitutional changes occurred in Athens that culminated in the Periclean democracy of the mid-fifth century, when Athens was the most democratic of the Greek states. As was the pattern in other poleis throughout the eastern Mediterranean, during the late seventh and early sixth centuries Athens experienced political turmoil as various factions contended for dominance. Into this arena stepped Solon (ca. 638–ca. 559 B.C.E.), elected archon for the year 594/593 and, two years later, commissioned to reorganize the government. His reforms included cancelling debt for poor farmers, economic changes that stimulated the export of such Athenian goods as olive oil and pottery, opening public offices to men of demonstrated ability rather than only to those of noble birth, empowering all citizens to serve as jurors, and creating a new council (*Boulê*) of four hundred, which took over the legislative responsibilities of the ancient Council of the Areopagus. It was such political innovations that earned for Solon a place among the Seven Sages (Plato, *Prot.* 343a).[5] Solon's laws and administrative changes had diminished the dominance of the ancient aristocracy by giving the common people a place—albeit a limited one—in the governance of the city. They thus laid the groundwork for the more far-reaching democratic reforms that would take place at the end of the sixth century, under the guidance of Kleisthenes.

Solon and the tyrant Peisistratus may have laid the groundwork for democracy, but the reforms of Kleisthenes actually put legislative power into the hands of the common man. Throughout the sixth century, under Solon's reorganization of the Athenian government, the political structure had rested on the four traditional Ionian tribes. This arrangement, based on birth and an assumed common ancestry, did not allow the average (male) citizen to participate in political decision making. Between 510 and 507 Kleisthenes elevated the common citizen's place in the state by replacing the four old tribes with ten new ones based on residence rather than on birth. The effect of this was to open the door to a genuinely popular democracy, albeit one limited to male citizens. As Hooper observes, "so long as the old tribal system persisted at Athens, the city was dominated by a minority of families whose influence through custom and wealth was sufficient to secure for them a disproportionate power—one inconsistent with any truly democratic government" (1978, 148–49). Members of a newly created Council of Five Hundred (the *Boulê*) were selected by lot from among names nominated by each tribe. Ultimate legislative sovereignty was vested in the *Ekklêsia*, the assembly of all citizens, which was open to all male citizens over the age of eighteen.[6] Thus was political power in Athens spread equally among the aristocracy and the commons; and thus were mechanisms of open debate and discussion created that would, in their turn, nurture robust intellectual activity. Fredal observes that "Cleisthenes's appeal [to the Athenian people] gave birth to the ideal of political equality (*isonomia*) and free speech (*isêgoria;* see Herodotus 5.78) and acted as a model for the popular pursuit of honor (*time*) through political oratory appropriate to a democracy" (2006, 108).

Athens in the mid-fifth century, then, attracted thinkers from throughout the Greek world and provided a setting in which problems pursued by Presocratic thinkers were augmented by new inquiries. Questions concerning the connection between *nomos* and *physis* were accompanied by skepticism about the existence of the gods. Debates arose concerning the nature of virtue (*aretê*) and about whether it could be taught. Indeed, the spirit of debate—the *agôn* between competing ideas—engendered intense discussion about the nature of morality and about the possibility of genuine moral knowledge. The expansion of democratic governance in Athens created an appetite for instruction in the speaker's art, an appetite that engendered a demand for professional teachers of this art. As much as any other single factor, this is what attracted to Athens such men as Protagoras of Abdera, Gorgias of Leontini, Prodicus of Ceos, and others. As de Romilly observes, "it is certainly true that the development of their teaching programme was linked with that of the Athenian democracy. The rhetorical and political training that they purveyed only made sense if the skill of public speaking truly did make it possible for individuals to play an effective role" (1992, 213; also see Ober 1989, 1996; Fredal 2006). Moreover it was the teachings of these men that gave Socrates an opportunity to interrogate and argue with whomever he happened to encounter in and around the agora. "The status of laws and moral principles," writes Guthrie, "the theory of man's progress from savagery to civilization replacing that of degeneration from a past golden age, the idea of the social compact, subjective theories of knowledge, atheism and agnosticism, hedonism and utilitarianism, the unity of mankind, slavery and equality, the nature of *aretê*, the importance of rhetoric and the study of language": these were the topics that dominated intellectual inquiry and debate in the Athens of Socrates and the Sophists.[7]

Sophistical Wisdom

It would be imprecise to speak of "sophistical doctrines" or of a "sophistical view" of wisdom as representing a generally held set of principles, since "sophist" applies to a rather wide range of professional teachers of civic philosophy and the art of public speaking. Hunt, for example, notes that "such terms as a sophistic mind, a sophistic morality, a sophistic skepticism, and others implying a common basis of doctrine, are quite without justification" (1965, 71). Similarly Lloyd observes that

> the activities of Protagoras, Gorgias, Hippias, Prodicus, and the sophist Antiphon no doubt have certain features in common, but these men form no self-contained group, let alone one that constituted itself self-consciously as a movement or school. Rather, their work, and that of many others, should be set against a wider background of intellectual, social, and political developments in the late fifth century—developments that include (1) an increasing interest in rhetoric and dialectic . . . , (2) some spread in the demand for more than merely elementary instruction in such subjects as mathematics, medicine, and natural philosophy, as well as (3) the developments of those subjects themselves, in addition to (4) a growing interest in political and moral questions, including the relativisation of moral judgments and other aspects of the complex set of issues often debated under the rubric of the controversy between nature and convention. (1987, 93n152)[8]

Nonetheless, there are certain features of some Sophists' views that have come to be identified with sophistical thought generally and that have particular significance here. I concentrate especially on their conceptions of political wisdom, their theological/ontological skepticism, their epistemological relativism, and on the role of persuasive speech in the acquisition and exercise of "wisdom." Although the fullest characterizations of sophistical doctrines are to be found in Plato's writings, we must be cautious in accepting his accounts. Plato's antipathy toward the Sophists is well recognized. Even so, we can discern something of their ideas in Plato's dialogues as long as we compare his characterizations with other textual evidence for their teachings.

What is a "Sophist"? We have seen that the terms *sophos* and *sophia* were in common use at least since the time of Homer and Hesiod to denote skill in a particular craft. Through the "stretching" of these terms by such thinkers as Heraclitus and Pythagoras, by the fifth century they had come to be associated both with general wisdom or knowledge about the workings of the cosmos and with practical sagacity about politics and good sense in the enterprise of living. Accordingly the verbs *sophizô*, "to make wise or to instruct," and *sophizesthai*, "to practice *sophia*," were accompanied by the noun *sophistês*, "a wise, prudent or statesmanlike man" and "one who gives lessons."[9] By the mid-fifth century the term *sophistês* had come to be associated principally with a number of practitioners and teachers of a certain kind of wisdom. It had also acquired unfavorable associations. The verb *sophizomai*, following its connection with being skilled or clever, came to mean "playing subtle tricks" and "devising verbal contrivances" that could deceive others. "Thus in the hands of conservative Aristophanes," writes Guthrie, "[*sophistês*] became a term of abuse implying charlatanry and deceit" (1971b, 33). Xenophon has Socrates compare Sophists to prostitutes because they take money for teaching wisdom "to all comers" (*Mem.* 1.6.13).

Generally the Sophists of the fifth century were professional educators who offered instruction to young men for a fee (though not all took fees) and whose teaching typically focused on imparting political and practical sagacity and on developing skill in the art of *logos* (speech, argument, reasoning).[10] For example, of Mnesiphilus, who was admired by the Athenian statesman Themistocles, Plutarch says the following: "This man was neither an orator nor one of the so-called natural philosophers, but had made a special study of what at that time went by the name of 'wisdom.' This was really a combination of political acumen and practical intelligence, which had been formulated and handed down in unbroken succession from Solon, as though it were a set of philosophical principles. His successors combined it with various forensic techniques and transferred its application from public affairs to the use of language and were termed Sophists. It was Mnesiphilus, then, whom Themistocles made his mentor at the beginning of his political career" (*Themistocles* 2, in Plutarch 1960, 78).[11] Likewise, Plato has Protagoras describe the instruction he provides: "A pupil coming to me will learn . . . sound judgment (*euboulia*) in his domestic affairs, so that he may best manage his own household, and also in the affairs of the city, so as to become a real power in the city, both in acting and in speaking" (*Prot.* 318e, my translation).[12] Prodicus, too, may have provided instruction in politics and personal management. Other Sophists, including Thrasymachus and Antiphon, wrote or taught on such political topics as the nature of justice, slavery, and social equality.[13] Thus the *sophia* of the Sophists consists in the first instance of "political acumen and practical intelligence," of good sense and sound judgment in managing both personal and civic concerns.

Plato's *Protagoras* yields additional insight into sophistical wisdom. Socrates interrogates Protagoras about the subject of the latter's teachings and, following Protagoras's description of what his students will learn, concludes that the Sophist teaches "the art of politics, . . . promising to make men good citizens." "That," Protagoras replies, "is exactly what I profess to do" (319a). Civic excellence (*politikê aretê*) is at the heart of Protagoras's teaching. By way of a quasi-mythic tale about the origins of civilization (320d–22d), he identifies as components of the "political wisdom"—the keystone of civic virtue—moral qualities that enable us to "bring order to our cities and create a bond of friendship and union." These qualities—"respect for others (*aidôs*) and a sense of justice (*dikaiosynê*)"—are the foundation of political wisdom (322c).[14] To these Protagoras adds "moderation" or "self-control" (*sôphrosynê*), "holiness of life" or piety (*hosiotês*), and "courage" or "manliness" (*andreia*). He concludes that "everyone shares a sense of justice and civic virtue. . . . [For] a man cannot be without some share in justice, or he would not be human" (323a–c). These qualities are the "parts of virtue" (*aretê*), and "wisdom indeed is the greatest of the parts" (330a).

For Protagoras, then, wisdom is linked to traditional Greek virtues, and guided by these, it enables a person to act "rightly and advantageously." Moreover, though the capacity for such knowledge is innate in humans, it must be nurtured through instruction (323c–26e). Schiappa observes that "the process of education occurs throughout life. The family teaches the child to excel, then the schools do the same, then the state itself through its laws (*nomoi*)" (2003, 181). Thus the proper aim of the citizen's education, in Protagoras's view, is to cultivate these innate virtues and enhance the capacity for wise, efficacious action in both personal and civic endeavors.[15] Moreover civil laws are socially constructed rules that must be observed if human societies are to avoid degeneration toward our natural state of savagery.[16]

Prodicus seems to have offered advice in the same vein, stressing the importance of self-discipline, hard work, and service to the community. He was "a Sophist in the full sense of a professional freelance educator," says Guthrie, "whose name is coupled with that of Protagoras as teaching the art of success in politics and private life" (1971b, 275). His principal emphasis seems to have been on the "correctness of names," but he apparently included logic, ethics, and related subjects in his teachings. The Suda describes him as "a natural philosopher and sophist, a contemporary of Democritus of Abdera and Gorgias, a student of Protagoras" (DK 84 A 1). Stewart, introducing his translation of Prodicus's fragments, observes that "non-Platonic sources . . . give us rather an impression of a wide-ranging dilettante whose interests included ethics and physiology, cosmology and anthropology—and, of course, rhetoric, the chief preoccupation of all the sophists" (Sprague 1972, 70).[17]

Xenophon (*Mem.* 2.1.21–34) recounts the Sophist's cautionary tale about the moral life and the dangers of self-indulgence, told in the form of a story about Heracles.[18] "When Heracles was setting out from childhood to manhood," says Prodicus, "at the age when the young become independent and show whether they are going to approach life by the path of goodness or . . . of wickedness, he went out to a quiet spot and sat down considering which way he should take" (21). There he met two female figures, one with a noble bearing, "clean-limbed and modest in expression, and soberly dressed in a white robe," while the other's figure bespoke "fleshiness and softness." Her face colored by makeup, she wore clothing that "revealed as much as possible of her charms." As the two women approached Heracles, the "soft" woman barged ahead of the other and accosted the young man. "If you take me as your friend," she said, "I will lead you by the easiest and pleasantest road; you shall not miss the taste of any pleasure, and you shall live out your life without any experience of hardship" (23). After the woman described the various pleasures to which she would lead him, Heracles inquired as to her name. "My friends call me Happiness," she replied, "but people who don't like me nickname me Vice" (26).

At that moment the second woman approached Heracles and addressed him. "If you will only take the path to me," she told him, "you may become a very effective performer of fine and noble deeds. . . . I will not delude you with promises of future pleasure; I shall give you a true account of the facts, exactly as the gods have ordained them. Nothing that is really good and admirable is granted by the gods to men without some effort and application. If you want the gods to be gracious to you, you must worship the gods; if you wish to be loved by your friends, you must be kind to your friends; if you desire to be honoured by a State, you must help that State; if you expect to be admired for your fine qualities by the whole of Greece, you must try to benefit Greece; if you want your land to produce abundant crops, you must look after your land; . . . if you want to be physically efficient, you must train your body to be subject to your reason, and develop it with hard work and sweat" (27–28). This, of course, is the path of virtue and wisdom. Indeed, the wisdom that Prodicus teaches is the knowledge that both in one's personal affairs and in civic matters one must exercise self-discipline and moderation, that one must tend to the practical demands of one's aspirations, that true happiness comes only through "hard work and sweat," and that the greatest rewards in life come to those who benefit their community and their people.

The wisdom Antiphon taught takes a somewhat different tack, but one not necessarily at odds with the foregoing.[19] He was one for whom the distinction between *nomos* and *physis* was of primary interest. The idea of *physis* as an abstract "nature" emerged from the speculations of the Presocratic thinkers, as we have seen. In contrast to *nomos*, it comes to designate what is "real," what exists apart from human perception and convention. *Nomos* is something that is believed in, practiced, or held to be right (*nomizetai*). As long as there was a link between *nomos* and the divine—as there was in Hesiod, for whom Zeus laid down the law of justice for all men (*Works and Days* 276), and in Heraclitus, for whom human laws are sustained by a divine law (DK 114)—there could be *nomoi* that were valid for all people, wherever they lived. However, once the existence of the gods was called into question by Protagoras (DK 80 B 4) and others, this link no longer obtained. Since different people and societies believe in different things, *nomos* is a matter of *doxa* or opinion rather than "reality," and thus it has no universal legitimacy. When *nomos* is divorced from *physis*, what exists by custom, belief, or convention is no longer grounded in the "real" or "natural." Thus did questions arise during the fifth century concerning whether the gods existed by *physis*—in reality—or only by *nomos* or custom; whether states arose by divine ordinance, by natural necessity, or by convention; whether civil law had any validity outside the community that adhered to it by agreement; and so on. If laws and moral standards are not god-given or natural but rather are created by agreement and enforced by public opinion, then the "right" and the "just" will vary from one community to another and even from one time to another within a single community. The implications of such ethical relativism will be considered later in this chapter, but for now it provides a context for sophistical and Socratic conceptions of wisdom.[20]

In *On Truth*, Antiphon holds that "justice . . . is a matter of not breaking the laws and customs (*nomima*) of the city in which one is a citizen. So a man would make use of justice most advantageously for himself if he were to regard the laws as important when witnesses are present."[21] Note the concluding qualification: to act justly or virtuously, one must adhere to the *nomoi* of the society in which one lives *when others can observe your actions*. And when one can act unobserved? Laws, which are upheld by convention, are often opposed to nature, and one should follow the dictates of nature when doing so will not be detected by others: "When on his own without witnesses, [he should regard] the demands of nature [as important]. For the demands of the laws are adventitious (*epitheta*), but the demands of nature are necessary (*anankaia*); and the demands of the laws are based on agreement, not nature, while the demands of nature are not dependent on agreement. So if a man transgresses the demands of law and is not found out by those who are parties to the agreement, he escapes without either shame or penalty; but if he is found out, he does not. . . . If, on the other hand, a man does what is really an impossibility and violates one of the inherent demands of nature, . . . the injury he suffers is not in appearance but in truth. . . . [For] many of the things which are just according to the law are at variance with nature."[22]

If wisdom incorporates a capacity for taking care of "one's personal affairs and the affairs of the city," then on Antiphon's account it involves knowing when to act in accordance with the laws and when to follow the dictates of nature. In this respect, it is practical and pragmatic; wisdom is best understood under the rubric of *phronêsis*—prudence or practical wisdom. It is a sense of pragmatic discernment, a capacity in a given set of circumstances for judging what will be advantageous to oneself or one's fellow citizens—that is, what will preserve life and well-being.[23] In some cases, advantage comes through following law or custom for the sake of appearances; in others, it comes through following the dictates of nature, which are the source, says Antiphon, of *true* advantage. "The advantages which are prescribed by the laws," he says, "are fetters of nature, whereas the advantages which are prescribed by nature make for freedom" (DK 87 B 90, fr. B4). True wisdom, accordingly, is recognizing where the genuinely beneficial lies in a particular situation—whether in observing the *nomoi* or in following *physis*. At least implicitly, it is also understanding the principles of nature so as to maximize its benefits through one's practical actions. Thus, for Antiphon, complete wisdom includes both *sophia* (grasping the universal laws of *physis*) and *phronêsis* (sound practical judgment). In sum, wisdom is a capacity for apprehending, in situations where choice is possible, opportunities for securing the greatest benefit for oneself and for others. This power of observing what is possible in a given set of practical conditions is a central feature of sophistical wisdom.

Like Protagoras and Prodicus, Antiphon also holds that the prudent person exercises self-discipline, controlling the natural impulse to pursue pleasure. "Good sense," he says in *On Concord*, "might be said to belong to that man and to no other who makes himself withstand the immediate pleasures of his heart and has succeeded in overcoming and conquering himself. The man who intends to satisfy his heart's desire immediately intends what is worse rather than what is better" (DK 87 B 58). On the basis of such sentiments, de Romilly concludes that "Antiphon turns out to be the most moralistic of all the Sophists and, in this domain of ethics, possibly the closest of all of them to Socrates" (1992, 184). Again we are invited to perceive a link between wisdom and virtue, *sophia* and *aretê*, a connection that suffuses Greek thought from beginning to end. There is in this wisdom a kind of moral sense, an ability to apprehend the path of moderation in a given situation and an inclination to subject one's natural desires to this apprehension. Sophistical wisdom, then, perceives in private and public circumstances opportunities for just and advantageous action, both for oneself and for the community as a whole. It is rooted in a certain strength of character, most particularly in innate human capabilities for moderation and self-discipline, respect for others, and courage. It is also the capacity for distinguishing what is "natural" from what is merely customary, for understanding and applying the fundamental laws of nature, and for perceiving in a given set of circumstances what would be truly beneficial or advantageous.

In contrast to Antiphon's belief in a common "nature" that links all people, sophistical wisdom was also inflected by a pervasive skepticism concerning both the existence of the gods and the reality and intelligibility of natural principles or universal truths. Both subjectivity and a rhetorical sensibility were thereby introduced into the idea of wisdom. When Protagoras acknowledged his own religious agnosticism in saying, "Concerning the gods I cannot know either that they exist or that they do not exist, or what form they might have, for there is much to prevent one's knowing: the obscurity of the subject and the shortness of man's life," he opened the door to the *human* ground of both being and knowledge: "Of all things the measure is [the] human (*anthrôpos*), of things that are that they are, and of things that are not that they are not."[24] Likewise, Gorgias's ostensible denial of objective reality as existent, knowable, or communicable had the effect of privileging speech itself as ontogenic and epistemic.[25] Thus the person skilled in *logos* is also *sophos* (wise) or *phronimos*—prudent, sensible, or clever in the conduct of personal and public/civic affairs. The idea of wisdom again embraces a practical, moral element, and it is rooted in the power of persuasive speech to shape belief or opinion (*doxa*). Indeed, a specifically Protagorean/Gorgianic view of wisdom as practical and political knowledge holds that the only "realities" that exist and are apprehensible by humans emerge through the rhetorical negotiation of social experience.

Protagoras's "human-measure" statement is provocatively ambiguous, and its meaning has been hotly debated.[26] On the most general level, it appears to say that human beings provide the standard by which the existent can be identified as such and by which it and the nonexistent can be distinguished.[27] The interpretive issues focus on *in what capacity* humans provide the "measure" of existence (that is, as individuals or as a collectivity), what human capability constitutes the "measure," and on the nature of the "what is" and its "is-ness." Some readings of these texts illuminate what was, in the fifth century B.C.E., an unprecedented conception of being-in-the-world.

The term *anthrô*pos can be read either as an individual "human" or as "humankind" generally (Schiappa 2003, 119). Guthrie maintains that Protagoras "had chiefly the individual in mind" (1971b, 183). This reading, he observes, invites the conclusion that "Protagoras adopted an extreme subjectivism according to which there was no reality behind and independent of appearances, no difference between appearing and being, and *we are each the judge* of our own impressions. What seems to me *is* for me, and no man is in a position to call another mistaken" (187, my italics). This also appears to be Sextus's understanding of the fragment. In *Against the Schoolmasters* (7.60) he writes that "some also reckoned Protagoras of Abdera in the company of those philosophers who do away with the [objective] standard of judgment, since he says that all appearances and opinions are true and that truth is a relative matter because a man's every perception or opinion immediately exists in relation to him."[28] On this reading, each *individual*'s perception or judgment is the criterion according to which the existent is distinguished from the nonexistent: I live in my world, and you live in yours; there is no reconciling the inconsistencies between them.

An alternative reading recognizes the ambiguity of the term *anthrôpos*—it can signify either the individual person or humanity as a collective—and holds that Protagoras, like Heraclitus before him, sought to exploit this very ambiguity in expressing a subtle and sophisticated conception. Gomperz writes that "'man,' as opposed to the totality of objects, was obviously not the individual, but mankind as a whole" (1901, 1:451). However, Untersteiner concludes that "Protagoras must have identified this 'Man' equally with the man understood in an individual sense and with man in general. We have here not an inept vacillation on the part of Protagoras' speculative ability, but two movements of a dialectical process of which the two termini are laid down as 'individual man' and 'universal Man'" (1954, 42). Likewise, Schiappa maintains that "the most reasonable interpretation is to assume he intended the word *anthrôpos* to convey both senses" (2003, 120). Thus we might read the fragment as saying, "Of all things the measure is human(ity)," indicating thereby that the standard lies in something essential to the human being *as* human. There is something common to all humans and within each human that provides the "measure" of being and nonbeing.[29]

From Heraclitus and Parmenides we have seen that what is "common" and "shared by all" is *logos*—speech, language, thought, and reason, all considered as aspects of the same thing. Thus one reading of Protagoras's fragment maintains that the *metron* or standard by which the existent is distinguished from the nonexistent is the logic of language: the *logos* of the *logos*, so to speak. This is consistent with Parmenides' belief that existence is coextensive with "what is there to be said and thought." What Protagoras might be taken to intend here is that "what is" is what humans construct through the language they use. Every "thing" that exists does so *as* a "thing" because it exists in language. It has been named. It is speech itself that confers "is-ness" on what we name, describe, characterize, appraise, and relate to other "things-that-are." For Protagoras, there is quite literally no-thing beyond the perimeter of language, and what exists is precisely what has been invoked by speech. Asking whether there is a "reality" beyond our linguistically mediated perceptions is a meaningless question, akin to asking if there is empty space into which the universe is expanding: there is no "space" outside the universe into which it can expand. Similarly there is no "existence" outside the universe of "existences" that are brought into being by utterance.

On this reading, there is a clear sense of the individual person creating the reality in which he/she lives and acts, and it is inviting to conclude that each of us thus lives in a world that is wholly private or personal. However, Protagoras seems to hold that the process of reality-construction involves not merely the act of expression but also the contest between alternative expressions or statements about "what is." Diogenes Laertius (9.51) reports that "[he] was the first to say that on every issue there are two arguments opposed to each other" (*Kai prôtos ephê duo logous einai peri pantos pragmatos antikeimenous allêlois;* trans. O'Brien, in Sprague 1972, 21).[30] Competing accounts (*logoi*) of the "existent," consequently, can always be given, and any particular account is always open to question, always a matter of debate and negotiation among individuals whose actions must be adjusted to one another's. A "true" account, on this view, is ultimately a matter of what a particular social/political/linguistic community finds most persuasive at any given moment in the absence of an extrapsychological criterion. "Knowledge" of the "real" comprises just the convictions to which one is led by the "persuasives" that compel belief. Knowledge is always a matter of opinion (*doxa*) and is always contingent on the particular account of "what is" that arguments (*logoi*) have rendered persuasive at a particular moment. Consigny (2001), like Hawhee and Fredal, emphasizes the importance of *agôn* in the polis and argues that *logos* is inherently competitive. To be a *rhêtôr* is to be engaged in a competitive game. It is to be a player who wields *logos* in seeking the prize of "truth." In this account, truth is found neither in reference to objective reality nor in subjective assertion but in the adherence of a community of citizens for whom a given argument is persuasive.[31]

This interpretation of the "two-*logoi*" fragments leaves open the possibility that Protagoras also intended an ontological proposition. Schiappa (2003), for example, advances a "Heraclitean" reading of Protagoras's doctrine, arguing that "Protagoras' claim is not only a description of human argumentative prowess, but also a claim about the world. 'Reality' (*pragma*) is such that there are two opposing ways (*logoi*) to describe, account for, or explain any given experience" (92). He sees Protagoras as extending Heraclitus's thinking about the relationship between language and reality, and he offers two translations of Diogenes Laertius's text. A "locative" reading gives that "Two accounts [*logoi*] are present about every 'thing,' opposed to each other"; a "veridical" reading yields, "Two contrary reports [*logoi*] are true concerning every experience" (100). In both cases it is the "existent" itself that requires opposing accounts, just as Heraclitus would have it. Both are legitimate, but one may be more compelling than the other, and thus may exercise greater power over opinion.

For Protagoras a principal benefit of his teaching would be equipping the student to "make the weaker argument stronger" (DK 80 B 6b; Aristotle, *Rhetoric* 1402a). This fragment has typically been interpreted pejoratively (Schiappa 2003, 104–7), but in the context of Protagoras's teachings it is more accurately understood in a positive sense—as enabling "the substitution of a preferred (but weaker) *logos* for a less preferable (but temporarily dominant) *logos* of the same 'experience'" (109). The aim of his instruction in *logos* is to enable the rhetor to render persuasive accounts of what is better for the community and to refute what is worse. Protagoras's speech in Plato's *Theaetetus* suggests exactly this:

> By a wise man I mean precisely a man who can change any one of us, when what is bad appears and is to him, and make what is good appear and be to him. . . . It is not that a man makes someone who previously thought what is false think what is true, for it is not possible either to think the thing that is not or to think anything but one's experiences, and all experiences are true. Rather, . . . when someone by reason of a depraved condition of mind has thoughts of a like character, one makes him, by reason of a sound condition, think other and sound thoughts, which some people ignorantly call true, whereas I should say that one set of thoughts is better than the other, but not in any way truer. . . . Moreover wise and honest public speakers substitute in the community sound for unsound views of what is right. For I hold that whatever practices seem right and laudable to any particular state are so, for that state, so long as it holds by them. Only, when the practices are, in any particular case, unsound for them, the wise man substitutes others that are and appear sound. (166d–67c; trans. Cornford, in Plato 1961m)

The wise person, on this account, seeks to change through *logos* the public's judgment as to what is conducive to their common good, especially when they have been persuaded by a competing *logos* to embrace what is not good. Since two opposing arguments can be put forward on any matter, wisdom enables its possessor to challenge accepted views (*nomoi*) through counterargument.

The ontological and epistemological potency of persuasive speech is a central tenet of Gorgias's surviving writings. Described by tradition as a student of Empedocles, Gorgias recognized that, in a world where both the existence and comprehensibility of universal, fixed truths are dubious at best, "speech is a powerful lord (*logos dynastês megas estin*)" and "persuasion has the form of necessity (*anankê*)."[32] He lays the groundwork for this view in his treatise *On the Nonexistent or On Nature*.[33] His motives in writing this work are not altogether clear. As Guthrie observes, "a great deal of ink has been spilt over the question whether this was intended as a joke or parody, or as a serious contribution to philosophy, but it is a mistake to think that parody is incompatible with serious intention."[34] It seems likely that Gorgias had both ironical and philosophical aims in the work. In the former case, we can regard the treatise as a response to the Eleatic (and particularly to the Parmenidean) logic that sought to demonstrate that if something exists, then it follows necessarily that only Being exists, that it is singular and indivisible, that it can be known by the mind, and that it can be described in speech. Turning the title of the treatise by Melissus (*On Nature or On Being*) on its head and arguing that "nothing exists," Gorgias constructs "a highly ironical *reductio ad absurdum* of the Eleatic philosophy," showing that, using the same argumentative form as the Eleatics, it was as easy to prove that "nothing exists" as that "only Being exists."[35] If this is so, then the presumed connection between language and absolute reality (Being) is severed; that is, objective Being is not embedded in the logic of language.

Beyond a response to Parmenidean logic, Gorgias's treatise also advances a substantive argument concerning the nature, intelligibility, and communicability of "the existent." In Sextus's rendition of the treatise's gist, these points are expressed as follows: "First and foremost, [Gorgias proposes] that nothing exists; second, that even if it exists it is inapprehensible to man; third, that even if it is apprehensible, still it is without a doubt incapable of being expressed or explained to the next man" (DK 82 B 3 65). The first of these points is "demonstrated" using what amounts to a mirror-image of Parmenides' arguments: "If [anything] exists, either the existent exists or the nonexistent or both the existent exists and the nonexistent. But . . . neither does the existent exist nor the nonexistent, . . . nor the existent and [the] nonexistent. . . . It is not the case then that anything exists" (66). Now, what is the "existent" whose existence is denied in these arguments? Understanding the treatise in the context of Gorgias's Presocratic predecessors, he may be read as denying the existence of objective, stable, absolute realities behind the phenomena of experience.

Thus he would be rejecting the reality of the *Physis* or the *Logos* according to which all things come to pass. This interpretation is offered by Guthrie, who notes that "by saying that 'nothing is' Gorgias was denying the assumption underlying all their [the Presocratics'] systems, that behind the shifting panorama of 'becoming' or appearances there existed a substance or substances, a *physis* of things, from the *apeiron* of Anaximander to the air of Anaximenes, the four 'roots' of Empedocles and the atoms of Democritus. All such permanent 'natures' would be abolished on Gorgias' thesis" (1971b, 194; also see 196–97, 199–200).[36] Accordingly, only the constant shifting of appearances has any "reality," and there is nothing permanent behind them. Putting the matter in Heraclitean terms, there is no bedrock of *Logos* or *gnômên* beneath the surface of the flowing river; there is only the surface, only the flow. In rejecting Parmenides' arguments about what *is*, Gorgias embraces "the other path," an "indiscernible track," the path of *appearance* and *becoming*.

Alternatively, if we read the first thesis against the background of Protagoras's "human-measure" postulate, Gorgias denies the existence of extrapsychological realities (McComiskey 2002, 34–38). Thus, to maintain that "nothing exists" is to hold that nothing exists outside human consciousness and that all "realities" are the products of perception and thought. This does not mean that just anything thought of must be a "real" object (that is, what can be thought of may not necessarily be perceptible), for "Scylla and Chimaera and many other nonexistent things are considered in the mind" (80). It means, rather, that to be "real" is to be perceptible, or that perceptions are the only "realities" to which humans have access. Once again, Gorgias embraces the realm of appearance, in direct contrast to Parmenides' preference for Being.

A third reading of Gorgias's first thesis comes from considering his point in the context of what McComiskey terms "the deeds and circumstances of everyday communal life that are beyond our direct control and [that] condition our social personalities."[37] Gorgias was not merely a theorist of *logos*. He was also a practitioner. He served his native Leontini as an ambassador; he wrote and delivered funeral orations and was famous for speeches he gave at the Olympic and Pythian games. Thus it is reasonable to think that his ontological critique could apply to the realm of praxis, to the sociopolitical sphere. When the proposition that "nothing exists" is understood in terms of the "realities" of our social, communal lives, Gorgias could intend that there are no absolute, fixed realities in the sphere of human affairs and social action. In this social/political/moral realm, all truths are particular rather than universal, contingent rather than necessary, transitory rather than immutable.

Gorgias's first thesis can be understood most fully if we read all three of these interpretations into it simultaneously. With Gorgias it is reasonable to think that his was a complex mind, and consequently that he conceptualized his critique of existing ontological positions on several levels (Schiappa 1999, 147). At the most abstract level, he problematized the presumption on which all Presocratic inquiry was based: that there is some permanent, stable *physis* constituting and steering the flow of events we experience. However, he has extended this challenge from the cosmic to the social realm and thus has called into question established conceptions of justice, morality, and virtue. In neither the natural/physical/divine nor the social/political/moral realms are there objectively existing, unchanging, universal realities that undergird the particulars of human experience. Thus, both ontologically and morally, we humans are adrift on a sea of particularity and subjectivity, with no fixed anchorages by which our ontological and practical judgments can be secured.

The second of Gorgias's three propositions intensifies the estrangement between human beings and the realm of permanence and universality. He maintains that, even if objective realities did exist, the human could not know that they exist nor their nature. His reasoning for this is that since we can think about "things" that do not exist in perception (such as "a man flying or chariots racing in the sea"), and since we have no criterion by which to distinguish *in thought* the subjectively from the objectively existing, we cannot know if what we take to exist objectively actually does so. The argument takes the following form: 1) "if things considered in the mind are not existent, the existent is not considered. And that is logical," 2) "for if things considered are existent, all things considered exist, and in whatever way one considers them. Which is absurd"; 3) "Therefore, the existent is not considered in the mind," and 4) "things considered in the mind will exist even if they should not be seen by the sight nor heard by the hearing, because they are perceived by their own criterion" (DK B 3 77–81). As Guthrie summarizes the argument, "if our thought of something is not sufficient to prove its [objective] existence, then, even if we think of something real, we have no means of distinguishing it from the unreal. Gorgias has indeed 'abolished the criterion'" (1971b, 198). This is how Sextus apparently understood Gorgias's meaning, inasmuch as he concludes his exposition of the treatise by observing that "such being, in Gorgias' view, the problems, insofar as they are valid, the criterion [of independent existence] is destroyed. For there would be no criterion if nature neither exists nor can be understood nor conveyed to another" (DK 82 B 3, 87).[38]

Accepting this argument commits one to some degree of epistemological skepticism and relativism.[39] How can one ever know if what one *thinks* is an objective reality *actually is one*? Gorgias's position on this question, as evidenced by his argument here, is that one cannot know. Thus are human beings forced to live their lives on the basis of what *appears to them to be real*. Gorgias has provided a rationale for Protagoras's view that the criterion of "what is" lies in humanity itself, since objective "reality" cannot be known as such. We must make our judgments and choices based on what appears to us to be so, for we have access to nothing beyond our own perceptions.

This being said, Gorgias appeals to what must ultimately function as "rational" criteria by which one can distinguish "authentic" from "inauthentic" perceptions. His argument rests on an appeal to the apparent "logic" of *logos* and to a shared sense of what *makes sense* in the flow of appearances. Consider first Gorgias's appeal to logic. As he develops his argument (sec. 77–81), Gorgias concludes each line of reasoning by saying that a proposition is "logical" (*kata logon*, 77) or that it is "sound and logically follows" (*hygies kai sôzon akolouthian*, 78). The "logic" of the argument, as it happens, is fallacious. Nonetheless, the "demonstration" presents the *form* of logical proof even as it commits the fallacy of equivocation. The argument rests on the following sorts of propositions and on the relationships between them: If A ("things considered in the mind") is not-B (not "existent"), then B ("the existent") is not-A (not "considered in the mind"). There is a subtle shift here in the meanings of the terms being used. We go from "if A (subject) is not-B (attribute)," to "then B' (subject) is not-A' (attribute)." Similarly, if A ("white"—attribute) *is an attribute of* B ("what is considered"— subject), then B' ("being considered"— attribute) *is a possible attribute of* A' ("what is white"—subject). Finally, if not-A (not "to be existent"—attribute) *is an attribute of* B ("what is considered"— subject), then not-B' (not "to be considered"—attribute) *is a possible attribute of* A' ("what is existent"—subject). In all these arguments the operative terms in each proposition shift in function from subject to predicate.

This is precisely the sort of verbal sleight of hand that Aristotle describes when he explains the fallacy of equivocation.[40] The "logic" and "rationality" of the argument are illusory, and so the "proof" is deceptive. This is the point Gorgias makes in the *Helen* about the nature of persuasive speech. We might also take this as further evidence of his desire in the treatise to "refute" Parmenides and the other Eleatics by demonstrating that, using the logical form of their arguments, it was as easy to prove that "nothing exists" as it is to prove that "only being exists." On Gorgias's view, all such "proof" is ultimately illusory. Even so, the "criterion" by which authentic perceptions can be distinguished from inauthentic includes "what seems to be reasonable"—that is, what *appears* to be supported by reasoning. If no "reasoned account" (*logos*) can be given about a perceived "reality," then one has no "reason" to believe that it is an authentic perception.

A second aspect of this criterion is disclosed in Gorgias's repeated appeal to the reader/auditor's sense of the plausible. If what is thought about actually exists, he says, then all things thought about must exist, "and in whatever way anyone considers them." For then anything one might think about—including a man flying or chariots racing in the sea—would exist, "*which is absurd*" (79, italics added). Likewise, since "opposites are attributes of opposites, and the nonexistent is opposed to the existent" (80), if what is thought about must exist, then the nonexistent cannot be thought about. *"But this is absurd*, for Scylla and Chimaera and many other nonexistent things are considered in the mind" (80, italics added). Again, if one believes that chariots are actually racing in the sea just because one thinks about this event, even if one does not see them, *"this is absurd"* (82, italics added). This presumed "common sense" of what is plausible and what is "absurd"—of what is within and outside the realm of possibility— serves as a standard by which the authentic can be distinguished from the fantastic in experience. Thus not all perceptions will carry the same weight in the formation of belief or opinion. Only those conceived as being possible or plausible are to be accepted as valid for practical purposes. It is the task of persuasive speech/argument/reasoning (*logos*) to render events in a plausible way.[41]

The third proposition in the treatise explicitly invokes *logos*. Gorgias contends that human speech could not express the objectively real even if the latter existed and could be grasped intellectually ("it is . . . incapable of being expressed or explained"). The supporting argument reveals much about how he conceives the function and significance of speech. Gorgias reasons, assuming for the moment that external things exist and can be apprehended by the mind, that "*logos* arises from external things impinging upon us, that is, from perceptible things" (DK 82 B 3 85). He elaborates, "from encounter with a flavor, *logos* is expressed by us about that quality, and from encounter with a color, an expression of color." Here is an overt recognition that "external things" exist in some sense; that is, there are realities outside human consciousness (see Consigny 2001, 48–49). However, because each of us perceives such things directly and personally, they cannot be revealed to another person. Moreover the act of perception itself alters the "reality" of what is perceived. As McComiskey writes, "External realities remain external, and when perceived through human eyes and ears, these external realities become something· different altogether from the realities themselves; thus, what we communicate when we speak about realities is not the realities themselves but a representation of those realities, that is, a *logos*" (2002, 36). All we can do is to reveal our *logoi*—we can only convey our words to others, not our perceptions. Speech, as Gorgias sees it, does not have "substance in the way visible and audible things have, so that substantial and existent things can be revealed from its substance and existence. For . . . even if *logos* has substance, still it differs from all the other substances, and visible bodies are to the greatest degree different from words. What is visible is comprehended by one organ, *logos* by another" (86).[42]

If speech cannot convey the content of one's perceptions to another, we are left with the idea that when we speak we are not re-presenting external "reality."

Rather our experienced "reality" is brought into being through speech. As Gorgias purportedly put the matter, "*Logos* is not evocative of the external, but the external becomes the revealer [*mênutikon*] of *logos*" (85). Speech is what gives significance to the events that impinge on our senses. The character of the "real," therefore, is constructed by the language employed in expression arising from personal perception. More precisely, the "real" is what a given group of listeners can be persuaded by speech at a given moment to believe it is. Segal notes, "'Reality' for [Gorgias] lies in the human psyche and its malleability and susceptibility to the effects of linguistic coruscation ['sparkling' or 'shining']" (1962, 110). The effective use of persuasive speech, consequently, is the key to creating the "realities" in terms of which members of a community live together. McComiskey remarks that "Gorgias offers a nascent social constructionist view of language in which perceived realities (*ta pragmata*) condition the generation of statements (*logoi*) about the world" (2002, 34). Similarly, Consigny argues that "Gorgias construes language as an array of maneuvers or tropes that people use in various socially sanctioned agons or games; . . . [and] he depicts *truth* as a label of endorsement, a prize awarded by the audience or community to the accounts they find most persuasive" (2001, 60; also see Poulakos 1984, 218).

Gorgias illustrates this conception of the power of speech in his *Encomium of Helen* and *Defense of Palamedes*. Though the aims of these speeches have been matters of considerable scholarly discussion, there is agreement that they embody Gorgias's sense of the potency of *logos* in shaping opinion and thus in constructing the "realities" in terms of which human beings must live their lives.[43] Both take the ostensible form of judicial speeches—they defend accused persons and seek to acquit them of guilt. The fact that those to be defended were long-since dead (if, indeed, they were not altogether fictitious), however, means that the speeches were not truly forensic; no actual legal matter was at issue. Rather, they appear to have been composed partly for use as models to be imitated by students, partly as a means of demonstrating to prospective students the sort of skill they could expect to develop through studying with the "master *rhêtôr*," partly as virtuoso oratorical performances for an appreciative public audience, and perhaps partly as public demonstrations of the efficacy of *logos* in matters of opinion and practical judgment. The speeches represent a kind of oratorical exercise that, a century later, would be subsumed under the genre of *epideixis*.[44] What seems clear, in any case, is that the speeches serve to demonstrate the power of *logos* in shaping how people think about "reality."

Gorgias opens the *Helen* with a promise to speak "the truth" about her abduction from Sparta, for "what is becoming to . . . a speech [is] truth (*alêtheia*)," and so "it is the duty of one and the same man both to speak the needful rightly and to refute the [unrightfully spoken]" (DK 82 B 11, sec. 1–2). The "truth"

Gorgias proposes to speak, in accordance with the conclusions reached in *On the Nonexistent*, must be how the case appears to him; that is, it will be *his genuine opinion* of the case that is to be spoken.[45] His stated purpose is, "by introducing some reasoning (*logismos*) into my speech, . . . to free the accused of blame" (2). Gorgias then advances a form of apagogic argument through which he reasons by alternatives. He puts forth the only four possible reasons (in his view) as to why Helen did what she did and then proceeds to show how each in its turn requires that we hold Helen blameless: "For either by will of Fate and decision of the gods and vote of Necessity did she do what she did, or by force reduced or by words seduced [or by love possessed]" (6).[46] Three of these four lines of argument are discharged in relatively short order. If Helen acted under divine compulsion, she had no choice in the matter and so cannot be held responsible. If she was violently forced to return to Troy with Alexander (Paris), she is not the one to be held accountable. If she was constrained by love to act as she did, Helen cannot be blamed (15–19).

The most fully developed (8–14) of the four alternatives reasons that "if it was speech which persuaded her and deceived her heart, not even to this is it difficult to make an answer and to banish blame" (8). The justification lies in the fact that, according to Gorgias, "speech is a powerful lord (*dynastês megas*), which by means of the finest and most invisible body effects the divinest works: it can stop fear and banish grief and create joy and nurture pity." The use of the term *dynastês* here is particularly telling, for as a "lord," "master," or "ruler," *logos* is something that must be obeyed. Gorgias then offers "proof to the opinion (*doxa*) of [his] hearers": the "agency of words" rests upon their power to "beguile . . . and persuade . . . and alter [the soul] by witchcraft" (10), a potency that "is comparable to the power of drugs over the nature of bodies" (14). Gorgias's account of this power illuminates the role of speech in coming to judgment and composing belief. Forms such as poetry (which Gorgias defines as "*logos* with meter") and "sacred incantations" are capable of producing in hearers "the divinest works": they can stop fear, banish grief, create joy, nurture pity, induce longing, create suffering, bring pleasure, and so on. Speech exercises on its hearers what Gorgias describes as a kind of "magic."

De Romilly elaborates the idea: "The terms [that speech] uses evoke incantations, magic, charms, drugs, witchcraft. The implication can only be that, by seemingly irrational means, words have the power to enthral the reader, affecting him despite himself. . . . The use of rhetoric is justified by the uncertainty of knowledge. It works because our knowledge is imperfect. That is how speech comes to acquire such absolute power. . . . If Helen was persuaded to follow Paris, she was simply obeying the compulsion of all-powerful speech. From poetry, to magic, to constraint: in the space of a single page, we have moved on from a kind of emotional pleasure to a power of persuasion that nothing can arrest" (1992, 66–67). I think de Romilly has erred in attributing such power to the *written* word (suggested by her reference to the "reader"). Given the historical context in which he composed and performed the speech, Gorgias was addressing an audience still attuned more to orality than to written speech (Ong 1982; Lentz 1989). Implicit in his conception of *logos* is the recognition that it is the *spoken word* which has such power. Although he calls attention to his having written the speech, it is only the rhythms and cadences of Gorgias's words *as spoken and heard* that can have the bewitching, intoxicating effects he attributes to poetry and incantation.[47] In order to understand the power of speech, we must appreciate the significance of its aurality. Like the poets and rhapsodes whose heir he was, Gorgias grasped the impact upon the soul of how language *sounds*. As Segal writes, "Gorgias regarded his rhetoric as having more than a superficial effect on the ear, as actually reaching and 'impressing' the psyche of the hearer" (1962, 105). Later he observes that "the purely aesthetic reaction of *hedone* (delight, enjoyment) leads to a powerful motivational response which immediately and strongly moves the psyche and produces direct action" through a series of emotional reactions that culminate in the "necessity" (*ananké*) of persuasion (125).

Gorgias's own verbal style—renowned for its use of rhythm, repetition, and other auditory patterns—is clear evidence of this.[48] As a speaker, Gorgias was conspicuously attentive to the sounds and cadences of speech. De Romilly appears to appreciate this fact, writing that, although he displayed "virtuosity when it came to playing with intellectual concepts, . . . it was not to these procedures of argumentation that his contemporaries tended to draw attention. It was his style that seems to have been considered particularly important. . . . Even in the ancient world people would already refer to 'figures in the style of Gorgias'; and in all the various texts by him that have come down to us, every line is studded with them. Like many others, he frequently used antitheses, . . . final assonances or rhymes, balanced numbers of syllables, the use of terms that were parallel either by virtue of form, or of *sound or metre*" (1992, 63; my italics). When he invokes the power of poetry and incantation, Gorgias is invoking the power of the human voice to enthrall its hearers through the employment of aural patterns. *Incantation* is speech that is chanted rhythmically, and the effect of listening to such vocal rhythms is *enchantment*, indicating that speech can put the hearer into a suggestible, trancelike state of mind. The association of incantation with enchantment, and thus with fascination and bewitchment, leads Gorgias to maintain that speech is like *magic:* it has the power of producing illusions. The magical power of speech is rooted in the psychological effects of the *sounds of words* when they are spoken and heard.

For Gorgias, the magical power of *logos* arises primarily from how the sounds of speech affect the emotions, particularly the sense of aesthetic pleasure. Like the influence of drugs on the body, these sounds can have a physical impact on the soul, inducing shuddering and tears, bringing pleasure and banishing pain, for "through the agency of words, the soul is wont to experience a suffering (*pathos*) of its own" (9).[49] Just as pictures, creating "a single figure and form" through the use of "many colors and figures, . . . delight (*terpsis*) the sight" (18), so too is one affected by the "pleasure (*hêdon*) of words" (DK 82 B 23). It is this aesthetic pleasure, for Gorgias, that gives speech its power to enchant and bewitch the hearer. Segal concludes, "Successful persuasion . . . works through the aesthetic process of *terpsis* and the emotions connected with it. . . . The fully effective impact of *peitho* involves the emotional participation of the audience, which is made possible by and takes place through the aesthetic pleasure of *terpsis*" (1962, 122). Thus *logos* works its magic on the soul first and foremost through the production by the speech's sounds of aesthetic pleasure in the hearer.

The aesthetic potency of persuasive speech also derives from its inherent deceptiveness. As Gorgias explains it, all persuasion promotes illusion because it rests on a "false argument" (*pseudê logon*, DK 82 B 11, 11). It makes things seem to be true absolutely or necessarily that, in fact, are always matters of appearance and opinion. If we want to understand how persuasive speech "is wont to impress the soul as it wishes," we can consider the words of astronomers who, "substituting opinion for opinion, . . . make what is incredible and unclear seem true to the eyes of opinion." Then we can study "logically necessary debates" that, while they are crafted so as to have "the form of necessity," are "not spoken with truth" or sincerity. Even so, such speeches sway crowds with their apparent logical force. In addition, we should regard "the verbal disputes of philosophers" wherein the fleetness of thought makes "belief in an opinion subject to easy change" (13). McComiskey contends that "these three contexts for *peithô*—astronomy, public debate, and philosophical argument—all demonstrate the tremendous power of *logos* to move the *psuchê* and elicit action in an audience, and the power of language in these discourses" (2002, 46). Persuasive speech gives the appearance of necessity to what must remain a matter of belief or opinion. Indeed, says Gorgias, "on most subjects most men take opinion as counselor to their soul" (11). However, because opinion "is slippery and insecure," those who take its counsel cannot look for more than "slippery and insecure successes" (11). Persuasive speech, because it creates an impression of stability and permanence where no such qualities are possible, is inherently deceptive.[50]

One who recognizes this and is willingly deceived is "wiser" (*sophôteros*) than the undeceived (DK 82 B 23), who does not recognize the inherent deceptiveness in all language (Segal 1962, 130–31). Consigny concludes, "In Gorgias' construal, there is no objective, nonsituated, or nonrhetorical way of seeing 'things as they really are,' because every . . . account is always a partial and partisan assertion by a rhetor engaged in a specific agon. In some cases, clever rhetors are able to conceal their own situatedness and, consequently, the rhetoricity of their texts. In so doing, they effectively efface themselves before what appears to be an objective truth, . . . and in this respect they deceive their unwitting audiences. But this does not mean that, as members of the audience, we must necessarily be deceived by clever rhetors; it only means that we may be deceived if we forget that there will always be alternative ways of construing the situation and that we, as situated members of the community, ultimately decide what is true" (2001, 92). Perceiving the deceptiveness and illusoriness of speech, like the sounds of words themselves, is a source of aesthetic pleasure, inasmuch as the auditor cannot help but enjoy the skill with which a speech is crafted.[51] In its power both to generate emotional responses and to create a transitory stasis in the unfolding of opinion, speech can enchant hearers' souls and lead them to take one kind of action rather than another. However, the ground of such action is always unstable and ephemeral.

A key element in Gorgias's view of persuasive speech is the playfulness with which it is to be deployed (de Romilly 1992, 97; Schiappa 1999, 138). This is shown implicitly in the reasoning he uses in *On Non-Being* and explicitly in his conclusion of the *Helen*. In the former, Gorgias "plays" with language and forms of reasoning in order to create the impression of "proof" and logical demonstration. He employs wordplay in his equivocal use of key terms, and he toys with the logic of the Eleatics' arguments in advancing his own parodies of those arguments. There is, indeed, a spirit of amusement permeating the entire treatise, revealed most conspicuously in Gorgias's invocations of "a man flying" and "chariots racing in the sea." The closing words of the *Helen* disclose this spirit more overtly. "I wished," he says, "to write a speech which would be a praise of Helen and a diversion to myself" (*eboulêthên graphai ton logon Helenê men enkômion emon de paignion;* 21). The final word of the Greek text—*paignion*—is translated by Kennedy as "diversion." It can also be translated as "trifle," "recreation," "game," "sport," or "plaything." Gorgias's use of *paignion* need not invite us to view the *Helen* as a trivial "diversion" to be dismissed from serious consideration. Rather, I see him making explicit the general spirit in which all persuasive speech is to be used. An important idea is expressed in this term: because language has no inherent connection to objectively existing, stable, universal "truths," because all "truth" is a matter of opinion, and because opinions are always susceptible to the enchantments and illusions of speech, the entire enterprise of persuasion is ultimately a kind of "play" or "game." It is, to be sure, a very serious game, since both personal and collective decisions about practical action are shaped by the play of language, but it is a game nonetheless.

Poulakos writes that "in rhetoric, one plays both specific games, as in the case of a legal battle or a political race, and the broader game of language," and he describes Gorgias as "toying with language and with his readers" throughout the *Helen* (1995, 65–66). He proposes that "no argument or position, no matter how entrenched, can dominate the mental world of an audience once and for all. In and through the interplay of language use, any one argument can be overthrown and replaced by another." He concludes that Gorgias "is content to have diverted himself by playing with language, playing, that is, with a malleable medium of dynastic powers and deceptive qualities. Put another way, he is content to have participated in the game of words, to have demonstrated to his audience that he is a splendid player, and to have tried to bring them into the game" (67; compare Segal 1962, 119–20). There is an element of irony in Gorgias's conception of the speaker's art: in the realm of human affairs, everything rests on our linguistic constructions of the "true" and the "real," and yet such constructions are themselves as unstable, as fleeting, as chimerical as light on the surface of the sea. This insight is demonstrated nowhere more clearly than in the *Helen*.

Within the boundaries of our linguistic constructions, nonetheless, some interpretations of events can be shown to be more "likely" or "probable" (*eikota*) than others, again based on appeals to what is believed to be "possible" or "plausible." Indeed, it is in the field of the probable that we live our lives and that we must seek to persuade one another. Moreover probabilistic argument enables a speaker to make the weaker case stronger and the stronger case weaker, so that one might overturn an accepted opinion and persuade an audience of what is in their true interest. The origins of "argument from probability" in Greek discourse are unclear. Kennedy identifies what he calls "apparently the earliest specific example of argument from probability" in the *Hymn to Hermes*, a poem in the Homeric style, "probably composed in the sixth century B.C." (1994, 14). Plato (*Phaedrus* 267a, 273a–b) attributes to Tisias of Syracuse the earliest instruction in this form of argument, whereas Aristotle (*Rhetoric* 1402a) attributes the doctrine to Tisias's teacher Corax.[52] Gorgias's *Defense of Palamedes* illustrates this tenet of sophistical thought, though arguments about what is likely or probable play a central role in Antiphon's *Tetralogies* as well.[53]

Though humans can never be *certain* that "facts" and "realities" are what they appear to be, it can be argued that some interpretations of events are more likely or plausible than others. What makes one view of events appear likely is that it is consistent with what is generally believed about how things happen. Though they may have rejected much of what the Presocratics proposed about the character and intelligibility of nature and objective reality, sophistical teachings nonetheless presupposed that there are regularities in our perceptions of what occurs in the world—that is, human beings tend to behave in somewhat consistent ways, and our perceptions of natural events likewise exhibit regularities. It is precisely because things appear to happen in recurrent ways, and because there is general agreement about such patterns, that some occurrences can be viewed as being more "likely" or "probable" than others (Poulakos 1995, 180). If one cannot give an adequate account of a particular event—if one cannot advance a *logos* of it that is consistent with what is believed to be the normal patterns of things—then the event will not appear likely to those who are asked to believe it.

Palamedes was credited in myth with being clever and resourceful and with having invented the alphabet. He served with Agamemnon at Troy but came into conflict with Odysseus. In revenge, the latter forged a letter from Priam to Palamedes arranging for Palamedes to betray the Greeks, and he hid gold in Palamedes' tent as "evidence" of a payoff. On this evidence Palamedes was found guilty and put to death by the army (Hyginus, *Fabulae* 105). De Romilly considers Gorgias's use of argumentation in the speech and elaborates her view that "verisimilitude and human psychology" and "a technique of a priori analysis" functioned persuasively in sophistical speech (1992, 61–63). Gagarin notes that "virtually the entire case is an attempt to refute the direct, but false, evidence of Odysseus by means of probability arguments in support of the truth. By arguing in this fashion Gorgias does not imply that probability arguments are a better guide to the truth than direct evidence; rather, he shows that probability arguments, though not always effective, are sometimes the only means available for supporting a true case" (1994, 54–55). McComiskey sees in the *Palamedes* precursors of Aristotle's formal delineation of logical demonstration (*logos*), argument from character (*êthos*), and appeals to audience emotions (*pathos*) as means of persuading from probabilities. He argues on this basis that, in the *Palamedes*, Gorgias articulated the basic elements of his own *technê* of persuasive speech (2002, 47–52). Indeed, he concludes that "considering the many significant theoretical and pragmatic parallels between Aristotle's *Rhetoric* and the extant Gorgianic texts (especially the *Palamedes*), it would be remarkable to consider one a *technê* and not the other, regardless of what Plato thought" (52).

Palamedes is made by Gorgias to defend himself by advancing a series of arguments from probability. If he had betrayed his fellow Greeks, Palamedes contends, such an action must have begun as a discussion with the opponent (DK 82 B 11a, sec. 6). In order for a discussion to have taken place, moreover, there must have been a meeting. But "how could there have been a meeting" without an intermediary, and "how does it take place? Who is with whom? Greek with barbarian. How do we listen and how talk to each other? By ourselves? But we do not know each other's language" (6–7). Palamedes then introduces a series of conditions (7–9) under which his collusion with the enemy might have taken place—that there was an interpreter present (but this would have added a witness to "things which need to be hidden," thus making it unlikely that the meeting would have remained secret); that a pledge was given and received, perhaps in the form of an oath (but "who was apt to trust me, the traitor?"); that hostages were exchanged ("but these things, if they happened, would have been clear to you all"); that money was offered and accepted, either a small amount ("but it is not probable that a man would take a little money for a great service") or a large one (but "who was the go-between? How could one person bring it?"). In this way, Palamedes argues that "it is not probable" (*ouk eikota einai*) that he could have betrayed his countrymen to the barbarians, for such events are unlikely to have happened, or at least to have gone undetected. Such an interpretation of events, he implies, is not reasonable or plausible given the way that things tend to happen and that people tend to behave.

The remainder of this speech follows much the same pattern. Palamedes' argument is predicated on the presupposition that the events required for him to have betrayed his fellows are either impossible or unlikely, given the way that the world appears to operate. The same sort of reasoning undergirds his arguments concerning his presumed motives for having taken the action of which he is accused. "What reason," he asks (13), "was there to wish to do these things?" He then considers a number of possible motives he might have had if he had sought to betray the Greeks, and he argues in each case that it was either impossible or improbable that he could have acted from such a motive (13–19). "That I would most hurt myself," he concludes, "in doing these things is not unclear. For in betraying Greece I was betraying myself, my parents, my friends, the dignity of my ancestors, the cults of my native land, the tombs of my family, and my great country of Greece" (19). The implicit assumption here is that, given the costs that would accrue to anyone who betrays his countrymen, it is unlikely that Palamedes would have done so. Indeed, "would not my life have been unlivable if I had done these things? . . . Therefore, that I would not if I could, nor could if I would, betray Greece has been demonstrated by what has been said" (20–21).

As a final warrant for his argument Palamedes invokes his own life (29). Not only was he blameless in his past actions, he says, but he is also "a great benefactor of you and the Greeks and all mankind, not only of those now alive but [also] of those to come" (30). Why does he remind his hearers of his contributions to their well-being? The answer is, in order to make it clear that he applies himself to such things and that he abstains from "shameful and wicked deeds," for "it is impossible" that one would have done both good and evil to his fellow Greeks (31). At the very least, it is unlikely that a person could have behaved in such inconsistent ways. This implicit appeal to what is probable is, once again, the foundation of Palamedes' argument.

Gorgias's defense of Palamedes demonstrates how persuasive speech employs reasoning to create a sense that some events and actions are more likely than others to have happened. In matters of opinion—which, according to Gorgias, is "a most untrustworthy thing" (24)—where sure knowledge is impossible, humans must rely on such reasoning and on their sense of what appears to be likely in the flow of perceptions. Reasoning and persuasive speech about events and human conduct aim finally at what de Romilly terms "psychological verisimilitude," an account that resonates with how hearers actually experience the world (1992, 61). This is the same idea that Fisher describes in his account of the "narrative paradigm": "Rationality [with respect to what constitutes "good reasons" for practical decision making] is determined by the nature of persons as narrative beings—their inherent awareness of *narrative probability*, what constitutes a coherent story, and their constant habit of testing *narrative fidelity*, whether or not the stories they experience ring true with the stories they know to be true in their lives" (1985, 65). Particularly where people cannot have firsthand knowledge of events and must depend on others' words to form their judgments, they must rely on what seems to be likely, given their previous experience of how events occur and of how people typically behave in particular circumstances. Poulakos observes that "probability . . . requires a broad knowledge of human nature as well as a keen sense of how similar events have turned out. By extension, rhetorical discourse based on probability depends on historical knowledge, which forms the base upon which one can predict the outcome of an issue" (1995, 180; also see Kennedy 1994, 25; McComiskey 2002, 48–49).

The foundation of probabilistic reasoning, then, is the presupposition that, because there are recurring features in the sorts of situations in which human beings find themselves, a present circumstance is in some respects "like" (*eikos*) previously occurring circumstances, and what took place then is "likely" (*eikota*) to take place again.[54] Similarly reasoning from probabilities concerning human feelings, motives, and actions presupposes that people are, at some level, "like" each other and that in all of us there are tendencies to behave in similar ways when confronted with similar circumstances. These presuppositions are the foundation of such reasoning, and they are exhibited clearly in Gorgias's arguments, both in the *Helen* and in the *Palamedes*.

The word-wisdom of the Sophists involves several important qualities. It requires attentiveness to the "given" in experience—to the perceived facts or circumstances that can be employed in constructing plausible accounts of events and thus used in persuading auditors to embrace one opinion over others. As Gorgias indicates, *logos* and *doxa* arise "from external things impinging upon us, that is, from perceptible things" (DK 82 B 85). In using speech to influence the opinions of others, a speaker is constrained by the others' beliefs about what is "given," about the commonly accepted facts of the case. What was believed, after all, by those who heard Gorgias deliver his *Encomium* was that Helen had left Sparta with Paris and had gone with him to Troy. These were the "givens" within which Gorgias-the-wordsmith had to practice his craft. What was not given were the causes of her action, and here is where a speaker who possesses *logos-sophia* can craft from the realm of possibility an account of Helen's actions that strikes hearers as plausible.[55]

Another aspect of sophistic word-wisdom is the ability to envision, from the given facts of a case, accounts that are sufficiently coherent and plausible as to compel belief. In other words *logosophia* involves a capacity to see within the givens of a case how a coherent, verisimilar account can be constructed, and how language and reasoning can be employed to render that account more likely seeming than its competitors. This capacity itself includes an ability both to conjure sets of circumstances that will render an event comprehensible and to articulate those circumstances to make them appear more likely than other possibilities ("either by will of Fate and decision of the gods and vote of Necessity did she do what she did, or by force reduced or by words seduced [or by love possessed]").

Thus the *sophia* emphasized by such Sophists as Protagoras and Gorgias included the ability to invent counterarguments to theses advanced by others. This is eristic, verbal debate aimed at silencing competitors—the *agôn* of public argument. Skill (*sophia*) in eristic is an ability to see in a given case the argument that can be made *against* what is proposed, of which Gorgias's proofs in *On Not-Being* are examples. In this sense, sophistical wisdom includes an awareness of the alternative, an ability to perceive in a given situation *both* opposing arguments that can be advanced regarding a particular issue, question, or experience. This is why the Sophists are characterized by Plato (for example, *Theaetetus* 167e) as being masters of eristic. Kerferd writes, "as Plato uses the term, eristic means 'seeking victory in argument,' and the art which cultivates and provides appropriate means and devices for so doing. Concern for the truth is not a necessary part of the art—victory in argument can be secured without it, sometimes more easily so. . . . Eristic as such is not strictly speaking a *technique* of argument. It can use any . . . of a series of techniques in order to achieve its aim, which is success in debate or at least the appearance of such success. Fallacies of any kind, verbal ambiguities, long and irrelevant monologues may all on occasion succeed in reducing an opponent to silence and so be appropriate tools of eristic" (1981a, 62–63). The association of such Sophists as Protagoras, Gorgias, and Antiphon with the practice of eristic (*eristikê*, from *eris*, strife) and counterargument (*antilogikê*) is widely recognized, even if these technical terms themselves did not come into use until the fourth century (Schiappa 1999, 15). Indeed, Kerferd maintains that "the true nature of antilogic . . . is in many ways the key to . . . understanding the true nature of the sophistic movement" (62). Protagoras's "two-arguments" fragments encapsulate the principle, while the *Dissoi Logoi* and Antiphon's *Tetralogies* illustrate its techniques. Aristotle's *On Sophistical Refutations* embodies his critique of the fallacious reasoning employed in sophistical antilogies, but he still endorses the capacity for arguing on opposite sides of a question, "not in order that we may actually do both (for one should not persuade what is debased) but in order that it may not escape our notice what the real state of the case is and that we ourselves may be able to refute if another person uses speech unjustly" (*Rhet.* 1355a, trans. Kennedy 2007).[56]

Insofar as it embodies a capacity for seeing in existing circumstances the materials from which alternative accounts and arguments can be constructed regarding a particular issue or event, sophistical word-wisdom is fundamentally opportunistic and particularistic. It includes perceptiveness about what words could be uttered in the present moment to persuade a particular group of listeners to embrace a certain way of viewing a given matter. In this respect, *logosophia* involves adeptness in the use of time and in the selection of the right words when speaking. Indeed, central in sophistical conceptions of word-wisdom are the ideas of *kairos* (the opportune moment), *to prepon* (appropriateness), and *orthos logos* (correct language).[57] *Kairos* is particularly important in understanding sophistical word-wisdom, inasmuch as it denotes the sense of timeliness that we often associate with "playing things" as they present themselves. It refers to the *exact* or *critical time* at which something happens or should be done, as well as to the *opportunity* for doing something. *Kairos*, in Greek mythology, was the youngest son of Zeus and was personified as Opportunity. The term comprehends a sense of "due measure, proportion, or fitness" (Liddell and Scott 1996, *s.v. kairos*) and thus appears to be conceptually, if not etymologically, related to both *logos* and *harmonia*. In connection with the practice of medicine, it refers to the challenge of "seizing the right moment" for treatment, as well as of treating the right place on the body (Lloyd 1987, 118, 129–30). The term also signifies the *season*, as when storms happen "in season" or when the "season is right" for planting. From the constellation of such associations comes the more abstract idea of "the opportune moment" for utterance as applied to the speaker's art. As an element of *logosophia*, *kairos* signifies an awareness of how the act of utterance can fit into the present experience of an audience. Writes Poulakos, "The rhetor who operates mainly with the awareness of *kairos* responds spontaneously to the fleeting situation at hand, speaks on the spur of the moment, and addresses each occasion in its particularity, its singularity, its uniqueness" (1995, 61).[58] The term indicates the sense of timing that a skilled speaker brings to the speech situation—a sense of the right time to speak and of the opportunities that present themselves for articulating an account of events that will be persuasive to a particular audience in that moment. It may also suggest a readiness to speak on any subject, exhibited through a skill in ex tempore speaking. Indeed, Philostratus comments that "Gorgias [seems] to have begun extemporaneous oratory. For coming into the theater of the Athenians he had the boldness to say 'suggest a subject,' and he was the first to proclaim himself willing to take this chance, showing apparently that he knew everything and would trust to the moment to speak on any subject."[59]

Closely related to the speaker's sense of the opportune is his/her sense of the fitting or the appropriate—*to prepon*. Schiappa observes that there is little textual evidence that *to prepon* was a consciously held theoretical concept among fifth-century Sophists generally, but "both *kairos* and *to prepon* may be appropriate terms to describe choices made by sophistic speakers in *practice*" (2003, 73–74).[60] This is precisely the point to be drawn from Plato's account in the *Phaedrus* (267b) of Prodicus as the one who "had discovered what sort of speeches the art demands—to wit, neither long ones nor short, but of fitting length" (trans. Hackforth, in Plato 1961h). The term *to prepon* appears in Gorgias's *Funeral Oration* (DK 82 B 6), where he praises Athenians killed in the Peloponnesian War for being "gentle in regard to the fitting (*euorgêtoi pros to prepon*)." The idea is also invoked in the *Palamedes*, where Gorgias has the speaker say, "I wish to say something invidious, but true about myself, not appropriate to one who has [not] been accused, but fitting to one who has been accused" (DK 82 B 11a, sec. 28). The word-wisdom practiced and taught by at least some Sophists, accordingly, includes a feeling for what *logoi* would best fit into and harmonize with the present situation and moment. *Sophia* comprehends a capacity for saying the right thing, in the right way, at the right time (Untersteiner 1954, 197–98; Poulakos 1983b, 41–43; 1995, 60–61).

It is no surprise that sophistical teachings also emphasized the importance of using the "right word" (*orthos logos*) in any given case. A preoccupation with the proper use of language can be detected in the doctrines of several fifth-century Sophists. Protagoras, for example, was described by Plato (*Crat.* 391c) as being concerned with "the fitness of names." He was credited by Diogenes Laertius (DK 80 A 1) with being "the first to distinguish the tenses of the verb," while Aristotle (*Rhet.* 1407b) remarks that he was noted for distinguishing words by gender (see Schiappa 2003, 34; Guthrie 1971b, 179–80, 205). Kerferd notes that a treatise on *Orthopeia* is listed among the works of Democritus and concludes that "the topic 'correctness of names' was something of a standard theme in sophistic discussions" (1981a, 68). Similarly Prodicus was well known for his interest in definitions and the correct use of language, variously referred to as *orthos logos*, *orthotês onomatôn*, and *orthopeia*.[61] The *Dissoi Logoi* treatise states that "the man acquainted with the skills (*technai*) involved in argument (*logos*) will also know how to speak correctly (*orthos legein*) on every topic" (DK 90 8.3).[62] Sophistical word-wisdom, accordingly, is marked by a concern for precision and accuracy in the use of language.

Given an attentiveness to the potential psychological impact of how language sounds, sophistical *logosophia* includes an astute sense of *harmonia*, of how words can be fit together so as to harmonize with the soul's tendencies to respond to the aesthetic elements of aurality. When we observe of a speaker that he/she has "struck a chord" with an audience, we are speaking more than metaphorically. If Gorgias was right about how the *psychê* responds aesthetically and emotionally to the sounds of words, then we must see the word-craft of the Sophists as including a kind of musical sensibility, an attunement to how the soul's natural tendencies can be engaged by the rhythms, cadences, and other sound-values of speech.[63]

What is disclosed additionally in sophistical teachings about *logos* is a distinctive form of consciousness, a way of being-in-the-world that embraces chance, circumstance, instability, and particularity. It prefers the path of *seeming* and *becoming* to that of *Truth* and *Being*, favored by Parmenides. A sophistical consciousness is rooted in an awareness of the ultimate inaccessibility and unfathomability of Reality, and of the role language plays in the construction and perception of the "realities" and "truths" in terms of which we must live our lives. It holds that reasoned opinion is the closest we can come to "knowledge" about the world and that opinion is subject to persuasion through speech. A sophistical *sophia*, consequently, reverts to the *poeia* of the wordsmith: facility with *logos* in the realm of social experience, skill in speaking, word-wisdom. When the power of speech is used with excellence or *aretê* in the political sphere, sophistical teachings are fulfilled. As Havelock comments, "the Elder Sophists sought to rationalize the process by which opinion is formed and then effectively expressed, and by which leadership is imposed and followed, sentiment crystallized, and common decisions reached" (1957, 156).

If sophistical wisdom is fundamentally a combination of political excellence (*politikê aretê*), sound practical judgment (*phronêsis*), and skill in the art of speech/argument/reasoning (the *logôn technê*), how did these professional educators propose that it can be acquired? A survey of their own teaching practices reveals both a broad range of subjects to be mastered and a close connection between speech and the acquisition of *sophia*.[64] The Sophists of the fifth century viewed themselves principally as educators for citizenship, as teachers of the sort of wisdom that would prepare students for participation in the public/political life of Athens. Their teachings were eminently practical in aim: to provide the (male) citizen with the knowledge and skills needed "to persuade with speeches either judges in the law courts or statesmen in the council-chamber or the commons in the Assembly or an audience at any other meeting that may be held on public affairs" (Plato, *Gorg.* 452e). Civic education begins at birth and progresses in both informal and formal ways throughout life. Protagoras is portrayed by Plato as holding that such education proceeds "from earliest childhood and [continues] throughout their lives. As soon as a child can understand what is said to him, nurse, mother, tutor, and the father himself vie with each other to make him as good as possible, instructing him through everything he does or says" (*Prot.* 325c–d). When boys were sent to school, they received instruction in "good behavior" and letters, music, and physical training.[65]

Though there was no standardized course of study among the many Sophists who taught in Athens and elsewhere, if one chose to attend the lectures of several of these teachers, one could receive instruction in such varied subjects as geometry, astronomy, music, rhythms, painting, sculpture, mythology, history, laws, ethics, the function of letters and syllables, the meanings of words, and grammar. Kerferd observes, "From time to time in the past, attempts have been made to argue that the sophists were wholly or predominantly concerned with a single area of study and teaching, which concern was then taken as the distinguishing mark of a sophist as such—the educational idea of rhetoric, the opposition of nature and convention, political success, the idea of education in general, the rejection of physical science, a turning away from religion, the humanistic view of man as at the centre of the universe, man as a tragic figure of destiny. All these in turn or in combination have been suggested by different modern scholars. . . . The actual references that we have to sophistic teachings suggest that these covered an extremely wide range" (1981a, 34–35; also Lloyd 1987, 92n). Hippias is reported to have lectured on a particularly wide range of subjects and is credited by Guthrie as being a "serious ethical thinker" (1971b, 284).[66] As we have already seen, "correct diction" (*orthoepeia*) and "correctness of words or names" (*orthotês onomatôn*) are said to have been discussed by Protagoras and Prodicus, while Thrasymachus and Antiphon are reported to have professed "accurate expression" and appropriateness of diction (DK 85 A 3, 13). There is evidence in Cicero and elsewhere that Hippias, Prodicus, Thrasymachus, and Protagoras may even have written and lectured on natural philosophy.[67] It appears that at least some of the Sophists wrote and taught about things divine. Certainly this is where we should include Protagoras's treatise *On the Gods* (DK 80 A 1, B 4), and both Prodicus (DK 84 B 5) and Critias (DK 88 B 25) wrote about the origins of human belief in the gods. A "sophistical" educational program taken as a whole, then, would have provided the basis of what Cicero would later describe as "the liberal education of a gentleman" (*De Oratore* 3.32.127). From training such as this, the student of civic affairs might be expected to develop the sorts of understandings and sensibilities that would equip him to excel in the "art of politics"—that is, to develop "civic virtue" (*politikê aretê*).

The culmination of sophistical education was training in the *logôn technê*, the art of speech/argument/reasoning. Indeed, in order to exercise the civic excellence for which the citizen was to be educated, and thus to become "a real power in the city," the prime necessity, as Guthrie observes, "was to master the art of persuasive speaking. . . . It has even been argued (by Heinrich Gomperz) that the whole teaching of the Sophists is summed up in the art of rhetoric. That is a considerable exaggeration; the *aretê* which Protagoras claimed to impart consisted of more than that. But one of them, Gorgias, did indeed laugh at the professed teachers of civic virtue. The art of clever speaking, he said, . . . was the master art" (1971b, 20; also see 176ff.; Kerferd 1981a, 34–35). The Sophists' emphasis on the speaker's art is well attested, and it was instruction in this art that was most directly connected to the *logosophia* at which sophistical teachings ultimately aimed.

Then there was the use of eristics or "contests in argument" (*logôn agônas*). We have already considered Protagoras's "two-arguments" doctrine, applied in his teaching, it seems, by conducting debates and by "attacking any thesis" through the method of questioning, a practice that was also used by Socrates.[68] It was this technique that Plato disparaged as mere verbal wrangling or trickery (for example, in *Euthydemus* 277d–e, 278b–c, 288b) and that he equated with sophistry generally (*Sophist* 225c, 231e). However, Grimaldi writes that "eristics is not something to be readily dismissed as trickery. . . . First of all, in a good sense it is a kind of intellectual dueling that develops a sharpness of mind, clarifies problems, and helps to specify and define issues. Even in this bad sense it encourages the person subjected to the trickery to develop these qualities in self defense" (1996, 29; also Kerferd 1981a, 59–67; de Romilly 1992, 81–82). Kerferd notes:

> One feature . . . distinctive of all sophists as such [was] that there were *Antilogikoi* who opposed one Logos to another. This means that what I have been calling the method of Protagoras has a base in [his] own theorising, and this surely does suggest that his method is likely to have been his own rather than simply derived from Socrates. . . . The Socratic method, to the extent that it may have originated with Socrates, nonetheless originated from within the sophistic movement, if only because Socrates himself was a part of that movement. Once it is granted that sophists other than Socrates did use the question and answer method, and this surely we must grant, then the degree of Socrates' originality and the degree to which he was influenced by other sophists is both an unanswerable question, and also one of subordinate importance." (1981a, 34)

Sophistical wisdom, in both exercise and its acquisition, centered on the use and mastery of speech. While there were various conceptions of wisdom to which individual Sophists were committed, sophistical teachings problematized the traditional connection between *sophia* and knowledge of the divine or universal realm. As Schiappa puts it, "The way to wisdom was not divinely inspired poetry but contrasting human prose arguments" (2003, 162). Both in their rejection of divine knowledge and in their concentration on practical, prudential knowing as the key to a successful public life, the Sophists promoted an interest in the circumstances and challenges of *human* existence that was pursued by Socrates, Plato, Isocrates, and Aristotle. If we can characterize a conception of *sophia* as "sophistical," we might note the following: it begins with the paradoxical admission of ignorance—all we can know (for certain) is that we cannot know anything (for certain); what "knowledge" there is concerns the world of experience, praxis, and communal life; in this world, all knowledge and belief are ultimately contestable, and the construction of social reality is communal, linguistic, and argumentational; the *sophia* most essential to such a worldview includes civic virtue, practical judgment, and mastering the art of reasoned speech.

Socratic Wisdom

Such a conception of wisdom would not be altogether foreign to Socrates (ca. 469–399 B.C.E.).[69] Certainly his acknowledgment of his own ignorance (*Apology* 23b and elsewhere), his apparent indifference toward the sorts of physical and cosmological speculations engaged in by the natural philosophers (*Apol.* 19b–c), his acute interest in politico-moral questions, and his devotion to reasoned discourse as a means of investigating such questions are quite compatible with the sophistical view of *sophia*.[70] However, Socrates was seemingly uncomfortable with the epistemological and, most especially, the ethical problems created by sophistical subjectivism and relativism. Indeed, he sought to address these problems by searching after stable, logically coherent moral concepts that could guide human conduct. While he did not claim to have discovered any such concepts himself, Socrates did develop and employ a discursive technique of inquiry by means of which he thought they could be discovered. His inquiries and the account he gave of his own life disclose the senses of wisdom that he envisioned.

The extent to which Socrates' views were shaped by his reactions to sophistical teachings is difficult to determine. Kerferd writes that "the very idea of including Socrates as part of the sophistic movement is at best a paradox and to many absurd. . . . Yet Socrates was a human being living in a particular period in time. He can only be understood if he is seen in his own contemporary world" (1981a, 55). He concludes that "it is . . . clear that Socrates *was* quite widely regarded as part of the sophistic movement [by his contemporaries] . . . , and his intellectual and educational impact on the aspiring young men at Athens was such that *in function* he was correctly so regarded. The fact that he took no payment does not alter his function in any way" (57). Brickhouse and Smith discuss the evidence that Socrates may have been the pupil of the sophist Prodicus but conclude that he "was never a student of any of the more malignant humanistic Sophists. . . . Although it would be a mistake to say that Socrates' interest in moral philosophy was merely a reaction to the moral skepticism and relativism of some of his adversaries, it would also be a mistake to think that Socrates' thought was not shaped, at least to some extent, by the formidable opposition these views presented" (2000, 21). Guthrie further characterizes the relationship between Socrates and the Sophists: "Socrates was the initiator of a revolution, and the first step in a philosophical revolution has two characteristics: it is so rooted in the traditions of its time that its full effects are only gradually realized, and it is presented in a simple and absolute form, leaving to future thinkers the job of providing the necessary qualifications and provisos. The tradition in which Socrates was caught up was that of the Sophists, and his teaching would have been impossible without theirs, much of which he accepted. They based their lives on the conviction that *aretê* could be taught, and he concluded that therefore it must be knowledge" (1971a, 138; also see 1950a, 71).

For the ancients Socrates represented a watershed in the development of Greek speculative thought. More systematically than the Sophists, he turned intellectual inquiry away from the concerns of the nature-philosophers and concentrated instead on what it means to be a human being and on the ground of individual action. Cicero, for example, says that "ancient philosophy up to Socrates, who was taught by Archelaus the pupil of Anaxagoras, dealt with number and movement, and the source from which all things arise and to which they return; and these early thinkers inquired zealously into the magnitude, intervals and courses of the stars, and all celestial matters. But Socrates first called philosophy down from the sky, set it in the cities and even introduced it into homes, and compelled it to consider life and morals, good and evil" (*Tusc.* 5.4.10).[71] Xenophon reports that, although Socrates was conversant about the nature-speculations of some of his contemporaries, "he himself always discussed human matters, trying to find out the nature of piety and impiety, honor and dishonor, right and wrong, sanity and lunacy, courage and cowardice, State and statesman, government and the capacity for government, and all other subjects the knowledge of which he thought marked truly good men" (*Mem.* 1.1.16). Whatever may be concluded about Socrates' role in the redirection of intellectual inquiry from *physis* to *anthrôpos*, it is undeniable that his interests were markedly different from those of the cosmologists, and this he shared with contemporaries such as Protagoras, Gorgias, and Prodicus.

Several interpretive issues attend any effort at reconstructing Socrates' thought. The most fundamental, of course, is that we have no direct record of his views because he left no writings.[72] Our efforts at understanding the thinking and teaching of this unique person rely on the writings of men whose character and motives vary widely. Portrayals of Socrates range from Plato's consistently respectful treatment of him in the dialogues to Aristophanes' lampooning of "philosophy" via the ludicrous character of "Socrates" in the *Clouds*. Consequently we must construct a composite portrait of the man and his ideas from disparate sources. Guthrie observes that "two things are frequently said about him which, if they both were true, would preclude us from making any significant remarks about him at all. It is claimed on the one hand that his teaching is indissolubly linked with his whole personality, and on the other that we can know nothing about this historical person Socrates because the accounts of him which we have not only are somewhat distorted . . . by being filtered through the minds of his pupils or opponents, but were actually never intended by their authors to be anything but fiction" (1971a, 6). He accepts the former of these statements and rejects the latter. Indeed, Guthrie goes on to note that "for myself . . . I do not think that our position concerning knowledge of the historical Socrates is as hopeless as is sometimes alleged. . . . He was a complex character, who did not and could not reveal every side of himself equally to all his acquaintances. . . . If then the accounts of, say, Plato and Xenophon seem to present a different type of man, the chances are that each by itself is not so much wrong as incomplete, that it tends to exaggerate certain genuine traits and minimize others equally genuine, and that to get an idea of the whole man we must regard them as complementary" (8–9; also see Scoon 1928, 151–53).

Brickhouse and Smith propose six interpretive rules for studying the textual evidence about Socrates: the *Principle of Interpretive Cogency*, the *Principle of Interpretive Plausibility*, the *Principle of Textual Fidelity*, the *Prohibition of Anachronism*, the *Principle of Contextual Coherence*, and the *Principle of Charity* (2000, 3–5). Two of these are particularly germane here. The *Prohibition of Anachronism* stipulates that "no adequate interpretation can provide an understanding of the text that required the assumption of application of some fact or concept that came about or was generated later in history and would not have been available to or known by the author of the text" (4). This is a principle, of course, that I have tried to observe throughout this study. The *Principle of Charity*, which the authors say is "often very controversial both in its conception and in its application," reads, "Other things being equal, the interpretation that provides a more interesting or a more plausible view is preferable" (5).

Recognizing that this rule can easily conflict with one or more of the others, the authors still argue that "the basic perception it captures is not particularly controversial. . . . We study Socrates because he is *interesting* and because his positions and arguments usually seem to be at least *plausible*, almost always philosophically significant, and sometimes even exactly right. Other things being equal, an interpretation that results in a picture of Socrates . . . that is less interesting or less plausible will be to that degree less satisfying than one that yields a more interesting or more plausible picture, precisely because the less interesting or plausible picture will seem to us to be less accurate concerning the Socrates . . . we found to merit our attention in the first place" (6).

In general, our sources are Plato, Xenophon, Aristophanes, and Aristotle. Plato's accounts of Socrates and his teachings are by far the most extensive, and it is on these that we must principally rely. In doing so, we must recognize that the portrayal of Socrates changes as we move from Plato's early dialogues to his middle and later ones.[73] Plato was but twenty-eight when his teacher and friend was put to death, and it is likely that his aims in the early dialogues were to defend Socrates' reputation and to preserve his teachings. In the early and transitional dialogues, the character "Socrates" is concerned almost exclusively with such moral issues as the nature of justice, courage, or piety and not with the metaphysical and epistemological issues that are taken up in the middle and later dialogues. Since these teachings were intimately bound up with Socrates' personality, it seems inevitable that Plato would have employed the dialogue form to portray Socrates as a person and to present his thinking. Taylor develops his account of the historical Socrates on the assumptions that "Plato's picture of his Master is substantially accurate, and that the information he supplies about him is intended to be taken as historical fact" (1953, 34). Guthrie comments,

> Reading our authorities on Socrates gives a vivid impression of a highly individual character whom one feels one knows not only as a thinker but as a whole person. In this of course the dramatic form of Plato's writings, far from being a hindrance, is a tremendous help. This feeling of personal acquaintance gives a certain encouragement (may I even say a certain right?), when a particular philosophical point is in question, to say: "No, I can't imagine that Socrates himself would have put it like that," or "Yes, that is just what I should have expected Socrates to say." If this sounds an impossibly subjective criterion, I can only say that, provided it is based on a reading of all the sources, I do not believe that any better one presents itself. (1971a, 30–31)[74]

Indeed, the early dialogues provide a compelling portrait of Socrates' character as well as giving insight into his thinking. In any event, we may feel somewhat secure in drawing conclusions about these matters from the early works, while some of the middle dialogues provide additional insight. The middle and late dialogues are generally taken to be more representative of Plato's own thought than of Socrates'. In these works we encounter the ideas of the mature Plato, the man who pursued the trajectories of his teacher's inquiries, who brought Socrates' presumed insights to their fruition, and who created the first comprehensive philosophical system in the Western world. We shall consider this Plato in the next chapter.

Xenophon was roughly contemporary with Plato. He was not a philosopher but rather was a soldier and farmer whose writings are decidedly more pedestrian than Plato's. Xenophon wrote about Socrates in four works: the *Oeconomicus*, a practical treatise on estate management and farming; the *Symposium*, which, like Plato's dialogue of the same name, portrays Socrates at a dinner party among friends; the *Apologia* (dismissed by Guthrie as a "rather pathetic little work"), which purports to demonstrate Socrates' reverence toward the gods and justice in his dealings with people; and the *Memorabilia*, which was written, says Xenophon, to support "my opinion [that] he benefitted his associates, partly by practical example and partly by his conversation" (1.3.1). Guthrie details Xenophon's reliability as a guide to the historical Socrates (1971a, 15–28): "Much that he saw in Socrates was, I am convinced, characteristic of the real man. When however we find in the Socrates of Plato something far less commonplace, far more paradox[ical], [with] humour and irony and above all a greater profundity of thought, it would be wrong to suppose that these were foreign to Socrates simply because they do not appear in Xenophon's portrait. The impression of uniqueness, and the powerful impact, favourable or unfavourable, which he made on everyone who met him . . . , are more comprehensible if we suppose that he had in him much of what Plato discovered as well as what appealed to the prosaic commonsense of Xenophon" (15).[75] In comparing the portraits of Socrates presented by Plato and Xenophon, Waterfield describes four important ways in which the two are incompatible (Xenophon 1990, 12–18), concluding that "ultimately, the choice of Plato over Xenophon is largely a matter of prejudice. Plato's Socrates is simply a far more provocative and brilliant character" (18). Even so, Waterfield advances a methodology for resolving the apparent incompatibilities between the two portraits based on the assumption that "Socrates taught principle rather than applied principle" (22). Thus, "wherever possible, we would have to consider what his followers said on any issue, and then generalize what they said to discover the underlying principle. Needless to say, the results of such a methodology will always be speculative" (23).

The only other of Socrates' contemporaries whose writings about him survive is the comic playwright Aristophanes.[76] Opinions vary concerning the veracity of Aristophanes' portrayal of the person Socrates through the character "Socrates" in the *Clouds*, ranging from those who maintain that it represented common perceptions of Socrates, Sophists, and nature philosophers with whom he was identified in the popular mind, to those who hold that the characters, though bearing historical names, were intended as satirical send-ups of certain types of persons. Schiappa writes that "most commentators agree that Aristophanes used Socrates as his central character for primarily dramatic purposes, and that his portrayal was not necessarily historically accurate" (2003, 106). Taylor maintains that "the Old Attic Comedy dealt throughout in personal burlesque, not in satire on generalized social 'types,' and . . . it was essential to the comedian's success that the object of the burlesque should be a public notoriety. We may therefore be perfectly certain that Socrates was already a well-known figure when Aristophanes attacked him, and that the poet counted upon the excellence of the caricature as something which the audience would recognize. Also we have to remember the general principle that a successful burlesque must be founded on notorious fact, or what is believed to be such. It must be a distortion, for comic effect, of something which is not the mere invention of the caricaturist" (1953, 20–21).[77] On this view, Aristophanes' portrayal is useful insofar as it reveals aspects of Socrates' character as he was commonly perceived by his fellow citizens. However, as Waterfield points out, his Socrates "is a catch-all character who displays features which popular prejudice and the collective unconscious attribute to intellectuals; he can hardly, therefore, be used as evidence for what the historical Socrates was really like" (Xenophon 1990, 10). Aristophanes' representation, accordingly, may reveal more about sophistical teachings than about Socrates himself (Sciappa 1999, 2003).

Though Aristotle (384–322 B.C.E.), unlike the earlier writers, had no personal acquaintance with Socrates, he had the advantage of having worked for twenty years in the Academy under Plato's tutelage. This afforded him a unique opportunity for knowing just what we want most to understand: the relation between the philosophies of Socrates and Plato. As Guthrie observes, "Aristotle, whose interest is purely philosophical, tells us in a few crisp sentences where in his opinion the thought of Socrates ends and that of Plato begins. He if anyone ought to know, and his contribution to the problem is invaluable" (1971a, 35–36).[78] Particularly in the *Metaphysics* but occasionally elsewhere, Aristotle provides guidance in distinguishing Socratic from Platonic thought. Stone remarks that Aristotle's references to Socrates are valuable "because Aristotle distanced himself from the cult of Socrates and treats his contribution to philosophy with a precise astringency, in striking contrast to Plato's adoration" (1989, 5).

These issues lead me to a somewhat conservative reading of the sources. Particularly, I am reluctant to attribute to the historical Socrates all the intellectual positions and doctrines that Plato has put into the mouth of "Socrates" in the dialogues and that Xenophon has Socrates articulate in the *Memorabilia* and elsewhere (see Stone 1989, 3–4, 16). This suggests, among other things, that we must take Socrates' professions of "ignorance" largely at face value, for reasons given below.

Socrates' thought was shaped by the historical circumstances through which he lived. Born in 470 or 469 B.C.E., Socrates spent his youth during the first decades of Athens's ascendancy following its victories over the Persians. During his childhood and adolescence, Anaxagoras was teaching in Athens and the Sophist Protagoras first settled there. The doxographical tradition holds that he was a student of Archelaus (himself a pupil of Anaxagoras), and he was roughly contemporary with the Atomists Leucippus and Democritus, with whose works he may have been familiar. His early study of natural philosophy may have invited Aristophanes to present a parodied "Socrates" in the *Clouds* as one who "speculated about the heavens above, and searched into the earth beneath," as Socrates himself put it in his trial defense (*Apol.* 18b).[79] He was still a young man when Pericles initiated the great building program that yielded such monuments as the new Parthenon and the Propylaea on the Acropolis and other temples throughout Attica. The decades of the Periclean "Golden Age"—the 440s and 430s—coincided with Socrates' twenties and thirties, a period during which he may have turned away from natural philosophy in favor of studying human affairs. In any case, it is the latter study for which Socrates is now chiefly remembered, and it emerged during a time when he likely had numerous opportunities to converse with intellectuals from Athens and throughout the Greek world.

It seems probable that the events dominating his last three decades—the Peloponnesian War (431–404) in which he served, the death of Pericles (429) from a plague, the rise of such demagogues as Cleon the Tanner, the treacheries of Alcibiades, Athens's eventual defeat, the tyranny of "The Thirty" (404–403), and the restoration of a democracy bent on eliminating any vestiges of possible oligarchic sympathies—affected Socrates' views of wisdom, virtue, and "the life worth living." It was a time of great turmoil, when traditional beliefs were challenged and ancient customs violated, when both collective and personal violence tore at the social fabric, when moral questions occupied intellectual debate and inquiry. Socrates' own intellectual quest must be understood in this context.[80]

How does Socrates conceive wisdom? In what is perhaps the most detailed account of his thinking on this matter, Plato's *Apology* introduces us to a complex

conception of *sophia* that we may connect with the historical Socrates. In opening his defense, Plato's "Socrates" acknowledges that he has gained the notoriety on which the charges against him are based as a result of his quest for
wisdom. "I have gained this reputation, gentlemen, for nothing more or less
than a kind of wisdom. What kind of wisdom do I mean? Human wisdom, I
suppose. It seems that I really am wise in this limited sense" (20d).[81] This wisdom is clearly some sort of knowledge, and Socrates appears to recognize that
there are different sorts of knowledge that can be termed "wisdom." We can
see these in his accounts of the wisdom he has and that he seeks.

Socrates follows his acknowledgment of possessing some "limited" wisdom
by recounting the story of his friend Chaerephon's visit to the oracle of Pythian
Apollo at Delphi, during which Chaerephon inquired of the god whether there
was anyone wiser than Socrates.[82] The priestess of Apollo, who pronounced
the god's answers to questions put to him, replied that there was not. "When
I heard about the oracle's answer," says Socrates, "I said to myself, What does
the god mean? Why does he not use plain language? I am only too conscious
that *I have no claim to wisdom*, great or small. What can he mean by asserting
that I am the wisest man in the world? He cannot be telling a lie; that would
not be right for him" (21b; emphasis added). Determined to "check the truth"
of the god's assertion, Socrates set out to interview various men who enjoyed
reputations for wisdom—first the politicians, then the poets, and finally the
craftsmen. However, in each case he discovered that, whereas each believed in
his own wisdom, none could give a coherent account of the matters about
which he professed to be wise. After each of these encounters, says Socrates,
"I reflected as I walked away, Well, I am certainly wiser than this man. It is
only too likely that neither of us has any knowledge to boast of, but he thinks
that he knows something which he does not know, whereas I am quite conscious of my ignorance. At any rate it seems that I am wiser than he is to this
small extent, that I do not think that I know what I do not know" (21d). In the
first instance, then, Socratic wisdom consists in knowing that one does not
know. To be wise is to be aware of one's own ignorance.

Socrates' characteristic use of irony has led some commentators to conclude that he was being ironic, too, in professing a lack of wisdom (Stone 1989,
80–81). However, the early Platonic dialogues suggest that he is being sincere
in maintaining that he does not possess "truth" about the matters in which
he is most interested. Virtually all of these dialogues end by leaving unsettled
the questions under investigation. Socrates offers no knowledge of his own
concerning, for instance, the nature of justice (*Gorgias*), piety (*Euthyphro*), temperance (*Charmides*), courage (*Laches*), friendship (*Lysis*), or virtue (*Protagoras*).
These and the other early dialogues end inconclusively, in *aporia* or perplexity.

Aristotle tells us that "it was the practice of Socrates to ask questions but not to give answers, for he confessed that he did not know" (*Soph. Refutations* 183b). Matthews (1999) writes:

> There are several things to say about such professions of Socratic ignorance [for example, at *Meno* 71a–b]. For one thing, Socrates isn't claiming any special, or unusual, gap in his knowledge. As he says here, he has never met anyone who *does* know what virtue is. So he thinks of the ignorance he is professing as a widely shared ignorance, perhaps even as a universal ignorance. Second, since the ignorance Socrates professes is quite compatible with his being able to ask astute and revealing questions about virtue, or whatever the matter under discussion is, it has to be a very special kind of ignorance. The picture we get from Plato's aporetic dialogues is that Socrates knows at least as much about the matter under discussion as his discussion partners know; but he, unlike them, realizes that there is some profound difficulty in what they otherwise naturally take themselves to understand perfectly well. His interlocutors have been unaware of this difficulty, but as they become aware of it, they begin to lose confidence that they can even use the ordinary words they had earlier used to express their easy-going intimations of knowledge. This is the phenomenon of having one's own words slip and slide around until one isn't sure any more what one is saying. . . . I am convinced . . . that his disclaimers of knowledge have a deeply philosophical purpose. We are meant to realize, it seems, that matters we *all* assume we understand perfectly well may be philosophically problematic. Socrates' professions of ignorance are apparently meant to warn us of this important fact. (1999, 44–45)[83]

Thus it is reasonable to take Socrates at his word when he asserts his ignorance about the ethical and moral matters others have claimed to understand. This intellectual modesty is a mark of Socratic wisdom.

If Socrates were to acquire the sort of wisdom that he disclaims, in what would it consist? In the opening section of his defense speech, Socrates mentions such Sophists as Gorgias, Prodicus, Hippias, and Evenus, noting ironically that they presumably possess the wisdom he lacks, a "wisdom that is more than human" (19e–20e). What constitutes such superhuman—divine—wisdom? Socrates gives us some sense of this. Though he does not claim to have the highest sort of wisdom, he does admit to having some knowledge of moral matters. He knows, for instance, that it would be wrong for him to escape from prison, since to do so would violate the laws of Athens and would "return wrong for wrong, evil for evil" (*Crito* 54c); and he knows that "it is wicked and shameful to do wrong, to disobey one's superior, be he god or man" (*Apol.* 29b). Yet such knowledge about the moral status of particular acts does not constitute, for Socrates, the superhuman wisdom that others claim, and to which he apparently aspires.

For assessing claims to such wisdom, he has one simple criterion: if a person had authentic knowledge about moral matters, he or she could give a coherent rationale—a *logos*—for it. In other words, it is not enough to be able to say that a particular act is wrong; one must be able to explain *why* it is wrong, and this explanation must be made in terms of a general conception of rightness and wrongness, justice and injustice, virtue and vice, and of how the particular act is subsumed by this conception. In order to say *with knowledge* that a particular action is just or unjust, for example, one must be able to provide a coherent definition of "justice" and show how this definition applies to the action in question. In the *Symposium* (202a) Diotima, a "wise woman" from Mantinea, asks Socrates, "Haven't you realized that there's something between wisdom and ignorance?" "What is it?" asks Socrates. "It is having right opinions," Diotima responds, "without being able to give reasons for having them. Don't you realize that this isn't knowing, because you don't have knowledge unless you can give reasons; but it isn't ignorance either, because ignorance has no contact with the truth? Right opinion, of course, has this kind of status, falling between understanding and ignorance" (Gill's translation, in Plato 1999).[84] A wisdom that is "more than human," for Socrates, lies in being able to define accurately the moral terms one uses in rendering and justifying moral judgments (Scoon 1928, 160–61). Grasping such definitions is the highest form of knowledge. Whether human beings can actually attain it, however, is uncertain.[85] There is enough ambiguity in our evidence that a firm conclusion is difficult. Whatever Socrates may have believed about the possibility of attaining divine wisdom, he seems nonetheless to have devoted his life to its pursuit and to have encouraged others to do the same, so evidently he believed that such knowledge might at least be approached.

Logically coherent, rationally defensible definitions are central in the Socratic quest for wisdom. This is demonstrated by virtually every dialogue in which he is a character, and most especially by the early dialogues. When he engages an interlocutor about some claim to knowledge the latter has made, Socrates inevitably inquires as to the form (*eidos*) or essential nature of the quality under consideration.[86] In the *Euthyphro*, for instance, in which the topic is piety or holiness, we find the following exchange:

> SOCRATES: Well, bear in mind that what I asked of you was not to tell me one or two out of all the numerous actions that are holy; I wanted you to tell me what is the essential form (*eidos*) of holiness which makes all holy actions holy. I believe you held that there is one ideal form by which unholy

things are all unholy, and by which all holy things are holy. Do you remember that?

EUTHYPHRO: I do.

SOCRATES: Well then, show me what, precisely, this ideal is, so that, with my eye on it, and using it as a standard, I can say that any action done by you or anybody else is holy if it resembles this idea, or, if it does not, can deny that it is holy. (6d–e; Cooper's translation in Plato 1961b)

The *Meno* contains a number of other terms Socrates may have used in his quest for definitions. He asks for the *ousia* (being, essence, 72b) of a thing; the *en ti eidos* (single form) which all the instances of a thing possess (72c and d); the *en kata pantôn, dia pantôn,* or *epi pasi* (the one thing said of them all, running through them all, in them all, 73d, 74a, 75a); or *to epi pasi tauton* (what in them all is the same, 75a).[87] This pattern is repeated in almost all the early dialogues, and in virtually every one of them Socrates himself acknowledges that he lacks the knowledge of definitions his interlocutors initially presume. Still, whether the subject of inquiry be virtue, courage, piety, beauty, justice, friendship, or some other such matter, Socrates' efforts are directed toward inducing the others present to generate logically coherent statements that define the moral concepts under discussion.

Underlying his quest for the "form" or "essence" of the concepts Socrates examined is the unspoken assumption that each has a substantial, stable nature that enables it to be apprehended, described, and distinguished from other forms. In this we find the implication of Socratic thought of which his student Plato made the greatest metaphysical and epistemological use. Moreover it represents a view that is diametrically opposed to the ontological relativism of some sophistical teachings. Whereas Gorgias might have denied the existence of such transcendent moral ideas, Socrates was convinced that without a belief in the objective reality of the *meanings* of moral terms, human beings could not live together in harmony. Without objective grounds upon which to base moral arguments, justice does become "nothing else than the advantage of the stronger," as the Sophist Thrasymachus may have put it (*Rep.* 338c); or it becomes a matter of personal perception and opinion, which can be altered by the intoxicating words of the speaker, as Protagoras and Gorgias might maintain. Thus would the administration of justice be vulnerable to the vagaries of the public mood. In either case, thought Socrates, there is no truly rational way of adjudicating conflicts between fellow citizens, and a harmonious, well-ordered community would be impossible to maintain.

A true definition must not only state the essential attributes of a concept but also—and primarily—be linked to the proper work (*ergon*) or function of the thing or activity to which the concept is connected. Everything that exists by design and not by chance, Socrates maintains, has a proper function, and its characteristic excellence or virtue lies in the fulfillment of that function. In the first book of the *Republic*, for instance, we find this exchange between Socrates and Thrasymachus (353b):

> SOCRATES: Do you not also think that there is a specific virtue or excellence of everything for which a specific work or function is appointed? Let us return to the same examples. The eyes, we say, have a function?
>
> THRASYMACHUS: They have.
>
> SOCRATES: And was there not a function of the ears?
>
> THRASYMACHUS: Yes.
>
> SOCRATES: And so also a virtue?
>
> THRASYMACHUS: Also a virtue.
>
> SOCRATES: And what of all other things? Is the case not the same?
>
> THRASYMACHUS: The same. (trans. Shorey, in Plato 1961j)

The Socrates of the early dialogues often draws on such examples. He speaks of the *ergon* and the *aretê* of cobblers, weavers, joiners, metalworkers, and others in illustrating his point that the essential character of a thing or an activity lies in its proper work or function, and that the particular virtue of each thing is the condition that allows it to do its work well. Thus it might be reasoned, the excellence of a cobbler consists in the knowledge that permits him to do his job well—knowledge, that is, of the uses to which different kinds of footwear are to be put, of leather and hobnails and stitching and other materials, and of the workings of the human foot. Likewise, the weaver finds her excellence (and thus her wisdom) in knowing the properties of different fibers and of different weaves, how the loom works, and so on. So it is with each of the various crafts that Socrates so often uses to illustrate his ideas about moral concepts.

In the *Apology*, when he explains to the jurymen how he had tested the meaning of the oracle's statement that he was the wisest of men by interrogating politicians, poets, and others, Socrates says, "Last of all I turned to the skilled craftsmen. I knew quite well that I had practically no technical qualifications myself, and I was sure that I should find them full of impressive knowledge. In this I was not disappointed. They understood things which I did not, and to that extent they were wiser than I was" (22c–d). Socrates goes on to observe, however, that even the skilled craftsmen had the failing he had found in the others: they thought that they knew things about which they had, in fact, no knowledge (22d). Socrates recognizes the wisdom in being able to do things—in being able to produce what craftsmen produce—and in being able to explain *why* something must be done in a certain way. It is a kind of technical, expert knowledge that encompasses both the *how* of making something and the end or purpose for which it is to be used. The *sophia* of the craftsman, then, is proficiency or expertise in making something and knowledge of its proper function. By extension, the highest form of *sophia* comprises expertise or proficiency in the most important craft of all: living well and rightly. Indeed, knowledge of moral concepts is particularly important to this craft.

Skill in the art of living requires the same conditions as with any craft. One must have knowledge of the function or end of the activity; hence one must know the function or purpose of human life. Just as individual crafts and actions have their proper ends, and so their proper virtues, for Socrates the human *psychê* has its own function: to guide one in living to the best of human capability. Thus it must be with the most important form of virtue. *Sophia* encompasses knowing the proper end or purpose of human life. Cornford notes that "this question—what is the end of life?—is one that, then as now, was rarely asked. . . . So we go on from day to day, contriving means to settled ends, without raising the question whether the ends are worth striving for. That is precisely the question Socrates did raise, and forced others to consider, thereby causing a good deal of discomfort. Taking life as a whole, he asked which of the ends we pursue are really and intrinsically valuable, not mere means to something else we think desirable. Is there some one end of life that is alone worthy of desire?" (1950, 33–34). Moreover one must know the conditions and resources out of which the means of fulfilling a particular function can be constructed. In the case of the cobbler, this requires knowledge of leather, of the human foot, of the uses to which the shoe will be put, of the tools by which the shoe will be crafted, and so on; with the weaver, it means knowledge of fibers, weaves, and the loom. With the craft of living well or rightly, this knowledge involves a grasp of the meanings of moral terms, an apprehension of the moral concepts these terms express: Justice, Love, Righteousness, Piety, Virtue, Courage, and so on.

Another requirement for proficiency in a craft is being able to perform or enact one's knowledge of ends and means. The cobbler must be able to measure a human foot accurately, transfer those measurements to various pieces of leather, mark the patterns off, and so on. The weaver must know how to figure the weave and patterns she wishes to produce, determine how much yarn will be needed, and take account of the characteristics of the fiber and the loom. In the art of living, the same is true. *Sophia* in this art must include an ability to distinguish between true and false goods, between greater and lesser pleasures and pains, and, as with the cobbler and the weaver, *to measure* competing goods and evils against each other so as to determine the correct course of action. The power of wisdom to direct one toward right action, Socrates says, lies in a special ability: skill in "the art of measurement" or "the metric art." In the *Protagoras* (355e–58b), for example, when he and the old Sophist are considering how one can distinguish between good and bad pleasures and how one can determine which pleasures to pursue in preference to others, Socrates suggests that one must weigh pleasures against pleasures, pains against pains, and pleasures against pains in order to see the comparative magnitudes of each. "So," Socrates says, "like an expert in weighing, put the pleasures and the pains together, set both the near and distant in the balance, and say which is the greater quantity. In weighing pleasures against pleasures, one must always choose the greater and the more; in weighing pains against pains, the smaller and the less; whereas in weighing pleasures against pains, if the pleasures exceed the pains, whether the distant, the near, or vice versa, one must take the course which brings those pleasures; but if the pains outweigh the pleasures, avoid it" (356b–c, trans. Guthrie, in Plato 1956). He goes on to liken this skill to "the art of measurement used in judging the relative thickness, number, and loudness of things perceived from close at hand and at a distance." He concludes, "What would assure us a good life then? Surely knowledge, and specifically a science of measurement, since the required skill lies in the estimation of excess and defect" (356e–57a). This science of measurement, moreover, "must be a special skill or branch of knowledge" (357b), and it must also be a component of the sort of wisdom required for living well.[88]

The *sophia* of the life-craft, as with any craft, entails proficiency in execution, in the actual practice of the craft. The cobbler must be able to direct his hands properly in measuring and cutting the leather, in applying hobnails and stitching, and so on. So, too, must the weaver maintain a steady hand in order to keep the proper degree of tension on the yarn and a consistent pattern in the weave. The name that Socrates gives to this element of wisdom is *aretê*, a word that means "excellence" or "goodness" of any kind but that, as we have seen, is usually translated as "virtue." For the cobbler and the weaver, *aretê* consists in being able to translate knowledge of function and material into practical action that will produce something that is well suited to the end for which it was produced. In every craft—shoe-making, weaving, music-making, sculpting, painting, woodworking, stone-cutting, carpentry—one must control the movements of one's body with great precision and discipline if the product is to be of high quality. So it must be also in the life-craft. The *aretê* of the human *as* human, the technical proficiency required for living rightly, is precisely this sort of self-control or self-mastery. Socrates calls this virtue *sôphrosynê*—a capacity for controlling one's desires and impulses in choosing actions and a disposition to choose the path of moderation. This excellence of the soul stands in direct contrast to *akrasia*, self-indulgence, and is both the sine qua non of right living and a necessary condition for acquiring wisdom, as Socrates observes in Xenophon's *Memoirs:*

> SOCRATES: Don't you think that self-indulgence debars people from wisdom, which is the greatest good, and drives them into the opposite state? Don't you think that, by dragging them off in pursuit of pleasure, it prevents them from studying and apprehending their real interests; and that it often confuses their perception of good and bad and makes them choose the worse instead of the better?
>
> EUTHYDEMUS: That does happen.
>
> SOCRATES: And who, Euthydemus, can we say has less concern with self-discipline than the self-indulgent man? For surely the effects of self-discipline and self-indulgence are directly opposed.[89]

Thus, for Socrates as for some Sophists, self-mastery and moderation are both prerequisites for acquiring *sophia* and requirements for enacting it in daily life.[90]

Socratic wisdom—the wisdom he claims not yet to have acquired and that he finds lacking in everyone he interrogates—comprises knowledge of the soul's proper function and of the moral ideas that are invoked in fulfilling that function. It includes skill in estimating the relative magnitudes of pleasures and pains, and it requires the virtue of temperance or moderation for both its attainment and its practice. How is such wisdom is to be acquired? For Socrates, wisdom comprises *self-knowledge,* and so the quest for it is fundamentally a matter of examining and caring for one's own *psychê* (see Guthrie 1971a, 139, 147–53). This is reminiscent of Heraclitus's pronouncement that when he went in search of the *Logos* he went in search of himself (DK 101). The most revealing disclosure of this idea occurs in the *Apology:* "I say that it is the greatest good for a human being to discuss virtue every day and those other things about which you hear me conversing and testing myself and others, for the unexamined life is not worth living for a human being" (38a). Thus, in fulfilling what he takes to be his service to Apollo, says Socrates, "I spend all my time going about trying to persuade you, young and old, to make your first and chief concern not for your bodies nor for your possessions, but for the highest welfare of your souls" (30b; see Cornford 1950, 35–37).

For Socrates, then, the first step on the path to wisdom is a commitment to the care of one's soul. This means that, rather than being preoccupied with external matters and "trivialities"—with wealth, power, prestige, reputation, or one's physical appearance—a wisdom-seeker must instead look inward, examine his or her own beliefs continually, and take the moral improvement of his/her own soul as the highest calling.[91] Our first duty, consequently, is to obey the Delphic command to "Know Thyself." The effect of such self-examination will be an ordering of the soul according to the principles of justice and temperance (*Gorgias* 504b–d). Cornford remarks that "Socrates' discovery was that the true self is not the body but the soul. And by the soul he means the seat of that faculty of insight which can know good from evil and infallibly choose the good. Self-knowledge implies the recognition of this true self. Self-examination is a discipline constantly needed to distinguish its judgment from the promptings of other elements in our nature. . . . Self-rule is the rule of the true self over those other elements—an absolute autocracy of the soul. . . . The true self is a faculty, not only of intuitive insight, but of will—a will that can override all other desires for pleasure and seeming happiness" (1950, 50–51).

Moral self-examination is carried out through discourse, most particularly through conversation with others. The philosophical process is fundamentally *dialogical* for Socrates, and it is therefore no accident that Plato chose to adopt this form both to portray the historical Socrates and, later, to advance his own philosophical views. In the give and take of verbal intercourse, when each interlocutor is confronted by the persistent questioning of the other, one is invited to examine one's own fundamental convictions and is called to account—to give a *logos*—for them. Through such self-examination and self-justification, Socrates apparently believed, one can formulate and put to the test a sequence of propositions that might approach a true definition of some moral concept or principle. Socrates' conversations with his companions demonstrate his rejection of the idea that wisdom can be taught; rather, talking is the way in which it can be awakened in ourselves and in our interlocutors. The fact that he advances no "truths" of his own in the early dialogues and his description of himself as a spiritual "midwife" rather than as a teacher suggest that Socrates believed each of us has to find moral knowledge within. "I am the son of a midwife," he says in the *Theaetetus.*

> I practice the same art. . . . Consider, then, how it is with midwives. . . . I dare say you know that they never attend other women in childbirth so long as they themselves can conceive and bear children, but only when they are too old for that. . . . My art of midwifery is in general like theirs; the only difference is that my patients are men, not women, and my concern is not with the body but with the soul that is in travail of birth. And the highest point of my art is the power to prove by every test whether the offspring of a young man's thought is a false phantom or [an] instinct with life and truth. I am so far like the midwife that I cannot myself give birth to wisdom, and the common reproach is true, that, though I question others, I can myself bring nothing to light because there is no wisdom in me . . . , nor has any discovery ever been born to me as the child of my soul. Those who frequent my company at first appear, some of them, quite unintelligent, but,

as we go further with our discussion, all who are favored by heaven make progress at a rate that seems surprising to others as well as to themselves, although it is clear that they have never learned anything from me. The many admirable truths they bring to birth have been discovered by themselves from within. But the delivery is heaven's work and mine.[92]

Socrates philosophizes by a technique that has come to be known as *elenchos*, a cross-examining or testing for purposes of disproof or refutation. Vlastos writes:

> In Plato's earlier dialogues . . . Socrates' inquiries display a pattern of investigation whose rationale he does not investigate. They are constrained by rules he does not undertake to justify. In marked contrast to "Socrates" speaking for Plato in the middle dialogues, who refers repeatedly to the "method" (*methodos*) he follows (either in general or for the special purpose of some particular investigation), the "Socrates" who speaks for Socrates in the earlier dialogues never uses this word and never discusses his method of investigation. He never troubles to say why his way of searching is the way to discover truth or even what this way of searching is. He has no name for it. *Elegchos* [*elenchos*] and the parent verb *elegchein* [*elenchein*] ("to refute," "to examine critically," "to censure"), he uses to describe, not to baptize, what he does. Only in modern times has *elenchus* become the proper name. (1994, 1–2)

Socrates' *elenchos* appears to carry forward the Presocratics' use of discussion and debate as the principal instrument of philosophical inquiry. It is yet another embodiment of the spirit of *agôn* that permeated the masculinist culture of Greek society from its beginnings (Fredal 2006, 15ff.).

Like the sophistical employment of *eristic*—a method of challenging a speaker's thesis by asking questions and advancing refutative arguments—the Socratic *elenchos* is a technique of question-and-answer that seeks to determine whether a speaker can sustain a logically coherent position on some moral question. When someone with whom Socrates is talking makes a moral claim, Socrates will "test" his interlocutor's moral knowledge by asking questions and by insisting that these questions be answered honestly. Using these answers as premises, Socrates will logically deduce the propositions that follow from them, pursuing the chain of reasoning until a conclusion is reached that contradicts the initial claim. An illustration occurs in the *Euthyphro* (15c):

> SOCRATES: And are you not aware now that you say that what the gods love is holy? But is not what the gods love just the same as what is pleasing to the gods?
>
> EUTHYPHRO: Yes, certainly.

SOCRATES: Well then, either we were wrong in our recent conclusion, or if that was right, our position now is wrong.

EUTHYPHRO: So it seems.

SOCRATES: And so we must go back again, and start from the beginning to find out what the holy is. As for me, I never will give up until I know.[93]

Thus is the interlocutor reduced to a state of *aporia* or perplexity (literally being at a loss or an impasse), because s/he cannot maintain both her/his initial position and the later propositions to which the argument has led her/him to assent. This is precisely the aim of the Socratic *elenchos*, because before one can truly seek wisdom, one must be aware of one's own ignorance. It is to this state of perplexity that Socrates' persistent questioning seems to be most consistently directed, for the beginning of wisdom must be silence, emptiness, and humility (Benson 2000, 258). This is precisely the outcome of his conversation with Euthyphro (11a–b):

SOCRATES: Consequently, Euthyphro, it looks as if you had not given me my answer—as if when you were asked to tell the nature of the holy, you did not wish to explain the essence of it. You merely tell an attribute of it, namely, that it appertains to holiness to be loved by all the gods. What it *is*, as yet you have not said. So, if you please, do not conceal this from me. No, begin again. Say what the holy is, and never mind if gods do love it, nor if it has some other attribute; on that we shall not split. Come, speak out. Explain the nature of the holy and unholy.

EUTHYPHRO: Now, Socrates, I simply don't know how to tell you what I think. Somehow everything that we put forward keeps moving about us in a circle, and nothing will stay where we put it.

Socrates himself is the first to acknowledge his own *aporia* when his inquiries yield no coherent answers to his questions, as in the *Meno*. When describing his method of testing the people he meets, Socrates says, "It isn't that, knowing the answers myself, I perplex other people. The truth is rather that I infect them also with the perplexity I feel myself. So with virtue now. I don't know what it is. You may have known before you came into contact with me, but now you look as if you don't" (80c–d, trans. Guthrie, in Plato 1961g). Guthrie writes, "The essence of the Socratic method is to convince the interlocutor that whereas he thought he knew something, in fact he does not. The conviction of ignorance is a necessary first step in the acquisition of knowledge, for no one is going to seek knowledge . . . if he is under the delusion that he already possesses it" (1950a, 74). Matthews notes that "philosophy arose for Socrates in the astonished recognition that the attempt to offer definitions of basic ethical terms generates puzzles, or perplexities, that one doesn't know how to resolve. This hypothesis, as it turns out, accords quite well with the picture Plato gives us of Socrates in several of his early dialogues. If, like most commentators, we take the early dialogues to be our best guide to the historical Socrates, we may even want to give credence to the idea that the historical Socrates came to philosophy by this route" (1999, 20–21; also see 1–10, 121–30).

In order for the *elenchos* to serve its purpose, participants in the conversation must give sincere answers to questions posed. Speaking genuinely is essential if conversation is to lead to genuine insight. The aim of philosophical dialogue is to permit interlocutors to examine their own convictions and to test those convictions against the standards of self-consistency and logical coherence. This cannot be accomplished if partners in discourse do not offer their genuine opinions regarding the matters under consideration. In the *Gorgias*, for example, Socrates and Callicles come to a moment when, in frustration, the latter takes a position he does not embrace merely in order to avoid inconsistency with what he had said earlier. Socrates objects that the inquiry cannot proceed unless both participants are willing to speak their opinions genuinely (495a–b):

> SOCRATES: But enlighten me further as to whether you say that the pleasant and the good are identical, or that there are some pleasures which are not good.
>
> CALLICLES: To avoid inconsistency if I say they are different, I assert they are the same.
>
> SOCRATES: Then you ruin your earlier statement, Callicles, and you can no longer properly investigate the truth with me, if you speak contrary to your opinions.
>
> CALLICLES: You are doing just the same, Socrates.
>
> SOCRATES: Then I am not acting rightly, if I am so doing, nor are you.

In book 1 of the *Republic*, similarly, Socrates emphasizes the need for honesty in the common quest for true knowledge: "Well," says Socrates, "I mustn't flinch from following out the logic of the inquiry, so long as I conceive you to be saying what you think. For now, Thrasymachus, I absolutely believe that you are not 'mocking' us but telling us your real opinions about the truth" (349a). The principle at work here is what Vlastos (1991) has called the "say what you believe" requirement (also see Brickhouse and Smith 2000, 89).

Just as the spirit and form of our conversation must adhere to certain principles if it is to function philosophically, so must our talk center on matters "of the greatest importance," rather than on "trivialities." The early dialogues give us a sense that the content of one's conversation plays a central role in the search for self-knowledge and thus for wisdom. We must "discuss virtue every day and those other things about which you hear me conversing and testing myself and others" (*Apol.* 38a). What these "other things" are is disclosed in the subjects about which Socrates talks with his companions. From Plato, as we have seen, these include such ideas as virtue, friendship, piety, justice, the good, love, and the like. From Diogenes Laertius, we find such additional topics as "Of the Gods," "On the Beautiful," "On Guiding the People," "Of Honor," "Of Poetry," "On Music," "On the Art of Conversation," "Of Judging," and "On Doing Ill."[94] The quest for wisdom, then, requires that one converse about and inquire into topics having moral significance. They will not be matters of gossip or deal with superficial aspects of daily life. Rather, they will involve questions about the principles according to which we ought to conduct our daily lives.

Although it is not clear from our evidence that Socrates believed he or any other human being could actually acquire genuine knowledge of moral concepts, he did employ a conversational practice that might culminate in such knowledge. Certainly Plato thought it could, and he deployed it in his later dialogues, where he has "Socrates" induce his interlocutors to articulate just the sorts of definitions that the historic Socrates appears to have sought in his own inquiries. This constructive aspect of the "Socratic method" (in contrast to the deconstructive function of the *elenchos*) employs two techniques: induction and reasoning by analogy. In connection with the first of these, Aristotle states, "There are two things which may justly be credited to Socrates, inductive argument and general definition" (*Meta.* 1078b). He tells us (*Topics* 105a) that induction involves a movement from the particular to the universal, and he illustrates this with an example that Socrates himself might well have used: if the best navigator is the one with expert knowledge, and the best cart driver is the one with expert knowledge, and so on, then we can infer that in general the best in any occupation is the one with expert knowledge. As Guthrie summarizes the process, "The mind is 'led on' (as the Greek word for induction, *epagôgê*, may signify), from the observation of particular instances to grasp a general characteristic shared by all the members of a class" (1971a, 106–7).[95]

As Socrates employs this technique, the quest for moral definitions involves two stages. The first is to collect instances to which it is agreed that, for instance, the term "just" (or "pious" or "beautiful") can be applied; then the collected examples are examined in order to discover in them some common quality by virtue of which they are rightly called by the name "just" (or "pious" or "beautiful"). This common quality constitutes their essential nature—their *eidos*—as just acts. Perceiving a shared quality or complex of qualities—that is, intuiting the abstraction that can subsume the particulars—bespeaks an intellectual capacity for making an inductive leap from particular to universal, from concrete to abstract. It may be that Socrates was unsure of the human's ability to make this leap, and thus ever to arrive at the essences of moral concepts that are expressed in their definitions. I am satisfied that he believed in the existence of such essences, at least as logically coherent linguistic constructs. It is a major leap from this to Plato's theory of Forms, which we will encounter in the next chapter, and we must be cautious about imputing too much clarity to this aspect of Socrates' thinking. Certainly the germ of Plato's theory is detectable in Socrates' mode of inquiry. Carried to its logical conclusion, the process of induction, if practiced thoughtfully and subjected to logical scrutiny, invites one to ask about the ontological status of the "essences" that can be expressed in true definitions, and Plato accepts the invitation with enthusiasm, as we shall see.

In the meantime, we may want to take to heart Diotima's recognition that Socrates' own philosophical activities could take him only so far and that the mysteries of the Forms may have been beyond his capabilities. In the *Symposium* (209e–10a), after having described connections between Eros, the perception of beauty, and the soul's procreative impulse, Diotima says, "even you, Socrates, could perhaps be initiated in the rites of love I've described so far. But the purpose of these rites, if they are performed correctly, is to reach the final vision of the mysteries; and I'm not sure you could manage this. But I'll tell you about them, and make every effort in doing so; try to follow, as far as you can" (following Gill's translation in Plato 1999). With Cornford, I am inclined "to agree with those scholars who have seen in this sentence Plato's intention to mark the limit reached by the philosophy of his master. Socrates had been the prince of those educators who can beget spiritual children in others' minds and help them to bring their own thoughts to birth. Had he gone further? . . . If I am right in believing that Socrates' philosophy was a philosophy of this world, while Plato's was centered in another world, here is the point where they part company" (1967, 75; compare Guthrie 1971a, 77n).

The other key aspect of the Socratic "method" for seeking true definitions, and one that is intimately tied to the inductive process, is reasoning by analogy. Socrates, of course, was notorious for his use of analogies to illustrate and argue for things. The drunken Alcibiades, in his speech of praise for Socrates in the *Symposium* (215a–22a), turns from the latter's exploits in battle to his personal character and its effects on others and concentrates on the "way he talks":

> If you're prepared to listen to Socrates' discussions, they seem absolutely ridiculous at first. This is because of the words and phrases he uses, which are like the rough skin of an insulting satyr. He talks about pack-asses, blacksmiths, shoemakers and tanners, and seems to be always using the same words to make the same points; and so anyone unused to him or

unintelligent would find his arguments ridiculous. But if you can open them up and see inside, you'll find they're the only ones that make any sense. You'll also find they're the most divine and contain the most images of virtue. They range over most—or rather, all—of the subjects that you must examine if you're going to become a good person. (221d–22a)

Somehow Socrates is able to find sufficient connection among "pack-asses, blacksmiths, shoemakers and tanners" to permit him to draw a general point from a consideration of the whole group, and this can happen only if the various cases share something fundamental. It is this essential similarity—for instance, that all are called "excellent" in virtue of their capacity to fulfill their proper functions well—that allows Socrates to infer the existence as a general quality of "excellence" or *aretê*.[96] Reasoning by analogy is a prerequisite for the process of induction, since the latter depends on being able to see in disparate cases a common quality or condition. This mode of reasoning was taken up by Aristotle and employed frequently in his politico-ethical works, as well as in his scientific and metaphysical speculations.

The Socratic conception of wisdom, including both the "human wisdom" of knowing one's own ignorance and the "superhuman wisdom" of knowing the essential natures of moral concepts, is a product of *logos* in many shades of its meaning. For Socrates, both kinds of wisdom come though talk, conversation, discourse, dialogue, argument, reasoning. *Logos* is the instrument of self-examination and self-knowledge. It is the means by which two lovers of wisdom can engage in the common quest. It is the method by which propositions are examined and the standard by which they are judged. It is the path by which genuine knowledge about moral ideas may be attained, if it can be attained at all. For Socrates, perhaps more fully than for any of his predecessors and certainly as fully as any of his contemporaries, the pursuit of wisdom is a social, cooperative, procreative, *communicative* enterprise.

The fifth century was extraordinarily important in the development of Greek thought and in the evolution of the Western intellectual tradition. For a variety of reasons—economic, political, linguistic, cultural, and intellectual—this century in Greece generally, and in Athens particularly, gave rise to ideas, problems, methods of inquiry, and terminologies that have affected Euro-American thought ever since. It is impossible, of course, to find uniformity in the views of Antiphon, Gorgias, Prodicus, Protagoras, Socrates, Thrasymachus, and other fifth-century teachers of moral philosophy, political wisdom, the speaker's art, and other humanistic subjects. Nonetheless, there are insights to be found in their teachings that make important contributions to emergent Greek conceptions of wisdom and its connections with speech and language.

Although we cannot draw a rigid distinction between the interests of Presocratic thinkers such as Pythagoras, Democritus, or Archelaus, on the one
hand, and those of Protagoras or Socrates, on the other, a shift in emphasis is
clearly discernible in the questions they asked and the problems they pursued.
Whereas the Presocratics as a whole were principally concerned with the origins and operations of the material world, participants in the fifth-century
"Enlightenment" were more interested in problems in the possibilities of human knowledge, most particularly of social/political/moral knowledge. While
Presocratic thinkers asked why the physical world works the way it does, the
"first humanists" in the Greek world asked practical questions: How should
one conduct oneself in life? What are the foundations of the laws and moral
principles by which human conduct should be governed and judged? What are
the processes by which disparate and conflicting political and moral opinions
can be reconciled, or by which the better opinions can be distinguished from
the worse? In their attempts to answer such questions, Socrates and his contemporaries articulated conceptions of knowledge, wisdom, speech, and the
connections among these that emphasized the limitations of human knowing
and the uncertainties that attend all human action.

Several important insights emerge concerning the nature, attainment, and
exercise of *sophia*. Perhaps most fundamental, both the Sophists and Socrates
conceived humans as dwelling not solely in the physical world but more
importantly in a socio-politico-ethical one. Protagoras's *Great Speech* provides
what may be the earliest Greek account of the idea that human beings live in
communities *by nature*, because they lack the size and strength to survive individually in a world full of wild beasts. The human, as Aristotle would put the
matter a century later, "is by nature a political animal" (*Pol.* 1253a)—designed
by nature to live in communities. The wisdom of fifth-century Athens, consequently, is a kind of practical, political knowledge that enables its possessor
to conduct him/herself skillfully and appropriately in the realm of communal
life.

There is considerable agreement among most of our fifth-century thinkers
about the components of this knowledge, even as there is diversity of opinion
regarding how it is acquired. For Protagoras, Gorgias, and Socrates most
conspicuously, wisdom and virtue are profoundly interconnected. To be wise
is to be capable of prudent action both "in one's personal affairs" and in "the
affairs of the city," and this capability is identified as the highest excellence
(*aretê*) of the human soul. It is *politikê aretê*—excellence in dealing with communal affairs—and *phronêsis*—excellence in practical judgment. This composite virtue—excellence in the "art of living"—enables its possessor both to give
sound advice to his/her fellow citizens about shared concerns and to choose
his/her own actions well. Moreover it resides in a character whose other virtues

include self-discipline, courage, and respect for whatever is held to be sacred in one's own community.

There are important differences among the Sophists, and between at least some of them and Socrates, regarding the sources and nature of the ideas in terms of which political and practical decisions ought to be made. Nonetheless, we can also see a widely shared belief in the importance of how we use language in our communal and personal endeavors. Ranging from Gorgias's ostensible denial that there are any objective, stable grounds on which moral decisions can be made, to Socrates' belief that there are enduring, transcendent moral concepts that must anchor our moral reasoning and judgment, the character of moral knowledge was highly contested. What is perhaps most intriguing about this contest, however, is the lesson it provides: what constitutes moral "truth" is always a vexed question, so uncertainty and ambiguity inhere in all moral choice and practical action.

What may be most significant in the teachings of Socrates and the Sophists is the idea that human beings live in a politico-moral world that is ultimately of their own construction, a construction rooted in their speech practices. Whether it is held that the "real" and the "true," the "just" and the "good" are matters of shifting opinion in the polis or of fixed Being in the natural order of the universe, how humans can conceive these ideas will always be shaped by language. It is no accident that figures as diverse as Protagoras, Prodicus, Hippias, Antiphon, and Socrates emphasized in their teachings the importance of using words properly. The logocentricity of Gorgias implies the same point: practical, political, and moral judgments that are arrived at through reasoning will necessarily turn on the meanings of the terms we use, because reason (*logos*) and words (*logoi*) are two aspects of the same thing. For Socrates no less than for Gorgias and Antiphon, the moral universe in which human beings must dwell is grounded in language and in the persuasive uses to which it is put. What distinguishes them is the origin of the meanings that moral terms invoke. Socrates held these meanings to exist in the nature of things (*physis*), and they are stable, absolute, and universal. For Gorgias, Protagoras, and Antiphon, they are matters of convention (*nomos*) and are transitory, mutable, and particular to the circumstances in which language is being used. Accordingly the *sophia* Socrates seeks lies in apprehending the "true" meanings of moral terms, while sophistical wisdom resides in the ability to use words so as to gain adherence to a particular set of meanings, by a particular audience, at a particular moment. In both cases the practice and acquisition of wisdom centers on speech, reasoning, and argument.

Especially implicated in the quest for wisdom, for both Sophists and Socrates, is the use of language to challenge existing opinions or beliefs about political and moral issues. They thus carry forward an impulse first disclosed in the teaching methods of the Presocratics. The use of eristic by the Sophists and of *elenchos* by Socrates echoes the Presocratics' emphasis on discussion and debate, argument and counterargument as means by which the mind can be prepared for wisdom. In the case of the Sophists, the use of eristic aims both at disabusing the interlocutor of the notion that his/her position could be demonstrated beyond challenge and at illustrating the fact that for every argument there is an equally plausible counterargument. Thus is the mind opened to the possibilities created by speech and to the *logosophia* of the wordsmith. For Socrates, the *elenchos* has two purposes: reducing to perplexity an interlocutor who claims to know the true meaning of a moral term; and testing moral propositions in order to determine the extent to which they withstand critical scrutiny and have a claim to validity. In the first case, by demonstrating one's own ignorance to oneself, refutative speech can open the mind to the possibility of knowing the true essences of moral ideas. In the second, with Socrates' departure from sophistical epistemologies, the *elenchos* is an instrument by which one can come to apprehend true moral ideas. Running through the teachings of both Sophists and Socrates is the spirit of competition, the public contest, *agôn*.

In these teachings we also see origins of the divisions and dichotomies that, for some, came to define the relationship between philosophy and rhetoric: knowledge vs. opinion; truth vs. deception; speculative reason vs. practical reason; dialectic vs. rhetoric; certainty vs. probability. While Isocrates rejected these distinctions, Plato sharpened them, and in Aristotle's writings they are codified, as we shall see.

The contributions of Socrates and the Sophists to Greek thinking about *sophia* center finally on the appropriate use of language and speech in the conduct of personal and communal life. These thinkers feature the role of *logos* in both the acquisition and the exercise of wisdom, just as several of their Presocratic predecessors had done. In the hands of these fifth-century "humanists," this role emphasizes the power of *logos* (speech and reasoning) in affecting opinion and in revealing the rational character of the moral universe, rather than the centrality of *Logos* (proportion, balance, and reciprocity) in the physical transformations of the natural world. In the generation that succeeded them, both emphases endure in the teachings of Isocrates and Plato, and they are finally integrated in the philosophic system of Aristotle.

FIVE

Civic Wisdom, Divine Wisdom

Isocrates, Plato, and Two Visions for the Athenian Citizen

Since human nature cannot attain knowledge that would enable us to know what we must say or do, . . . I think that the wise are those who have the ability to reach the best opinions most of the time, and philosophers are those who spend time acquiring such an intelligence as quickly as possible.

Isocrates, *Antidosis* 271

When [the soul] investigates itself, it passes into the realm of the pure and ever-lasting and immortal and changeless, and . . . when it is once independent and free from interference [by the body], consorts with it always and strays no longer, but remains in that realm of the absolute, constant and invariable. . . . And this condition of the soul we call wisdom.

Plato, *Phaedo* 79d

The decades from the birth of Isocrates in 436 B.C.E. to his death in 338 were among the most tumultuous in Athenian history. When Isocrates was born, Athens was at the pinnacle of its military, economic, and cultural power in the Aegean world. When Plato was born almost a decade later, the Peloponnesian War was already under way. At the time he died in 347, the Greek world was still embroiled in interpolis rivalries and military conflicts that continued to sap its energies and to distract from what may have been the greatest threat against Greek political and cultural autonomy: the Persian king's expansionist impulses. In the year of Isocrates' death, Athens and most other Greek states fell under the hegemony of Macedon's king Philip II, whose overriding ambition was to defeat the Persians once and for all.

During these years the three principal threads of Greek philosophical thought—the Sophists' emphasis on civic and practical excellence and on linguistic dexterity, Socrates' pursuit of moral universals, and the Presocratics' naturalistic investigations—found their fullest development and expression in the teachings of Isocrates, Plato, and Aristotle. In several important ways Isocrates carries forward the interests and outlook of the older Sophists, though he explicitly rejects their teachings in his own writings. Plato, who became Socrates' most illustrious and influential student, took his teacher's inquiries to what he believed were their logical conclusions. In Aristotle's writings, as we will see in the next chapter, we find an integration of Presocratic, sophistical, and Socratic thought in the first comprehensive philosophical system produced in the Western world. The writings of each of these thinkers express distinctive views of the relationship between wisdom and speech, philosophy and rhetoric. For Isocrates, philosophy and rhetoric merge into a single intellectual discipline aimed at educating the democratic statesman and at reforming the Athenian political culture. Plato, in contrast, draws a sharp line between them, identifying philosophy with the pursuit of immutable moral truths and subordinating a "true art" of rhetoric to this pursuit. Aristotle's response to these divergent conceptions will be to identify two realms of "reality" in which philosophy and rhetoric find their proper applications and to articulate two conceptions of wisdom to which each is linked. What follows presently is an illumination of the conceptions of wisdom and its relation to *logos* that emerge from the writings of Aristotle's two teachers, Isocrates and Plato.

The historical events through which these two men lived shaped their thinking and teaching. Before either of them reached the age of forty, Isocrates and Plato would witness the rupture of public morality in Athens, the rise of demagogues in civic life, acts of great brutality at the hands of the *dêmos*, the city's military defeat by the Spartans and their allies, the rule of a ruthless tyranny, a bloody civil war, the execution of Socrates by a restored democracy, and the reemergence of Athens as an aspiring imperial power. This was a traumatic period, not just for Athens as a whole but perhaps especially for youthful citizens such as Isocrates and Plato as they sought their places in Athenian life. Isocrates was some nine years older than Plato (and outlived him by the same number), but his formative years were spent enduring the same upheavals, brutalities, and uncertainties that affected his younger compatriot. However, whereas Plato left Athens for an extended period following the execution of Socrates in 399, Isocrates remained, earning a living by writing speeches for others to deliver in the law courts and by teaching the civic arts to aspiring Athenian leaders. His political outlook and philosophical interests were shaped to a greater degree than were Plato's by public affairs in Athens during the early fourth century. The ongoing strife between Athens and other Greek poleis, renewed Persian military threats, and the growing power of Philip encouraged Isocrates to participate actively in Athenian political discussions, albeit through his writings rather than as an orator.

Plato's response to the disruptions of the Peloponnesian War and its aftermath, and especially to the execution of his friend and teacher Socrates, was to shun public affairs, at least in Athens. Though his aristocratic birth entitled him to play a prominent role in civic life, Plato withdrew from Athenian politics altogether. Soon after the death of Socrates in 399, he left his native city and traveled, first to Megara and thence to Cyrene (in modern Libya), Egypt, Italy, and Sicily. In about 387 he returned to Athens and established his school at the Academy, where he taught and wrote for the remaining forty years of his life. There is no record of Plato having played an active role in Athenian political affairs during all these years, though he provided counsel to his friends in the Greek city of Syracuse.

The tumult and ferment of these decades help to explain the disparate careers and philosophies of these two men. Athens's progression from a second-tier polis at the beginning of the fifth century to an imperial power by its midpoint was accompanied by increased tensions with such cities as Thebes, Corinth, and Sparta (long the unrivaled military power in the Peloponnesos). This is the world in which Socrates spent his youth and early adulthood, in which Pericles exercised his military and political prowess, and in which Athenian artistic expression flourished. By the time the Parthenon was dedicated in 438, Athens's efforts at expanding its influence on the mainland and its increasingly high-handed treatment of its erstwhile "allies" in the Delian League had exacerbated old ill feelings toward the Athenians and created new animosities. In 431 these feelings erupted in a conflict that would dominate the Greek world for a generation and irretrievably transform Athens.[1]

It is beyond my present scope to describe this conflict in detail, but certain crucial events illuminate how the effects of the war and its aftermath may have shaped the philosophical and pedagogical views of Isocrates and Plato and perhaps explain why these views diverged as they did. The military and political details of the conflict are recounted by Thucydides up to the year 411 B.C.E., by Xenophon from that point through the death of Socrates and beyond, and in several modern accounts. Insofar as events in Athens during these three decades shaped the attitudes and interests of Isocrates and Plato during their adolescence and early adulthood, it was because of the social and moral consequences that flowed from them.

Dissension arose among the Athenians about the conduct of the war. Moreover tensions were exacerbated by the fact that the population of much of Attica withdrew for months at a time to within Athens's walls and thus had to endure overcrowding, poor sanitation, and ultimately a plague that killed nearly a third of the population, including Pericles.[2] These conditions led finally to a general disintegration of the social compact and thus to what Thucydides describes as "the beginnings of a state of unprecedented lawlessness":

Seeing how quick and abrupt were the changes of fortune which came to the rich who suddenly died and to those who had previously been penniless but now inherited their wealth, people now began openly to venture on acts of self-indulgence which before then they used to keep dark. Thus they resolved to spend their money quickly and to spend it on pleasure, since money and life alike seemed equally ephemeral. As for what is called honour, no one showed himself willing to abide by its laws, so doubtful was it whether one would survive to enjoy the name for it. . . . No fear of god or law or man had a restraining influence. As for the gods, it seemed to be the same thing whether one worshipped them or not, when one saw the good and the bad dying indiscriminately. As for offences against human law, no one expected to live long enough to be brought to trial and punished. (2.53, trans. Warner, in Thucydides 1972)

There ensued in Athens a cycle of cruelty and retribution culminating in a collapse of the customs, institutions, shared convictions, and social sanctions that are the foundations of a civilized existence: schoolboys slaughtered by hired troops, civilian populations murdered and enslaved, suppliants assaulted at altars, bodies left to rot on the battlefield.

The 420s saw a change in the character of Athenian government. Though no legal distinctions separated social classes, until the war the *dêmos* had felt most secure with political power in the hands of men from old, wealthy families, men such as Cimon and Pericles. In the aftermath of the plague (which took Pericles in 429), the governance of Athens fell to men whose fathers and grandfathers had recently made money in business. These "demagogues" or "leaders of the people" (*dêmagôgoi*), through both brash advocacy and conspicuous displays of public generosity, persuaded the assembly to pursue policies that ultimately cost Athens its empire. Thucydides describes in some detail the political careers of such figures as Cleon and Alcibiades, both of whom represent the tenor of Athenian leadership during the years of war.[3] The ruthlessness and arrogance of the Athenians during the remainder of the war are shown in their decisions regarding Mytilene (427 B.C.E.), Mende (423), Scione (421), and Melos (416/415) and in their conduct of the ill-fated expedition against Syracuse in Sicily (415–413).[4] As Thucydides portrays them, the Athenians fell prey to hubris—the belief that they were bound by neither the law of Zeus nor the law of nature. *Dikê* and *Logos*—justice and the principle of proportionate reciprocity—mandate that, in the words of Anaximander, "they [who violate this principle] pay penalty and retribution . . . for their injustice" (DK 12 A 9). In their conduct toward friends and adversaries alike, the Athenians appear to have invited their own downfall. As Munn writes, "The Athenians were acutely aware that the gods were implicated in their political community. . . . An underlying tenet of public piety was that the gods upheld a system of justice that transcended justice by human reckoning. . . . Although a wrongdoer might evade human justice, divine retribution would bring redress in the end" (2000, 120).

Owing both to overextended military resources and to growing civil strife at home, the last decade of the war, when Isocrates and Plato were young men, was principally one of instability and fear. Athens's former allies, the increasingly bitter subjects of her empire, started to plot insurrections with hopes of Spartan support (Thucydides 1972, 8.2). Within the city political conflict simmered until, in the late spring of 411, it boiled over as an oligarchic coup supplanted the democracy, if only briefly. A restored democracy continued its prosecution of the war until the final, decisive battle in 405 at Aegospotami in the Hellespont. In the spring of 404 B.C.E. the victorious Spartans installed in Athens a governing council of wealthy and powerful men (2.3.1–10). The Thirty Tyrants promised to restore the ancient laws of the city fathers (2.3.2) but instead presided over a lawless reign of terror, assassinating leaders of the democratic faction, confiscating the property of the wealthy (citizens and noncitizens alike), and intimidating would-be opponents into silence or exile (2.3.11–56).[5] When the exiled democrats were strong enough, they marched back against Athens, and a reconciliation was engineered. Thus the democratic rule of law was restored, and the Thirty, with the last of their followers, were banished to Eleusis (2.4.30–42). The Athenians agreed to the first recorded amnesty in history; grievances arising out of the civil strife were to be forgiven (2.4.43). So it was that peace returned to the city, harbor town, and countryside. It was, nonetheless, a troubled peace. Decades of war followed by months of fear under the Thirty had taken their toll on civility and the capacity for forgiveness (Svoboda 2002). In such an environment, it is perhaps not surprising that Socrates, who had made a career of challenging democratic politicians to explain and defend their claims to wisdom and knowledge, became a target of resentment and animosity. Moreover the distrust of radical democracy that was expressed in some of his conversations and his association with the likes of Critias (a leader of the Thirty) may have induced some of his fellow citizens to impute oligarchic sympathies to him (Stone 1989). However this may be, in 399 B.C.E. Socrates was indicted, tried, and executed.

The first half of the fourth century B.C.E. was, for the Greek world, as troublesome as the previous half-century had been—what Norlin terms a period of "extraordinary vicissitudes and disenchantments" (1972, 196). Continuing conflicts among such traditional adversaries as Athens (which by 378 had formed a second maritime league), Sparta, Thebes, and Corinth perpetuated the general instability that marked the Peloponnesian War. Moreover, as the century progressed, disputes between and within these poleis about how to respond to the increasingly hegemonic actions of Philip of Macedon sowed discord that threatened to fragment the social bonds on which the very ideal of the polis was based.[6] Eventually the growing disparity of wealth in Athens between the fortunate few and the many who worked for a living accelerated the breakdown of community ties, weakening the sense of shared interests that makes political agreement and concerted action possible. Thus, as Isocrates and Plato entered their primes, the Hellenic states and their own home city presented them with the same sorts of issues and challenges as had shaped their earliest experiences. They responded in very different ways. Both seem to have perceived the conduct and outcome of the war as reflecting an Athenian political culture that was intellectually and morally bankrupt. It was a city in which both *rhêtores* and the *dêmos* lacked the wisdom and temperance required for prudent governance. Each in its own way, the subsequent careers of these two men reflected their commitments to address these deficiencies in the political life of their city.

Plato departed Athens in his quest for a tyrant-in-waiting whom he could train in philosophy and equip for sound governance. He returned, his experiment a failure, to establish in 384 the philosophical institute that became known as the Academy, dedicated to pursuing the timeless, universal moral concepts that should guide both personal and collective action. In contrast, Isocrates, after earning money for a time as a professional speech writer, by 392 had established in Athens his own school of philosophy that centered on his conception of *paideia*—an educational culture founded on practical, political wisdom embodied in rhetorical excellence and devoted to the preparation of the citizen-statesman for participation in public deliberation and advocacy.

Against this background we can examine the views of Isocrates and Plato and discern their conceptions of wisdom and the means of its attainment. These two figures represent highly contrasting philosophical visions, both of which suffused Greek intellectual culture generally in the early fourth century. As Jaeger remarks, "Greek literature of the fourth century reflects a widespread struggle to determine the character of true paideia; and within it Isocrates, the chief representative of rhetoric, personifies the classical opposition to Plato and his school. From this point on, the rivalry of philosophy and rhetoric, each claiming to be the better form of culture, runs like a leitmotiv throughout the history of ancient civilization" (1944, 46).

Isocrates and Civic Wisdom

Isocrates appears to have been affected by the conflicts of the late fifth and early fourth centuries both personally and philosophically. The long Peloponnesian War was disastrous for him. He lost his inheritance and so was forced to begin earning a living as a speech writer for litigants in the courts.[7] Though he later repudiated this phase of his career, Isocrates appears to have been sufficiently successful in it to have opened his own rhetorical school in Athens in 392.[8] The aim of his educational program was to equip (male) Athenian citizens for advocating wise political decisions in the public arena—and thus to rectify the conditions that, in his judgment, contributed to the disastrous policy choices that culminated in Athens's defeat in the war.[9] "He lived," writes Jebb, "in times of which the deadly disease in public and social life was a narrow, dishonest and impudent selfishness; the spirit which animates his writings was in itself wholesome as a protest against this corrupt and abject cynicism" (1893, 42). In addition to his teaching, Isocrates participated in the fourth-century debates—albeit as a writer of political pamphlets (in the form of orations) rather than as a rhetor in the assembly—that shaped Athenian policy toward other Greek states and toward the Macedonians. A recurring theme in these political "speeches" was the need for Greek unity—that is, for the cessation of intra-Hellenic rivalries and conflicts—so that a united Greek world could confront what Isocrates viewed as the most serious threat to its autonomy and well-being: the Persian Empire. Thus the lesson Isocrates appears to have taken from the conflicts he witnessed during his life was that what Greeks needed most was internal harmony and the exercise of civic wisdom in determining public policy.

Isocrates was born just five years before the beginning of the Peloponnesian War. His father was a wealthy flute maker who provided his son with an excellent education (*Antidosis* 161). Indeed, Isocrates is said to have studied with Socrates and with such Sophists as Protagoras, Gorgias, and Prodicus, among others, as well as with Tisias, the Syracusan expert in the use of probability arguments.[10] Thus, as Benoit observes, "It appears that Isocrates had a powerful educational foundation upon which to construct his own rhetorical school" (1984, 110). In his writings and teachings we find clues to his conception of wisdom and of the political role of the rhetor, whose speech embodies the union of *sophia* and *logos* that was the aim of Isocrates' *paideia*.

Isocrates—"that Old Man Eloquent," as Milton dubbed him (tenth sonnet)— was one of the greatest teachers of rhetoric in antiquity, propounding a conception of the ideal citizen centering on a union of political wisdom and eloquence in both speech and writing. This conception, reflecting the influence of Protagoras and Gorgias, inspired such successors as Cicero, who calls him "the Master of all rhetoricians" (*De oratore* 2.94), and propagated a vision of liberal education that persists into our own time. Isocrates' teachings have been a subject of scholarly interest since Jebb's early study of the Attic orators (1893), with considerable attention having been paid to his educational program (*paideia*), his political and social thought, and his views concerning rhetoric.[11] Here I examine the conception of wisdom that emerges from his writings and its relationship to his ideas about the nature and functions of *logos*. What results is a vision of practical and political wisdom that draws on the lessons of history, ethical principles, and insights drawn from experience, providing a fund of knowledge that can be applied to practical needs, both personal and political. Most important, Isocrates' teachings reflect a profound belief in the values that defined Hellenic—and particularly Athenian—culture. Thus he professed a wisdom reflecting those values.

Despite his apparent repudiation of sophistical teachings in *Against the Sophists*, Isocrates can be regarded in many ways as the inheritor of their educational philosophy (T. Poulakos 1997, 24–25; 2004). Jaeger remarks that "Isocrates . . . was the post-war representative of the sophistic and rhetorical culture which had flourished in the Periclean period" (1944, 49). It appears that in at least two respects Isocrates was particularly influenced by Gorgias (Norlin 1972, 200; Jebb 1893, 5). His emphasis on the aesthetic aspects of oratory reflected Gorgias's well-known employment of a style that was "akin to poetry: rhythmical, ornate, and making its appeal not to the intellect alone but to the senses and imagination as well" (Norlin 1972, 197). The influence of Gorgias on Isocrates is shown partly in the latter's view that the language of oratory should be as aesthetically pleasing as that of poetry (*Antid.* 47). Still, as Norlin concludes, "Isocrates did not attempt the grand manner, and did, in fact, avoid the Gorgian excesses of style. He uses the Gorgian antitheses both of language and of thought with better effect and with more concealing artifice; and he employs alliteration and assonance with greater continence" (199). In characterizing "the sort of eloquence . . . which has occupied me and given me so great a reputation," Isocrates describes deliberative oratory—the type that deals "with affairs of state, and . . . [is] appropriate to be delivered at the Pan-Hellenic assemblies"—as "more akin to works composed in rhythm and set to music than to the speeches which are made in court. For they set forth facts in a style more imaginative and more ornate; they employ thoughts which are more lofty and more original, and, besides, they use throughout figures of speech in greater number and of more striking character" (*Antid.* 43–47). He goes on to observe that "all men take as much pleasure in listening to this kind of prose as in listening to poetry, and many desire to take lessons in it, believing that those who excel in this field are wiser (*sophôterous*) and better and of more use to the world than men who speak well in court" (47–48).

Like Gorgias in his speech at the Olympic Games (DK 82 A 1.4, B 7–9), Isocrates extolled the virtue of concord among Greek poleis and promoted the superiority of Hellenic culture, most conspicuously in his *Panegyricus* and *Panathenaicus*. Of his extant discourses, at least six can be classified as "political" insofar as they addressed civic themes and promoted specific policies. Norlin, in the general introduction to his translation of Isocrates' works,

categorizes the discourses as "forensic speeches," "hortatory" or ethical treatises, "encomia" or "epideictic" speeches, "educational essays," "political" treatises, and "letters." He observes that the *Panathenaicus*, which he classifies as
epideictic, could be placed "just as properly among his educational or his political works" (Isocrates 1928, xxxi). In his approach to both the nature and the
proper function of rhetoric, then, Isocrates appears to reflect the general views
of the older Sophists whose student he had been, particularly those of Gorgias.

The other great influence on Isocrates' intellectual and philosophical development appears to have been Socrates. In his closing conversation with
Phaedrus in Plato's dialogue of that name, Socrates speaks with warmth and
admiration of Isocrates, predicting for him success in both oratory and philosophy (278e–79b). The passage, as Norlin observes, suggests that there was at one
time a close relationship between the young Isocrates and his teacher. Moreover "the studied effort with which he echoes the striking features of Socrates'
defense in his . . . *Antidosis* . . . is evidence enough of the high regard" in which
he held the philosopher (1972, 202).[12] Jebb writes that "the companionship of
Socrates has left a broad mark upon his work, in his purpose of bringing his
'philosophy' to bear directly on the civic life" (1893, 4; also see Jaeger 1944,
301n18).

Isocrates might be said to have pursued both careers that Socrates prophe-
sied for him. As Jebb notes, although "want of nerve and weakness of voice . . .
kept Isocrates out of public life," he nonetheless wrote a number of political
essays or "orations" that were notable for their rhetorical artistry and stylistic
polish, as well as for the political counsel they expressed (1893, 5; also see
Jaeger 1944, 51). These essays dealt with contemporary political affairs and
served as vehicles by which Isocrates could counsel his fellow Athenians—and
his fellow Greeks generally—concerning particular matters of public policy.
For example, the *Plataicus* (373 B.C.E.) and the *Archidamus* (366) addressed,
respectively, Athenian policies toward Thebes and Spartan intentions toward
the newly established polis of Messene. Similarly the *Areopagiticus* (355 B.C.E.)
urges the Athenian Assembly to restore the powers of the ancient Council of
the Areopagus as being necessary to the welfare and safety of the city. *On the
Peace* (355 B.C.E.), as Norlin characterizes it, urges Athens to "throw away her
dream of empire, and recognize once and for all the right of each Hellenic
state to be free and independent."[13] In his most famous political essay, the *Panegyricus* (381 B.C.E.), Isocrates addresses the Greek world as a whole, arguing
that competing poleis must overcome their rivalries and internal conflicts and
unite under the leadership of Athens in a war against the Persians. Isocrates'
political activities reflected his commitments to the idea of Hellenic cultural
superiority and to a political philosophy predicated on the unity of the Greek

city-states, and his belief that the proper role of the orator in democratic governance is to advise the polis on matters of public policy and law.

These views are also disclosed in Isocrates' career as a philosopher. He often refers to his teachings as a *philosophia* (for example, *Antid.* 50, 181, 183) and to his students as *philosophian diatribontes*—those who are occupied with philosophy (for example, *Antid.* 41). Though not a "speculative seeker for truth" (Jebb 1893, 35)—as Socrates, Plato, and Aristotle were—Isocrates professed a *paideia*: a theory of culture, a course of study, a discipline, and a way of life.[14] It is in his work as a *paidagôgos* or educator that Isocrates' philosophy—and his *sophia*—are embodied. Isocrates' school was designed to equip young Athenian men to conduct their own affairs competently, to take part in the political debates and other processes of democratic governance, and to contribute to such liberal studies as rhetoric, philosophy, and history. The curriculum emphasized studies that "allow them to manage well their own homes and the city's commonwealth—for which one must work hard, engage in philosophy, and do everything necessary" (*Antid.* 285, trans. Too).[15] According to Jebb, "Isocrates was the most illustrious teacher of his day; he educated the best youths of his own city and of all Greece—distinguished, some as politicians, some as advocates, some as historians; and made his school the true image of Athens" (1893, 12).

An important focus of his curriculum was the art of speech. Isocrates' understanding of the speaker's *technê* and his conception of civic education have been the subjects of much study. He seems not to have used the term "rhetoric" (*rhêtorikê*) but instead writes of the "arts of speech" (*technai tous logous*, at *Ag. the Soph.* 19, *To Alex.* 4) of those who can exercise the "power of words" (*dynamis tôn logôn*, as at *Ag. the Soph.* 14) and of "the study of discourse" (*tên peri tous logous philosophian*, at *Panegyricus* 10). These *technai* were at the core of the *philosophia* he professed.[16] The training of the citizen-statesman-orator was a principal goal of his *paideia*. However, it was not mere technical competence in the speaker's art at which this education aimed. Rather, as Wagner observes, "its purpose is to make practical 'philosophers' of its students" (1922, 328). "Let a single man attain to wisdom (*phronêsis*)," Isocrates himself writes, "and all men will reap the benefit who are willing to share his insight" (*Panegyricus* 2; trans. Norlin). His educational program, accordingly, emphasized the development of the whole intelligence as a precondition for responsibly employing the powers of speech. The course of study at his school featured what may fairly be called the "liberal arts"—a study of such subjects as history, political philosophy, literature, grammar, and argument, all aimed at equipping the citizen for participation in political affairs and governance.[17] If it was practical and political wisdom at which Isocrates' *paideia* aimed, we can appreciate

his contributions to rhetorico-philosophical education most fully if we can
delineate the elements of this wisdom.

Isocrates emphasizes the preeminence of natural aptitude and the importance of his pupils becoming "versed and practiced in the use and application
of their art" (*Antid.* 187; trans. Norlin). He then notes the necessity of submitting to training (*paideuthênai*) and of mastering the subject-matter knowledge
proper to students' interests. Isocrates' conception of wisdom can be discerned
in the "training," the *paideia*, although his account of it is, for the most part,
tantalizingly vague. In describing his approach to tutelage in "the culture of
discourse (*ê tôn logon paideia*)," he begins by observing that human nature "is
composed of body and soul. No one would deny that of these two, the soul is
superior and more valuable, for its task is to deliberate about matters private
and public, while the body's is to serve the soul in carrying out its decisions"
(*Antid.* 180; trans. Too). Whereas training the body is the aim of "gymnastics,"
the discipline responsible for training the mind is "philosophy" (181). It is the
latter to which Isocrates' *paideia* is principally devoted, aiming to train the soul
to deliberate and decide well. Teachers of practical philosophy, he says, "impart
all the forms of discourse in which the mind expresses itself" (183; trans. Norlin), which might include "the genealogies of the demi-gods . . . , studies of the
poets . . . , histories of wars . . . , [and] dialogue (*antilogoi*)" (45–46), as well as
the particular subjects on which deliberation and decision may focus (187).
The practical utility of these studies lies in their ability, insofar as any science
can, to enable students to perceive the consequences that most often follow
from the various occasions when sound thinking must be applied (184–85).

Acknowledging that "no system of knowledge can possibly cover [all] these
occasions," Isocrates maintains that those who have studied practical and
political matters "will most often meet these occasions in the right way" (184).
In his most explicit account of wisdom and philosophy "properly perceived,"
Isocrates writes that "since it is not in the nature of man to attain a science
(*epistêmê*) by the possession of which we can know positively what we should
do or what we should say, in the next resort I hold that man to be wise who is
able by his powers (*dynamai*) of conjecture (*doxa*) to arrive generally at the best
course, and I hold that man to be a philosopher who occupies himself with the
studies from which he will most quickly gain that kind of insight (*phronêsis*)"
(*Antid.* 271).[18] Takis Poulakos remarks that "in the context of public deliberation, whether he uses *sophia* or *phronesis*, Isocrates is . . . suggesting the kind of
insight or judgment necessary for orators to deal with the uncertainties of
the deliberating situation. For any advocacy of action involves the future, and
the course of action endorsed as the best-case scenario is a mere guess until the
events unfolding in the future determine whether the action taken was . . . correct or incorrect and whether the guess . . . was lucky or unfortunate" (1997,

79). Commenting on Isocrates' use of *doxa* and *epistêmê* (*Antid.* 184) to contrast "theories" with "system of knowledge," Norlin writes that "the distinction usually drawn, in Plato for instance, between [these terms], the one 'opinion,' the other 'knowledge,' is not exactly that made by Isocrates. *Doxa* is here, not irresponsible opinion, but a working theory based on practical experience" (Isocrates 1929, 290n). At *Antidosis* 271 Norlin translates the same term as "conjecture," carrying forward the notion that a "theory" or rational account of an event permits one to speculate reasonably about future consequences that might flow from that event. In this respect, Isocrates' teaching anticipates the thinking of John Dewey (1922), Dewey and James Tufts (1932), and other pragmatists some twenty-three hundred years later who emphasized that the function of intelligence in determining conduct is to anticipate the consequences that would likely accrue to various possible courses of action (Schiappa 1999, 180–84).

Chief among Isocratean studies is history, for knowledge of the past is the best guide to what will result from the various courses of action about which we deliberate and from among which we must choose. "When deliberating," he advises, "make past events models for the future, for the unseen is most quickly comprehended from the seen" (*To Demonicus* 34; trans. Mirhady). Similarly at *To Nicocles* 35 he recommends that one "consider current events and their consequences for both private citizens and kings. If you recall the past, you will plan better for the future" (trans. Too). Proussis notes that "Isocrates was the first educator to introduce history as an academic discipline," and the importance of historical knowledge in addressing practical problems has been a recognized aspect of civic education ever since (1965, 68).

Isocrates proceeds—albeit hesitantly, because his views are "so far moved from other people's ideas" (*Antid.* 272; trans. Too)—to describe the sorts of lessons that enable a person to speak both eloquently and wisely. "In my view," he writes, "people improve and become worthier if they are interested in speaking well, have a passion for being able to persuade their audience, and also desire advantage (*pleonexia*)—not what foolish people think it is but that which truly has this power" (275). For Isocrates, then, wisdom turns not only on the ability to anticipate the probable consequences of various courses of action, but also on the power of discerning in any given set of circumstances—present or future—what will be "truly advantageous" to the state (*Nicocles* 2). This, in turn, is a matter of avoiding "topics that are unjust or insignificant or that deal with private arguments but [selecting instead] those public issues which are important and noble and promote human welfare" (*Antid.* 276). The capacity for seeing in any given case what will most fully conduce to the commonweal is cultivated, Isocrates tells us, by selecting "from all the [past] actions of men which bear upon his subject those examples which are the most illustrious and the most edifying; and, habituating himself to contemplate and appraise such examples, he will feel their influence not only in the preparation of a given discourse but in all the actions of his life. It follows, then, that the power to speak well and think right will reward the man who approaches the art of discourse with love of wisdom and love of honour" (277; trans. Norlin).[19]

In the *Panathenaicus* (30–32), Isocrates includes among the traits of "educated" persons (*pepaideumenos*) the ability to "manage well the daily affairs of their lives"; the power to "form an accurate judgment (*doxa*) about a situation (*kairos*) and in most cases . . . figure out (*stochazesthai*) what is the best course of action (*to sympheron*)"; behaving "appropriately and fairly toward people who are always with them, [enduring] the rudeness and unpleasantness of others calmly and easily, and [conducting] themselves as gently and modestly as possible toward those they come in contact with"; being "always in control of their pleasures and . . . not excessively overwhelmed by their troubles but [enduring] them with a stout heart and nature worthy of our common humanity"; and "most important," not being "corrupted by their good fortune, . . . not [abandoning] their true selves, or [becoming] arrogant." He concludes that those who "are wise and complete and possess all the virtues are those whose minds are well fitted not only for one of these areas of life but for all of them" (trans. Papillon).

For Isocrates, in sum, proper civic education aims at cultivating a wisdom that permits the individual to see where true advantage lies, both in personal affairs and in public policy; to foresee the probable outcomes of alternative courses of conduct, and thus to discern the truly expedient course; and to know both what must be said and when it must be said if one's fellow citizens are to be persuaded to pursue such conduct. This combination of practical sagacity and rhetorical skill is to be animated by a commitment to the common good and by an appetite for what is held to be honorable by one's fellow citizens. More particularly still, the *sophia* at the center of Isocrates' *paideia* equips a person to engage in intelligent speculation or conjecture about practical matters. Wisdom is nurtured in the soul through a study of politics (that is, through examination of great political discourses), ethics (primarily traditional Greek ethics, based on poetry and custom), and history (through examining the teachings of the poets and the works of Herodotus and Thucydides). Though Isocrates' immediate concern as an educator was to prepare Athenians for successful lives in the changing conditions of fourth-century Greece, his larger aim was the political and moral regeneration of Hellenic culture so that it might fulfill its leadership role in civilizing the world at large (Leff 2004, 236–37).

Central in Isocrates' conception of wisdom was his view of *logos*, encompassing the capacity to reason, the sense of rational speech and communication, and the power of judgment that enables a person to discern the truly honorable and beneficial when dealing with practical and civic affairs. For Isocrates, as Norlin observes, "*logos* is both the outward and the inward thought: it is not merely the form of expression, but reason, feeling, and imagination as well; it is that by which we persuade others and by which we persuade ourselves; it is that by which we direct public affairs and by which we set our own house in order; it is, in fine, that endowment of our human nature which raises us above mere animality and enables us to live the civilized life" (1972, 209).[20] Education in speech was no mere training in clever oratory, but a broad and rigorous cultural study covering almost all fields that form what has come to be termed "humanistic culture." It was the cultivation of expression, reason, feeling, and imagination, the training of the whole person so that one might live a genuinely cultured—that is, a Hellenic—life. Education in discourse ultimately focused on what was good, enduring, and universal in Greek culture, particularly as it was represented in Athens. In eloquent expression on political topics, says Isocrates, one can find the breadth of outlook, the nobleness of tone, the sense of justice, and the devotion to the general good that are the marks of wisdom. Thus it is first and foremost from *philêkoia*, "love of listening" (Haskins 2004, 70–71), and the study of great discourses from past ages that one can cultivate the inward outlook and sensibility that will express themselves outwardly in one's own *logoi*: "If you love learning, you will be very learned. . . . Apply your life's leisure time to a fondness for listening to discussion, for in this way you will easily learn what is discovered by others with difficulty" (*To Demonicus* 18; trans. Mirhady).

To this end Isocrates selected the most noble and serious subjects for his students to study, avoiding mythical and heroic topics and directing their attention to the themes on which he wrote in his own political and ethical "orations": the moral qualities of good citizens and leaders (in *To Demonicus, To Nicocles*), Greek unity (*On the Peace, Panegyricus*), and the traditional ideals of Hellenic culture (*Panathenaicus, Areopagiticus*). As Jebb comments, Isocrates' aim "is to enlarge the mental horizon of his pupils by exercising them on subjects wider and nobler than the concerns of any single city" (1893, 41). In describing the content of Isocrates' moral instruction, Proussis observes that "it concerned conduct toward the gods, parents, children, friends or enemies, society in general. . . . It asked many questions: Which are the really best things in life and how should one pursue them? What are the duties of the private citizen and the holder of public office? What is the power of example and culture?" (1965, 67–68). *Logos*—eloquent expression funded by the accumulated cultural wisdom of Greece—is both the repository of that wisdom and the instrument by which it is shared among citizens who comprise the polis.

The defining qualities of good oratory, says Isocrates (*Ag. the Soph.* 13), are "fitness for the occasion" (*kairos*), "propriety of style" (*prepon*), and "originality of treatment" (*kainôs echein metaschôsin*). The speech of the wise, accordingly, is guided by a due sense of timeliness and the fitting, reflecting the older Sophists' embrace of *kairos* and *prepon* in cultivating "word-wisdom" in their students. This sense is a product of reflection in deliberative situations, a matter of thinking before one speaks, and a particular awareness of the possibilities afforded by the circumstances for eloquent expression. It involves recognizing how well qualified one is to speak on a given subject and a responsiveness to the demands of the occasion. "Always when you are about to say anything," Isocrates writes in *To Demonicus* (41), "first weigh it in your mind; for with many the tongue outruns the thought. Let there be but two occasions for speech—when the subject is one which you thoroughly know and when it is one on which you are compelled to speak. On these occasions alone is speech better than silence; on all others, it is better to be silent than to speak" (trans. Norlin). The particular gift of the wise, he says elsewhere, is "to use the events [of the past] at an appropriate time, conceive fitting arguments about each of them, and set them out in good style" (*Panygyricus* 9; trans. Papillon). The quality of originality is emphasized in several places, as when Isocrates writes that "we must not avoid issues about which others have spoken before, but rather, we must try to speak better than they have" (8), and that we should "admire and honour . . . those who speak so wisely that no one else would be able to speak afterwards" (10).

Speech is also the instrument by which the individual citizen can interrogate and assess the competing *logoi* of the assembly. Describing Isocrates' *philosophia* as an art of criticism, Ober writes that he "invites his listeners/readers to embark upon his educational curriculum (*paideia*) . . . [presenting] a way of life and a mode of comprehension and expression (a *philosophia*) that will allow students to deal with the cacophony of critical speech. They will learn to counter and refute that which is slanderous or deleterious, embrace that which is meritorious, and avoid extremism of all sorts. Moreover Isocrates' *philosophia* holds out the promise of a political program (*politeia*) that will fulfill the needs and guarantee the just deserts of all decent persons, in the polis of Athens and in the broader realm of Hellas" (1998, 251). For Isocrates, then, *logos* is the embodiment of wisdom. Both in discoursing with fellow citizens and in private deliberations, one's words/thoughts manifest the practical insights gleaned from experience and the study of the past, express the ideals with which one has been enculturated, and evidence the sound judgment one brings to bear on practical matters.

Isocratean wisdom bespeaks a form of consciousness or mode of awareness that might be described as "civic" (Johnstone 2001b). A "civic consciousness" recognizes our fundamentally social, communal nature as human beings and the power of discourse to shape communal thought and action. The civilizing potency of *logos* rests on the fact that, in its best and most fully developed form, speech is funded by the noblest ideals that define a culture, and it functions to foster the communal identifications that are prerequisite to any form of cooperative action (Haskins 2004, 81–95). Accordingly the prudent employment of *logos* in the conduct of community affairs enacts our communal identity even as it fulfills our civic duty. Indeed, the essential act of citizenship in Isocrates' view is "performing" *logos*, and its most fundamental obligations are to participate in governance, to listen and respond to others, and to advocate for the commonweal above any personal or partisan interest.

Plato and the Quest for Divine Wisdom

Isocrates and Plato were not only peers and compatriots but professional rivals as well. They had much in common, even as they diverged in their thinking about how best to educate citizens for political life in Athens (Morgan 2004, 127–35). Both had schools in Athens in the early and mid-fourth century, and there were pronounced similarities between their pedagogical aims. "Like Plato," writes Konstan, "Isocrates had an ideal of political virtue that could be excogitated through systematic contemplation, albeit without the underpinning of metaphysics and mathematics that gives Plato's philosophy its special character. Like Plato, again, he believed that understanding is advanced by dialogue, when this is carried on in a proper spirit and away from the narrow interests and prejudices that are typical of public debate. Isocrates agreed with Plato finally that good government depends essentially on rule by a philosophically sophisticated elite" (2004, 121). At the same time, he differed from Plato "in his confidence that even a democracy like that of Athens might be reformed" (121). Whereas Isocrates responded to the political challenges confronting the Greek states by professing a form of practical wisdom rooted in the empirical facts of history and in the probabilities inherent in social experience, Plato sought the salvation of the polis in divinely inspired wisdom concerned with a transcendent, intellectual realm of metaphysical and moral certainty. Ontologically and epistemologically, Isocrates' views concerning wisdom and its connections with speech are akin to those of Gorgias and Protagoras, while Plato's philosophical thought owed much to the teachings of Socrates. Isocrates concentrated his *paideia* on preparing the citizen-statesman-orator for contributing practical sagacity and ennobling discourse to democratic debates about matters of law and policy; Plato's educational program aimed at producing philosophers who could rule the polis with the authority of a monarch (Morgan 2004; also see Atwill 1998, 122ff.). These contrasts help us understand the very different directions in which these two men were led by their experiences during the Peloponnesian War and its aftermath.[21] "Plato's response is to withdraw from political life," Morgan writes. "Isocrates too withdraws, but only far enough to give him space to model a different kind of audience and civic education" (2004, 151).

Plato was likely born during the fourth year of the war, in 427 B.C.E., in either Athens or Aegina, and he died at the age of eighty in 347.[22] His family claimed descent on his father's side from Codrus, supposedly the last king of Athens, and from Solon on his mother's side. Critias and Charmides, who became members of the notorious Thirty Tyrants in 404, were Plato's cousin and uncle, respectively, through his mother. "This has led many," Guthrie observes, "to conclude that family influence must have been responsible for instilling anti-democratic ideas into Plato from his earlier years" (1986a, 11), though Burnet vigorously denies this (1924, 209ff.). Field provides this account: "The rich and noble families which had been accepted in the Periclean regime and been proud to serve it, seem to have been driven in increasing numbers into the ranks of the extreme opponents of democracy by the financial oppression to which they were subjected to pay for the war policy of the democratic party. At any rate it is clear that during those susceptible years in which Plato was first coming to manhood those most near to him were becoming more and more hostile to the democracy and ready to go to any length to overthrow it" (1930, 5).

That the social turmoil of his first three decades was somewhat troubling to Plato might be inferred from his almost total omission of the war from his dialogues, which were set for the most part during the war years.[23] Even so, he was apparently not prevented by the war and its outcome, nor by the restoration of the democracy, from aspiring to take part in public life and in politics. "Once upon a time in my youth," Plato writes in the *Seventh Letter*,

> I cherished like many another the hope of entering upon a political career as soon as I came of age. It fell out, moreover, that political events took the following course. There were many who heaped abuse on the form of government then prevailing, and a revolution occurred. In this revolution, fifty-one men set themselves up as a government, eleven in the city, ten in the Piraeus, . . . and thirty came into power as supreme rulers of the whole state. Some of these happened to be relatives and acquaintances of mine, who accordingly invited me forthwith to join them, assuming my fitness for the task. No wonder that, young as I was, I cherished the belief that they would lead the city from an unjust life, as it were, to habits of justice and "manage it," as they put it, so that I was intensely interested to see what would come of it. Of course I saw in a short time that these men made the former government look in comparison like an age of gold. . . . [Then] came the fall of the Thirty and of their whole system of government. Once more, less hastily this time, . . . I was moved by the desire to take part in public life and in politics. To be sure, in those days too, full of disturbance

as they were, there were many things occurring to cause offense, nor is it surprising that in time of revolution men in some cases took undue revenge on their enemies. Yet for all that, the restored [democratic] exiles displayed great moderation.[24]

The execution of Socrates, however, induced Plato to turn away from active involvement in politics—especially Athenian politics—and to pursue his travels and his philosophical interests instead. "As it chanced," he continues in the *Letter*,

> some of those in control brought against this associate of mine, Socrates, . . . a most sacrilegious charge, which he least of all men deserved. They put him on trial for impiety and the people condemned and put to death the man who had refused to take part in the wicked arrest of one of their friends. . . . Now as I considered these matters, as well as the sort of men who were active in politics, and the laws and the customs, the more I examined them and the more I advanced in years, the harder it appeared to me to administer the government correctly. . . . The result was that I, who had at first been full of eagerness for a public career, as I gazed upon the whirlpool of public life and saw the incessant movement of shifting currents, at last felt dizzy, and, while I did not cease to consider means of improving this particular situation and indeed of reforming the whole constitution, yet, in regard to action, I kept waiting for favorable moments, and finally saw clearly in regard to all states now existing that without exception their system of government is bad. . . . Hence I was forced to say in praise of the correct philosophy that it affords a vantage point from which we can discern in all cases what is just for communities and for individuals. (325b–26b)

As he contemplated the loss of Socrates, the character of the men who then held political power in Athens, and the laws and customs generally, Plato could no longer see a place for himself in the governance of his home city. Accordingly he left Athens soon after Socrates' execution and traveled for some twelve years, staying first at Megara with other Socratics and then traveling to northern Africa before going to Italy and Sicily around 387.[25] After a visit of a few months, Plato returned to Athens and opened his philosophical school about a mile outside the city's walls—the school that became known as the "Academy." Here he taught for most of the remainder of his life, interrupted only by visits to Syracuse in 367–365 and again in 361–360 (Woodbridge 1957, 20–25; Guthrie 1986a, 26–31).

Plato's visits to Sicily—particularly the last two—afforded him opportunities to put his developing philosophical convictions to a test. In his disenchantment with Athenian politics, Plato had determined that "the human race will not see better days until either the stock of those who rightly and genuinely follow philosophy acquire political authority, or else the class who have political control be led by some dispensation of providence to become real philosophers" (*Seventh Letter* 326b). During his first visit in 387, Plato had initiated an abiding friendship with Dion, a well-born citizen of Syracuse. Through Dion, he had become acquainted with Dionysius I, then tyrant of the city. In 367, however, Dionysius died and was succeeded by his son, Dionysius II, Dion's nephew. Having considerable influence on the young ruler, and in the belief that sound philosophical training would equip him for his responsibilities as overlord of Syracuse's empire in Sicily and Italy, Dion arranged to have Plato invited for a second visit to oversee his education (*Sev. Let.* 327d–28a). Albeit with misgivings (328b), Plato (who was now about sixty) went again to Syracuse in hopes that "the world will . . . see the same man both philosopher and ruler of a great city" (328a). It was an unsuccessful enterprise owing to the intrigues that surrounded Dionysius and to his preoccupation with a war in which Syracuse was then engaged (338a). Therefore, in 365 Plato returned to Athens, accompanied by Dion, only to be recalled once more by Dionysius for his third and final visit in 361. "Never," writes Guthrie, "can a journey have been undertaken more unwillingly. . . . So the third act of the tragedy began" (1986a, 27).

Plato determined that Dionysius was unprepared for genuine philosophical study, due both to his own conceits and intemperance and to the difficulty of the task. "Those," Plato writes, "who are not genuine converts to philosophy, but have only a superficial tinge of doctrine—like the coat of tan that people get in the sun—as soon as they see how many subjects there are to study, how much hard work they involve, and how indispensable it is for the project to adopt a well ordered scheme of living, they decide that the plan is difficult if not impossible for them, and so they really do not prove capable of practicing philosophy. Some of them too persuade themselves that they are well enough informed already on the whole subject and have no need of further application. This test then proves to be the surest and safest in dealing with those who are self-indulgent and incapable of continued hard work" (*Sev. Let.* 340d–41a). In the end, Plato escaped Dionysius's enforced "hospitality" and returned to Athens for good, and his friend Dion was killed by agents of Dionysius during a thwarted attempt to overthrow the tyrant. The effect of this misadventure on Plato's own philosophical mission may have been to turn his attention from the realization of the ideal state to concentrate instead on the "state within us," the state of individual students' souls at the Academy.[26]

Owing both to the inspiration of Socrates' quest for fixed, universal moral concepts that could guide personal and communal action and to his disenchantment with Greek political life generally, Plato's search for wisdom emphasized a withdrawal from the realm of practical, political action and a rejection of the uncertainty and transience of sensory experience, in favor of a realm of pure thought and rationality. The philosophy he professed was rooted in his conviction that there is a way of Truth leading to apprehensions of the unchanging, universal, immaterial Ideas or Forms (*eidoi*), and that these Forms constitute the fundamental meanings of the terms we use to communicate with one another. Echoing Parmenides' thought, Plato envisioned a path to knowledge that rejects the evidence of the senses for the insights of a disembodied Reason. Platonic *sophia* lies precisely in these insights, acquired through a particular practice of *logos*. Plato's educational program aimed at inculcating this wisdom, and it was animated by his belief that those who possessed it would best be suited to direct the conduct of the polis (Atwill 1998, 129–33).

Plato's dialogues are generally grouped into three periods—early (*Apology, Crito, Laches, Lysis, Charmides, Euthyphro, Hippias Minor* and *Major, Protagoras, Gorgias,* and *Ion*); middle (*Meno, Phaedo, Republic, Symposium, Phaedrus, Euthydemus, Menexenus,* and *Cratylus*); and late (*Parmenides, Theaetetus, Sophist, Politicus, Timaeus, Critias, Philebus, Laws*).[27] His early dialogues aim principally at creating a portrait of Socrates as a teacher and thinker, and so it was to them that we turned in an effort at discovering a Socratic conception of *sophia*. Here we saw Socrates' method of inquiry represented in his interactions with various characters about such topics as friendship, virtue, justice, and piety, but no positive philosophical doctrines were advanced. These conversations typically ended in *aporia*, and from this it was inferred that the historical Socrates advanced no positive philosophical doctrines of his own. In the middle and later dialogues, however, we encounter (usually, though not always) in the character "Socrates" statements that can be taken as representations of Plato's own emerging thought. It is primarily in the latter two groups, therefore, that we should seek insight into his thoughts about wisdom and its attainment.

We must be cautious about attributing to Plato a generally coherent, systematic philosophy such as we will find for his student Aristotle. As Sallis remarks, "It is . . . questionable to propose to present, in whatever form, something called 'the philosophy of Plato.' Why? Because it is highly questionable whether there is any such thing as the philosophy of Plato—that is, whether philosophy as presented in the Platonic writings is such as can ever be appropriately spoken of in such a phrase" (1986, 1). Consequently an account of a Platonic *sophia* must draw on references across a variety of his writings, and we must seek whatever coherence there may be in his accounts.

Plato considers the idea of wisdom in many of his dialogues. In the *Greater Hippias* it is described as the most beautiful of all things (296a), while the *Phaedo* characterizes it as a "condition of the soul" in which one experiences a kind of communion with "the realm of the absolute, constant and invariable, through contact with beings of similar nature" (79d). In the *Laws* wisdom is described as a "concord" and "consonance" of the soul with what "judgment pronounces to be noble or good" (3.689a–d). According to the *Republic*, lovers of wisdom seek "true being" (480a), "reality and truth" (501d), "that which is eternal and unchanging" (484b). The *Phaedrus* describes wisdom in terms of apprehending universal, immutable truths that the human soul apprehends before birth and that remain imprinted there, though they are forgotten (247c–48e). In the *Symposium* we read that wisdom should govern the ordering of society generally (209a). In the *Meno* (88b), *Euthydemus* (281b, 282a), *Theaetetus* (145e), and elsewhere Plato uses *phronêsis* (practical wisdom or good sense) and *epistêmê* (knowledge) synonymously with *sophia*, suggesting that wisdom is a kind of knowledge that bears on the conduct of practical affairs. For Plato, then, true wisdom consists in a re-cognition of and a harmonizing of the soul with the most complete, most perfect of things: those timeless, fixed realities that exist in a realm of pure being and that should direct both individual conduct and the ordering of the polis.

For Plato, genuine wisdom lies in the soul's understanding of the essential natures—the "Forms" or "Ideas," the true meanings—of such concepts as the Good, Justice, Beauty, Love, Piety, and others invoked in the conduct of personal and communal life, "as they exist in the nature of things" (*Rep.* 501b). These essences, which transcend the senses and exist only in the mind (*Parm.* 132b, *Rep.* 509d, 537d), express the generalized nature of the experienced particulars we call by this or that name: "beauty itself" or "goodness itself" (*Parm.* 134c). The use of "essence" or "true nature" (*ousia*, literally "being") to describe the Forms of things can be seen, among other places, in the *Euthyphro* (5d, 11a) and the *Phaedo* (65d, 92d). Guthrie, in comparing Plato's conception of the Forms to Socrates' search for moral universals, writes that "Socrates' demands for universal definitions in the ethical sphere presupposed an unchangeable essence which could be the object of reason. Convinced by Socrates, Plato gave such realities the name 'Forms' (*ideai*) and said that sensible things were called after them because they owed their existence to 'sharing' in them" (1986b, 426). Thus, not only do moral qualities such as justice or goodness have their proper Forms or Essences, but so also do the various objects—trees, houses, chairs, and the like—that we encounter in our daily experience of the world.

Rogers contends that "Plato employs the terms *eidos* and *idea* with a wide variety of shades of meaning; but most frequently they stand for a class of objects or for the common nature which makes classes possible" (1935, 516n4).[28] Plato uses the term *eidos* and its cognate *idea* interchangeably (for example, *Rep.* 475e–76d). Both derive from the verb *eidô*, which means to "see." Accordingly the root meaning of the *eidos/idea* is "that which is seen, that which reveals itself to a seeing." "The reference of these words to a seeing, to something's showing itself to a seeing," writes Sallis, "is of utmost importance. If they are thoughtlessly translated as 'form' or 'idea' and regarded as meaning something like 'concept,' then the issue to which these words are addressed in the dialogues will simply be left untouched" (1986, 383). The transcendent realities the understanding of which constitutes Platonic wisdom are things that can be "seen" in the mind. They are disclosed in moments of "insight," in the soul's "vision" of an immaterial realm of pure thought.

Among the ideas that can be thus "seen," paramount is the form of the Good (*to agathon*), the *eidos* by which the others are subsumed or to which they direct the soul. Plato writes that "the greatest thing to learn is the idea of good by reference to which just things and all the rest become useful and beneficial. . . . Or do you think there is any profit in possessing everything except that which is good, or in understanding all things else apart from the good while understanding and knowing nothing that is fair and good?" (*Rep.* 505a–b).[29] The Good is "that . . . which every soul pursues and for its sake does all that it does, with an intuition of its reality," and its apprehension by the soul is what legitimizes any understanding of such other moral qualities as "the just" and "the honorable" (*Rep.* 505e–6a). "These [specific values]," writes Demos, "need to be validated by a study of ultimate principles, and this is the study of the Good as such" (1937, 245–46). It is equated with the Beautiful (for example, *Lysis* 216d, *Rep.* 452e, *Symp.* 201c) and is the object of the highest study (*Rep.* 504e). Moreover knowledge of the Good constitutes genuine human happiness (*Symp.* 204e).

Perhaps recognizing that the historical Socrates never claimed to have apprehended the Good directly, Plato has the Socrates of the *Republic* dismiss "for the time being" a search for the "nature of the good in itself"—that is, of its essence, its true meaning. Rather, Socrates proposes to describe "the offspring of the good" so that he and Glaucon, his interlocutor, might grasp its "likeness" (506d–e). He proceeds (508b–c) first to distinguish again between sensible and cognitive worlds, and then to compare the sun (as the source of illumination for the eyes in the sensible realm) to the Good (as the source of illumination for Reason in the realm of pure thought). Following these analogies, Socrates reasons that just as the light of the sun both reveals and nourishes the visible world, so does the "light" of the Good both reveal and sustain the forms of all other things, most especially including the moral standards of Justice and Virtue (508d–9c). The Good, then, functions architectonically to create and order the realm of the intelligible Forms. It is the "first principle" of that order (511d), the "self-authenticating principle and cause of all things . . . , [which] shows the intelligible world to be an ordered and organic whole" (Guthrie 1986a, 510).

Plato holds (*Rep.* 352e–53e) that the Good of any particular thing lies in the fulfillment of its proper function or purpose (*ergon*), thus endorsing the teleological outlook that runs through Socrates' teachings and is conspicuous in Aristotle's conceptions of wisdom and virtue. The human being's function in the rational order of the cosmos is to grasp and live harmoniously with the form of the Good, the originating principle of that order. This is the essence of wisdom, to understand and attune one's desires and actions to the ordering principle of the universe. Here we find echoes of Heraclitus and the Pythagoreans, who also linked wisdom and the "good life" to understanding and acting in harmony with the fixed principles that order the world.[30]

The fundamental nature of this principle—the true Form of the Good—is proportion, harmony, balance, symmetry. As Plato writes, "The qualities of measure and proportion (*logos*) invariably . . . constitute beauty and excellence" (*Phil.* 64e), for "the truth is akin to measure and proportion" (*Rep.* 486d). Here are reverberations of the Heraclitean *Logos*. Demos argues that, for Plato, "measure . . . is ranked as the highest in the list of perfections" (1937, 256) and that "Measure, and indeed the Good, are geometrical conceptions, mathematical ratios" (257). A central idea here is that the Good, and thus the rational principle that orders the cosmos, is to be understood in mathematical terms, as for the Pythagoreans. At the very least, the concept of *proportion* as a defining quality of Justice and the Good can be seen, writes Demos, as "like an algebraic formula, whose expression varies as the values given to the variables are different" (258).[31] *Sophia*, on this account, may be said to involve an intuitive grasp of the mathematical ratios or proportions that function as *kosmêtôr* (orderer, arranger) to the universe.

What follows is that wise action accords with these proportions. The "best life which the gods have set before mankind," Plato writes, consists in "learning the harmonies and revolutions of the universe" (*Tim.* 90d). The best life, that is to say, is lived in concord with the principle of proportion and balance that governs the cosmos and makes of it a unified, organic whole. Wisdom, then, is exercised in the soul's deliberations and choices concerning the conduct of life: "The soul has . . . a work which you couldn't accomplish with anything else in the world, as for example, management, rule, deliberation, and the like. . . . Of necessity, then, a bad soul will govern and manage things badly while the good soul will in all these things do well" (*Rep.* 353d–e). Knowledge of the Good—the principle of proportion according to which the world is organized—is what allows both individuals and states to deliberate well about practical matters and to manage their affairs wisely.

For Plato, knowledge of the Forms—and especially the Good—is fundamentally a product of self-knowledge and recollection, an apprehension of truths implanted in the *psychê* prior to birth. In the *Phaedrus*, Socrates recounts a myth describing the soul's nature in terms of a charioteer and two horses.[32] Before it is joined to a body, the individual soul (which is immortal) traverses the heavens with the gods, following them as they "pass to and fro, each doing his own work" (247a). Thus does the soul perceive absolute Reality, for "it is there [in the heavens] that true being dwells, without color or shape, that cannot be touched; reason alone, the soul's pilot, can behold it, and all true knowledge is knowledge thereof. . . . Wherefore when at last she [the soul] has beheld being she is well content, and contemplating truth she is nourished and prospers, until the heaven's revolution brings her back full circle" (247c–d). As the soul is borne through its revolutions around the realm of Being, it "discerns justice, its very self, and likewise temperance, and knowledge . . . , the veritable knowledge of being that veritably is" (247d–e). Similarly in the *Meno* (81c–d), we read that "the soul, since it is immortal and has been born many times, and has seen all things both here and in the other world, has learned everything that is. So we need not be surprised if it can recall the knowledge of virtue or anything else which . . . it once possessed. All nature is akin, and the soul has learned everything."[33] Since the human soul— specifically the thinking, reasoning part of the soul that "pilots" it—is imprinted before birth with the *Logos* that orders the cosmos, we can grasp the *Logos* because, in the end, it is the ordering principle of our own souls. We can glimpse the divine *archê* of the cosmos because our souls, in their deepest nature, are also divine. From Heraclitus and Pythagoras through Plato and thence to Aristotle, the identification of the soul's *logos* with the divine is a fundamental tenet of the wisdom-tradition. It is the ground of philosophical inquiry in both methodology—"rational" discourse governed by laws of logic, which themselves are rooted in the *Logos* that governs the cosmos—and content— concepts that are products of intellectual activity. In the end, much Greek philosophical inquiry is talking, writing, and thinking about thinking.

Plato's account of wisdom in the *Phaedrus* describes how the soul, when it is joined with flesh at birth, is pulled down from the heavenly realm by certain unruly passions and becomes "burdened with a load of forgetfulness" (248c). It thereby loses sight of the divine vision it once beheld. Knowledge of the true essences of things descends into the depths of the soul just as dreams recede from consciousness upon waking. Wisdom, then, requires a kind of "deep remembering," a recollection of the time before time when our souls beheld the unchanging truths of the cosmos. A person, Plato writes, "must needs understand the language of forms, passing from a plurality of perceptions to a unity gathered together by reasoning (*logismôi*)—and such understanding is a recollection (*anamnêsis*) of those things which our souls beheld aforetime as they journeyed with their god, looking down upon the things which now we suppose to be, and gazing up to that which truly is (*to on ontôs*)" (250b–c).

This process of recollection requires that one transcend, or at least master, one's physical being. The seeker for wisdom must "get rid of the body and contemplate things by themselves with the soul by itself" (*Phaedo* 66d–e), using the "unaided intellect, . . . cutting [oneself] off as much as possible from [one's] eyes and ears and virtually all the rest of [one's] body, as an impediment which by its presence prevents the soul from attaining to truth and clear thinking" (65e–66a). Here a disembodied *logos*—the soul's pilot—pursues wisdom by returning to its divine origin. In the *Republic* (514a–17b), with his allegory of the cave, Plato describes the coming of wisdom in terms of being released from the bonds of the senses, compelled to turn away from their "passing shadows," and then being "dragged by force" up a rough, steep path, out of the cave's darkness and into the light of being, where the true Forms reveal themselves to be "seen" by Reason's vision. Elsewhere the body is somewhat less problematic—indeed, it can play an important role in the quest. In the *Phaedrus*, as the myth unfolds, the soul is likened (246a–b, 253c–e) to a union among a charioteer (Reason, which steers the soul) and two winged horses (our bodily element), one representing the noble passions (such as the love of honor, temperance, and decency) and the other symbolizing such base appetites as wantonness, avarice, and gluttony (also see *Rep.* 4.439d–41a). The tendency of the noble steed is to respond to the presence of physical beauty by pulling the soul upward toward the heavens, where it may again dwell in the presence of divine truth. However, with most of us the erotic desire kindled by the perception of another's beauty leads the chariot to be pulled downward by the lure of physical pleasure and the appetite for sensual gratification (hence the body as "impediment" to wisdom). When such souls are led to "deeds of unrighteousness, . . . they [forget] the holy objects of their vision" because their intellectual sight has dimmed (250a). Only when the charioteer can break the willful "ignoble steed" are one's fleshly desires tamed and their energies harnessed with those of the noble passions. Working now in harmony and under the guidance of Reason, the passionate elements lift the soul to the heavens so that it may once again gaze upon pure being (254 a–e).

The lesson in these accounts is that in order to attain wisdom, one must subjugate one's carnal yearnings to the guidance of reason and free the soul from the realm of change and appearance. When it is thus liberated from physical sensation, the soul can seek the truths residing in its own deepest nature. "When the soul . . . investigates by itself," Plato writes, "it passes into the realm of the pure and everlasting and immortal and changeless, and being of a kindred nature, when it is once independent and free from interference, consorts with it always and strays no longer, but remains, in that realm of the absolute, constant and invariable, through contact with beings of a similar nature. And this condition of the soul we call wisdom" (*Phaedo* 79c–d).

The idea that true wisdom involves recovering or remembering (Plato's term is *anamnêsis*, literally "unforgetting") truths hidden deep within the soul is a central doctrine in Plato's mature dialogues (for example, *Meno* 8cff., 86b, 98a; *Phaedo* 72e, 75, 92; *Rep.* 621a), including most conspicuously the *Phaedrus* and the *Symposium*. The process of recollection culminates in an intuitive "seeing" of Truth, which "bursts upon" one in a "wondrous vision" of absolute Beauty and Goodness (*Symp.* 210e). Guthrie writes that "*Nous*, the highest intellectual faculty, is not the ability to reason things out to a conclusion: it is (for both Plato and Aristotle) what gives an intuitive and immediate grasp of reality, a direct contact between the mind and truth" (1986a, 253). When the soul has turned away from the distractions of the senses and appearances, toward the realm of pure reality, and after a "long period" of study and companionship with other wisdom-seekers, "suddenly, like a blaze kindled by a leaping spark, [wisdom] is generated in the soul and at once becomes self-sustaining" (*Sev. Let.* 341c–d).

In general, the soul's path to these moments of epiphany involves a laborious course of dialectical and discursive reasoning, beginning with the particulars of sensory experience and then concentrating one's inquiries on ever more abstract conceptions until one is led finally to the realm of pure intellection and the moment of *noêsis*—a direct perception of "what is." This is the process of dialectical investigation, which Plato learned from Socrates (*Rep.* 537d). Typically it begins with either a judgment ("That was a just action," "This is a beautiful scene," and so on) or a question ("Was that a just action?" or "Is it beautiful?"). Both openings invite a further question: "In virtue of what can an action be called 'just?'" or "By what standard of 'beauty' can something be adjudged 'beautiful?'" This, of course, initiates a consideration of what constitutes "the just" or "Justice," "the beautiful" or "Beauty"—the ideas owing to which a given action, thing, or event can be described appropriately in such terms. As we saw earlier, Socrates' inquiries appear to have been devoted to the investigation of such questions, though he seems not to have claimed such knowledge for himself. For his part, Plato appears more optimistic, and indeed, he ultimately advances his own answers.

A dialectical investigation of such terms proceeds, as we saw with Socrates, by considering a collection of concrete instances of a thing, action, or event that is called "just" or "beautiful" and then seeking what they have in common—a "gathering together" (an archaic meaning of *logos*) of specific cases and then an identification of the essential quality that permits them to be collected under one term (*Timaeus* 83c, *Phaedrus* 265d). Through a rigorous analysis of the logical implications of terms used to define a given concept, dialectic aims at constructing a conception that is free from self-contradiction or internal inconsistency. As Plato has Socrates explain the process in the *Republic*, the realm of the purely intelligible is "that which the reason itself lays hold of by the power of dialectic, treating its assumptions not as absolute beginnings but literally as hypotheses, underpinnings, footings, and springboards so to speak, to enable it to rise to that which requires no assumption and is the starting point of all, and after attaining to that again taking hold of the first dependencies from it, so to proceed downward to the conclusion, making no use whatever of any object of sense but only of pure ideas moving on through ideas to ideas and ending with ideas" (511b–c). The process employs the Socratic *elenchos*—the technique of statement and refutation that determines whether a stance on some question can be sustained in a logically coherent way. For Plato as for Socrates, then, the pursuit of wisdom involves considering the logical implications of the meanings of words (*logoi*) we use to describe our experience of or judgments about the world. The process seeks finally conceptions/definitions of such ideas as Justice, Beauty, Piety, Courage, or Love that can withstand reasoned challenge and thus that are free from self-contradiction. Guthrie observes that dialectic "aims directly at knowledge of beauty and goodness, for so seen, they reveal the underlying harmony, proportion and order of the cosmos" (1986a, 524–25; also see Sallis 1986, 439–43).

For Plato, there are two interrelated forces under whose influence a soul can be induced to turn away from the attractions of the sensory realm and to seek a true understanding of the Forms: Beauty and Love. These, indeed, identify the spirit of philosophical dialogue. The perception of beauty in the face or body of another awakens in the soul a shadowy recollection of "beauty in all its brightness," seen in the time before birth when "we beheld with our eyes that blessed vision . . . [and were] initiated into that mystery which is rightly accounted blessed beyond all others" (*Phaedrus* 250b). The apprehension of another's physical beauty stirs the soul, and one yearns for some sort of reunion with what was once possessed—perfect, divine Beauty. For a soul whose initiation into the mystery of beauty is long past, however, or who has been corrupted by corporeal existence, the perception of another's physical beauty may engender impulses toward physical union and procreation: "he looks upon [the beauty of the other] with no reverence, and surrendering to pleasure he essays to go after the fashion of a four-footed beast, and to beget offspring of the flesh, . . . consorting with wantonness" (250e). By contrast, "when one who is fresh from the mystery, and saw much of the vision, beholds a godlike face or bodily form that truly expresses beauty," the noble passions lead the soul to regard the other with "reverence as at the sight of a god" and to ascend toward the divine realm of pure beauty (251a).

The tension between the base and the noble passions is fundamental in Plato's conception of the soul and in his view of the path to wisdom. When these passions have been "bridled" and "broken," they become obedient to the commands of Reason and are made to work in harmony with the virtuous desires.[34] In this case, in the presence of another's beauty the soul seeks not physical but spiritual union with the other, for beholding the other's beauty with "reverence and awe," the soul is reminded of what it grasped before birth—the realm of divine truth. Significantly, in the beauty of the other one beholds one's own beauty, for the beloved "is as it were a mirror in which he beholds himself" (255d). When we perceive our deepest selves in the other, we are in fact glimpsing our shared link with the immortal world. In this moment of self-recognition, this flash of vision into the deepest core of our beings, we are open to true wisdom, to a reminder of the knowledge that resides in the depths of our souls. "And so," Plato concludes, "if the victory be won by the higher elements of mind guiding them into the ordered rule of the philosophical life, their days on earth will be blessed with happiness and concord, for the power of evil in the soul has been subjugated, and the power of goodness liberated; they have won self-mastery and inward peace" (256a–b; also see Sallis 1986, 149–75; Cross 1954).

The attainment of genuine wisdom—recollecting the eternal truths of the cosmos—requires that erotic impulses released in the soul by an encounter with beauty be channeled from a desire for physical union to some corresponding form of spiritual intercourse. The central ideas in this account are developed most fully in the *Symposium*, where the essential role of eros is linked with the activity of conversation. Particularly in the image of erotic love, the organizing metaphor of this dialogue, Plato directs our attention to those features of conversation that render it capable of leading two souls to insights that constitute genuine wisdom. The *Symposium* features a series of speeches given at a dinner party attended by Socrates and some of his friends. The diners decide that, instead of the normal after-dinner entertainment, the company should amuse themselves with talk and that this should take the form of a speech by each participant in praise of love (eros). The diners speak in their seating order, starting with Phaedrus. Socrates is the last to speak. Though the views of the other speakers are ultimately rejected by Socrates when he tenders his own account, each contributes some element to the comprehensive view he articulates, one presumably embraced by Plato. Illuminating the metaphorical force of these elements discloses Plato's idea of "erotic" conversation as the method by which wisdom can be acquired.[35]

The conception of Eros is constructed progressively throughout the dialogue. The first two speakers, Phaedrus and Pausanias, confine themselves to a treatment of erotic love in its most obvious sense. Phaedrus advances the view that "Love is the oldest and most glorious of the gods, the great giver of all goodness and happiness (*aretês kai eudaimonias*) to men, alike to the living and the dead" (180b). Two points in this speech recur throughout the discussion of

Eros and find their way into Plato's ultimate vision: Love's divinity and its beneficence toward humankind. The latter idea is a constant in the speeches that precede Socrates' address, and it is a central feature of the conception of love he articulates. Eros is a positive force in human life; it improves rather than weakens the human condition. The former feature—Love's divinity—undergoes some modification by the time Socrates considers it. Nonetheless, Eros retains its association with the divine, and this connection is central to its characterization. In Plato's lifetime the philosophical idea of divinity emphasized the qualities of immortality or timelessness, omnipresence, and omnipotence. Thus, when Plato identifies Eros as *theos*, he likely intends that it is an eternal, pervasive force in the world (as it was for Empedocles) and that it affects all people in one way or another. This idea is carried forward in the remaining speeches.

Pausanias introduces a distinction between nobler and baser kinds of love that further prepares the way for Socrates. He identifies Love with Aphrodite, distinguishing between two incarnations of the goddess (180d): "One, the elder, sprung from no mother's womb but from Heaven (*Ouranos*), whence we call her Heavenly, while the younger, daughter of Zeus and Dione, we call Popular (*Pandemos*), the earthly Aphrodite." Pausanias concludes, following this, that there are two kinds of love, one "heavenly" and divine and the other "earthly" and human. The latter "governs the passions of the vulgar" (*phauloi*); "their desires are of the body rather than of the soul" (181b). Heavenly love, on the other hand, is "innocent of any hint of lewdness." Two points in from this speech later find their way into Socrates' account of the matter and are keys to understanding Plato's conception of "heavenly eros" as the impetus toward wisdom. One is the distinction between physical and spiritual love, which marks two paths along which one may be led by the force of erotic desire. The other occurs later in the speech, after Pausanias further contrasts base and noble lovers. He considers the question of whether it is possible to submit to any form of servitude to one's beloved "without offending our ideas of decency." He concludes that "just as the lover's willing and complete subjection to his beloved is neither abject nor culpable, so there is one other form of voluntary submission that shall be blameless—a submission which is made for the sake of virtue (*aretê*) . . . [and] increase of wisdom (*sophia*)" (184c). The noble lover, then, may yield without shame to the beloved in the pursuit of moral excellence and divine knowledge. This linkage of heavenly eros with the pursuit of virtue and wisdom and the idea of yielding to the beloved in this pursuit become for Plato defining features of the best sort of erotic relationship between two people. It will be taken up again by Socrates.

Eryximachus speaks next. Though much of his speech is unremarkable, it makes its contribution. Love, he says, "besides attracting the souls of men to human beauty, . . . has many other objects and many other subjects, and . . . his influence may be traced both in the brute and the vegetable creations, and I think I may say in every form of existence—so great, so wonderful, and so all-embracing is the power of Love in every activity, whether sacred or profane" (186a–b). This treatment of love as a cosmic principle operating through the whole of existence marks a significant transition from the narrow sense of physical desire expressed by Phaedrus, and to that extent it prepares for the ascent from physical to intellectual love foreshadowed by Pausanias and developed fully by Socrates.

This idea of Eros as a cosmic force, timeless and universal, permeating human experience as a kind of profound yearning or desire, is deepened by Aristophanes. Using as his vehicle a fantastic myth about the first humans and their rebellion against the gods, Aristophanes portrays love as a longing for the restoration of a lost state of unity with another person, and he describes happiness as the result of this restoration. Speaking of "the whole human race, women no less than men," he says that happiness "is to be found in the consummation of our love, and in the healing of our dissevered nature by finding each his proper mate" (193c). Though the tale he tells describes this longing in physical terms—as the desire for reunification with one's bodily "missing half"—the imagery suggests that love is experienced as an excruciatingly intense yearning for restoration to a primordial condition of unity, a return to one's original nature. On the level of physical love, this yearning is a desire for bodily consubstantiality. Aristophanes speaks of being "fused" (*syntêxai*) and "welded" (*symphysêsai*) into "the closest possible union" (192d–e). This yearning, however, can also be understood on a spiritual level as a longing for the fusion of soul with soul, as a hunger for a psychic union in which one's personal identity is either expanded to include the other or is lost altogether in a new consciousness of selfhood (Levy 1979). In his account of the nature of love, Erich Fromm writes that "the deepest need of man . . . is the need to overcome his separateness, to leave the prison of his aloneness" (1956, 9). The full answer to the problem of separateness, he concludes, lies in "the achievement of interpersonal union, of fusion with another person, in *love*. This desire for interpersonal fusion is the most powerful striving in man, it is the most fundamental passion, it is the force which keeps the human race together, the clan, the family, society" (18; also see 52–57). This conception is invited by the imagery Aristophanes introduces.

Agathon's account also contributes to the evolving idea of Love. Through a consideration of the youth and delicacy of Love, Agathon demonstrates the beauty and goodness of the god. Indeed, he is the most beautiful and best of the gods (195a–97d), and it is he who governs us in both drinking and speaking (197e). While Agathon is prone to exaggeration and ornamentation, he nonetheless introduces ideas that emerge as central in Socrates' account. Here, for the first time, we observe the linkage of Eros with both beauty and goodness and see him as manifesting his power in speech.

We turn now to the discourse of Socrates, the fullest expression of Plato's conception of Eros and its role in the quest for wisdom. The discussion between Agathon and Socrates that follows the former's speech is a dialectical exchange establishing certain preliminary conclusions about Eros (199c–201c). The positions are that Love is a relative name like Father or Mother, in that it implies the existence of an object loved; that Love desires its object; that desire is not felt for what is already possessed; and that since the object of Love, on Agathon's own showing, is beauty, Love cannot be beautiful—nor, by the same reasoning, can it be good. The point is thus settled that Love is the consciousness of a desire for a good not yet acquired or possessed. A hint of this has already been given in Aristophanes' fantasy, but it is now laid down on rational grounds as a foundation for the exposition of Plato's own view.

Against the backdrop constructed by the other speakers, Socrates develops a view of Eros that includes—albeit in modified forms—some of their ideas and that has important implications for the practice of conversation as a path to wisdom. Eros retains its linkage with the divine, the beautiful and the good, the improvement of humankind, wisdom and virtue, intense yearning for communion with another and for restoration of a lost unity, and our noble and base natures. Socrates articulates a conception of Eros in which conversation between two people is the method of spiritual procreation and where wisdom and virtue—the progeny of such a union—reside in the recovery of knowledge acquired when the soul was in its primordial state but forgotten. Particularly interesting is what we can infer about the character of such conversation by illuminating the sexual metaphor in terms of which it is described.

Using the narrative device of a secondhand account provided by "a Mantinean woman, called Diotima" (201d), Socrates explains that Eros, while not divine himself, bridges the gap between divine and human worlds. He is a "very powerful spirit (*daimôn megas*), and spirits . . . are halfway between god and man." Eros, then, is one of many messengers or envoys "that ply between heaven and earth, flying upward with our worship and our prayers, and descending with the heavenly answers and commandments, and since they are between the two estates they weld both sides together and merge them into one great whole" (202e–3a).[36] Eros gives humans access to the divine realm— that is, the realm of timeless, universal, absolute truths that order the cosmos. As an intermediate being (and being an intermediary), he provides means by which humans can come to understand divine things, including Beauty (*to kalon*), the Good (*to agathos*), and Resourcefulness (*euporia*) (204b–e).

All of the previously considered elements—the connections with the divine, with beauty and the good, with wisdom and virtue; the longing or yearning for what one lacks; the physical and spiritual expressions of this yearning—come together in Diotima's extended exposition of the sexual metaphor: Love as the procreative impulse. The function (*ergon*) of love, she says, "is begetting in beauty both bodily and spiritually. . . . All humans are pregnant . . . both in body and in soul; on reaching a certain age our nature urges us to procreation, never in ugliness but only in beauty. . . . It is a divine affair, this engendering and bringing to birth, an immortal element in the creature that is mortal . . . because this is something ever-existent and immortal in our mortal life" (206c–7a, my translation).[37] Diotima distinguishes, as Pausanias had, between "those whose procreative impulse is physical" and those whose creative desire is "of the soul" (208e–9a)—a key dichotomy in understanding Plato's view of the quest for wisdom. In both cases, Diotima tells Socrates (as he recounts the conversation in his speech), the longing for immortality—and thus for participation in the divine—is the motive force at work. Men whose impulse is physical, she says, "turn to women as the object of their love, and raise a family, in the blessed hope that by doing so they will keep their memory green 'through time and through eternity.' But those whose procreancy is of the spirit rather than of the flesh . . . conceive and bear the things of the spirit. And what are they? you ask. Wisdom (*phronêsis*) and all the other virtues" (209a–b).

For Plato, the ideal love—Heavenly Eros—is a yearning in the human soul for a procreative fusion with another soul, a union to be undertaken and carried out in beauty and to issue in the intuitive apprehension by both of absolute Beauty, Justice, Virtue, and all the other divine essences manifested in the particulars of human experience. Especially important here, turning again to the imagery of "begetting" and pregnancy, is that these apprehensions or insights already dwell, if only embryonically, in the individual soul. We are, each of us, already pregnant with the seeds of wisdom, and it is the act of loving in and through beauty that brings these to fruition so they can show forth in speech as our spiritual offspring. The form of action through which gestation is achieved is also *talk*. Through their conversation with one another, two lovers can pro-create within themselves and one another the insights and understandings that constitute the highest form of human knowledge.

The "ascent passage" in Diotima's speech (210a–11c) illuminates this interpretation of Plato's views. Without detailing this well-known section of the dialogue, we can readily see that it traces the movement of the spiritual lover from the first encounter with physical beauty in another individual, "so that his passion may give life to noble discourse" (*logos kalos*), through a realization that all physical beauty is one and the same no matter in whom it is perceived.

This leads to an acknowledgment that "the beauties of the body are as nothing to the beauties of the soul, so that wherever he meets with spiritual loveliness, even in the husk of an unlovely body, he will find it beautiful enough to fall in love with and to cherish—and beautiful enough to quicken in his heart a longing for such discourse as tends toward the building of a noble nature" (210b–c).[38] It is precisely such discourse that delivers the two lovers of those "soul-children" with which they have been pregnant. As Guthrie observes, "a man pregnant in *his own* soul, when he converses with a fair youth, brings forth what he has long been pregnant with, and the two cherish it together" (1986a, 390). If we are always already pregnant, then both lover and beloved will bring forth their insights and "cherish [them] together."

From the apprehension of spiritual beauty, the lover proceeds to contemplate the "beauty of laws and institutions," thence to the branches of knowledge (*epistêmai*), and thence to the final epiphany, the moment of deepest insight, when "there bursts upon him that wondrous vision which is the very soul of the beauty he has toiled so long for" (*Symp.* 210e). Cornford notes that "Eros now becomes the philosophic impulse to grasp abstract truth and to discover that kind of beauty which the geometer finds in a theorem and the astronomer in the harmonious order of the heavenly bodies. By now we have lost sight of individual objects and the temporal images of beauty, and we have entered the intelligible world. . . . The Beautiful . . . is revealed to intuition 'suddenly.' The language here recalls the culminating revelation of the Eleusinian mysteries—the disclosure of sacred symbols or figures of the divinities in a sudden blaze of light" (1967, 77). Beauty is seen as "an everlasting loveliness which neither comes nor goes, which neither flowers nor fades, for such beauty is the same on every hand, the same then as now, here as there, this way as that way, the same to every worshiper as it is to every other. Nor will his vision of the beautiful take the form of a face, or of hands, or of anything that is of the flesh. It will be neither words, nor knowledge, nor a something that exists in something else, such as a living creature, or the earth, or the heavens, or anything that is—but subsisting of itself and by itself in an eternal oneness, while every lovely thing partakes of it in such sort that, however much the parts may wax and wane, it will be neither more nor less, but still the same inviolable whole" (211a–b).

This vision, Diotima concludes, reveals the kind of life that is "ever worth the living"—in the contemplation of "the very soul of beauty" (211d). In the moment of aesthetic rapture, one's soul is in a state of wonder and worshipfulness, and in this state it can "see" into the deepest nature of Beauty. As two interlocutors are drawn ever deeper into their own souls through the process of opening themselves to one another, they come ever closer to the divine reality at the center of their beings. The flash of insight, the moment of epiphany, occurs when the mind seizes and is seized by the vision of the forms of the Beautiful and the Good.

What might we take from Plato's account that illuminates the process of remembrance by which true wisdom is acquired? Clearly the role of beauty and of the aesthetic experience is central. When we encounter and are taken by beauty—in a face, a figure, a piece of music, a landscape, a sunset, a thought, a mind—we yield to it, open ourselves to it, and it fills us with wonder and awe. It also awakens a deep longing to be taken into it, to be possessed by it, to become one with it. We long to lose ourselves in the face, the music, the sunset, the thought, the mind, and to dwell where there is only the Beautiful. The *erotic* is our response to the beautiful, whatever form it takes. When two people respond to beauty in each other, the willingness to yield and the longing for communion create opportunities for insight and deep remembering. The experience of wonder—*thauma*—opens a portal through which we may glimpse the eternal. If the truths of the cosmos are imprinted on the souls of all humans before birth, then when two lovers engage in "spiritual intercourse," as they ascend toward the "wondrous vision" of the very essence of Beauty and the Good, they are also descending toward the depths of their own souls. Indeed, in the end ascent and descent arrive at the same place: the cosmic *Psychê* that is the life force of the universe. One cannot help but be reminded here of Heraclitus's saying that "the way up and down is one and the same" (DK 60). To be brought to a state of wonder by an encounter with beauty is to be opened to the highest/deepest truths of the universe.

Significantly each stage of this ascent/descent involves the use of "beautiful speech," "words that will tend to the betterment of the young," and "the most fruitful discourse." It is *logos*, talk, conversation, through which the procreative quest for wisdom occurs. Indeed, later in the evening, when he arrives at the dinner party drunken and loquacious, Alcibiades describes Socrates' unique personality and his erotic effect on others (most notably on Alcibiades himself) in terms of his *logoi*—his "talk," "arguments," and "speeches" (221d–22a). The character of this talk is *erotic*, and the centrality of the sexual metaphor invites us to see in philosophical conversation a form of eros and to consider its nature. Hints about this nature can be gleaned from what Plato has said here and from what he said about the true lover in the *Phaedrus*, but it is the image of spiritual "love-making" that is particularly suggestive.

While the truths to be remembered and grasped are universal, the erotic process by which they are apprehended is particular and personal. It centers on the uniqueness of the souls who seek fusion with one another through dialogue. The art of erotic conversation must be attentive to the psychological particularities of the interlocutors. One must engage the other in terms of her/his own *êthos*, her/his "customary dwelling place." In this respect, philosophical conversation is always situated, embodied, local, immediate, particular. Spiritual intercourse requires an acute sensitivity and responsiveness to the particularity and uniqueness of the other even as it carries us toward the realm of the universal.

The qualities of philosophical conversation that make the universal accessible to the individual provide prescriptions for philosophically productive conversation—guidelines for "fruitful discourse." What is "love" in conversation? Fromm writes, "Love is not primarily a relationship to a specific person; it is an *attitude*, an *orientation* of *character* which determines the relatedness of a person to the world as a whole, not toward one 'object' of love" (1956, 46). The lover's soul is characterized first and foremost by a willingness to submit to Beauty, a readiness to yield to the experience of fusion and transcendence, an openness to the journey on which eros leads one. Nussbaum writes that "knowledge of love is not a state or function of the solitary person at all, but a complex way of being, feeling, and interacting with another person. To know one's own love is to trust it, to allow oneself to be exposed. It is, above all, to trust the other person" (1990, 274). In the context of Plato's conception, love is trusting oneself to Being and to the divinity and goodness of Beauty. When Plato writes of love that it involves a willingness to submit, yield, or surrender to the governance of Beauty, he implies that it involves a readiness to be vulnerable, to risk oneself. Henry Johnstone Jr., proposing ethical principles for practicing "rhetoric *con amore*," describes the "duty of Openness" as a willingness to *listen* to the other, and so as a willingness to be affected by the other (1981, 310).[39] Lao Tzu casts this idea in gendered terms to emphasize the quality of *receptiveness:* "Can you hold the door of your tent wide to the firmament? . . . Can you, mating with heaven, serve as the female part?" (1944, 30). Consider the sexual metaphor here: "Can you, mating with heaven, serve as the female part?" Can you receive the gifts of the cosmos, taking them into yourself? Can you surrender yourself to the flashes of light, so that within your soul might be kindled the sparks of knowledge that will grow, with proper care, into the vision that is wisdom?

A corollary to the idea of *openness to the other* is *openness with the other,* willingness to share one's own soul with the other. If eros manifests itself as a longing for fusion with another soul, then one must both be open to the other's soul and be ready to reveal one's own deepest insights and sentiments in the course of conversation. Fromm writes, "In the most general way, the active character of love can be described by stating that love is primarily a *giving*, not receiving" (1956, 22). What does one person give to another? "He gives of himself, of the most precious he has, he gives of his life . . . of that which is alive in him; he gives . . . of his joy, of his interest, of his understanding, of his knowledge, of his humor, of his sadness—all expressions and manifestations of that which is alive in him. . . . He does not give in order to receive; giving is in itself exquisite joy. But in giving he cannot help bringing something to life in the other person, and this which is brought to life reflects back to him; in truly giving, he cannot help receiving that which is given back to him" (24–25).[40] Thus is eros projective as well as receptive. Just as the erotic consciousness involves a willingness to yield to the other's spiritual beauty and to be kindled by it, so does it include the impulse to reach out to the other, to disclose oneself to him/her. Moreover the impulse to give oneself to the other is neither an effort to "impress" the other nor to guide or direct her/him toward some self-conceived "truth." Rather, it is a willingness to extend oneself toward the other, to put oneself out for the sake of the other, and to be guided by the other's movement toward her/his own sense of the ultimately Real. Even in extending one's self into the psychic space of the other, one is simultaneously expressing oneself authentically and adjusting or adapting oneself to the other.

Related to both conceptions of openness is the idea of *responsibility*—that is, willingness to be *for the other* rather than for oneself. This attitude of responsibility is essentially a commitment to the spiritual well-being of the other and a willingness to subordinate oneself to her/him in the ascent/descent toward wisdom. In the *Theaetetus*, Plato has Socrates describe himself as *maieutikos*, skilled in the art of midwifery, by which art he assists others in giving birth to the wisdom with which they are pregnant (150c–d). Truly to love the other is to devote oneself to bringing *the other*'s soul-children to full term and to assist in "delivering" them in moments of profound insight. One embarks on the path of spiritual eros, accordingly, not for the sake of one's own ascent toward wisdom but for the sake of the other's. Love is a fundamentally selfless act. Moreover it is not *one's own* understanding that the other is to grasp; rather, one must commit oneself to helping the other discover *within her/himself* the fundamental realities of the cosmos. Plato is sometimes viewed as portraying a conception of philosophical conversation in which a person who already possesses wisdom (the lover) leads another (the beloved) to "truths" and "realities" that the lover has grasped even before the encounter begins. The interpretation offered here is predicated on the assumption that even if the lover has glimpsed for her/himself some of the universal truths that dwell in the depths of her/his soul, they cannot be "implanted" in the soul of the other. One cannot impregnate the beloved with one's wisdom. Rather, one loves the other in order to assist her/him in giving birth to her/his *own* insights, her/his *own* incarnations of the truths that dwell within us all. As we talk and listen to one another, we lead each other and ourselves to the threshold of the inexpressible, to the core of existence. It is up to each of us to be enlightened in our own way by this, and thereby to behold the one Truth to which our different souls have led us.

As important as the spirit of erotic dialogue is the content. What should we talk about if we would move toward the most profound truths humans can grasp? Two ideas are central here. One is that philosophical conversation must concentrate on the moral ideas that manifest themselves in the particulars of daily life. Plato's dialogues are full of examples, as we find Socrates conversing with this or that person about the nature of such concepts as justice (*Gorgias, Republic*), friendship (*Lysis*), love (*Phaedrus, Symposium*), piety (*Euthyphro*), beauty (*Hippias Major*), virtue (*Protagoras, Republic*), the good (*Theaetetus, Republic, Philebus*), and evil (*Crito*). Since such terms invoke general concepts, their use in ordinary conversation presents us with opportunities for inquiring into the concepts they invoke, and thus for embarking on a shared quest for true knowledge of the Forms in which they participate. The second key idea concerning the content of philosophical converse is that it must be *authentic, honest, truthful*. When we engage and are engaged by others in meaningful conversation about moral ideas, we are to express our own true thoughts, uncertainties, insights, and puzzlement (*aporia*). Love is not a game—we do not play with words and ideas when we encounter another in a spirit of eros. Rather, love demands that we "bare our souls" to one another, that we share our deepest senses of the things we talk about.

As to the forms of spiritual intercourse, two features suggest themselves from Plato's portrayals. One is the centrality of *questions*. In order to assist the other in delivering whatever deep insights might be gestating within, one must continually invite him/her to go beyond/deeper than where s/he is at the present moment. What *do* you mean by "piety"? What *do* you think "beauty" is? As we explore our own thoughts and feelings about these matters, as we work to articulate this or that sense of the idea under consideration, we must continue to ask questions, to probe, to penetrate into the deeper layers of our souls, to create openings for us and our interlocutors to go more deeply still. The Platonic/Socratic eros is largely an art of asking the right question at the right time as the conversation unfolds, even as one submits to the questioning of the other. As we reciprocate questioning and disclosure, the conversation leads us ever deeper into ourselves and each other until, perhaps, we recognize ourselves in one another, we encounter some fundamental truth to which we both have been led, and we confirm our shared insight even as we grasp that "existence is beyond the power of words to describe."

The other feature of wisdom-generating conversation emphasizes the role of analogical or metaphorical expression. Again drawing on Plato's Socrates as the exemplar of erotic dialogue, we can see as a recurring element in his talk the employment of analogies as a way of stimulating deep thinking about abstract concepts. Certainly the vivid analogies in the *Phaedrus* and *Symposium* are instrumental in allowing conversational partners to envision the deeper natures of the subjects under consideration. Most conspicuously the analogy between physical and spiritual procreation creates important opportunities for understanding how conversation can yield profound insight into the nature of things. Metaphorical thinking, supplemented by analytical modes, seems to be fundamental to the generation of insight (Verene 1981, 117). The metaphor liberates the mind from literal, analytical ways of thinking about the world, creating an opportunity for synthesis that induces insight. The metaphorical vision creates an opening in experience, a portal on the unities underlying the flow of events.

If the use of *logos* to obtain wisdom falls under the domain of dialectic for Plato, the employment of speech to lead others toward just and prudent conduct is the purview of rhetoric. A "true art" of rhetoric, accordingly, is concerned with the construction of "good speech" that can "influence men's souls" in matters both public and private. Plato's conception of rhetoric has been examined by numerous scholars, many of whom conclude that a "true art" must be some form or application of dialectic. Brownstein (1965), Quimby (1974), and Guthrie (1986a, 414–17), for example, maintain that "the genuine art of rhetoric . . . [is] dialectic" (Guthrie, 414). Black argues that "Plato conceived a true art of rhetoric to be a consolidation of dialectic with psychogogia . . . to influence men's souls. . . . Dialectic was Plato's general scientific method; rhetoric is a special psychological application of it" (1958, 369). Hikins concludes that rhetoric serves to "*evoke* knowledge already within the self [of the hearer] via the process of *anamnêsis*" (1981, 170), identifying Plato's conception of "rhetorical knowing" as "*rhetorical dialectic*" (172). In contrast, Kauffman argues that for Plato, "rhetoric depends on a prior dialectic to discover its language and its content," concluding that it "embraces falsehood, deception, and censorship" in order to "guarantee doctrinal conformity and social control" (1982, 353–54). For my part, I have concluded that for Plato, dialectic and rhetoric have distinct functions, but I agree with Hikins's conclusion that while words "do not *themselves* impart knowledge," they may "help the soul (mind) in *its* generation of knowledge via the process of recollection" (174).

What is good speech? In the *Phaedrus* (258d–78e) Plato has Socrates take up this question. In describing those who speak not "beautifully (*mê kalôs*)" but "shamefully and badly (*aischrôs te kai kakôs*)" (258d), Socrates uses the word *kalôs* to describe "good speech." Good speech, in the first instance, is spoken (or written) in accord with the beautiful.[41] It is speech that reveals or discloses Beauty (*to kalon*) as it appears "in the midst of the visible to which man is attached in his embodied condition" (Sallis 1986, 163). Indeed, it is speech "which is appropriate to the condition of man, which consists in his having access to being only through the shining of the beautiful and the recollection which that shining is capable of provoking [in the hearer]. Beautiful speech

must be [that] which contributes to the shining forth of the beautiful to provoke a genuinely human re-enactment of the divine banquet" (164)—that is,
of the soul's converse with the gods before birth.

In order for a person's speech to be "fine" or "beautiful," it must proceed
from "a knowledge in the mind of the speaker of the truth about his subject"
(*Phaedrus* 259e). A speaker must know the *ousia* ("being," 237c) of a subject in
order to persuade others toward right action regarding that subject. In the
assembly this means, first and foremost, that a speaker must know what the
Good is in order to advocate what will be beneficial for the community, while
in a law court the speaker must grasp the essence of true Justice in order to
advocate what is just in particular cases. "When a master of oratory," Socrates
asks Phaedrus (260c–d), "who is ignorant of good and evil, employs his powers of persuasion on a community as ignorant as himself . . . by extolling evil
as being really good, and when by studying the beliefs of the masses he per-
suades them to do evil instead of good, what kind of crop do you think his oratory is likely to reap from the seed thus sown?" Phaedrus replies, "A pretty
poor one." It is precisely Gorgias's and his followers' inability to articulate a
coherent and defensible conception of "right" and "wrong" that leads Socrates
to describe (their) rhetoric as being a mere "knack acquired from experience"
rather than as a true *technê* or art (*Gorg.* 447a–62c). This view of rhetoric is
portrayed vividly in Plato's *Laws* (937d–38a):

> Life abounds in good things, but most of those good things are infested
> by polluting and defiling parasites. Justice, for example, is undeniably a
> boon to mankind; it has humanized the whole of life. And if justice is such
> a blessing, how can advocacy be other than a blessing too? Well, both
> blessings are brought into ill repute by a vice which cloaks itself under the
> specious name of an art. It begins by professing that there is a device for
> managing one's legal business—in fact that it is itself a device for managing
> such business of one's own and assisting another to manage his—and that
> this device will ensure victory equally whether the conduct at issue in the
> case . . . has been rightful or not. And it then adds that this art itself and the
> eloquence it teaches are to be had as a gift by anyone who will make a gift
> in money in return. Now this device—[whether] art or mere artless empiri-
> cal knack—must not, if we can help it, strike root in our society.

While the targets of this attack may well have been certain of Plato's contemporaries, it is not difficult to discern some pointed references to the *sophia*
claimed by such predecessors as Protagoras and Gorgias.

A speaker practicing a true art of rhetoric, then, must be a philosopher first
(*Phaedrus* 261a), for only after having acquired true *sophia* through dialectical
training and philosophic conversation with fellow lovers of wisdom is one

competent to persuade those who have not yet attained this level of knowledge. In this, Plato stands in direct contrast to the Sophists, of course, for whom the "truth" and "knowledge" that humans can acquire are *products* of persuasive discourse rather than preconditions for its appropriate practice, and for whom *sophia* resides partly in the effective use of language to create plausible accounts of things instead of in the apprehension of absolute, objective truths of which the objects of sensation are mere shadows or reflections.

On Plato's conception, then, wise rhetorical discourse follows from the dialectical/erotic process through which wisdom is acquired; it does not produce wisdom itself. Still, as Hikins argues, it may be that "the *art* of rhetoric moves the soul to *reflection*" (1981, 174) and that "causing the individual to *reflect* [leads him/her to] discover the truth from *within*" (176). This is a speculative conclusion, because there is no direct textual evidence in Plato's writings to support it, but insofar as true definitions mimic the true Forms, they may very well provoke hearers to look more deeply into themselves and to recover their forgotten knowledge of these Forms. In his account of why Plato wrote dialogues, Hyland remarks that "like the best works of art, these imitations may lead the beholder to the reality itself. The image of philosophy which is presented in the dialogues may lead us to *be* philosophers. Thus . . . the dialogues function both as imitations of and as invitations to philosophy" (1968, 43). So it may be with "beautiful speech." The "true art" of rhetoric is not dialectic, but insofar as it reflects or imitates the Form of the beautiful, it can invite hearers to turn away from the shadows in the cave and toward the brightness of the Good.

Plato seems not to have been especially optimistic about the prospects that a philosophical practitioner of rhetoric would be well received by those who continue to dwell in the cave. After having been freed from the fetters of sensation and having perceived things in their true natures, if the philosopher "should go down again and take his old place" in the cave (516e), he would "provoke laughter," and those still dwelling below would say of him that his vision had been ruined. Moreover, "if it were possible to lay hands on and to kill the man who tried to release them and lead them up, would they not kill him?" (517a). This seems a clear reference to the fate of Socrates at the hands of the Athenians, whom he had spent a lifetime trying to convince of their own ignorance and of the need to seek out the true meanings of the terms they used in the everyday business of the city. Thus, while a philosophically grounded art of rhetoric might be possible in an ideal world, it was perhaps "as far from the possibilities of mankind as his Republic was from Athens" (Hunt 1920, 42).[42]

At the outset of this chapter I suggested that in the writings of Isocrates, Plato, and Aristotle we find the most mature and comprehensive articulations of several motifs we can discern in the written Greek wisdom-tradition. One theme—prominent in Homer's *Odyssey*, in Hesiod's *Theogony* and *Works and Days*, in the moral teachings associated with Pythagoras and Democritus, in the practical doctrines of the Sophists, and in the moral teachings of Socrates—concerns practical matters, the formation of moral character, and the exercise of a sort of wisdom that allows us to conduct our own affairs competently as well as to provide wise counsel in civic debates and decisions. This conception of wisdom sometimes links practical sagacity with a knowledge of divine Justice (as with Hesiod and Socrates) and the immortal harmonies and principles that order the universe (as with Pythagoras). Plato is a clear advocate of this conception. Sometimes, however, there is no such linkage of moral wisdom with the divine. Instead, practical intelligence involves understanding human nature and the use of speech to affect people's beliefs and actions (as with such Sophists as Gorgias and Protagoras). Isocrates is in many respects the representative of this impulse.

A second theme in this tradition, also originating in the mythopoetic vision of divine wisdom, emphasizes the importance of understanding the universal, unchanging laws or principles that direct the unfolding of the natural world. Even as the conception of "the divine" was altered by the Presocratics, the idea persists that the highest wisdom involves apprehending the eternal *archai* of the physical world. This idea is clearly discernible in the thinking of Anaximander and Heraclitus, in Parmenides and Empedocles, and in Anaxagoras. As he adopts a Parmenidean rejection of "appearance" in favor of "true existence," Plato represents this quest for the eternal, the immutable, the absolute. Like Heraclitus and Parmenides, he distrusts the evidence of the senses; but like the more empirically minded among his forebears, he embraces the idea that beyond the flow of perceptions there is a fixed and enduring realm of Being that can be apprehended by the human intellect. Thus does he bring this theme to bear on questions of ontology and epistemology.

Plato's conception of *Sophia* shares with that of Isocrates a wide-ranging set of intimate connections to the practice of *logos*, even as their views of the nature of wisdom are diametrically opposed. In the development of Greek thought about wisdom, these two thinkers represent two distinct threads in the tradition. Plato has carried to a kind of culmination not only Socrates' search for fixed, absolute, universal ideas that can ground our practical decisions in the world, but also the Presocratics' quest for an indwelling, timeless cosmic principle of proportion, balance, and harmony in accordance with which all things come to pass. Isocrates, in contrast, carries forward the Sophists' emphasis on the world of sensory perception and contingency, of probability and uncertainty, of empirically based practical reasoning. Even with this divergence in views, however, an important feature in the thinking of both is the importance of beauty and the aesthetic dimensions of language in acquiring and speaking with wisdom.

Emerging from the teachings of Plato and Isocrates is a conflict between speculative and practical inquiry that has been codified in the antagonisms between "philosophy" and "rhetoric" that persist to this day. Despite the fact that both depicted their doctrines as "philosophy," Plato's appropriation of the term to denote speculation and theory, and the relegation of "rhetoric" to practical affairs, succeeded in delegitimizing Isocrates' use of it to describe the arts of citizenship and statecraft on which his pedagogy was based. Nonetheless, central in the quest for wisdom—speculative and moral, theoretical and practical—are the variegated operations of *logos*. Reasoned inference, argument and debate, a sense of proportion, and linguistic dexterity are for both Isocrates and Plato instruments of philosophical inquiry and manifestations of one's sagacity. It remained for Aristotle, Plato's most illustrious student, to find a way of reconciling the contradictions between these two perspectives and of integrating them into a single, unified philosophical system.

SIX

Speculative Wisdom, Practical Wisdom

Aristotle and the Culmination of Hellenic Thought

So if the intellect is divine compared with man, the life of the intellect must be divine compared with the life of a human being. . . . We ought, so far as in us lies, to put on immortality, and do all that we can to live in conformity with the highest that is in us. . . .

But such a life will be too high for human attainment; for any man who lives it will do so not as a human being but in virtue of something divine within him. . . . Life in conformity with [moral] virtue will be happy in a secondary degree, because activities in accordance with it are human.

Aristotle, *Nichomachean Ethics* 10.7–8

If Thales can justly be called the father of Greek philosophy, Aristotle was his most fecund descendant. In his hands (and mind) the philosophic impulse initiated by Thales and nurtured by other Presocratic thinkers, challenged and redirected by the Sophists and Socrates, honed and extended by Plato, and applied by Isocrates attained its fullest expression in the classical era. His philosophizing, indeed, represents the culmination of the Hellenic intellectual tradition, a masterful synthesis of the various lines of inquiry that preceded him. Building on the naturalistic inquiries of the Presocratics and the Atomists, he wrote treatises (or left extensive lecture notes) on cosmology, metaphysics, physics, chemistry, and zoology. From the teachings of the Sophists he took up problems in psychology (including dreams and their meanings), ethics, politics, and the uses of language in its rhetorical and poetical applications, as well as epistemological matters. Similarly his interests in questions of knowledge, logic, and reasoning echo those of the Sophists and Socrates, even as his metaphysical investigations draw on and depart from the writings of thinkers ranging from Parmenides and Empedocles to Plato. In all, he authored some thirty-two philosophical works that have come down to us wholly or in part, as well as an unknown number now lost, and a poem that survives.[1] He was the first Greek thinker to provide comprehensive, systematic theoretical accounts of many arts and sciences now recognized as informing the academic disciplines that define the modern university. My aim here is to discern in his writings how he conceived wisdom, its attainment, and its expression. In particular, his conceptions of "speculative wisdom" (*sophia*) and "practical wisdom" (*phronêsis*), and their relationships to the language arts involved in scientific and practical reasoning, give rise to his views concerning the natures and functions of dialectic and rhetoric.

Though his name is closely associated with Athens, Aristotle was not a native Athenian.[2] He was born in 384 B.C.E. in Stagira, in what is now northern Greece. When he was born, this region was part of the dominion of the kings of Macedon. His father, Nicomachus, became friend and personal physician to the Macedonian king Amyntas II. Both he and Aristotle's mother, Phaestis, claimed descent from Asclepius, son of Apollo and god of healing. This suggests that both came from a long line of physicians, who were the principal representatives of empirical inquiry among the Greeks. These facts might also have affected the methods and directions of Aristotle's future studies. Moreover both his parents were of Ionian origin. Bearing in mind that the tendency of Ionian thought was toward scientific investigation of nature and its physical elements and living types, we may speculate that Aristotle's upbringing impelled him toward the preoccupation with nature that marks so much of his own thinking. Additionally his father, as a physician, was practiced in the art of dissection (which Aristotle afterward pursued) and was probably versed in the writings of the Hippocratic school, with their close observations of the symptoms of diseases, their records of particular cases, and their prescriptions for remedies and treatments. All this may have helped to kindle Aristotle's interest in biology, which he began to study around 345 and on which he wrote and lectured after 335.

Aristotle was orphaned early in his life, and his upbringing and childhood education were supervised by his guardian Proxenus, apparently a native of the Anatolian city of Atarneus, with which Aristotle became well acquainted later in his life. In 367, at the age of seventeen, Aristotle went to Athens. Though its political power in the early fourth century was not as all-encompassing as during the Periclean era, by the time Aristotle arrived in Athens the city had already formed a second confederacy by means of which it again controlled the Aegean. It was the recognized cultural center of Greece—the home of Greek drama, of the Attic dialect that was becoming common to all educated Greeks, and of at least two institutes of higher learning (Plato's Academy and Isocrates' school of politics) that attracted students from throughout the Greek world. Though this stage of his education is most often associated with the Academy, Haskins notes that, according to ancient biographies, "Aristotle probably received a well-rounded 'liberal education' from the school of Isocrates before joining Plato's Academy" (2004, 1). Chroust proposes that, due to his early study at Isocrates' school, Aristotle's "first literary effort was concerned with rhetoric, and . . . at a relatively early stage of his 'academic career,' he was considered fully qualified to take issue with Isocrates' particular brand of rhetoric and, hence, was entrusted with offering in the Academy a full-fledged independent 'course of lectures' on rhetoric" (1973, 102; also see Guthrie 1990, 24n1). In any event, he remained at the Academy until Plato's death.

Aristotle's time at the Academy was an important formative influence on his interests and on the development of his own philosophy. Though Plato was often absent in Syracuse during the first ten years of Aristotle's studies, the young pupil was influenced by the master's thought through reading the dialogues, evident in the numerous references to them in his surviving works (as well as in some that have been lost).[3] In any event, Aristotle spent some twenty years studying in Athens, meeting regularly with some of the most eminent thinkers of the time. There he engaged in dialectical discussion, taught, and wrote. It was during his time there, presumably, that his interest in metaphysics, political theory and ethics, psychology, epistemology, and logic was added to the scientific curiosity he had inherited from his parents.

Upon Plato's death in 347, Aristotle left the Academy and Athens and, with his fellow student Xenocrates, moved to the city of Atarneus on the northwestern coast of Asia Minor. There he organized a small Academic circle, got married, and became a father. It was there that his friendship with the local tyrant Hermias (whose niece he married) may have intensified Aristotle's interest in political philosophy and ethics. In any case, Hermias was sufficiently receptive to the efforts of this "little colony of Platonists," as Guthrie describes them, to "modify considerably the usual administration of a petty tyranny. . . . As Didymus succinctly expresses it (probably quoting Hermippus): 'He deliberately turned his tyranny into a milder form of government, and thus added to his domain all the surrounding territory as far as Assos; wherefore he was greatly pleased with the said philosophers, and allotted to them the city of Assos'" (1990, 28).[4] Here they spent their time doing philosophy.

Aristotle spent almost three years in Assos and in 345 moved across the narrow strait to the island of Lesbos, where he took up residence in the main town, Mytilene. Here he studied marine biology and became acquainted with the native scholar Theophrastus, who was to become Aristotle's most famous disciple and his successor as head of his school in Athens. In 343 B.C.E. Philip of Macedon, the son of Amyntas II, summoned Aristotle to Pella. For some six years (342–336) he served as tutor to Philip's son Alexander, starting when the future king was a boy of thirteen. Little is known about the content of his instruction or about its later influence on Alexander. It is pleasing to believe the story that when Alexander embarked on his conquest of the Persian Empire, he arranged to have biological specimens shipped back to his old teacher.[5]

About 335 Aristotle returned to Athens and founded a school of his own, at the Lyceum (the gymnasium in the precinct of Apollo Lykeios), which he directed from 335 until 323. Here, with a coterie of advanced students, he lectured and wrote on the entire range of human knowledge at the time: logic, metaphysics, theology/cosmology, history, politics, ethics, rhetoric, drama and poetry, psychology, anatomy, biology, zoology, botany, astronomy, meteorology, physics, and chemistry. Teaching as he strolled, perhaps, with his students through the covered walkways (*peripetoi*) that surrounded the gymnasium, Aristotle entered upon the most productive period of his life, writing most of the scientific and philosophical treatises we still possess and a far greater number of works that have been lost. He is said to have assembled a collection of manuscripts and scientific specimens that was unprecedented in his own time. There was also a collection of constitutions from all the Greek city-states, the names of all winners in the Olympic Games, and other important items. Strabo calls him the first known collector of books (which probably meant that he was the first to establish a properly arranged collection of writings in its own building), and Demetrius of Phaleron, a member of the Lyceum, later became an adviser to Ptolemy Soter, the Hellenistic ruler of Alexandria who established the famous Mouseion on his royal estate. Thus it was said by Strabo that Aristotle "became the instructor of the kings of Egypt in the arrangement of a library" (see Guthrie 1990, 40–41, 59–60; During 1957, 382, 431).

In 323 Alexander died at Babylon, and the anti-Macedonian sentiment that had been developing for some time in Athens erupted in a wave of hostile acts: the Athenian Assembly declared war, and Athens committed itself to the general cause of liberating Greek poleis from Macedonian hegemony. Aristotle was known to have Macedonian connections, and as Socrates before him had been, he was charged with impiety. Unwilling to permit the Athenians to put a second philosopher to death, he went to his mother's hometown of Chalkis on the island of Euboea, where he died in 322. His school, the Lyceum, survived for some five hundred years after its founder's death, stimulating and challenging intellectual inquiry well beyond that of its own members.

The trajectories of Aristotle's thought and the diversity and extent of his philosophical investigations are products not only of the period in which he came of age but also of a unique combination of personal aptitudes and the educational experiences of his early development. Perhaps unlike such predecessors as Socrates, Isocrates, and Plato, Aristotle seemed not to be heavily affected by the political events that swirled around him during his life. Rather, his thought appears to be a result of original genius, of a particularly powerful intelligence at work on the myriad questions presented by the world in which he lived.

Several important factors must be borne in mind as we examine Aristotle's writings. One, of course, is the question of precisely what he wrote. Diogenes Laertius (*Lives* 5, 22–27) lists more than 150 items, running to some 550 books in all—the equivalent, says Barnes, of about 6,000 modern pages (1995, 9). Barnes reproduces Diogenes' list and says that "it is not complete—it omits some of Aristotle's most celebrated surviving works. It contains some things which were surely not written by Aristotle. . . . It includes a number of 'doublets'— that is to say, the same work may be included twice, under two different titles" (7). Of the 32 surviving works (running to fewer than 2,000 modern pages), some are incomplete. Nonetheless, "our modern corpus represents most of Aristotle's main interests and all of his main philosophical concerns" (10).

Another challenge arises when we consider the character and purpose of Aristotle's surviving writings. He apparently wrote two types of works, with different aims and intended for different kinds of audiences. One set comprises his so-called "esoteric" works, prepared for his advanced students and perhaps created as notes for Aristotle's use during his lectures in the Lyceum. These appear to be represented in the manuscripts that have come down to us. The other set—the "exoteric" writings—were more literary compositions intended for a wider public audience. Except for some fragments, these have been lost. The esoteric writings were constantly being reworked, revised, edited, added to, and simplified in collaboration with his colleagues (Guthrie 1990, 50). Thus it would be a mistake for us to regard these as finished "treatises" representing a polished expression of Aristotle's theoretical views. Moreover, because they were constantly undergoing revision, these "notes" contain restatements of various points in different terms, which may or may not have been corrections, and even wholly different treatments of some ideas. These inconsistencies and other discontinuities present problems in interpreting Aristotle's thinking.[6] Thus caution is warranted as we examine Aristotle's writings in illuminating his thoughts about wisdom, its acquisition, and its manifestations in conduct and speech. That said, we must work with the evidence we have, and with it alone. We may not find the degree of consistency and coherence across the entire corpus we would like, but we find information sufficient for constructing a comprehensible, coherent interpretation of Aristotle's thinking concerning the matters at issue here.

Aristotle inherited from his predecessors a rich tapestry of philosophical doctrines, multiple threads of inquiry, and a challenging set of problems, to all of which he set his formidable intellect. On the one hand, from the Presocratic thinkers ranging from Thales to Democritus, he took up questions concerning the fundamental constitution of the world we know through experience—what it is made of, why it behaves as it does, and what causes the changes we observe. These matters were addressed in such works as the *Physics, On the Heavens, On Generation and Corruption,* and *Meteorology.* From certain of these thinkers—most particularly from Anaximander, Heraclitus, Parmenides, and Anaxagoras—and from his teacher Plato, Aristotle took up inquiry into the ultimately real, the fixed and enduring entities that underlie the flowing world of appearance. This is the realm of unchanging, universal reality and of epistemic certainty, and Aristotle's investigation of it is reported in his *Metaphysics.* On the other hand, by the teachings of such thinkers as Protagoras, Gorgias, Isocrates, and other Sophists, Aristotle was invited to consider the realm of change, appearance, opinion, probability, and practical action. He did so in such treatises as the *Nicomachean Ethics,* the *Politics,* and the *Rhetoric.* The tensions between these two realms presented him with an especially challenging problem: how can a unified, comprehensive, coherent philosophical account of existence integrate these diametrically opposed ways of viewing the world? Moreover how can one sustain a coherent conception of wisdom in light of these two forms of consciousness—the absolutist/universalist and the relativist/particularist? It is a measure of Aristotle's genius that he developed a philosophical system accomplishing precisely this.

Using the philosophical contrasts between Plato and the Sophists as a template for examining Aristotle's synthesis of these divergent approaches, we can see how he sought to integrate key elements in both. Indeed, he resolved the conflict between Platonic and sophistical conceptions of wisdom by proposing two realms of existence—one universal and immutable, the other particular and transitory; and two kinds of wisdom—one speculative or theoretical, the other practical or moral. In his accounts of *sophia* (speculative wisdom) and *phronêsis* (practical wisdom), Aristotle incorporates key elements from his predecessors' thinking. Moreover, in his explanations of the means by which wisdom is acquired and exercised, he synthesizes and extends many of his forebears' thoughts about the nature and efficacy of *logos.* Thus in Aristotle we find the fullest expression of a classical conception of wisdom and of its relation to speech.

Aristotle's views of wisdom developed in the context of philosophical problems he inherited. One involves the relationship between the flow of appearances—the realm of "becoming and passing away"—and the quest for an unchanging, universal "reality" that underlies and directs this flow—the realm of a "being" that is constant and universal. A second problem concerns the supposed distinction between "knowledge" (*epistêmê*)—certain and unerring—and "belief" or "opinion" (*doxa*)—probable and contingent. Thus, for Aristotle, a central aim of philosophical investigation was to discover how, if at all, such tensions and contradictions might be reconciled, or at least integrated, in a single philosophical system. This is what he sought to accomplish, and examining his manner of doing so shows how he conceived wisdom and its connections with speech.

Aristotle's familiarity with the teachings and writings of those who preceded him is shown by his treatment of the Presocratics (from Thales through the Atomists), Socrates, and Plato in book 1 of the *Metaphysics* and elsewhere, as well as by his consideration of the views of such Sophists as Protagoras (*Meta.* 1007b, 1009a), Gorgias and Thrasymachus (both in *On Sophistical Refutations*), and Isocrates (for example, *Rhet.* 1368a, 1399a). In many ways the development of his own views was a response to these doctrines, and it resulted in his construction of an ontology and an epistemology aimed at resolving the problems he encountered in them. Aristotle conceived two realms of existence, each with its proper forms of knowledge and its own kind of wisdom. On the one hand, there is the realm of the universal, necessary, and unchanging—the sphere of things whose causes are absolute and immutable. On the other hand, we find the realm of the particular, contingent, and variable—the sphere of things that may be other than they are. In the realm of the universal and immutable, wisdom is *sophia*, an apprehension of first causes and of what logically follows from them in nature. For the realm of the particular and variable, wisdom is *phronêsis*, an ability to perceive what practical actions will benefit humans generally and what specific actions will serve in particular circumstances. Let us turn, then, to this integrative view of existence and wisdom.

Aristotle's most prominent statements concerning the nature of *sophia* are in the *Metaphysics*.[7] He discusses this idea at length in the first book, noting that "wisdom (*sophia*) is concerned with the primary causes (*aitia*) and principles (*archai*)" of things (981b). Wisdom is knowledge (*epistêmê*) of these causes and principles (932a); indeed, it is "the most sovereign and authoritative (*archikôtatê kai êgemonikôtatê*) kind of knowledge" (996b). He elaborates the idea in his *Nicomachean Ethics*, and it is here that he introduces the distinction between two kinds of existence and differentiates between speculative and practical wisdom. In his discussion of the Good and human happiness, Aristotle suggests that we might understand it by considering the human being's proper function in the natural scheme of things, which requires a consideration of how the *psychê* is structured (1097b). He maintains that the human soul is part rational and part irrational. Of the irrational element, one aspect is common to all life—namely, the "vegetative (*phytikos*), . . . that which causes nutrition and growth" (1102a). He dismisses "the mere act of living" as our proper function, since this is shared even by plants, "whereas we are looking for the function peculiar to man; we must therefore set aside the vital activity of nutrition and growth" (1097b–98a).[8]

A second irrational element—the "sentient" (*aisthêtikê*) or "appetitive" (*orektikê*) part of the soul—is common to all beings capable of sensation. This element is responsive to pleasure and pain, and it initiates actions aimed at procuring the former and avoiding the latter. However, the "sentient life . . . appears to be shared by horses, oxen, and animals generally" (1098a), so it cannot belong properly to the human being as such. "There remains therefore," Aristotle continues, "what may be called the practical life (*zôê praktikê*) of the rational part (*tou logon echontos*)" (1098a)—that is, the part of the soul "having a *logos*" or rational principle.[9] "Let us now similarly divide the rational part," he writes, "and let it be assumed that there are two rational faculties, one whereby we contemplate those things whose first principles are invariable, and one whereby we contemplate those things which admit of variation. . . . These two rational faculties may be designated the Scientific Faculty (*to epistêmonikon*) and the Calculative Faculty (*to logistikon*) respectively; since calculation is the same as deliberation, and deliberation is never exercised about things that are invariable, so that the Calculative Faculty is a separate part of the rational half of the soul" (1139a).

Both rational faculties aim at discovering truth (1139b), both fall under what Aristotle calls "Intellectual Virtues" (*aretas dionoias*, 1139a), and each finds its proper excellence in the discovery of its distinctive form of truth. However, they direct their inquiries at different forms. The scientific or speculative intellect is concerned with matters that are "eternal," that exist "of necessity," and thus that do not "come into existence or perish" (1139b). It pursues truth in two ways, deductively and inductively. Strictly speaking, "scientific knowledge" (*epistêmê*) is "the quality whereby we demonstrate (*apodeiktikê*)" or proceed "by way of deduction" to the particular facts that follow logically from the first principles of nature (1139b). In the *Posterior Analytics*, Aristotle writes, "We suppose ourselves to possess unqualified scientific knowledge of a thing, as opposed to knowing it in the accidental way in which the sophist knows, when we think that we know the cause on which the fact depends, as the cause of that fact and of no other, and, further, that the fact could not be other than it is. . . . What I now assert is that at all events we do know by demonstration (*apodeixis*). By demonstration I mean a syllogism productive of scientific knowledge" (71b).[10] Later in this treatise Aristotle observes, "Since the object of pure scientific knowledge cannot be other than it is, the truth obtained by demonstrative knowledge will be necessary. And since demonstrative knowledge is only present when we have a demonstration, it follows that demonstration is an inference from necessary premises" (73a; see Guthrie 1990, 170–78). Accordingly, because scientific knowledge is demonstrated from first principles that are necessarily true and are known with certainty, what logically follows from them is also known with certainty (*Ethics* 1139b). Moreover it is the soul's *logos*, its reasoning ability, that equips humans to acquire such demonstrative knowledge.

The "necessary premises" themselves, of course, cannot be known through demonstration, since they would themselves have to be derived from prior causes, and these from still prior causes, and so on ad infinitum. In order to avoid this infinite regression, there must be a second method and another intellectual faculty by which the first causes, the ultimate premises of demonstration, are apprehended (*Meta.* 994a–b). Thus does Aristotle introduce the process of induction and the faculty of *nous* or "intuition." As Aristotle explains in the *Ethics*, "demonstrated truths and all scientific knowledge (since this involves reasoning) are derived from first principles (*archai*). Consequently the first principles from which scientific truths are derived cannot themselves be reached by Science (*epistêmê*)" (1140b). Instead, the originating principles or causes of existing things can be known only as a result of inductive reasoning from sense-perception, culminating in a direct apprehension through intuition (*Post. An.* 100a–b).[11] These *archai* disclose themselves directly to the "intelligence" or "understanding" (other meanings of *nous*) as being self-evidently true. They cannot be doubted, for they are true necessarily, and the mind's essential *logos* enables us to perceive this immediately. The first principles of nature, though they are the farthest removed from sensory perception, are the objects most readily apprehended by human reason. The last chapter of the *Posterior Analytics* (1009aff.), Guthrie remarks, is "a confession of his epistemological faith, a statement of the source from which in the last resort all knowledge springs" (1990, 179). "Moreover," he writes later, "*nous* for both [Aristotle and Plato] was not a purely human faculty, but a link between man and divinity, for pure *nous* is God" (186).

Following this, for Aristotle, *sophia*—what we might call "theoretical" or "speculative" wisdom—"must be the most perfect of the modes of knowledge (*ê akribestat ê tôn epistêmôn*). The wise man therefore must not only know the conclusions that follow from his first principles, but also have a true conception of those principles themselves. Hence Wisdom must be a combination of Intelligence (*nous*) and Scientific Knowledge (*epistêmê*): it must be a consummated knowledge of the most exalted objects" (*Ethics* 1141a, 1141b). *Sophia* involves both an intuitive understanding of the "causes" or "principles" of natural objects and events, and a demonstrative understanding of all that can be deduced from them, for "the wise man knows all things, so far as it is possible, without having knowledge of every one of them individually" (*Meta.* 982a). Theoretical wisdom is a comprehensive understanding of how the natural world works and of why it works as it does. It is, in sum, the most complete form of "cosmic consciousness," a pervasive awareness of the "way" of the universe.

Moreover, as an apprehension of the eternal, unchanging causes at work in the universe, *sophia* is knowledge of the divine realm.

The counterpart of *sophia* is the sort of wisdom proper to the other part of the rational soul—the calculative or practical intellect (*to logistikon*)—namely "prudence" or "practical wisdom" (*phronêsis*). It is the mark of the prudent person (*o phronimos*) "to be able to deliberate well about what is good and advantageous for himself, not in some one department [for example, for health or strength] . . . , but what is advantageous as a means to the good life in general" (*Eth.* 1140a). Since no one deliberates about things that cannot be other than they are, *phronêsis* considers "things whose fundamental principles are variable [and] are not capable of demonstration" (1140a). Since "matters of conduct admit of variation," practical wisdom is not *epistêmê*, but it still must be "a truth-attaining rational quality, concerned with action (*einai exin alêthê meta logou praktikên*) in relation to things that are good and bad for human beings" (1140b). The "first principles of action (*archai tôn praktôn*) are the end to which our acts are means"—*to ou eneka ta prakta*, literally "that for the sake of which actions [are done]" (1140b). It is the aim of practical wisdom to envision these ends and determine the best means to their attainment. This knowledge will always be a matter of opinion, "for Opinion (*doxa*) deals with that which can vary, and so does Prudence" (1140b). Consequently *phronêsis* can never provide knowledge of universal principles because it must always take account of particular facts—it is concerned with action, and action deals with particulars. Nonetheless, good deliberation can yield what Aristotle terms "practical knowledge," a perception of the right course of action in a particular set of circumstances.

Elsewhere Aristotle elaborates the distinction between theoretical and practical knowledge, and thus between *sophia* and *phronêsis*: "The end of theoretic knowledge (*theôrêtikês*) is truth (*alêtheia*), while that of practical knowledge (*praktikês*) is action (*ergon*); for even when they are investigating *how* a thing is so, practical men study not the eternal principle but the relative and immediate application" (*Meta.* 993b). Whereas Aristotle uniformly uses the term *epistêmê* when referring to "scientific" or "theoretical" knowledge, he offers no specific analogy for practical knowledge, though he does employ *praktikês* and variations of *gignôskô*—signifying "to learn, to perceive, to form a judgment about, to understand"—in discussing the sort of insight at which *phronêsis* aims.[12]

The role of *logos* is prominent in the methods, objects, and activities proper to each form of wisdom. As we have seen, *sophia* is a combination of intuited first principles and causes—the *archai* and *aitia*—according to which the natural world operates, and a demonstrative understanding of the specific natural events and objects that logically follow from these. Accordingly we must examine both the upward-directed quest for originative principles and the downward-directed demonstration of particulars if we are to grasp this conception of wisdom. In the end, both modes of inquiry lead us to the same place: we begin from sensation in seeking the *archai* of things, and from these *archai* we return to the perceived world through logical demonstration, where we understand particulars in terms of their ultimate causes. As T. S. Eliot puts the matter, "The end of our exploring will be to arrive where we started and know the place for the first time."

The first principles of nature are grasped through induction (*epagôgê*), which Aristotle defines as "a passage from particulars to universals" (*Topics* 105a).[13] This holds true in all fields of scientific inquiry—biology, chemistry, physics, mathematics, astronomy, ontology—in which empirical inquiry (*historia*) begins with appearances (*phainomena*). "In each science the principles which are peculiar [to it] are the most numerous. Consequently it is the business of experience (*empeiria*) to give the principles which belong to each subject. I mean for example that astronomical experience supplies the principles of astronomical science; for once the phenomena were adequately apprehended, the demonstrations of astronomy were discovered. Similarly with any other art or science" (*Pr. An.* 46a). Similarly "in the knowledge of nature [the starting point is] the unimpeachable evidence of the senses as to each fact" (*On the Heavens* 306a). Discussing the empirical starting points of inductive inquiry, Irwin remarks that Aristotle "does not say that we can distinguish these authoritative sensory appearances in advance of inquiry. The rule 'Begin from authoritative appearances' cannot be a practical guide for the initial conduct of inquiry, and we cannot assume that we have eliminated false sensory appearances at the start of inquiry. But though Aristotle must allow that some of the appearances we begin from are false or misleading, he does not draw attention to this possibility as often as we might expect. Indeed, he appeals quite confidently to appearances, on the assumption that they are plainly true" (1990, 31). Thus, for Aristotle, "empirical inquiry begins from the particulars grasped in perception, and proceeds to the universal grasped by reason" (43), from what is known immediately to what can be known remotely.[14]

Guthrie (1990, 181) writes that sensation, viewed by Aristotle as "'a congenital power of distinguishing one thing from another,'" is common to all animals, "but only some have the capacity to go beyond sensation. In these the mental process ascends first to memory, then (in mankind only) to the making of a generalization" (for which Aristotle's word is *logos*; see 181, note 2). Induction moves from a direct awareness (*gnôsis*) of individual things through a process of ascending generalization, first to an understanding of what is common to all members of a class, next to what is shared by all classes subsumed in a more general class, and thence to the most general class of all, the universal (*to katholou*). The process is one of abstracting (or, as Guthrie says, "extracting") what is common to a given set of particular objects, "separating from their matter a set of common properties which mark off those particulars from the rest of nature as belonging to the same species (*eidos* again). Without this 'one over the many,' discernible in the flux of becoming, science would be impossible. So far Aristotle reasons as a Platonist, but he sees no need to suppose it a transcendental unity *outside* the world" (190).

This process of abstraction, classification, and definition is termed *logismos*— thinking through the similarities and differences among particular things and thereby arriving at a higher-order understanding. It is also *logos*, deploying the resources of language in distinguishing one class of things from others in terms of their essential properties and their differentiae. In order to accomplish this classificatory and descriptive enterprise, Aristotle develops a technical vocabulary and a set of conceptual categories to do the necessary work. These are the principal focus of the *Catagories* and *On Interpretation*. In the former, he considers such matters as the use of names (1a), the forms of speech (1a–b), the nature of predication (1b), and the classes in which the objects of thought can be placed: substance, quantity, quality, relation, place, time, position, state, action, and affection (1b–11b). He then turns to "the various senses in which the term 'opposite' is used" (11b–14a) and thence to the meanings of the terms "prior" (14a–b), "simultaneous" (14b–15a), and "to have" (15b), with a brief digression (15a–b) on the six types of movement. *On Interpretation* is still more fundamental, defining the parts of speech (noun, verb, and so on) and of the sentence (subject, predicate), and then considering the ways in which propositions may be used and their relationships to truth and falsehood, possibility and impossibility, contingency and necessity. Such are the tools of induction: description, differentiation, definition, and classification. The upward-directed search for principles and causes is fundamentally an activity of *logos*, for only through the prism of language can the observations of particular things and events be sorted (one meaning of *logos*) and the relations (another meaning) among them be identified and stated (yet another).

Illustrations of the inductive method at work can be found in Aristotle's scientific writings, where he describes characteristics of various individuals and, based on the essential traits shared by some but not by all, distinguishes one species from another. Thus, for instance, in *On the Parts of Animals* he notes, "the individuals comprised within a species, such as Socrates and Corsicus, are the real [individual] existences; but inasmuch as these individuals possess one common specific form, it will suffice to state the universal attributes of the species, that is, the attributes common to all its individuals. . . . But as regards the larger groups—such as Birds—which comprehend many species . . . it will be well, if practicable, to examine [the] ultimate species separately, just as we examine the species Man separately [from other mammals, for instance]; to examine, that is, not the whole class Birds collectively, but the Ostrich, the Crane, and the other indivisible groups or species belonging to the class" (644a; trans. Ogle, in Aristotle 1941g). As one moves up the ladder of generalization, observation of particular species leads to a more general classification (for example, birds, fishes, and humans are all types of animals). This can lead to a still more general classification (for example, both animals and plants are types of living things); thence to a higher-order classification (living and nonliving things are types of existing things or beings); and finally to the ultimate object of inductive inquiry: being as such, the subject of "first philosophy" or metaphysics. Each specific science aims at its proper set of first principles and causes, but the "science of being itself" aims at the apprehension of the *archai* of all existence—that is, at the nature of being qua being (*Meta.* 995a–97a, 1003a).

Since each particular science seeks demonstrative knowledge about the kinds of individual things proper to it, each must have its own specific set of propositions or principles that are logically prior to the deductive conclusions at which each aims. Thus, for example, in a science such as zoology there must be a set of definitions that distinguishes one species of animal from all others. For mathematics and geometry, there must be definitions, axioms, and postulates that can serve as premises from which particular theorems can be deduced. In the science of logic, there are principles without which reasoning cannot be carried out.[15] In physics, which studies the nature and motion of bodies, there must be a set of primary causes from which specific bodies and their movements arise. In the science of being, there must be a set of principles from which the characteristics of all existing things can be deduced. Thus, in introducing the *Physics*, Aristotle writes, "When the objects of an inquiry, in any department, have principles, conditions, or elements, it is through acquaintance with these that knowledge, that is to say scientific knowledge (*epistêmê*), is attained. For we do not think that we know a thing until we have carried our analysis as far as its simplest elements. Plainly therefore in the science of Nature (*ta physika*), as in other branches of study, our first task will be to try to determine what relates to its principles. The natural way of doing this is to start from the things which are more knowable and obvious to us [sensory perceptions] and proceed towards those which are clearer and more knowable by nature [first principles]" (184a; trans. Hardie and Gaye, in Aristotle 1941j).

Above and beyond the principles proper to each of the other sciences, physics and metaphysics identify a set of causes that must be grasped in order for us to understand how a thing comes into being, either naturally or artificially, and what it is. These causes (*aitia*) are answers to "why" a thing is what it is, comes to be what it is, or does what it does (*Phys.* 198a), and they are four in number (194b–95a): the material cause ("that out of which a thing comes to be and which persists, . . . e.g. the bronze of the statue"); the formal cause ("the statement of the essence . . . and the parts in the definition"); the efficient cause ("the primary source of the change or coming to rest; e.g. . . . the father is the cause of the child"); and the final cause ("'that for the sake of which' a thing is done, e.g. health is the cause of walking about") (also see *Meta.* 983a–b). In order to understand and explain any natural or artificial thing or event in any specific branch of knowledge, one must be able to identify each of its causes (*Meta.* 1044a–b). Thus, whether we seek to "know" a specific animal, a celestial body, or a piece of pottery, we must be able to explain it in terms of what it is made of, what kind of thing it is, by what means it came to be, and the purpose for which it exists. Moreover, whereas the material and efficient causes of a thing might be grasped through simple observation, the formal and final causes can be apprehended only through an intuitive leap following the inductive ascent from the particulars of observation.[16]

When we consider formal and final causes, we enter the realm of "first philosophy" for Aristotle: the study of essences and ends. This involves investigating what we now term "ontology," following Aristotle's study of "what is" (*to on*) and of "things that are" (*ta onta*) in terms of what it means "to be" (*einai*).[17] Introducing this subject, he says (*Meta.* 1003a–b) that though the term "being" is used in many senses, it is used "always with reference to one principle": the idea of substance, *ousia*, "that which is one's own." Thus, to ask of a thing, "what is it?" is to ask, "what is its substance, its essential nature?" As we learn from the *Catagories* (2a), "substance" can be either primary—the subject of all predication and never itself predicated of anything else (such as "man" or "horse"); or secondary—a thing's essence or definable form, represented by the genus and species to which its primary substance belongs. The essence or form of a thing is independent of human action; it exists "by nature." Moreover this is what gives to matter a particular form of existence, so essence is logically prior to material existence. Thus is essence "substance" without matter (*Meta.* 1032b), and it is grasped through an intuitive movement from experience with particular things to that in virtue of which one species of thing can be distinguished from all others—its essential nature.[18] To grasp a thing's formal cause is to grasp one of its first principles, an *archê*. This is a component of speculative wisdom.

It remains, then, to consider the highest and most complete of the four causes—the *archê* or *aitia*—that can be grasped by *nous*. This is the final cause, the purpose or end for which a thing exists, its *telos*, upon which all its other principles and causes rest. A fundamental tenet Aristotle inherited from his predecessors was that the universe is fundamentally rational—it is ordered by a rational principle, a *logos* in accordance with which all things come to pass. We inhabit a teleological universe, wherein the natural tendency of any particular thing is to fulfill its purpose or to attain its "perfection" in the context of the cosmic order. We shall return to these themes shortly, but it will be helpful to keep them in mind as we consider Aristotle's conception of final causes, especially the most final of all.

Aristotle's teleological orientation applies equally to artificial and natural objects. In the case of "man-made objects" (for example, houses, ships, shoes, statues, states) or human activities (for example, flute-playing, medicine, military strategy, shipbuilding, governing), the final causes are the purposes for which they are to be used and for which they were made or done. Houses exist in order to shelter people and their possessions (*Meta.* 1043a). Tools exist in order to perform particular functions such as cutting, pounding, or shaping. Medicine aims at restoring or maintaining health (*Eth.* 1102a, 1137a). States exist in order to secure the good for their citizens (*Pol.* 1252a). Military strategy aims at securing victory (*Eth.* 1094a). Thus, in the case of such things, the ultimate "reason" for the existence of each is what it was meant to do, its proper function or "work" (*ergon*). This "meaning" or purpose, moreover, is a human construction, as we determine the ends at which our buildings, implements, and actions are aimed.

In the case of natural objects and events, the same attitude prevails but with important differences. It is clear, Aristotle maintains (*Eth.* 1097b–98a), that not only do such human activities as carpentry, flute-playing, sculpting, and shoe-making have their proper work; so also do "the eye, the hand, the foot and each of the various members of the body" exhibit purposes set by nature. Moreover, just as the specific organs of the body have their own unique functions, so must the complete creature have its proper "work"—that is, a function set by nature for the creature to perform. For plants, this work is manifestly "the vital activity of nutrition and growth," each particular species being naturally suited to fulfill this end in its own way. For animals, which are capable of sensation and movement, the proper functions consist in general physical health and well-being (as with plants too), but also in the form of activity at which each type of animal is designed to excel. Thus multiple observations of horses in action, coupled with an intuitive grasp of what they have in common and of what defines them as "horses," might lead to the insight that the *telos* of the horse is to run fast over great distances. So it is with all living organisms, as well as with the purely physical entities in the cosmos—the planets, stars, and other heavenly bodies. So, indeed, it is with *anthrôpos*, for "are we to suppose that while the carpenter and the shoemaker have definite functions and activities (*erga kai praxeis*) . . . , man as such has none, and is not designed by nature to fulfil any function?" (1097b).

Consequently each "natural object or action" must be understood in terms of its proper function in the rationally ordered scheme of the universe. Left to its own "design," each object or action would naturally tend toward its *telos*, "striving" to fulfill its proper function and to realize its natural end. Indeed, Aristotle writes, "There are some who, while they allow that every animal exists and was generated by nature, nevertheless hold that the heaven was constructed to be what it is by chance and spontaneity; the heaven, in which not the faintest sign of hap-hazard or of disorder is discernible! Again, whenever there is plainly some final end, to which a motion tends should nothing stand in the way, we always say that such a final end is the aim or purpose of the motion; and from this it is evident that there must be a something or other really existing, corresponding to what we call by the name of Nature" (*On the Parts of Animals* 641b).[19]

Accordingly Nature does nothing without a purpose: "everything that Nature makes is means to an end. For just as human creations are the products of art, so living objects are manifestly the products of an analogous cause or principle, not external but internal, derived like the hot and the cold from the environing universe. And . . . the heaven, if it had an origin, was evolved and is maintained by such a cause" (*On the Parts of Animals* 641b; compare *On the Soul* 415b). All natural existences, then, strive to realize the purposes that Nature has set for them, and in doing so each, "as far as its nature allows, . . . may partake in the eternal and divine" (*On the Soul* 415b). If the final cause of any particular thing or action is the end toward which it naturally tends, then in order to understand how a thing "fits into" the rational order of the universe one must grasp the *telos* of that order. What for Aristotle constitutes the purpose and end of the universe as a whole? Here we enter the realm of eschatology—of ultimate existence or Being. What is the *telos* toward which the universe tends according to its own "internal" or indwelling nature, its own *entelechia*? "The *telos* of the whole world," writes Guthrie, "is of course God, according to Aristotle's own rather individual conception of divinity, and the development of things in the natural world, each in its own restricted sphere, is, to borrow Plato's phrase, assimilation to God as far as possible" (1990, 118).

The final cause of the cosmos is what Aristotle terms the "prime mover," "which always moves that which is moved, and the 'prime mover' is itself unmoved" (*Meta.* 1012b) and "exempt from all change" (*Phys.* 258b). Again, this is Nature, "the internal drive which Aristotle detected in all natural products toward achieving their own proper form and activity . . . , an endeavor to emulate, so far as the limitations of their matter will permit, the one pure form whose perfection is unsullied . . . by any taint of matter at all" (Guthrie 1990, 258). This, Aristotle tells us, "is the first principle upon which depend the universe and the world of nature (*o ouranos kai ê physis*)" (*Meta.* 1072b). This principle is "mind (*nous*) thinking itself through a participation in the object of thought" (1072b). Moreover it is "divine" (*theion*) and "life itself" (*energeia zôê*), for "the actuality of thought is life, and God (*o theos*) is that actuality; and the essential actuality of God is life most good and eternal. We hold, then, that God is a living being, eternal, most good; and therefore life and a continuous eternal existence belong to God; for that is what God is" (1072b).[20]

God's essential activity is the contemplation (*theôria*, as at *Meta.* 1072b) of his (its) own essential nature, for in this activity he/it animates all other, subordinate beings to strive for their own perfection or completion in the "orderly arrangement" (*taxis*, as at 1075a) of the cosmos. What is the "essential nature" of God? We know that it is pure "substance" or "form" without matter—unadulterated *entelecheia*, pure *telos*, singular and unitary (1074a)—and that it is pure "mind (*nous*) . . . thinking (*noei*)." "What does it think?" Aristotle asks (1074b). Well, "Mind thinks itself, if it is that which is best; and its thinking is a thinking of thinking (*estin ê noêsis noêseôs noêsis*)" (1074b). So, the divine Mind that is the first principle of all existence and whose thinking is the prime cause of all movement—the Mind of God—thinks about its own thinking. We are left by Aristotle with this somewhat unsatisfying conundrum: what is the content of the thought of the Mind that thinks only about its own thinking? What is the fundamental principle—the *archê*—on which the mind of God is concentrated?[21] To grasp this is to attain the highest wisdom.

I am not content to leave this matter unaddressed, though it may have to remain unresolved in any final sense. In what follows I argue for one way of answering the question just posed, fully cognizant of the fact that Aristotle does not answer it directly. In any event, in order to consider this matter we must turn momentarily to Aristotle's consideration of the best life for a human being—that is, to the Good whose realization constitutes the fulfillment of our natural function and thus that constitutes human happiness or well-being.[22] What that function is, we have already seen: "In men rational principle (*logos*) and mind (*nous*) are the end toward which nature strives" (*Pol.* 1334b). The activity of *logos* is the highest excellence of which humans are capable; it is the activity of the highest thing in us, our *nous*, which we share with God. Thus it is not too big a step to infer that the essential activity of *nous* is *logos* or *logismos*: thinking under the guidance of a rational principle. If this may be applied to the *noêsis* of God, then, we can conclude that what God thinks about is his/its own *logos*—the principle according to which the universe is ordered. What, for Aristotle, is the nature of this fundamental principle? It is proportion, an "equality of ratios" (*analogia isotês esti logôn; Eth.* 1131a).[23] It is not too much to say that for Aristotle, as for his Presocratic forebears, the ruling principle of the cosmos is a law of proportion, reciprocity, balance, and harmony according to which all things tend by their own natural inclinations to "fit together" (the literal meaning of *harmonia*) in ways that maintain or fulfill the natural proportions and balances that govern the universe as a whole.

If this interpretation of Aristotle's thinking is fair, then we can conclude that the source of theoretical wisdom (*sophia*), which comes through insight into the mind of God, is an intuitive apprehension of the *Logos* according to which the cosmos is ordered, for this *Logos* is the final cause of the cosmos, the foundation of the plan or design that "steers all things through all."[24] When God contemplates his/its own mind, we can reasonably infer that he/it is thinking about the cosmic "orderer" (*kosmêtôr*) that is the essence of his/its thought. To borrow a later expression of the same idea: "In the beginning was the *Logos*, and the *Logos* was with God, and the *Logos* was God" (*en archê an o logos, kai o logos an pros ton theon, kai theos an o logos,* John 1.1). Thus does human *sophia* rest on an intuition of the divine *Logos*, the "word of God," in a distinctively "rational" conception of divinity.

Speculative wisdom, for Aristotle, comprises a combination of the intuitively grasped *archai* of existence and a demonstrative understanding of what follows logically from these. Therefore we turn now to "scientific knowledge (*epistêmê*) . . . , the quality whereby we demonstrate (*exis apodeiktikê*)" (*Eth.* 1139b). Once one has grasped the first principles and causes of a particular object or event, one must deduce from these principles (which function as premises of arguments) the particular conclusions or facts that necessarily follow from them. The method of scientific demonstration involves "showing forth" or "making known" the logical connections between premises and conclusions (Liddell and Scott 1996, *s.v. apodeiktikê*). These conclusions constitute the content of scientific knowledge, which grasps particular things in terms of their ultimate causes and principles (*Post. An.* 71b). There are two aspects of this idea that invite examination: the method by which scientific knowledge is acquired—"demonstration"; and the contents of this knowledge, which will be the conclusions to which demonstration leads. Both will bear on the character of Aristotle's *sophia*.

The method of demonstration is essentially the method of deductive reasoning. In contrast to the ascent through induction toward the first principles of nature, Aristotle describes "reasoning" (*logismos*) as "an argument in which, certain things being laid down, something other than these necessarily comes about through them. It is a 'demonstration' (*apodeixis*) when the premises from which the reasoning starts are true and primary, or are such that our knowledge of them has originally come through premises which are primary and true" (*Topics* 100a).[25] The fundamental structure of a demonstrative argument is syllogistic, consisting of a major premise and a minor premise that, owing to the logical implications of the terms used and to the necessary connections among the terms of the two premises, lead necessarily to a third proposition— the conclusion or particular fact (*Post. An.* 85b). As he explains the matter, "the positing of one thing—be it one term or one premise—never involves a

necessary consequent: two premises constitute the first and smallest foundation for drawing a conclusion at all" (73a). An apodeictic syllogism (in contrast
to a dialectical or merely formal syllogism) is a true proof, proceeding from
various types of "primary premise" or "basic truth"—that is, from premises
that "predicate a single attribute of a single subject" (72a7–9). Each science has
its particular set of such premises or truths: the four causes of motion in the
case of physics, the axioms and definitions of geometry and mathematics, the
principles of logic in the science of reasoning, definitions in the sciences of
biology and zoology, and so on. Starting, then, with a particular set of premises
in a given science, one can (in principle) demonstrate all that must follow from
them, culminating in particular facts we could observe in the world around us.

Aristotle's examples in the *Posterior Analytics* generally take the form of
purely symbolic proofs. However, when the form is applied to the world of
actual experience, factual conclusions follow from the premises or "basic truths"
already apprehended through an inductive/intuitive grasp of causes—material,
efficient, formal, or final.[26] For example, we might envision the following:
1) "All humans are capable of reasoning" (major premise, drawn from a definition of what it means to be "human"); 2) "Socrates is human" (minor premise,
based on another chain of inference from both empirical facts and classification); 3) Therefore, "Socrates is capable of reasoning" (conclusion, a statement of fact). Similarly we might argue in the following way: 1) "All humans
are capable of reasoning"; 2) "Horses are incapable of reasoning"; 3) Therefore, "Horses are not human." These conclusions—the content of scientific
knowledge—can be known with certainty if the premises are necessarily true
and if the reasoning is sound. The object of pure scientific knowledge, Aristotle tells us, "cannot be other than it is [because] the truth obtained by demonstrative knowledge [from necessary premises] will be necessary" (*Post. An.* 73a).

In principle, scientific reasoning can also yield conclusions about facts that
have not yet come to pass. If the laws of nature (the cosmic *archai* and *aitia*)
are universal, immutable, and inviolable, the conditional conclusions that follow necessarily from them must hold conditionally—that is, even when the
minor premise has not yet been actualized. Using the examples above, then,
one might reason as follows: 1) "All humans are capable of reasoning"; 2) "If
Socrates is human" (a conditional minor premise), then 3) "He will be capable
of reasoning." Similarly 1) "All humans are capable of reasoning"; 2) "If horses
are incapable of reasoning," then 3) "The horse will not be human." Taking
this application (only implicit in Aristotle) a bit further, we might deploy the
predictive power of syllogistic reasoning in another way: 1) "Matter preventing
solar energy from escaping the earth's atmosphere causes heating on the earth's
surface" (a material cause, ascertained inductively from observation and/or
from related cause-effect demonstrations); 2) "If matter preventing the escape

of solar heat is permitted to accumulate in the earth's atmosphere," then 3) "The earth's surface will become hotter." In fact, it is the logical force provided by syllogistic reasoning that has permitted modern science to predict how human activity will affect the rate of global climate change, how the human body will respond to various chemicals, how vehicles in space will be affected by gravity, and how different substances will affect the growth and nutritional value of plants.

In short, the enterprise of modern empirical science is an application of principles underlying Aristotle's conceptions of inductive and deductive reasoning. It may be that our understanding of "first principles" (the laws of nature) is somewhat more tenuous than he envisioned in his account of induction and *nous*, but there is little debate now about the laws of gravity, motion, thermodynamics, the conservation of energy, and similar principles, all of which were derived through inductions based on empirical observations. Moreover our ability to predict how various natural objects and processes will behave under specified conditions is rooted in our ability to deduce from natural laws how these will work out in particular instances. This is precisely how Aristotle envisioned the acquisition of *epistêmê* or scientific knowledge. So, while we go beyond his explicit accounts in tracing out these ideas, they are clearly implied in his writings. Accordingly Aristotle's conception of *sophia* recurs in this way to the *sophia* of the seer, the prophet, the soothsayer: it entails the ability to foretell the future. This is what knowledge of nature aims at, an aim embraced by the Greek wisdom-tradition from its inception.

The counterpart of theoretical or speculative wisdom in Aristotle's philosophical system is "practical" or "moral" wisdom—*phronêsis*. If intellectual virtues such as scientific knowledge, intuition, and speculative wisdom concern objects and events that cannot be other than they are, *phronêsis* as a form of wisdom is proper to the realm of the variable, contingent, and uncertain. It is the excellence of the "calculative" or "deliberative" intellect (*to logistikon*), and it aims at "practical knowledge"—that is, "moral truths" that should guide practical decisions (Johnstone 1980). The mark of the *phronimos* is "to be able to deliberate well about what is good and advantageous . . . as a means to the good life in general" (*Eth.* 1140a). Two key elements figure in the acquisition and exercise of *phronêsis:* knowledge of the "first principles" of praxis, the final ends or causes of human action; and knowledge about means to attaining these ends, which rests on excellence in deliberating. The uses of *logos* that lead to these forms of knowledge are dialectic and rhetoric, respectively.

The overarching objective of the *Nicomachean Ethics* is to discover the final end—the Good—at which all human activities aim (1094a), for "a knowledge (*gnôsis*) of this Supreme Good [will] be . . . of great practical importance for the conduct of life." Thus Aristotle sets out to determine "what exactly this

Supreme Good is" so that, like archers, we might have a target at which to aim in our deliberations. What constitutes a "good life" for a human being? The method of investigating this question is dialectical inquiry, a procedure Aristotle inherited from Plato, just as Plato had learned it from Socrates' practice of interrogating the opinions of people he encountered in public and private around Athens. Dialectic is the subject of the *Topics*, as well as of *Sophistical Refutations*, which Guthrie calls "a kind of appendix to the *Topics* sometimes referred to as *Top*. bk. 9" (1990, 150n2). It involves reasoning to general conclusions from commonly held opinions or beliefs (*endoxa*) about questions in law, politics, ethics, and even (when employed as an instrument of criticism) the natural sciences.[27] The procedure, as we saw in Socrates and Plato, starts from stated opinions (held either by "the many" or by one's interlocutor) and, using these as premises and applying syllogistic reasoning to derive the conclusions that follow from them, determining whether the logical implications of the stated beliefs are compatible with the premises or with other beliefs also held. Thence arise the various puzzles or *aporiai* that require either rejection or modification of at least one of the original propositions. In such inquiries, moreover, since we are dealing "with subjects and starting from premises thus uncertain," we must be content if we succeed "in presenting a broad outline of the truth: when our subjects and our premises are merely generalities, it is enough if we arrive at generally valid conclusions" (*Eth*. 1094b).

In the *Ethics*, Aristotle illustrates how this method can be used to identify the final end of all human action—the Good for the human being, for the sake of which action is undertaken. What is the "highest of all the goods that action can achieve?" he asks. "As far as the name goes, . . . the great majority of mankind are agreed about this; for both the multitude and persons of refinement speak of it as Happiness (*eudaimonia*), and conceive 'the good life' or 'doing well' to be the same thing as 'being happy.' But what constitutes happiness is a matter of dispute" (1095a). Following this, Aristotle examines a number of opinions concerning what happiness is—that it is pleasure, wealth, honor, health, or knowledge, for example. All of these are rejected because they conflict with yet another conviction, for "we instinctively feel that the Good must be something proper to its possessor and not easy to be taken away from him" (1095b). Thus does the analysis unfold, Aristotle considering in turn what is generally "felt" or "believed" to be essential to happiness—namely that it must not be dependent on the actions of others, that it must be "final" and "self-sufficient," that by itself it makes life worth living, and that it must be enduring rather than transitory—until at last he arrives at a comprehensive conception. The Supreme Good attainable through human action is "the active exercise of [the] soul's faculties in conformity . . . with the best and most perfect" of human excellences (1098a), carried on not in isolation but in the company of family, friends, and fellow citizens, "since man is by nature a social being" (1097b). In addition, "it is manifest that happiness also requires external goods . . . ; for it is impossible, or at least not easy, to play a noble part [in life] unless furnished with the necessary equipment" (1099a–b). What is "advantageous" to the "good life in general," therefore, will be precisely those actions that provide opportunities for the exercise of one's reasoning faculties (for *logos* is the highest element of the soul) in regard both to oneself and to family, friends, and fellow citizens, and with an adequate provision of external goods. The exercise of *phronêsis* itself, of course, satisfies the first of these requirements, but it also presupposes an awareness of the other constituents of human well-being. The exercise of practical wisdom begins with a perception of practical goods for oneself, one's family, and one's community, and this perception is a product of the dialectical process, reasoned discourse—*logos*.

Now to turn to the other aspect of practical intelligence—its use in deliberating about and choosing actions that will yield practical goods. In this, we need to examine both the nature of deliberation and the role of *phronêsis* in choosing good acts. Practical wisdom is the intellectual virtue whose excellence lies in deliberating well about the means to ends we can achieve through action. It aims at ascertaining "moral truth," identifying right action in practical situations. As to the nature of this deliberative process, Aristotle tells us (1142b) that it is not *epistêmê* or "skill in Conjecture (*eustochia*)" or "any form of Opinion (*doxa*)." It is "some form of correctness" resulting from "conscious calculation." The most extensive consideration of this process in the *Ethics* occurs in book 3 (1112a–b), where we learn that no one deliberates about eternal things, "such as the order of the universe, or the incommensurability of the diagonal and the side of a square." Nor do we deliberate about regular events in nature such as the solstices and the sunrise or about irregular occurrences such as droughts and rains or about chance events such as "finding a hidden treasure." "The reason why we do not deliberate about these things," Aristotle tells us, "is that none of them can be effected by our agency." Thus "we deliberate about things that are in our control and are attainable by action" (1112a). Moreover we deliberate about things where our actions do not always produce the same results—"for instance about questions of medicine and of business; and we deliberate about navigation more than about athletic training, because it has been less completely reduced to a science; and similarly with other pursuits also . . . because we are more uncertain about them" (1112b). The sphere of deliberation, consequently, concerns what happens "for the most part," where the result is obscure and the right course of action is not obvious, "and where, when the matter is important, we take others into our deliberations, distrusting our own capacity to decide [well]."

Deliberating about means to desired ends consists finally in determining what action must be taken first in order to set in motion a chain of events that will culminate in the result we seek. This requires knowledge of cause-effect relationships regarding matters where human agency can affect events, and it requires an ability to reason deductively from the first causes of certain things (efficient causes, typically, in the realm of practical affairs) to the particular acts that must be performed in order to initiate the chain of causes. This form of reasoning involves what Aristotle terms the "practical syllogism" (*syllogismoi tôn praktôn*, 1144a), and it may require the application of scientific knowledge to practical matters. The premises of practical reasoning will be general propositions such as "dry food is conducive to human health," and they may be drawn from the findings of biological, physical, or other scientific investigations.[28] Even so, because of the variability and uncertainty that attend projected outcomes in such matters—for example, different patients may respond differently to the same treatment—our practical knowledge can never attain the degree of certainty associated with scientific knowledge.

In cases where an end might be achieved through several means (this is the case in most practical situations), we must determine which of various courses of action is likely to accomplish this "most easily and best." This is the sort of activity we typically associate with the term "deliberation." It involves comparing the relative advantages and disadvantages of alternative courses of action, finding evidence to support one or another judgment about these things, making arguments that will reveal one set of outcomes and costs as more or less likely than others and one course of action as more efficacious than the alternatives, and then deciding on that one action. In this respect, private deliberations are analogous to the deliberative process occurring in the legislative assembly of the polis. They are activities wherein we discover or invent things that can be said for and against prospective lines of conduct—that is, we discover "demonstrative" and "refutative" practical syllogisms that allow us to determine the relative expediency of each projected action. On this basis, we make a choice and perform the act that our deliberation has identified as "best." This is the way in which Aristotle describes the construction of deliberative syllogisms (for "the Enthymeme is a syllogism") in the *Rhetoric*.[29] Thus the deliberative activity of the practical intellect—and so the exercise of *phronêsis* in determining right conduct—is fundamentally rhetorical. The activity of *logos* in practical decision making is the same, whether the decision is personal or collective, for the term refers equally well to "inward debate of the soul," "argument," "reasoned discourse," and a "reason or ground" for doing something.

The process of moral deliberation and choice, as Aristotle conceives it, involves more than a cost-benefit analysis regarding which of several competing courses of action will be most expedient in attaining a practical good. *Phronê-sis* is not just an intellectual virtue; it is also inherently connected to the idea of moral virtue—that "settled disposition of the mind (*hexis*) determining the choice (*proairesis*) of actions and emotions, consisting essentially in the obser-vance of the mean relative to us (*en mesotêti ousa têi pros êmas*), this being deter-mined by [rational] principle (*logos*), that is, as the prudent man (*o phronimos*) would determine it" (*Eth.* 1107a). Insofar as "right conduct" chosen as a result of deliberation must lie in a "mean" or intermediate position between ex-tremes, practical reasoning must inevitably include some assessment of what constitutes the mean in a given set of circumstances. It is precisely the *logos* of the prudent person that determines this intermediate point. Aristotle's doc-trine of the mean—that "to feel these feelings at the right time, on the right occasion, towards the right people, for the right purpose and in the right man-ner, is to feel the best amount of them, which is the mean amount" (1106b)—is a central element in his moral theory. The intermediate point between excess and defect in feeling and acting is determined through the activity of the soul's "logistical" reason (*to logistikon*).

One guide to understanding how this occurs is Aristotle's own comparison of the process to that of finding an arithmetical mean. In the latter case, he gives an illustration by determining the intermediate point between 10 and 2, arriving by a simple calculation at the number 6. "But," he says, "we cannot arrive by this method at the mean relative to us" (1106a), which is not one and the same for everybody nor in all circumstances. Determining the mean in practical matters is not a process of routine calculation. Still, this mean is a kind of proportion (*analogia*), a point that is neither too close to nor too far from the extremes of excess and deficiency regarding a particular emotion or action. It is identified by applying the rule or standard by which the prudent person would identify it. This standard is the soul's *logos*. This term signifies, among other things, "argument" and "inward debate of the soul." Accordingly the process of deliberation, insofar as it involves "inward debate" and the con-sideration of arguments for and against a specific course of action, is an activ-ity of the soul's *logos*. However, the term also denotes "proportion" or "ratio." It suggests, as we have seen, the idea of balance or equilibrium between oppos-ing forces. The "rational principle" by which the mean is determined, then, is balance or proportion.

In the virtuous person, practical deliberation and choice are guided by a rhetorical sense of the stronger and weaker arguments in considering the ad-vantages and disadvantages of a possible action. However, these activities are also directed by a sense of balance or proportion by which an action can be judged in terms of how fully it comports with the mean in a given situation. Sound judgment must consider the particular circumstances, the agent's own character, and the characters of those toward whom one is to act. In this way, the *logos* of the prudent person serves as a kind of moral gyroscope, enabling one to keep one's moral balance even as circumstances and people vary from one occasion to the next. It is, quite literally, an aesthetic sense, a heightened sensitivity to the composition and tendencies of practical situations and a perceptiveness regarding how best to proceed amid the various possibilities defining a particular situation. Aristotle observes that hitting the mean "is a difficult thing to do, and especially in particular cases" (1109b), and he states that in the end, "the decision [concerning the Mean in a given situation] lies with perception (*en tê aisthêsei ê krisis*)." The reference to an "aesthetic" sense here tells us much about how Aristotle understood the operation of *logos* in identifying the mean. The moral sense is both cognized and felt; it incorporates both rational elements of the soul—reason per se—and appetites and passions that are "obedient to reason." Moral knowing is a function of the whole person, not merely of "the divine element in us."

Aristotle's conception of practical wisdom involves multiple applications of the soul's reasoning and discursive faculties in the determination of conduct. In discovering ends toward which our actions should ultimately be directed, we engage in the reasoned discourse of dialectical investigation. In selecting the most efficacious course of conduct for the realization of these ends, we engage in a process of deliberation that is both syllogistic and rhetorical. Finally, in determining the point of balance or proportion between the "too much" and the "too little" in our conduct, we draw upon an inherent sense of proportionality (again, upon our *logos*), an aesthetic sensibility toward what is balanced and harmonious regarding action in particular circumstances.

Aristotle conceived two forms of "rational activity" in the soul that could fulfill the demand for the "exercise of . . . the best and most perfect" of the virtues, the soul's *logos*. One is practical reasoning, the proper activity of the "logistical" or "calculative" intellect. The other is *theoria*—"contemplation"— which is the *telos* of the speculative intellect. Of these, the latter is "more divine" because its objects are "by nature most precious" (1172b–73a). If we proceed by the logic that Aristotle has set down, the highest good for a human being will be an activity of the soul that involves thinking about immutable, universal, necessary truths. This is precisely what Aristotle proposes (1177a). However, he says, "such a life would be too high for a [human being]; for it is not in so far as he is [human] that he will live so, but in so far as something divine is present in him; and by so much as this is superior to our composite nature is its activity superior to that which is the exercise of the other kind of virtue" (1177b). "In a secondary degree," he concludes (1177a), "the life in accordance with the other kind of virtue [moral virtue] is happy; for the activities in accordance with it befit our human estate. Just and brave acts, and other virtuous acts, we do in relation to each other, observing our respective duties with regard to . . . all manner of actions and with regard to passions; and all of these seem to be typically human." In sum it would seem that, for Aristotle, a completely happy human life will involve a combination of contemplation and practical engagement, both of which involve the exercise of our rational faculty. Contemplation of eternal *archai* must always be a constituent of human well-being. However, humans are not purely rational beings, and we cannot live (as humans) in social isolation nor in continuous contemplation. We are also passionate, desiring, active beings; we share with the rest of the animal world a capacity for sensation, and thus a tendency to seek pleasure and avoid pain. Moreover we are "political" creatures; we live with one another in communities, and it is in our communal experience that we must seek the form of happiness corresponding most fully to our *human* nature. Thus the good life for a human being will involve both contemplation of first principles and practical action in the polis.

In Aristotle we find a complex conception of wisdom that assimilates and integrates many of the ideas he inherited from his predecessors. On the one hand, Aristotle acknowledges the existence of a rational, law-governed natural realm whose first principles are immutable, universal, and necessary, the understanding of which constitutes the highest form of human knowledge: speculative wisdom (*sophia*). This is ruled by a "rational principle" (*logos*) that finds its highest manifestation in the mind of god, the primary cause of all existence, motion, and change in the natural world. To the extent that humans can grasp this divine *Logos*, it is because "something divine is present in us." The human soul possesses a *logos* that enables it to apprehend the *Logos* of the cosmos, and thus the human soul partakes in the divine Soul that animates the universe.

On the other hand, Aristotle situates the human being as a sentient, social creature in the realm of change, particularity, possibility—the moral realm. This is the sphere of human association and intercourse, practical decision and action, desire and emotion. Although constant contemplation of the first principles of nature is envisioned as an ideal—for "perfect happiness is a contemplative activity"—such a life would be "too high for man; for it is not in so far as he is man that he will live so." Human action is played out in the realm of appearance, probability, opinion, controversy, persuasion, rhetoric. The wisdom humans can attain *as* human is the wisdom of insecurity, uncertainty, and contingency: *practical* or *moral* wisdom. As with the higher form, practical sagacity rests finally in the soul's possession of a *logos*, a principle by which the prudent person can identify in a particular moral situation the course of action that will conduce toward desired ends and be intermediate between extremes. This is action that is balanced, proportional to all the factors characterizing the situation. With both forms of wisdom the key is *logos*—the element of the human soul that participates in the universal, divine order.

Aristotle manages to synthesize these several motifs—an interest in practical knowledge, a recognition that the sensory realm can lead to knowledge of the absolute and unchanging, the quest for certainty and immutability within or behind the processes of change—into a coherent philosophical system. In doing so he has articulated a highly textured, multifaceted conception in which we can detect elements of the wisdom-tradition at whose head he stands. For Aristotle as for many of his predecessors, the universe is constituted and governed by a divine *Logos*, a principle of proportion, balance, and equilibrium. This *Logos* is connected to the divine *Nous*, the mind of god, and it is the final cause of the cosmic process. For Aristotle as for many of his forebears, the human mind possesses its own *logos*, a particular manifestation of the divine *Logos*. Thus, for him as for Heraclitus and Plato, when we go in search of wisdom, we go in search of ourselves. For Aristotle as for many before him, wisdom is inherently connected to speech, language, argument, reasoning, debate, and persuasion. Moreover, insofar as our speaking/reasoning/arguing/deliberating/persuading powers are innately linked to the rational principle that orders the universe, the path to wisdom is always by way of *logos*. Our words structure our knowledge and construct our understandings of the world in which we live and act. These understandings may be uncertain and pluralistic, but they are nonetheless products of our speech. *Sophia* and *phronêsis*, speculative and practical sagacity, together constitute the forms of wisdom to which humans can aspire. In this vision Aristotle brings to completion the intellectual wisdom-tradition of Hellenic culture.

Epilogue

I commenced this inquiry seeking, in the Greek wisdom literature of the archaic and classical periods, coherent accounts of how founders of the Western intellectual tradition conceived wisdom, understood its means of acquisition and expression, and viewed the role of *logos* (broadly conceived) in these processes. I was particularly concerned to discover not merely how these thinkers *described* the idea of wisdom but also the content of the wisdom they believed themselves to have sought and acquired. Granting for the sake of discussion that these wisdom-seekers actually arrived at legitimate insights about the natural world and human experience, what did they understand? Turning from the nature and contents of Greek wisdom to its connections with *logos*—proportion, speech, reasoning, rational principle, discussion and debate, argument, logical inquiry—I sought to illuminate how these activities are involved in the acquisition of the highest forms of human wisdom, and how wisdom manifests itself in speech. My aim in these closing pages is to distill from the foregoing discussions of these matters the principal conclusions and insights to which they point. I have argued here for no overarching thesis, but my examination of these texts and their contexts yields a number of important ideas.

Connections between *sophia* and *logos* presage relations between philosophy and rhetoric that emerged during the fifth and fourth centuries; these relations persist into our own time. The language arts that came to be identified with speculative inquiry (philosophy) and with political deliberation and practical decision (rhetoric) arose from the same set of cultural beliefs and practices. The distinctions between them appear most conspicuously in Plato and Aristotle. Their proper concerns, boundaries, and commonalities are considered by Western thinkers ranging from Cicero and Augustine to Vico, Erasmus, and George Campbell. Twentieth-century scholars in both philosophical and rhetorical studies have sought to clarify the issues and themes that link and divide the two fields. Yet, for all this, in the beginning there was no difference between philosophy and rhetoric; later theorists gave them names "to express appearances," as Lao Tzu might put it. *Logos* was the path to *sophia*, and *sophia* expressed itself as *logos*. After Plato, the relationship between two distinct disciplines has been a common and important theme in scholarly inquiry.

We can identify no single, comprehensive conception of wisdom in the reports of early Greek speculative thought. Yet, for all the multiplicity of views, there are points of coherence among the discontinuities and contradictions. We find from the outset a distinction between divine and human wisdom—between "perfect wisdom" and that which "befits our human estate," fraught as it is with imperfection and uncertainty. In both cases wisdom permits its possessor to foretell the future. The poets held that only the gods are capable of "true wisdom," for only they can know why world events happen as they do, and only they can foresee the destinies of these events and the fates of human beings. Yet, to the extent that humans are capable of apprehending the divine mind, we are capable of divining what lies ahead. Insofar as we can read omens and understand the gods' characters as revealed in myth, we can envision, however imperfectly, what the gods have ordained.

With the Presocratics the same impulse is at work. However much thinkers such as Anaximander, Heraclitus, Pythagoras, Empedocles, Anaxagoras, and Leucippus may have differed in their conceptions of the world's origins, the nature of matter, and the sources of motion and change, they are united in their conviction that the universe is directed by an indwelling rational principle—Justice, *Logos*, Reciprocity, Harmony, Mind, Thought. It is precisely the idea that the universe is rational, that it exhibits order and is law-governed, that permits reasoned explanation of natural events and reasoned prediction about their outcomes.

The same conclusion holds if, as with Aristotle, the highest wisdom is apprehending the "final causes" or "first principles" that direct the cosmic processes of creation and destruction, and knowing the particulars that follow logically from these principles. Speculative or theoretical wisdom enables its possessor to foresee the careers of natural events because they are bound by the laws of causation. One motif running through Greek wisdom-literature, then, is that *sophia* entails the power of foresight, the capacity for predicting the future. Whether this power comes through grasping the mind(s) of (the) god(s) or through understanding the *logos* of nature, one aspiration of the speculative thinker is to intuit the eternal, universal truths that are at work in natural processes and to project how these processes will unfold. Wisdom culminates in comprehending "the sense things make," in grasping how everything fits together, and from this being able to envision a likely future.

An important adjunct to this, original in European thought with the Greeks, is the idea that every existing thing is but an aspect of a single, all-encompassing entity: "all things are one," Heraclitus tells us. As an intellectual and scientific development, the discovery of a unitary Nature was as revolutionary as the Hebrews' monotheism was in the history of ancient religions. This insight marks the invention of a *uni-verse*, the conception of an indwelling unity behind the diversity in existing things. Moreover, because it is governed by its own law, nature operates in regular, consistent, and thus in predictable ways; it is never arbitrarily but always of necessity that natural events occur. If we can grasp the laws of the universe, we can reason out what will happen as a result of their operation. The idea that, in its essence, nature is singular and that all things are manifestations of one thing animates contemporary cosmological speculations known as "unified-field theories"—lines of research aimed at unifying the four fundamental forces in the cosmos (gravity, electromagnetism, and the strong and weak nuclear forces). We also see in Greek "nature-philosophy" an incipient ecological consciousness. All things in the world are interconnected, and the laws of cause and effect mean that movement and change are never isolated events; thus do human actions affect natural processes around the globe, because we are elements of the same natural system. We are heir to the Presocratics' intuitive leap into this awareness.

The intellectual instrument enabling this leap was analogical thinking. Thales' speculation began with the insight that the world is somehow like water, while Anaximenes saw a likeness in air. Seeing likenesses among things is the basis of thinking by analogy. Inferring that something unknown is like something known permits the mind to speculate about the nature of the unknown thing and to know it in terms of what it has in common with the known. When this mode of thinking is carried to its end, it comes to the recognition that all things are alike at some level because all things are, at the deepest/highest level, aspects of the same thing. Allied with analogical thinking is the metaphorical use of concrete terms. Metaphor is a form of expression that gives voice to analogies in the mind. It is the linguistic foundation of all speculation about nature.

Another legacy is the thought that *physis* is *theia*. "Everything is full of gods," Thales says, and thereby points the way to an abstract conception of divinity as a feature of nature itself, rather than as a force outside nature that can inject itself into the flow of events. To hold that nature is divine is to see it as eternal, omnipresent, and all-powerful. It is nature that rules the cosmos; thus it always was and will be. Seeing nature as divine also invites the idea that it is worthy of reverence. Nature-worship is often associated with pagan religions, insofar as they worshipped as gods the forces we now connect with nature. However, one legacy of early Greek philosophical thought may be the idea that nature should be worshipped directly, rather than through the medium of anthropomorphic or other deities. This is the outlook one finds in the thinking of Albert Einstein, for example, who reportedly wrote, "The religion of the future will be a cosmic religion. It should transcend personal God and avoid dogma and theology. Covering both the natural and the spiritual, it should be based on a religious sense arising from the experience of all things natural and spiritual as a meaningful unity" (1954). The idea of a "philosophical spirituality" is an implicit element of Greek thinking about wisdom.

˙If Greek wisdom embraces the ideas that all things are One and that the One is Nature, it also maintains that the human being is part of nature and is subject to its dictates. The unity of human and cosmic *psychai* means that understanding fundamental principles of nature is also knowing oneself. The idea that cosmic truths are imprinted in the soul's depths, central in the thinking of Heraclitus and Plato, resonates through Western philosophical and religious traditions into the present. While this insight might not be unique to Greek thinkers, it is an important element in the vision of wisdom they have bequeathed to us. Moreover, as an incarnation of the cosmic soul, the human also has a proper function within the cosmic process. This teleological element in the Greek wisdom-tradition emphasizes the idea that the "purpose of human life" is to fulfill our natural role in the order of things. For the thinkers examined here, we are designed by nature to understand, to know, to make sense of the world. Our purpose is to use our intellectual powers to grasp the ultimate source of our own existence, and thereby to enable the universe to become self-conscious. As Niels Bohr is said to have put this point, "a physicist is just an atom's way of looking at itself."

For all the emphasis on knowledge and understanding, Greek wisdom is also an awareness that the human capacity for knowledge is limited. Thinkers from Xenophanes and the Eleatics to the Atomists, the Sophists, and Socrates recognized that our comprehension of "the way things are" is always constrained by the deceptiveness of the senses and/or the imperfection of human intelligence. While Plato and Aristotle envisioned the possibility of absolute certainty regarding universal and absolute truth, an important aspect of this wisdom-tradition is the fundamental humility that must attend all knowledge-claims. The Sophists remind us of our epistemological limitations, especially regarding practical affairs. They invoke a consciousness of uncertainty, a recognition that all knowledge is mediated by the knowing subject and by language.

Perhaps one of the greatest ironies in this Greek wisdom-tradition is that speech both discloses and masks the realities that rule us and in terms of which we live our lives. *Logos* is and is not the revealer of what is. It is the orderer of the cosmos, the principle of proportionality that runs through the structure and operation of the universe as we know it. At the same time, human *logos* both expresses and creates cosmic order. The cosmos exists as a realm of logical possibility (for what cannot be, is not). Whatever comports with the laws of nature can happen, whether or not it actually occurs. What does not comport with these laws cannot happen. Language, when used sensibly, expresses the possible and so expresses a "truth" about the cosmos. To exist coherently in language and to exist as a possibility inherent in the cosmic order are two facets of the same thing. At the same time, humans use language to *give* order to the cosmos. We use speech to distinguish between what is and what is not, and to define what is. Speech is the measure of all things—of things that are, that they are; and of things that are not, that they are not. In our use of language to circumscribe and define the existent, we impose order on experience. We construct our "realities" individually and collectively through the words we use to explain, describe, and argue for alternative ways of ordering experience. This insight, original with the Sophists, reemerges in social constructionism and symbolic interactionism. Still, since human *logos* expresses the cosmic *Logos*, the order we impose is rooted in the cosmic order. However, insofar as speech creates the impression that "things that are" exist as we describe them, it creates the illusion that we have captured "reality" in our words. "Reality is beyond the power of words to define." The cosmos is and is not as we say it is. This conundrum is an essential feature of Greek wisdom.

The Greeks' cognizance of our intellectual limitations points to a distinction between knowledge and faith. We can "know" the cosmos only within the limits of probability because uncertainty is a necessary condition of all human understanding. When we seek more, we enter the realm of faith—the leap to certitude. The mathematician and philosopher Jacob Bronowski, describing the limitations of modern scientific knowledge, writes that "one aim of the physical sciences has been to give an exact picture of the material world. One achievement of physics in the twentieth century has been to prove that this aim is unattainable. . . . There is no absolute knowledge. And those who claim it, whether they are scientists or dogmatists, open the door to tragedy. All information is imperfect. We have to treat it with humility. That is the human condition" (1973, 353). This important insight is another legacy of the wisdom-tradition I have excavated here. In our own time, we would do well to acknowledge it.

For the Greeks wisdom is more than a purely intellectual understanding of natural principles; it also encompasses an active, practical understanding of their implications for human choice and conduct. The goal of the moral philosopher—a lover of practical wisdom—is to apprehend the moral truths that should guide our decisions about conduct. For most of the thinkers examined here, the distinction between the divine, natural realm and the sphere of human choice is one of emphasis rather than of substance. We are subject in our practical choices to the laws of nature, and so our wisdom must comprise a fusion of cosmological understanding and moral insight. Wisdom denotes an approach to living and a way-of-being in the world illuminated by an apprehension of the "way" of the cosmos.

These recur ultimately to the *Logos*, the principle of proportion, balance, harmony, symmetry, and equilibrium according to which the universe is unfolding and by which right action is determined. The natural tendency—the *entelechy*—at work in both natural and human realms is toward balance and reciprocity; arrangement and motion are ordered by fidelity to this principle. Pythagoreans found in mathematical ratios and musical harmonies the laws that govern the structure and movement of the cosmos. The idea of music also suggests a kind of rhythm, a reciprocal or alternating flow between equal and opposing tendencies—the ebb and flood of the tide, the annual revolution of the seasons, the counterpoint between darkness and light, sleeping and wakefulness, death and life. Nature is full of rhythms, vibrations, harmonies, balances. This is what constitutes the natural "order"—everything is tending toward the perfectly attuned system. Moral wisdom involves the discovery and application of this principle in our actions toward the natural world and each other. Acting in accordance with the "intelligence" or "plan" that steers all things through all is the key to living morally. This insight underlies Aristotle's doctrine of the mean—the idea that sound moral judgment arises from an interior sense of proportion that reflects the principle of proportion at work in the universe as a whole.

The practical implications of the wisdom-tradition include insight into the key to living a happy life. Since the life one lives is the product of the practical choices one makes in responding to concrete circumstances, ultimately one lives the life one has chosen. An essential condition for a good life, accordingly, is the ability to make wise choices—skill (*sophia*) or excellence (*aretê*) in the art of living. This art, like any other, involves understanding the principles and laws that constrain the activity. It requires understanding the "rules" governing the production of a particular kind of artifact—in this case, a person's life. These rules are the principles manifested in causal connections, at both the cosmic and social levels. Thus, following Antiphon, in order to live a good life one should understand both *physis* and *nomoi*, natural and human rules. To the extent that one grasps and applies these, one is enabled to make wise choices, so that the goods in life come through deliberate action rather than by chance.

We may trace the distinction between dialectic and rhetoric, and therefore between philosophy and rhetoric, to two complementary uses of discourse, argument, and debate—as an instrument of speculative inquiry into the nature of things, and as a practical activity aimed at deciding moral questions in public and private affairs. It is not clear how or whether the first nature philosophers viewed these two functions as discreet; nor was there any reason they should have. The intellectual inquiries of Thales, Anaximander, their associates, and their successors were conducted with small groups of fellow seekers who questioned, asserted, argued, and counterargued about theories of nature.

Later, Eleatic thinkers proceeded similarly to examine the nature of "the existent" and the idea of Being. Socrates and Plato, with their adherents, gathered themselves away from the agora, in private homes or gymnasiums, to debate the nature of Justice, the Good, Virtue, and Beauty. These activities, perhaps with Plato, came to be subsumed by "philosophy," and thus has it been since. At the same time, the Milesians, Ephesians, Eleatics, and Athenians convened in public to question, assert, argue, and counterargue about political questions, and they employed the same techniques in their private deliberations about practical problems. These activities, perhaps again beginning with Plato, are "rhetorical." At the same time, it is important to remember that the Sophists and Isocrates made no such distinction, and it remains a vexed question even now.

Whatever boundaries might be drawn between philosophy and rhetoric, and whenever these were first made, their commonalities are deep and enduring. Cosmological and naturalistic theorizing, metaphysical and ethical speculation share with political and moral discourse the *technai* of the verbal *agôn*—contesting arguments though eristic and elenchus. Debate and disputation are the procedures of both uses of *logos*, and these procedures are fundamentally agonistic. This model of speculative inquiry and practical judgment is the archetype for scientific and academic methodologies that are at the core of the Western intellectual tradition, and for the technique of public debate that is the essence of democratic decision making. Moreover argument and reasoning in the service of both theoretical inquiry and practical judgment appeared together with the advent of *logos* and the polis as alternatives to *mythos* and the Dark Age chiefdom. Thence were philosophy and rhetoric made possible.

The Presocratics in particular developed a worldview and a vocabulary that gave rise to the intellectual and linguistic architecture of both rhetoric and philosophy. How this occurred in the case of philosophy we have seen. For rhetoric, the contributions of Presocratic thinkers involved, most particularly, a vision of regularity in events that creates the possibility of probability, the forms of deductive reasoning on which the syllogism and enthymeme were based, and an abstract vocabulary that enabled the Sophists and Aristotle to theorize an art of persuasion. When the flow of events is seen as emanating from stable, universal laws rather than from the caprices of supernatural beings, the world becomes predictable to a greater degree, and the dependable regularities in the flow make it possible to anticipate—within the limits of probability—the outcomes of various happenings and actions. One can argue that some outcomes are more probable than others on the premise that cause-and-effect relations among events arise from fixed natural laws or stable patterns, and that the future will resemble the past (Aristotle, *Rhet.* 1394a). Argument from probability—a discovery credited to Corax/Tisias in the rhetorical tradition and a central feature of sophistical teachings about speech and reasoning—is a product of this conceptual shift. Aristotle, of course, held that all practical and rhetorical reasoning is based on probabilities. The idea of "the probable" is implicit in the insight that the universe is governed by law.

Similarly the principles and practices of deduction—a form of argument at the heart of both dialectic and rhetoric for Aristotle—rest on the terministic meditations of Parmenides and the logical play of Gorgias. Terms exhibit logical relations, and these relations compel the mind to move from premises to conclusions. Certainly prerhetorical and prephilosophical minds reasoned deductively, insofar as things and events functioned as signs from which a god's or goddess's preferences could be inferred, but this process does not appear as a form of argument until Parmenides' analysis of the "is." Subsequent refinements and applications in this form are found in Empedocles, Zeno, and most conspicuously in Gorgias's *Palamedes* and *Helen*. Its employment by Socrates and Plato in pursuing philosophical questions and its codification by Aristotle for use in both dialectic and rhetoric are made possible by the earlier developments.

The construction of an abstract vocabulary characterized by the use of metaphorically "stretched" terms drawn from myth and of the verb "to be" as the copula of analytic statement enabled both cosmological/metaphysical speculation by philosophers and a theoretical account of rhetoric's workings by Aristotle. It is precisely the availability of abstract terms such as *o logos* (as "rational principle," "reasoned discourse," and "argument"), *to eikos* (as "probability," that which is likely to happen), and *to katholou* (as "universal," that which happens "on the whole" or "for all") that permitted Aristotle to conceptualize dialectical and rhetorical proofs. Had such a vocabulary not been bequeathed to him by his Presocratic forebears, Aristotle would have had to invent it himself before his conceptualization of *apodeixis*—logical demonstration—could be explained. Had Socrates and the Sophists not deployed the abstract terms required for moral and epistemological discussion, Aristotle would not have been able to theorize rhetoric as the *technê* of practical deliberation and judgment.

Finally there is the centrality of *beauty* in the practice of both philosophy and rhetoric. For thinkers ranging from Heraclitus and Pythagoras to Plato, it is an apprehension of harmony, order, and unity in the world that awakens the aesthetic response, opening one to universal truths that underlie the surface appearances of events. For Gorgias, *terpsis*—aesthetic pleasure—gives speech its power over the human soul. Whether in cosmological speculation or political persuasion, the role of the beautiful is central. Even now scientific theories are assessed for their simplicity and elegance, and the aesthetic dimensions of speech have been central in the study of eloquence from Longinus and Cicero to Lord Kames and Hugh Blair.

Emerging from the ideas examined here are understandings of *sophia* and the role of *logos* in its acquisition and exercise that have shaped the Western intellectual tradition from the beginning. These earliest speculative thinkers conceptualized nature, the divine, wisdom, and speech in ways that gave birth to what we have come to identify as "philosophy" and "rhetoric." Havelock writes that "Europe still lives in their shadow, using their language, accepting their dichotomies, and submitting to their discipline of the abstract as the chief vehicle of higher education, even to this day" (1963, 305). I have sought to do justice to the predisciplinary character of Presocratic and sophistical thinking, even as I attempted to explain ideas and terms that gave direction and content to the speculations of Plato and Aristotle. Presocratic and sophistical teachings were both revolutionary and seminal, setting a course for the journey on which we are still embarked in our quest to understand the world in which we live and the epistemological potencies of language and speech. A central theme of this book has been that the Greek wisdom-tradition preserved in the surviving texts yields insights that remain important in our own time. While the historical circumstances shaping this tradition are rooted in the past, they engendered a culture of which we in the West are still inhabitants, practitioners, and custodians. Central tenets of this culture are that the universe makes sense, that it is governed by a *Logos*, that it speaks to us, and that we can grasp the sense it makes if we know how to listen to it.

A few months before concluding this writing, I had occasion to visit the sanctuary of Asclepius, the ancient god of healing, at Epidaurus in the northeastern Peloponnesus. As I walked through the site on a crisp spring morning, going from the sanctuary's ancient, monumental gateway toward the amphitheater, I heard birds singing as a cool breeze blew through the needles on the nearby pines. The place was infused with silence and music simultaneously, and I recalled a passage from Henry Miller's *Colossus of Maroussi:* "Nature can cure only when man recognizes his place in the world, which is not in Nature, as with the animal, but in the human kingdom, the link between the natural and the divine. . . . At Epidaurus, in the stillness, in the great peace that came over me, I heard the heart of the world beat. I know what the cure is: it is to give up, to relinquish, to surrender, so that our little hearts may beat in unison with the great heart of the world. . . . [But] Epidaurus is merely a place symbol: the real place is in the heart, in every man's heart, if he will but stop and search it."

Notes

Chapter 1. The Greek Stones Speak

1. Cherwitz and Hikins 1986; Gregg 1984; Scott 1967, 1976.

2. C. Johnstone 1980, 1981, 1983; Kneupper and Anderson 1980.

3. Cole 1991a; Lentz 1989; Poulakos 1995; Robb 1983; Schiappa 2003; Vernant 1982, 1983.

4. Several thorough accounts of this development have appeared in recent decades. See, for example, Kennedy 1963, 1994; Cole 1991a; Enos 1993; Schiappa 1999; Fredal 2006. Others have examined the first glimmerings of a preconceptual rhetorical consciousness in the poetry of Homer and Hesiod. See Kirby 1992; Atwill 1998; Walker 2000; Roisman 2007; Clay 2007.

5. See Dodds 1951; Havelock 1963; Snell 1982; Guthrie 1953; Hatab 1990.

6. Ong characterizes "consciousness" as "man's sense of presence in the human life-world, including the physical world and what man senses beyond" (1977, 9), and he writes that the "evolution of consciousness . . . can be understood with reference to the interior, psychic world and with reference to the exterior world. . . . Through the development of culture, a store of experience and knowledge that human beings can accumulate and hand on to succeeding generations, mankind as a whole gains more and more conscious access to and control over the cosmos and itself" (42–43). Also see Jaynes 1976, esp. 21–66, 204–22.

7. In his recent study of rhetoric's development as a form of agonistic action in Athens, Fredal (2006) laments the tendency of "logocentrism" in historical research to eclipse "questions about bodies, practices, identity, and privilege" (4). He focuses instead on the material and geographical contexts in which rhetoric emerged during the sixth to fourth centuries B.C.E., just as Hawhee (2004) identifies rhetoric with the "bodily arts." Such approaches to reconstructing ancient beliefs and practices are important, and they suggest that there are multiple "wisdom-traditions" to be discovered in Greek culture, including perhaps the "wisdom of the body," the "wisdom of the household," "women's wisdom," and the "wisdom of place." Studies of such traditions would be worthwhile. My present focus, nonetheless, is on how wisdom was *conceived* in Greece and on how *logos* figured in its acquisition and practice, so I will perforce be "logocentric" in my approach and in the evidence from which I reconstruct conceptions of wisdom.

8. On the necessity of interpretation in historiography, see White 1972–73.

9. Borrowing terminology from Rorty (1984) and Makin (1988), Schiappa (1990b, 2003) differentiates between the "historical reconstruction" of sophistic doctrines and the "[rational] reconstruction of neo-sophistic rhetorical theory and criticism" (1990b, 193). Whereas the former aims to "recapture the past insofar as possible on its own terms" (194), the latter seeks to "draw on sophistic thinking in order to contribute to *contemporary* theory and practice" (195; italics in original). Although McComiskey endorses this distinction, he provides a corrective: "the practice of neosophistic appropriation does not fall into the category of [either] rational [or historical] reconstruction, but instead . . . requires its own category" (2002, 8). Thus, he writes, "assuming a clear separation between historical interpretation (with historical . . . and rational reconstruction functioning as points on a continuum) and neosophistic appropriation, I proceed . . . with caution" to pursue both objectives (11). Schiappa adopts McComiskey's approach in the second edition of his *Protagoras and Logos* (2003, 65–68), substituting "contemporary" for "neosophistic" appropriation. I apply the distinction broadly to all interpretation of historical texts and thus prefer Schiappa's terminology to McComiskey's.

10. Schiappa 1990b, 194. Also see Schiappa 2003, 64–69; Makin 1988, 122; McComiskey 2002, 6–11.

11. See Ceccarelli 1998. She argues that texts are "polysemous"; that is, they admit of multiple readings as a result of either "resistive reading" by audiences or "strategic ambiguity" by authors. In either case, the interpreter must recognize that a plurality of meanings can legitimately be read into texts. Similarly, White observes of historical writing that "there is no such thing as a *single* correct view of any object under study but there are *many* correct views, each requiring its own style of representation" (1966, 130–31). Also see White 1972–73, esp. 300ff.; Veyne 1971, ix–x, 3–14.

12. See Ceccarelli: "ultimately, the power over textual signification remains with the author, who inserts *both* meanings into the text and who benefits . . . from the polysemic interpretation" (1998, 404).

13. Havelock is not without his critics. Halverson (1992), for instance, raises a number of provocative challenges to Havelock's hypotheses about the early development of Greek and the impact on it of the transition from orality to literacy. My sense is that Halverson has overstated his case and has underestimated the centrality of writing in the kind of mental operations he describes. This does not mean, of course, that all of Havelock's theses are to be accepted uncritically. What I do find compelling, however, is the idea that language evolves and that the emergence of a philosophical syntax and vocabulary out of linguistic forms that had been used principally in service of the oral preservation of cultural myths was made possible by, among several important factors, the appearance of the Greek alphabet. See Havelock's essay "The Linguistic Task of the Presocratics" (1983). The volume contains other essays that either challenge or endorse Havelock's position. Also see Vernant, "The Formation of Positivist Thought in Archaic Greece" (*Myth and Thought*, 1983) and "The Reason of Myth" (*Myth and Society*, 1990).

14. Havelock argues that a principal consequence of the advent of literacy was a "revolution . . . both psychological and epistemological" (1983, 87), culminating in "a new state of mind" (7). See also Snell 1982, 193ff.

15. See Havelock's (1963) discussion of the "Homeric state of mind" and Frankfort and Frankfort's (1977) account of "the mythopoetic mind." Also see Burkert 1985.

16. Plato, for instance, is notoriously lax in his quotations from all sources. See Kirk, Raven, and Schofield 1983, 1.

17. For a useful consideration of our sources for Socrates, see Guthrie 1971a, 7ff.

18. Schiappa 2003, 33–34, describes the process of "triangulation." Also see Guthrie 1971a, 29–35.

Chapter 2. Singing the Muses' Song

1. Liddell and Scott (1996), *s.v. entheos.* "Within is a god," according to Burkert 1985, 109.

2. Jacobs and Greenway 1966, x. A range of approaches to the study of myth is to be found in the work of such writers as Jung 1951; Cassirer 1953; Malinowski 1954; Eliade 1960, 1963; Kirk 1970; Campbell 1972; Frankfort and Frankfort 1977; Olson 1980; Strenski 1987; Ausband 1983; Vernant 1983, 1990.

3. Also see Frankfort and Frankfort 1977; Hatab 1990; Kirk 1970; Larson 1974; Leakey and Lewin 1992.

4. Ausband writes that "myths are tales which demonstrate the order that a [person] or a society perceives in natural phenomena. It is the role of mythology to make the world coherent and meaningful by demonstrating or imposing order on it. No society has existed that did not need some sort of structure, a system of belief, by which it could ask and answer questions about its relationship to the universal" (1983, 2). Also see Saggs 1989, 269; Eliade 1960, 1961, 1963; Dupre 1975.

5. *Mythos* means, first, anything delivered by word of mouth (in contrast to *ergon*— a *deed* or *act*). However, the term in Homer also signifies "a tale, story, narrative," for example, at *Od.* 4.214: "Tales (*mythoi*) there will be in the morning"; 4.597: "for wondrous is the pleasure I take in listening to thy tales (*mythoisin*)." Cognate terms such as *mythlogeô, mythologein,* and *mythologia* are used by Plato, Xenophon, and others to signify the telling of mythic tales or legends. Burkert defines myth as "a complex of traditional tales in which significant human situations are united in fantastic combinations to form a polyvalent semiotic system which is used in multifarious ways to illuminate reality" (1985, 120). Also see Vernant 1990, 203–4.

6. Also see Saggs 1989, 269; Vernant 1990, 219; Jaynes 1976, esp. 67–125.

7. See Saggs 1989, 269ff; Murray 1925, esp. chap. 1.

8. See Snell 1982; Vernant 1982, 1983, 1990.

9. See Burkert 1985, 19ff. See also Saggs 1989, 284 ff.; West in Hesiod 1978, 3–22; Vernant 1990, 216n13.

10. On the bardic tradition, see Finley 1979, 1981; Burkert 1985, esp. 47–53; Hooper 1978, chaps. 2–3.

11. Unless otherwise noted, quotations from the *Iliad* are based on Fagles's 1990 translation. Line numbers refer to the Greek text in the Loeb edition (1924).

12. Also see Jaynes 1976, 72–83.

13. For helpful accounts of the characters and special responsibilities of the Greek gods, see Burkert 1985; Barthell 1971; Bremmer 1987; Graves 1959; Guthrie 1950b.

14. As the episode involving Achilles and Athena has shown (*Il.* 1.216–18), this is certainly true of the *Iliad*, though less true of the *Odyssey*. Of the latter, Jaynes writes that "the contrast with the Iliad is astonishing. Both in word and deed and character, the Odyssey describes a new and different world inhabited by new and different beings. The bicameral gods of the Iliad, in crossing over to the Odyssey, have become defensive and feeble. . . . The bicameral mind by its very definition directs much less of the action. The gods have less to do, and like receding ghosts talk more to each other. . . . The initiatives move from them, even against them, toward the world of the more conscious human characters" (1976, 273). Also see Lentz 1989, 5; Mifsud 1997.

15. There is no agreement about Hesiod's exact date nor about the chronological relationship between him and Homer. Athanassakis (Hesiod 1983) remarks that "the best we can do is place him somewhere between the second half of the eighth century and the first quarter of the seventh. The prevalent opinion among Greeks of the Classical period was that Hesiod was among the earliest poets and teachers of the race. They usually placed him after the mythical Orpheus and Mousaios and before Homer. But . . . there is no compelling reason for the assumption that Hesiod either preceded Homer or even that he was his contemporary" (1). He places the composition of the *Theogony* during the last quarter of the eighth century and notes that "Hesiod definitely belongs to that transitional period when the oral tradition was slowly coming to an end and the written was taking its first, timid steps" (2). West (Hesiod 1978) provides a bit more precision: "The date of his birth cannot be determined with any exactitude, but it must be considered unlikely that it was earlier than 750 or later than 720" (30–31). Kirk, Raven, and Schofield place the composition of the *Theogony* in the early seventh century (1983, 34).

16. All line references to the *Theogony* are to Athanassakis's translation (Hesiod 1983). The opening lines of the poem were quoted at the outset of this chapter. *Chaos* is derived from *Cha*, meaning "gape, gap, yawn." See Kirk, Raven, and Schofield 1983, 37ff. The noun is not to be understood in its modern meaning, as disorder; nor should it be taken to indicate a "void." It is rather "a gap, . . . a bounded interval" (Kirk, Raven, and Schofield 38). This suggests that the first being was a kind of formless, inchoate thing—bounded, but open; empty, but fertile and full of potency.

17. See Finley 1979, 1981; Hooper 1978. All line references to *Works and Days* are to Athanassakis's translation in Hesiod 1983.

18. See Zielinski 1926, 15–37; Jaynes 1976, 67–83.

19. Also *Il.* 2.485: "O ye Muses. . . . You also are divine, you are present among us, and you know all things."

20. See Burkert 1985; Eliade 1963.

21. Eliade (1963) elaborates later (18) that "in general it can be said that myth, as experienced by archaic societies, (1) constitutes the History of the acts of the Supernaturals; (2) that this History is considered to be absolutely *true* (because it is concerned with realities) and *sacred* (because it is the work of the Supernaturals); (3) that myth is always related to a 'creation,' it tells how something came into existence, or how a pattern of behavior, an institution, a manner of working were established; this is why myths constitute the paradigms for all significant human acts" (italics in original). Also see Veyne 1988, esp. chaps. 6 and 7.

22. Hatab comments that "if we are to take myth seriously, we must also take seriously the fact that people have taken their myths seriously—people have believed in myths and their lives have been guided and shaped by myths" (1990, 18). He continues (20–21), "myths were not intended as 'speculation' or even [as] mere stories, because they were *functional*, woven into the concrete lives of a people. Myths established social and educational values; prescribed daily tasks and ceremonial responses; inspired painting, sculpture, music, dance, poetry, and architecture; gave meaning to birth, maturation, marriage, and death—in other words, myths shaped the cultural life of a society."

23. Also see Frankfort and Frankfort 1977, 6. I have discussed these matters elsewhere (Johnstone 2005), where I apply this reasoning particularly to Gorgias's views concerning the power of the spoken word over human thought, feeling, and action.

24. Also see 134ff. In chap. 3 ("Poetry as Preserved Communication"), Havelock advances the idea that poetry was *invented* as a means of preserving a culture's communication about itself. Also see Havelock, "The Linguistic Task of the Presocratics" (1983), esp. 7–15; Pomeroy et al. 1999, 51–53.

25. It should be noted that Ong's view is challenged by recent research in the cognitive sciences and in neuropsychology. For an excellent review of this research and its implications for the operations of language and other symbols, see Elder 1998.

26. Epic verse was often recited by bards and rhapsodes to the accompaniment of a lyre or a drum, but it was not until the development of lyric poetry during the seventh century that it was actually sung to a melody (Snell 1982, chap. 3). Havelock observes that "the regularity of the [poetic] performance had a certain effect of hypnosis which relaxed the body's physical tensions and so also relaxed mental tensions, the fears, anxieties, and uncertainties which are the normal lot of our mortal existence. Fatigue was temporarily forgotten and perhaps the erotic impulses, no longer blocked by anxiety, were stimulated" (1963, 152).

27. Also see Clay, who suggests, "with only a little tongue in cheek, that Hesiod might well be considered the father of rhetoric" (2007, 447). Roisman observes that "the *Iliad* anticipates the development of formal rhetorical theory in the fifth century and onward" (2007, 429) and derives from her reading of the poem "what may be termed Homer's theory of right rhetoric" (430).

28. Hatab observes that "receptivity may be the most illuminating characteristic of mythical thought in that it shapes both the form of the world and the human response to it. So little does primitive experience see itself in control that not only is the general course of the world seen to be bestowed and guided by sacred powers but even such mundane things as tools and skills are venerated, even worshipped, or seen as gifts grounded in sacred origins" (1990, 34).

29. Hatab continues, "a key distinction between myth and modern logic is that mythical coherence follows an existential form while conceptual logic follows an abstract form, but the fact that there *is* form in myth—that there is culture, communication, and agreement—undermines the accusation of irrationality often leveled against myth" (1990, 29). Likewise, Vernant states that "a mythology, that is to say, a unified, narrative corpus of stories, . . . [b]y virtue of its range and internal coherence, . . . represents an original system of thought as complex and rigorous in its own way as a philosopher's construction may be, in a different mode" (1990, 215).

30. *Sophos* in *Olympian* 1.9, *Pythian* 4.217; *sophia* in *Pyth.* 1.12, 4.248.

31. The traditional list of the Seven Sages begins with Plato (*Prot.* 343a), who names Thales of Miletus, Pittacus of Mytilene, Bias of Priene, Solon of Athens, Cleobulus of Lindos, Myson of Chen, and Chilon of Sparta. Diogenes Laertius (1.41ff.) records contrasting traditions concerning the membership of the Seven.

32. See, for example, *Il.* 1.175 and 2.197. The term is related to the verb *mêtiomai*, "to devise or contrive"; and to the noun *mêtis*, used by Homer to mean "wisdom," "counsel," "plan," or "skill" (*Il.* 2.407, 7.324; *Od.* 4.678).

33. The priestess of Pythian Apollo at Delphi was reputed by some to have listened to a brook sacred to Apollo and to have heard the voice of the god, but others have attributed her powers to the inhaling of vapors rising out of the earth. The most important literary evidence comes from Plutarch, who was a priest at Delphi. See Burkert 1985, 116. Likewise, the oracle of Zeus at Dodona—probably the oldest of all Greek oracles—was held by tradition to have heard sounds in the rustling of an oak tree sacred to Zeus (*Od.* 14.327ff., 19.296ff.; also Burkert 1985, 114). When her enraptured utterances had been interpreted by the priests of the shrine, the petitioner received an answer to his or her query, usually in verse. In the Dionysian cult, a wine-induced madness or ecstasy leads to frenzy, dancing, and direct experience of the god (Burkert, 109–10, 161–62, 412n2).

34. "Significantly," writes Burkert, "the Greek word for god, *theos*, is intimately related to the art of the seer: an interpreted sign is *thesphaton*, the seer is *theopropos*, and what he does is a *theiazein* or *entheazein*" (1985, 112).

35. Eliade continues, "we see, then, that the 'story' narrated by the myth constitutes a 'knowledge' which is esoteric, not only because it is secret and is handed on during the course of an initiation but also because the 'knowledge' is accompanied by a magico-religious power. For knowing the origin of an object, an animal, a plant, and so on is equivalent to acquiring a magical power over them by which they can be controlled, multiplied, or reproduced at will" (1963, 14–15).

36. Burkert notes that "Greek religion might almost be called a religion without priests" because there was no priestly caste and because the priestly functions of speaking the prayer and making sacrifice on cult occasions did not require the leadership of a special person. "Prerequisite for this role is a certain authority and economic power. The sacrificer is the head of the house, family, or village, the president of the council, the elected chief magistrate of the city, . . . or the army general." The special duties of a priest or priestess involved caring for the specific sanctuary for which he or she had responsibility and also preparing for and presiding over cult activities in the sanctuary "to ensure that everything is done in proper order" (1985, 95). Thus, there is no special "wisdom" that accrues to the priest or priestess as such, though their knowledge of rite and ritual was specialized and thus not altogether common.

37. It is worth noting that on several occasions in the *Iliad* (e.g., 2.169, 407, 636) Odysseus is said to be "equal to Zeus in counsel" (*Dii mêtin atalanton*). The key to his sagacity appears to lie in his capability for shrewd, cunning action. He is given the epithet *polymêtis*—having "many devices," being resourceful (e.g., *Il.* 3.200). For this reason he is a trusted adviser in the Achaean camp, both in council and before the assembled troops. The attribution of parity with Zeus in wisdom is surely honorific,

expressing the reputation for practical acumen Odysseus enjoyed among both Greeks and Trojans. However, it seems to me impossible that it can have been meant literally by Homer.

38. See Burkert 1985, esp. chap. 6.

39. Burkert says that "it is tempting henceforth to dramatize intellectual history as a battle with successive attacks, victories, and defeats in which myth gradually succumbs to the *logos* and the archaic gives way to the modern. And yet from the point of view of the history of religion this is a very strange battle: the decisive turn seems to have been taken from the very beginning, but it remains without effect in practice. The picture of the religion as practised changes hardly at all, in spite of the deeds of all the intellectual heroes" (1985, 305). This fact is illustrated clearly in the attitude toward the gods displayed by Aristotle's most famous student, Alexander the Great. Alexander's piety and reliance on divine guidance and support are well documented (Wilcken 1967).

Chapter 3. *Physis, Kosmos, Logos*

1. Guthrie 1953, 6, 1962, 26ff.; Burnet 1930, 2ff.

2. See Vernant 1983, 343–66. Hooper observes that "only a small minority of Greeks ever abandoned the magical, mythological and supernatural common beliefs in favor of a speculative approach toward the universe around them or their own behavior in it. Speculation about the origin of all that exists, the conflict between being and becoming and the essence of virtue, is not a popular pastime. . . . The majority of the Greeks . . . never gave up their belief in a god of the winds or a god of the sea. They lived, as do most Greeks in the modern world, by instinct, habit and faith" (1978, 124).

3. Guthrie writes, "even Aristotle, though he casts an enormous shadow forward, looks back to the other world too. He might be the founder of logic and accomplish work in zoology that still excites the wonder of experts; but he believed firmly in the divinity of the heavenly bodies, and has curious ideas about the primacy of the number three which clearly go back to a primitive origin" (1953, 6). Also see Vernant 1983, 346–47; Frankfort et al. 1977; Reale 1987.

4. Hooper writes that "Hittite records which are dated between the fourteenth and twelfth centuries mention the kings and the land of Ahhiyava, which for the time and place could only mean the Achaeans" (1978, 52). Also see Burnet 1930, 39ff.

5. Also see Jaeger 1947, 18; Burnet 1930, 39–40.

6. Kirk, Raven, and Schofield comment that "the Babylonian priests had made observations of eclipses of the sun, both partial and total, for religious purposes, at any rate since 721 B.C.; and by the sixth century they had probably established a cycle of solstices (or less plausibly of lunations) within which eclipses might occur at certain points. It is overwhelmingly probable that Thales's feat depended on his access to these Babylonian records" (1983, 82). Also see Burnet 1930, 21–24; Jaeger 1947, 18. It is worth noting that the historicity and precision of Thales' prediction are not unquestioned. At the very least it seems likely, as Herodotus's carefully chosen words suggest, that Thales did no more than indicate the year of the eclipse. Neugebauer calls the account a historical myth (1951, 114ff.). Mosshammer (1981) also raises serious questions. However, see Guthrie 1962, 48.

7. See Saggs 1989, 86–88; Havelock 1963, 49ff.; Johnstone 1978, 156ff., 162; Carpenter 1933; Cook and Woodhead 1959; McCarter 1975.

8. Cornford remarks that "the Ionian science of Nature—the germ from which all European science has since developed . . . [marks] the achievement of an attitude of mind in which the object has been completely detached from the subject and can be contemplated by thought disengaged from the interests of action. The fruits of this attitude were the first systems of the world that can claim to be rational constructions of reality" (1950, 29).

9. Vernant emphasizes the role of writing and prose composition in making possible "a more rigorous analysis and a stricter ordering of the conceptual material. . . . The writing of prose marks a new departure. . . . Prose composition—medical treatises, historical accounts, the speeches of the orators, and the dissertations of the philosophers—represents not only a different mode of expression from that of oral tradition and poetic composition but also a new form of thought" (1990, 205). Also see 206ff; Kirk 1983; Kahn 1983; Margolis 1983.

10. Hooper 1978, 81. Also see Jeffrey 1976; Starr 1961, 1977; Andrewes 1963.

11. See Fredal 2006, 36–55, 105–33; Camp 1986; Sealey 1976.

12. As distinct from the *boulê* or council of chiefs. Cf. *Il.* 2.53 and 93, *Od.* 2.69, etc. See Johnstone 1996, 7.

13. Aristotle, *On the Heavens*, 294a. Aristotle continues, "This, indeed, is the oldest theory that has been preserved, and is attributed to Thales of Miletos. It [i.e., the world] was supposed to stay still because it floated like wood and other similar substances, which are so constituted as to rest upon water but not upon air." See Kirk, Raven, and Schofield 1983, 25; Holscher 1970, 309–10. Ancient sources do not agree about Thales' exact dates, but a reasonable estimation puts them at 624–546 B.C.E.. See Kirk, Raven, and Schofield, 76n1; Guthrie 1962, 49–50.

14. Indeed, it is questionable whether Thales actually committed his speculations to writing. Kirk, Raven, and Schofield note that "there was profound doubt in antiquity about Thales' written works" (1983, 87). For example, Simplicius remarks (*Phys.* 23, DK 29) that Thales "is said to have left nothing in the form of writings except the so-called 'Nautical Star-guide.'" Likewise, Diogenes Laertius (1.23) says, "according to some he left no book behind." Guthrie comments that "it seems incredible that he should have written down nothing, and of course the word 'publish' had little meaning in his day; but at least the confusion of later writers and the testimony of Aristotle himself make it plain that no writings of his were available in Aristotle's time and probably long before" (1962, 54).

15. In Homer the term *archê* signifies the "beginning" or "starting" of something, as at *Il.* 3.100: "this quarrel of mine which Alexander began [*archês*]."

16. At least one later source attributed to Thales the idea that the "floating-earth" idea explains the cause of earthquakes. Seneca (*Qu. nat.* 3.14) observes that Thales "said that the world is held up by water and rides like a ship, and when it is said to 'quake' it is actually rocking because of the water's movement" (see Kirk, Raven, and Schofield 1983, 93n2). The notion that the solid continents float on a subterranean liquid is, of course, at the core of modern plate tectonic theory, which substitutes for "water" the

molten magma beneath the earth's crust. For a detailed yet accessible account of this theory and its ramifications, see McPhee 1998.

17. See Kirk, Raven, and Schofield 1983, 89ff. Also see Cherniss (1935) and Guthrie (1970) on the need to be cautious in relying on Aristotle's historical accuracy in representing Presocratic thought and fragments.

18. W. P. D. Wightman, as quoted in Guthrie 1962, 68.

19. Aristotle describes the universal substrate in the *Metaphysics*, for example, at 11042a–b. See Moravcsik 1983; Robb 1983.

20. Also see Jaeger 1947; Murray 1925.

21. Depending on whose version of Theophrastus's account we read: Simplicius's, Hippolytus's, or Plutarch's. See Kirk, Raven, and Schofield 1983, 106–7; Burnet 1930, 50; Jaeger 1947. Diogenes Laertius 2.1–2 cites the chronographer Apollodorus as saying that "Anaximander was sixty-four years old in the second year of the fifty-eighth Olympiad [547/546 B.C.E.], and that he died shortly afterwards." This puts the philosopher's birth in 611/610 and makes him some fourteen years Thales' junior. Also see Guthrie 1962, 72; Burnet 1930, 51.

22. Popper's view is not universally accepted. Kirk, for example, contends that "Popper overstates the probable coherence of the Milesian 'school' and the probable amount of discussion and mutual criticism within it" (1970b, 167n1). He also finds fault with Popper's interpretations of the views of Thales, Anaximander, and Heraclitus (163–77). Nonetheless, although controversy continues concerning such questions, it seems likely that the cultural climate in Miletos during the sixth century invited contention, debate, and discussion over matters both political and philosophical.

23. The Suda lists several titles for works by Anaximander, including *On Nature* (*Peri Physeôs*), *Circuit of the Earth* (*Gês periodon*), *On the Fixed Stars* (*Peri tôn aplanôn*), *Sphere* (*Sphairan*), "and a few more." See Kirk, Raven, and Schofield 1983, 100–101. Guthrie observes that "these [titles] probably came from the catalogue of the Alexandrian library and represent divisions of a single work which Anaximander himself would almost certainly, in accordance with the custom of his time, have left unnamed. . . . Throughout antiquity the title 'On Nature' (*peri phuseôs*) was given indiscriminately to the writings of the Presocratics" (1962, 73). He also notes that "with Anaximander human reason asserted itself and produced what, right or wrong, was for the most part an account in purely natural terms of the origin of the world and life" (1950, 29).

24. Simplicius, *Phys.* 23, 13; DK 12 A 9. See Kirk, Raven, and Schofield 1983, 106–8, for three versions of Theophratus's account, including both Greek texts and English translations. These authors contend that the passage, "according to necessity; . . . according to the assessment of Time," is a direct quotation by Theophrastus from Anaximander's original treatise (118). Also see Guthrie 1962, 76–77. Kahn, on the other hand, maintains that the quotation is somewhat longer. His translation inserts quotation marks around the passage "it is neither water nor any other of the so-called elements, . . . according to the ordinance of time" (1960, 166). Kahn's detailed presentation of and commentary on the doxography concerning Anaximander's views is interesting and helpful (11–71).

25. On this question, see Kahn: "Are we to understand that Anaximander was the first to introduce 'this very term of *archê*,' or 'this name *apeiron* for the *archê*'? Both constructions can be, and have been, defended" (1960, 30). He concludes that "the ambiguity which surrounds this expression is, I think, definitively resolved by two . . . passages in Simplicius, which show that he has himself understood it to refer to the term *archê*. . . . Since Simplicius is our best source for this section of the *Phys. Opin.*, his understanding of Theophrastus' remark must be definitive for us" (31). Also see Guthrie 1962, 77.

26. Kahn's detailed commentary on Anaximander's employment of the term is useful (1960, 231–39). Also see Burnet 1930, 57–58; Kirk, Raven, and Schofield 1983, 109ff.; Guthrie 1962, 83–89; Holscher 1970, 321.

27. Several modern commentators read Theophratus's introduction to the fragment as expressing Anaximander's own thinking, and they conclude that the latter actually held a conception of "*the* unbounded" (*to apeiron*), an abstract idea expressed through a neuter noun derived from an adjective (*apeiros*) that modifies the feminine accusative noun *physin*. The passage from Theophrastus, recall, opens by observing that "Anaximander . . . said that the principle and element of existing things was *to apeiron*." Following this, Kirk, Raven, and Schofield ask, "what did Anaximander mean by *to apeiron*?" (1983, 109). Holscher comments that what gives Anaximander's view of *apeiron* its "philosophical character is its conceptual quality. This was helped by the spirit of the Greek Language, which managed to catch the abstract in adjectives made nouns. . . . Now philosophy was made from language, and the 'Boundless' became a concept" (1970, 321). Likewise, Kahn argues that "in the historical experience of Greece, Nature became permeable to human intelligence only when the inscrutable personalities of mythic religion were replaced by well-defined and regular powers. The linguistic stamp of the new mentality is a preference for neuter forms, in place of the 'animate' masculines and feminines which are the stuff of myth. The Olympians have given way before *to apeiron*, *to chreon, to perichon, to thermon, ta enantia*" (1960, 193). Though it is true that the development of an abstract philosophical vocabulary by the Presocratic thinkers involved the derivation of abstract, neuter nouns from the gendered adjectives that appear in Homer (Havelock 1983), the evidence is scant that it was Anaximander who initiated this process with *to apeiron*. It seems to me that Theopratus's language here represents a Peripatetic gloss on Anaximander's fragment. If we grant Kahn's own claim that the actual fragment begins with "it is neither water nor any other of the so-called elements," then the most that can be directly attributed to Anaximander regarding the concept of *apeiron* is that the first principle is "some . . . unbounded/infinite/ undefined [*apeiron*] *physin*." In any event, we want to be cautious here.

28. Also see Cornford 1957, esp. 144–47.

29. My translation of this passage follows that of R. P. Hardie and R. K. Gaye in McKeon (see Aristotle 1941j), which includes the quotation marks, thus suggesting that these words are Anaximander's own. Kahn discusses this passage at some length (1960, 42–44) and remarks that "the epithets 'deathless and imperishable' . . . correspond to Hippolytus' description of the Boundless as 'eternal and unaging.' . . . Just which expressions were used by Anaximander can scarcely be determined, but at least the

Homeric *agêrôs* [ageless, undecaying, unfading] must be his" (43). On this point, also see Guthrie 1962, 87–89.

30. Heidegger's (1975) close reading of and commentary on this passage is provocative and challenging. However, since he dismisses the "vain hopes of calculating historically, i.e. philologically and psychologically, what was at one time really present to that man called Anaximander of Miletus which may have served as the condition for his way of representing the world" (18), Heidegger is less concerned than I am about avoiding the deployment of anachronistic terminology in translating the fragment. Thus, he can write that "the matter under discussion is *onta;* translated literally, *ta onta* means 'beings.' The neuter plural appears as *ta polla,* 'the many,' in the sense of the manifold of being. But *ta onta* does not mean an arbitrary or boundless multiplicity; rather, it means *ta panta,* the totality of being. Thus *ta onta* means manifold being in totality" (20). It is doubtful that Anaximander himself was able to conceptualize something as abstract as "the totality of being," so we are led by such an analysis farther away from rather than closer to the ideas that Anaximander may have entertained.

31. See Kirk, Raven, and Schofield 1983, 143–44; Guthrie 1962, 115. The former put the birth of Anaximenes "around the *acme* of Thales," that is, around 585 B.C.E., and his own *acme* the conventional forty years later.

32. Aetius (1.3.4) writes that "Anaximenes, son of Eurystratus, of Miletus, declared that the origin (*archê*) of existing things is air, for out of it all things come to be and into it they are resolved again. 'Just as our soul,' he says, 'which is air, holds us together, so breath [or wind, *pneuma*] and air surround the whole cosmos.' Air and breath are used synonymously" (after Guthrie 1962, 131; also see Kirk, Raven, and Schofield 1983, 158–59). On the divinity of *aêr,* Kirk, Raven, and Schofield include an elliptical passage from Aetius (1.7.13) that they translate thus: "Anaximenes [says that] the air [is god]" (150). Cf. Aristotle (*Phys.* 203b) concerning the *apeiron* of Anaximander: "of the *apeiron* there is no beginning . . . but this seems to be the beginning of the other things. . . . and this is the divine (*einai to theion*); for it is immortal and indestructible, as Anaximander says." See Kirk, Raven, and Schofield (1983, 144–62) for texts and commentary regarding *aêr* in Anaximenes, and esp. 150–51 concerning its divinity. Also see Guthrie 1962, 115–40.

33. DK 21 B. Fragments 24, 16, 15, and 23 are from Clement of Alexandria, *Stromateis* 5.109.2, 7.22.1, 5.109.3, and 5.109.1, respectively. Fragments 26 + 25 are from Simplicius, *Phys.* 23, 11 + 23, DK 20. I have followed the arrangement and translation of the fragments as presented by Kirk, Raven, and Schofield 1983, 170–71. Burnet observes that "this 'god' is just the world. . . , and the use of the word *theos* is quite in accordance with Ionian usage. Xenophanes regarded it as sentient, though without any special organs of sense. . . . What Xenophanes is really concerned to deny is the existence of any gods in the proper sense, and the words 'One god' mean 'No god but the world'" (1930, 128). Also see Vlastos 1970c. Xenophanes, also an Ionian if not a Milesian (he was from Colophon, an inland town about fifty miles north of Miletos), was born around 570 B.C.E. and may have lived until about 475 (see Kirk, Raven, and Schofield, 164; Guthrie 1962, 362–64). His attack on popular theology and on the views of Homer and Hesiod, and his "constructive theology," are usefully discussed by Kirk, Raven, and Schofield, 168–72; and by Guthrie, 370–83.

34. Fragment 18 is from Stobaeus, *Anthologion* I.8.2; fragment 34 is from Sextus Empiricus, *Adv. Mathmaticos* 7, 49, and 110. Both are translated in Kirk, Raven, and Schofield 1983, 179. Guthrie (1962, 395) translates the last clause in fr. 34, "but in all things there is opinion," emphasizing the contrast between *oide* (knowledge) and *dokos* (seeming or opinion; see n5). Popper translates the passages (DK B 34 and 35) with even more color: "But as for certain truth, no man has known it, nor will he know it; neither of the gods, nor yet of all the things of which I speak. And even if by chance he were to utter the final truth, he would himself not know it: for all is but a woven web of guesses" (1970, 152).

35. On Xenophanes' theory of knowledge, see Frankel 1993.

36. In his account of the emergence of a "new language of philosophy" in the work of the Presocratics, Havelock observes that consequent upon the search for a "single, comprehensive statement" that would reduce all world events to aspects of a single whole—to "a cosmos, a system, a one and an all"—there would arise "a felt need to replace the verbs of action and happening which crowded themselves into the oral mythos [with] a syntax which somehow stated a situation or set of situations which were permanent, so that an account could be given of the environment which treated it as a constant. The verb called upon to perform this duty was *einai*, the verb 'to be'" (1983, 21). "By implication," Havelock concludes, "the 'is' (*esti*) remains the only verb needed in any language designed for theoretic purposes to describe the system as such" (25).

37. Most of the details of Heraclitus's life are difficult to determine with precision. The chronographer Apollodorus puts his *acme*—when he was presumed to be about forty years old—during the sixty-ninth Olympiad (504–500 B.C.E.). Kirk (1954) concludes that his philosophical work was probably completed by 480. Beyond his membership in the royal clan at Ephesos, almost nothing is known concerning the circumstances of his life. Kirk's introduction (1–30) to his examination of the Heraclitean "cosmic fragments" assesses the evidence for our knowledge of Heraclitus. Also see Kahn 1979; Guthrie 1962; Kirk, Raven, and Schofield 1983.

38. I will take Kahn's (1979) inventory of the fragments as authoritative. He notes that of the 125 fragments appearing in ancient sources, "only 89 qualify as fully verbatim citations, and even this figure may be a bit too generous. The other 36 texts . . . include partial quotations blended with the citer's own text, free paraphrases that may or may not preserve some of the original wording, and some reports of doctrine that do not even claim to represent Heraclitus's words" (25). Kahn takes the Greek texts from Marcovich's edition (1967), though I have also consulted Wright 1985; Kirk, Raven, and Schofield 1983; Kirk 1954; Diels and Kranz 1951–54. Unless otherwise noted, I will examine only those fragments that Kahn counts as being direct quotations from Heraclitus's book.

39. Kahn goes on to observe that "a given text admits of several different 'readings,' where the readings differ from one another by imposing alternative syntactical combinations on the text or by taking the same word in different senses" (1979, 92). His general discussion "on reading Heraclitus" (87–95) is useful as a guide to the interpretive issues involved here. Likewise, Cherniss maintains that "it is possible to discern the intention and the main characteristics of Heraclitus' thought" (1970, 13). For a careful consideration of multiple readings of Heraclitus's *logos* fragments, see Ercolini 2000.

40. Both the text and the meaning of this fragment are, in the words of Guthrie, "hotly disputed" (1962, 429). Kahn, following Marcovich, gives the following Greek text: "*en to sophon, epistasthai gnômên okê kubernêsai panta dia pantôn*," which he translates as "the wise is one, knowing the plan by which it steers all things through all" (1979, 55). In a note (54), however, Kahn observes that "the plausible readings for *kubernêsai*" include *kubernatai*, which changes the voice of the verb from active to passive and the meaning of the key phrase from something *steering* something else to something *being steered by* something else. This is the reading and text preferred by Kirk, Raven, and Schofield 1983, 202; Kirk 1954, 386; Guthrie 1962, 429; Burnet 1930, 134; and Wright 1985, 5. Though Kahn remarks that this is not "an obvious correction," it has the obvious virtue of connecting *gnômên* with the directive principle of the cosmos.

41. Kahn's commentary on this idea is particularly interesting and provocative (1979, 130ff.). See also Guthrie 1962, 439–54; Kirk, Raven, and Schofield 1983, 186–97; Cherniss 1970, 15–16. It is worth noting that referring to Heraclitus's use of *logos* as either "principle" or "law" is somewhat problematic. In her translations of the *logos* fragments, Freeman consistently translates the term as "Law" and parenthetically as "the Law (of the universe)" (1983, 24ff.). Kahn generally translates it as "account" or "report," but in some contexts (e.g., DK 31 B) he translates it as "amount." Kirk, Raven, and Schofield often leave the term untranslated, but in at least one case (again, DK 31 B) it is translated as "proportion." Robinson (1987) also gives "proportion" for this fragment. The translation of *logos* as "principle," indicating either an ultimate source or cause of things (*archê*) or a law of nature according to which things operate, may go beyond what Heraclitus could have conceptualized, but it seems an appropriate representation of the idea that he sought to express. Once again, if we take Heraclitus as seeking to "stretch" existing terminology to express novel conceptions, this understanding of *logos* is suitable. Also see Kirk 1954, 37–40; Minar 1939; Ercolini 2000.

42. Kirk (1954, 386) and Kirk, Raven, and Schofield (1983, 202) give "true judgment" for *gnômên* in this fragment, while Guthrie (1962, 429) translates it as "Thought."

43. Compare the line "distinguishing each [thing] according to its nature and telling how it is" to the fifth-century treatise known as the *Dissoi Logoi:* "It is necessary for the man who intends to speak correctly to have a knowledge of whatever things he might discuss" (DK 90 8.6, trans. Sprague 1972). On this passage and a similar point in Plato's *Phaedrus*, see Schiappa 1999, 74. The connection between *understanding* a thing and being able to give a correct *logos* (account) of it, central in sophistical and Platonic views of the speaker's art, appears to have been first identified by Heraclitus.

44. Also see DK 44: "The people (*demos*) must fight for the law as for their city wall." Just as the wall protects and preserves the people physically, so the law protects and preserves the people politically; and thus does the *Logos* preserve them ontologically.

45. A useful discussion of the uses of *psychê* before Plato can be found in Claus 1981. See esp. 122–40 for consideration of *psychê* in Anaximenes and Heraclitus.

46. For useful discussions of this fragment, see Minar 1939, 335–36; Kirk 1954, 307–24; Kahn 1979, 132–38.

47. See Kirk, Raven, and Schofield 1983, 187–88; Minar 1939, 331. Cf. Heidegger 1975, 59–78.

48. Thus do we find the term developed later by Aristotle, as we shall see in chapter 6. See Minar 1939, 323–26.

49. Though an Ionian by birth (ca. 579 B.C.E.) and upbringing, Pythagoras came to represent the rise of philosophy in the western Greek world following his move to southern Italy in the 530s. He was a contemporary of Anaximenes and thus was a generation older than Heraclitus. He left no writings. Consequently, little can be attributed with certainty to the philosopher himself. He founded a quasi-religious order at Croton in southern Italy, a "school" that survived for two hundred years. Much Pythagorean teaching is associated with the names of philosophers of the late fifth and early fourth centuries B.C.E. In the judgment of Kirk, Raven, and Schofield, "much of it [is] worthless as historical evidence of Pythagoras's own teachings" (1983, 216; also see Guthrie 1962, 181). Nonetheless, with Aristotle (*Meta.* 985b), we may regard the body of Pythagorean doctrine as reflecting ways of thinking that were set in motion by the great teacher himself (Burkhardt 1963, 285). On the problems with evidence and interpretation, see Guthrie 1962, 146–72; Kirk, Raven, and Schofield 1983, 214–16; Burnet 1930, 92, 277–86. For useful accounts of Pythagoras's life and historical context, and of the activities of his school, see Guthrie, 173–81; Kirk, Raven, and Schofield, 222–32; Brumbaugh 1964, 30–42; Burnet, 84–92, 276–77.

50. Not in all cases, however. Though some of the rules for practical conduct enshrined in the *acusmata* express broad moral precepts, "the majority are easily recognizable as primitive taboos" (Guthrie 1962, 183). Judging from a list attributed by Diogenes Laertius (8.34–35) to a lost work of Aristotle's, they include not to eat beans, not to pick up what has fallen from the table, not to stir the fire with a knife, to rub out the mark of a pot in the ashes, not to spit on one's nail-parings and hair-trimmings, to touch the earth when it thunders, and so on. See Guthrie, 183–95; Burnet 1930, 93–96; Kirk, Raven, and Schofield 1983, 230–32.

51. Plato, *Rep.* 616b–17e. See Kirk, Raven, and Schofield 1983, 233, 235. Also see Cornford 1950, 67; Guthrie 1962, 212–26, 295–301; Burkhardt 1963, 284–85; Burnet 1930, 99–111. Brumbaugh remarks that, "according to tradition, Pythagoras made the discovery that led to the idea of 'the music of the spheres,' an idea that has inspired much later Western science and poetry. Measuring the lengths of a vibrating string that gave concordant sounds, Pythagoras discovered that the ratios of these lengths for the octave, fifth, and fourth were exactly 2:1, 3:2, and 4:3—the simplest possible set of integer ratios. And observation, within tolerable limits of error, showed that *these same ratios* related the periods of planetary motion. Thus, the celestial system was a scale, a harmony which, like music, had an order of extreme mathematical simplicity" (1964, 37; emphasis in original).

52. Aristotle (*Meta.* 1080b) explicitly rejects the possibility that Pythagoras envisioned numbers as incorporeal realities: "The Pythagoreans also believe in one kind of number—the mathematical; only they maintain that it is not separate, but that sensible substances are composed of it. For they construct the whole universe of numbers, but not of numbers consisting of abstract units; they suppose the units to be extended." For contrasting views on this matter, see Guthrie 1962, 234; Brumbaugh 1964, 34.

53. See Guthrie 1962, 212ff.; Kirk, Raven, and Schofield 1983, 232–35; Burnet 1930, 108–9; Cornford 1950, 67–68.

54. See Guthrie 1962, 234–44, 301–6; Burnet 1930, 107–8, 307–9.

55. See Guthrie 1962, 213; Burkhardt 1963, 285. Recent studies have illuminated the relationship between mathematical ratios and the "geometry" of music. See, for example, Lowman 1971a, 1971b; Norden 1964; Putz 1995.

56. See Aristotle, *Meta.* 985b–86a. On the design and proportions of the Parthenon, see Dinsmoor 1975, 159–61; Bruno 1974, 57–72, 76–77. On the role of mathematical ratios in Greek architecture generally, see Warren 1919; Lawrence 1957; Coulton 1977.

57. See Aristotle, *Meta.* 986a for one version of the "table of contraries" that was attributed to the Pythagoreans. For useful accounts of this system, also see Guthrie 1962, 206–9, 240–51; Brumbaugh 1964, 36–37, 40–41; Cornford 1950, 1952; Heidel 1910; Scoon 1928.

58. Also see Scoon 1928, 38; Guthrie 1962, 68; Kirk, Raven, and Schofield 1983, 348–50; Claus 1981, 111–21.

59. Porphyrius, in *Life of Pythagoras* 19 (DK 14, 8a), writes the following: "What he said to his associates, nobody can say for certain; for silence with them was of no ordinary kind. Nonetheless the following became universally known: first, that he maintains that the soul is immortal; next, that it changes into other kinds of living things; also that events recur in certain cycles, and that nothing is ever absolutely new; and finally, that all living things should be regarded as akin. Pythagoras seems to have been the first to bring these beliefs to Greece" (Kirk, Raven, and Schofield 1983, 238).

60. Useful contemporary discussions of these thinkers and their thought can be found in Curd 1998; Guthrie 1965; Kirk, Raven, and Schofield 1983. Also see Burnet 1930; Raven 1948. Translations of all surviving fragments can be found in Freeman 1983. Greek texts with commentary are collected in Wright 1985. Biographical information about Parmenides is not without inconsistencies, but it would seem (Plato, *Parmenides* 127a–c) that he was born ca. 515–510 and that he was at one time a Pythagorean (Diogenes Laertius 1.21). He ultimately set his own philosophical course. See Guthrie 1965, 1–3; Kirk, Raven, and Schofield 1983, 239–41; Burnet 1930, 169–71; Curd 2004, 15–18.

61. According to Guthrie, it was available in its entirety to Simplicius, who quotes fifty-three lines: "One may assume that on this supremely important topic he has given the relevant passage complete. Altogether we now possess 154 lines, unevenly distributed" (1965, 3). Kirk, Raven, and Schofield (1983, 241) also acknowledge Sextus Empiricus, who preserved the proem. In the proem Parmenides relates how he was carried by a horse-drawn chariot to the "gates of the paths of Night and Day," within which he encountered a goddess (never identified) who took him by the hand and offered to teach him about "all things, both the unshaken heart of well-rounded truth, and the opinions of mortals, in which there is no true reliance." See Kirk, Raven, and Schofield, 242–43; Curd 2004, 18–24.

62. My translation of fr. 2 follows that of Kirk, Raven, and Schofield (1983, 245), who do not include fr. 3. Guthrie, however, adds it to fr. 2 with the punctuation I have used (1965, 14). Burnet splices the two fragments together with a semicolon, and it is his translation of fr. 3 that I have adopted here (1930, 173). Also see Freeman's (1983, 42) and Curd's (2004, 24–25) translations, with Curd's (25–34) and Wright's (1985, 79) commentaries. In any case, the two fragments are linked conceptually and logically, so it is appropriate and useful to consider them as a single unit of thought. Kirk, Raven,

and Schofield note that "Ancients and moderns alike are agreed upon a low estimation of Parmenides's gifts as a writer. He has little facility in diction, and the struggle to force novel, difficult and highly abstract philosophical ideas into metrical form frequently results in ineradicable obscurity, especially syntactic obscurity. On the other hand, in the less argumentative passages of the poem he achieves a kind of clumsy grandeur" (241). Also see Guthrie 1965, 3–4. An excellent study of Parmenides' use of language can be found in Mourelatos 1970.

63. For discussions of this issue, see Furth 1993, 242–48; Kirk, Raven, and Schofield 1983, 245–47; Guthrie 1965, 14–15; Burnet 1930, 178–79; Curd 2004, 34–51. Curd contends that "beginning by searching for the correct sense of the verb 'to be' is a mistake . . . [because] Parmenides's concern was as much methodological as metaphysical. What, he asks, is the right way to ask and to answer certain questions?" (35).

64. Burnet remarks that "Parmenides does not say a word about 'Being' anywhere, and it is remarkable that he avoids the term 'god,' which was so freely used by earlier and later thinkers" (1930, 178–79). He maintains that when Parmenides says that *what is, is,* "There can be no real doubt that this is what we call body. It is certainly regarded as spatially extended" (178). In a note (4), Burnet argues that "we must not render *to eon* by 'Being,' *das Sein* or *l'être.* It is 'what is,' *das Seiende, ce qui est.* As to (*to*) *einai* it does not occur, and hardly could occur at this date." Curd's discussion of this point and various views on it is informative (2004, 39 and n42). Also see Mourelatos 1971, 1973, 1976, 1979; Kahn 1966, 1969/70.

65. Freeman's translation (1983, 42). Also see fr. 6. Cherniss remarks that "the whole argument of Parmenides proceeds by applying the law of the excluded middle to prove that the identity of what *is* precludes the possibility of any characteristic except just *being*" (1970, 21).

66. Fr. 8, 5–31, in Simplicius *in Phys.* 78, 5 (after Kirk, Raven, and Schofield 1983, 249–50). Earlier in the fragment Parmenides holds that "there still remains just one account of a way, that it is. On this way there are very many signs, that being uncreated and imperishable it is, whole and of a single kind and unshaken and perfect." See Kirk, Raven, and Schofield (248–53) for a useful discussion of this fragment. Also see Owen 1993, esp. 271–83; Guthrie 1965, 26–43; Curd 2004, 83–87.

67. See Kirk, Raven, and Schofield 1983, 250–51; Guthrie 1965, 31–34; Burnet 1930, 175. Curd's discussion of Parmendean monism and analysis of his arguments are illuminating and helpful (2004, 64–97).

68. Fr. 8, 42–49, Simplicius *in Phys.* 146, 5, after Kirk, Raven, and Schofield 1983, 252–53. Also see Guthrie 1965, 43–49.

69. Compare fr. 6: "What is there to be said and thought must needs be; for it is there for being, but nothing is not" (Simplicius *in Phys.* 86, 27–28; 117, 4–13; in Kirk, Raven, and Schofield 1983, 247). Also see Guthrie 1965, 17ff.; Cherniss 1970, 21–22; Curd 2004, 70n17.

70. Fr. 6, in Simplicius *in Phys.* 86, 27–28; 117, 4–13. See Kirk, Raven, and Schofield 1983, 247. See also Guthrie 1965, 25: "the goddess warns Parmenides . . . *not to trust the senses,* but instead to *judge by reason alone*" (italics in original). Parmenides, in any case, dismisses the "path of opinion" as comprising a "deceitful ordering of . . . words" (fr. 8, Simplicius *in Phys.* 30, 14, in Kirk, Raven, and Schofield, 254). Also see Curd

2004, 51–63, 98–126. The cosmology and physics of the section, which echo features of earlier Presocratic views, are presented not as a "way of inquiry" but as the most useful analysis of human experience. See Reinhardt 1993; Mourelatos 1970.

71. Simplicius *in Phys.* 25, 19 (= DK 31 A 7) and the Suda (DK 31 A 2), translated by Kirk, Raven, and Schofield 1983, 281, 282. "Although the years of Empedocles's birth and death cannot be determined with certainty," writes Guthrie, "the general opinion is well founded that they must have been approximately 492–432" (1965, 128). He was a native of the Sicilian town of Akragas, a port on the southern coast of the island, and came from a wealthy aristocratic family. He played a leading role in the transformation of Akragas into a democracy following the overthrow of the tyrant Thrasydaeus in 471 B.C.E.. Details about his life and character are well presented by Guthrie, 128–34. Also see Kirk, Raven, and Schofield, 281–82; Burnet 1930, 197–203.

72. Kirk, Raven, and Schofield 1983, 285. He wrote *On Nature* and *Purifications* in hexameter verse, the fragments of which reveal "a deep preoccupation with Parmenides' thought, both in what he denied and in what he asserted; verbal echoes of Parmenides' poem and allusions to it are correspondingly frequent in Empedocles' verses" (283). Also see Guthrie 1965, 166ff.; Burnet 1930, 227–28.

73. Sextus *adv. math.* 7.123 and 125, translated by Kirk, Raven, and Schofield 1983, 285 (after Guthrie). Cf. Freeman 1983, 51–52; Burnet 1930, 204–5.

74. Fr. 17, lines 1–13, Simplicius *Phys.* 158, 1, translated by Kirk, Raven, and Schofield 1983, 287. The authors note that this fragment "presents the principal doctrine of Empedocles' philosophy" (see 287–88). Also see Guthrie 1965, 167–85, for a careful analysis of the Cosmic Cycle portrayed in Empedocles' poem.

75. Empedocles' theological beliefs are somewhat more complex than this, as is suggested by his discussion of spirits and the soul in the *Purifications*. He appears to have recognized at least the following categories of gods: the four roots, Love and Strife, the Sphere in which the four elements are perfectly blended with Love, and the *daimones* or spirits who for their transgressions are imprisoned in mortal bodies but who may arise again "as gods highest in honor" if they learn to live in purity (fr. 146 and 147, Clement *Strom.* 4, 150, 1 and 5, 122, 3). See Kirk, Raven, and Schofield 1983, 313–17; Guthrie 1965, 257–65.

76. Fr. 17, lines 14–26 (Simplicius *in Phys.* 158, 13). See Kirk, Raven, and Schofield 1983, 289–94 for Greek texts and translations of these fragments, with commentary.

77. See Kirk, Raven, and Schofield 1983, 352–55; Guthrie 1965, 266–69.

78. The passages are found in Simplicius (*in Phys.* 155, 26; 34, 21; 163, 20) and are translated by Kirk, Raven, and Schofield 1983, 358. The extant fragments of Anaxagoras's book total about a thousand words, which "can hardly represent less than an eighth of the original whole and may well represent a considerably larger fraction" (Kirk, Raven, and Schofield, 356).

79. On Anaxagoras's theory of matter, see Cornford 1930; Kerferd 1969; Vlastos 1950.

80. The passages, all from Simplicius (*in Phys.* 300, 31; 35, 14; 157, 7), are translated in Kirk, Raven, and Schofield 1983, 363–64. I have deviated slightly from their translation by leaving *Nous* untranslated and by altering some wording in part of fr.12. Compare Guthrie's translation of the three fragments (1965, 273–74). See also Burnet 1930, 259–60.

81. Guthrie comments that "it would be perverse to argue that since philosophers themselves are at this time only on the threshold of an explicit distinction between mind and matter, others can have been conscious of no such distinction. . . . The point is that they were fully capable of using a word metaphorically" (1965, 277n1).

82. Simplicius *in Phys.* 27, 23 (trans. Kirk, Raven, and Schofield 1983, 386–87). Also see Hippolytus *Refutations* 1.10: "Natural philosophy lasted from Thales to Archelaus, whose pupil was Socrates" (trans. Guthrie 1965, 339); and 1.9.1. Archelaus's dates are uncertain, but the tradition that he was a pupil of Anaxagoras and a teacher of Socrates gives us at least an approximate date.

83. See, for example, Kirk, Raven, and Schofield 1983, 385; Guthrie 1965, 339; Burnet 1930, 358–60.

84. See Kirk, Raven, and Schofield 1983, 390–98; Guthrie 1965, 101–14. The title of the treatise is reported in Simplicius *in Phys.* 70, 16. Kirk, Raven, and Schofield remark that "the title . . . is probably as usual not the author's" (391), since the practice of giving titles to prose works seems to have begun in the sophistic age. Paraphrases of the treatise's argument are preserved by Simplicius and in the pseudo-Aristotelian treatise *On Melissus, Xenophanes and Gorgias.*

85. Simplicius *in Phys.* 109, 34 (trans. Guthrie 1965, 110). Cf. Kirk, Raven, and Schofield 1983, 400.

86. Simplicius, *in Phys.* 151, 24, (trans. Guthrie 1965, 363). Cf. Kirk, Raven, and Schofield 1983, 434–35. Diogenes' views were apparently known in Athens, judging from Aristophanes' parody of them in *Clouds* 227, but it is not known whether he actually lived or visited there. Translations of the surviving fragments of *On Nature* are given in Freeman 1983, 87–90.

87. Kirk, Raven, and Schofield echo this characterization (1983, 437, 440). Also see Burnet 1930, 352–58. Ever sensitive to the dangers of anachronism in characterizing Presocratic thought, Guthrie asks, "is it not unreasonable to deny the epithet 'teleological' to the doctrine that an intelligent being existed prior to the cosmos as *archê*, was its efficient cause, ordered it in the best possible way and is still active in the world? This is all in the text. Where Diogenes went beyond Anaxagoras was in removing Mind from its position of proud but inefficient isolation, 'mixed with no other thing,' and bringing it into continuous contact with the world" (1965, 362n1).

88. See, for example, Aristotle *Meta.* 985b, 1042b, 1069b; *On the Heavens* 303a–b.

89. For discussion of the lives, dates, and individual contributions of these two thinkers, see Guthrie 1965, 382–89; Kirk, Raven, and Schofield 1983, 402–6; Burnet 1930, 330–33; Furley 1967. Leucippus is identified with both Miletos and Elea and is said to have been influenced by Parmenides' thinking, though little was known about him even in antiquity. In contrast, Democritus was the subject of numerous anecdotes told by ancient authors, "but he remains a scarcely less shadowy figure," say Kirk, Raven, and Schofield. Writings attributed to him include the *Great World-System* (assigned by Theophrastus to Leucippus), the *Little World-system*, the *Cosmography*, and *On the Planets* (all four titles are attributed to Democritus by Diogenes Laertius 9, 45, DK 68 a 33). Freeman lists numerous titles for Democritus that were organized by Thrasyllus into tetralogies according to their subject matter. Included in this listing, under Ethics, are

such titles as "On the Character of the Sage," "On Those in Hades," "On Courage," and "On Cheerfulness or Well-Being." Titles under Natural Science and Logic include those mentioned by Diogenes Laertius, as well as "On Mind," "On Perception," "On Tastes," "On Strengthening Arguments," "On Logic" or "The Canon," and others. Additional tetralogies contained mathematical works and writings on music, while unclassified titles on "Causes" are also included in the list.

90. For Guthrie's (1965) detailed account of the atomic theory, see 389–404. Also see Aristotle *On Generation and Corruption* 325a–b; Kirk, Raven, and Schofield 1983, 406–9.

91. Fr. 9, Sextus *adv. math.* 7, 135 (after Kirk, Raven, and Schofield 1983, 410; Freeman 1983, 93). Also see Guthrie 1965, 438–51. For Leucippus's views, see Aetius 4. 9, 8 (DK 67 a 32). Also see Burnet 1930, 347 and n6; Guthrie 1965, 440n3.

92. Fr. 11, Sextus *adv. math.* 7, 138 (after Kirk, Raven, and Schofield 1983, 412). Cf. Freeman 1983, 93; Guthrie 1965, 459. The etymologies of the two key adjectives here (*gnêsia* and *skotia*) illustrate again how the process of "metaphorical stretching" enabled these early thinkers to develop a new vocabulary by deploying older terms in a new way. *Gnêsia* derives from *genos, belonging to the race*, thence *lawfully begotten, born in wedlock*, and thus *legitimate*. *Skotia* comes from *skotos, darkness* or *gloom*, and then (of persons) *done in darkness* or *in secret*, hence *clandestine*, thence *out of wedlock, bastard* and so *illegitimate* when applied to children, and used metaphorically by Democritus to signify *illegitimate* when applied to knowledge. Guthrie's use of "bastard" incorporates these origins more fully than would the term "illegitimate."

93. See Kirk, Raven, and Schofield 1983, 409–13.

94. See ibid., 431: "Most of [the surviving fragments], including the most substantial pieces, have come down to us in the anthology compiled by John of Stobi in the fifth century A.D. There is also a collection of 86 *gnomai* ascribed to 'Democrates,' which overlap with Democratean material in Stobaeus and are generally regarded, with five exceptions, as genuine. . . . [However,] the authenticity of almost any fragment can usually be attacked on some ground or other." Also see Havelock's discussion of Democritus's political theory (1957, 125–54).

95. Translations of the ethics fragments are taken from Freeman 1983. Compare fragments 59, 64, and 65 with Heraclitus: "Men who love wisdom must be good inquirers into many things indeed" (DK 35), but "much learning does not teach understanding" (DK 40).

96. There are discontinuities, disjunctions, and contradictions in "Presocratic thought." The phrase denotes not so much a single, coherent philosophical system as a general preoccupation with a particular set of questions, shared assumptions about the natural origins and fundamental rationality of world events, and reliance on observation, intellection, and logical coherence in language for investigating and explaining those events. We have seen, however, that the surviving body of Presocratic writings contain some fundamental disagreements, and my efforts here to synthesize a conception of *sophia* from these writings should not be taken to indicate that we find unanimity among them.

97. These ideas are credited to Anaxagoras in Hippolytus *Refutatio* I, 8, 3–10 (DK 59 a 42); translation after Kirk, Raven, and Schofield 1983, 380–82.

Chapter 4. Sophistical Wisdom, Socratic Wisdom, and the Political Life

1. Guthrie observes that "the causes of the reasoned rejection of tradition which marked the middle of the fifth century were exceedingly complex, and, even if the inflammable mixture can be analyzed, it may remain difficult to see why the spark was applied to it just when it was" (1971b, 17). Also see Kerferd 1981a, 15–23; de Romilly 1992, 1–29; Munn 2000, esp. 77–82; Armstrong 1949, 21–22; Brumbaugh 1964, 93ff.; Scoon 1928, 107–13.

2. Also see Munn 2000, 15–63; Bowra 1971; Zimmern 1931.

3. Guthrie's discussion of the *nomos-physis* antithesis (1971b, 55–134) is extensive and informative. Also see Untersteiner 1954, 209–21, 244–51, 281–94; Kerferd 1981a, 111–30; de Romilly 1992, 113–16, 148–74.

4. See also Grote 1888; Hammond 1959; Meiggs 1972; Munn 2000.

5. Ancient sources on Solon include Herodotus's *Histories* and Plutarch's *The Rise and Fall of Athens.* Among the better contemporary sources are Hignett 1952; Starr 1977; and Munn 2000. Fredal provides a detailed account of Solon's contributions to the development of Athenian democracy and to the emergence of the speaker's art as central in its political process (2006, 36–55).

6. On the history and theory of Athenian democracy, see Fredal 2006, esp. chap. 5; Ober 1989, 1996, 1998; Munn 2000; Hooper 1978; Finley 1985; Tejera 1984.

7. Guthrie 1971b, 25–26. Grimaldi comments that the Sophists "represent an intellectual movement that raised problems in critical areas: reality versus appearance (metaphysics); logic; epistemology (theory of knowledge); the nature of man (moral philosophy) and of society (sociology); the existence of the gods (theology); political philosophy; law; the relations of language, thought, and reality (rhetoric); the nature of education; and finally literature. . . . Much of this very likely resulted from the fact that the Presocratic philosophers were still active when the Sophists appeared" (1996, 23). Also see Munn 2000; de Romilly 1992; Kerferd 1981a; Untersteiner 1954.

8. Also see Untersteiner 1954, xv–xvi; Guthrie 1971b; Kerferd 1981a; de Romilly 1992; Schiappa 1990b, 1999, 2003.

9. Liddell and Scott (1996), *s.v. sophistês;* Havelock 1957, 158–59; Guthrie 1971b, 28; Kerferd 1950, 8 and 1981a, 24–41; Lloyd 1987, 83–98; de Romilly 1992, 1–2; Munn 2000, 78; Schiappa 1999, 50–53. According to Diogenes Laertius (1.12), *sophos* and *sophistês* were once synonymous. As Guthrie reports, "this appears especially in Herodotus, who applies the name 'sophist' to Pythagoras, Solon and the founders of the Dionysiac cult. . . . That the Seven Sages were called sophists we know from a fragment of Aristotle and from Isocrates" (28). Schiappa notes that "the term [*sophistês*] first appears in Pindar in the early fifth century and predates the appearance of the group of so-called Older Sophists" (50).

10. De Romilly notes that "one of them, Thrasymachus, hit on an admirable formula to convey this [claim]. The epitaph that he composed for his own tomb ran: 'Chalcedon was my country, knowledge [*sophia*] my profession [*technê*]'" (1992, 1). Questions about the motivations of these teachers and about the authenticity of the "wisdom" they taught arose even during their own lifetimes. The present portrayal of sophistical wisdom is also in Johnstone 2006. I take my list from those mentioned by Guthrie 1971b

and Sprague 1972. They include Protagoras of Abdera (ca. 490–ca. 420), Xeniades of Corinth, Gorgias of Leontini (ca. 485–ca. 380), Lycophron, Prodicus of Ceos (ca. 470–ca. 399), Thrasymachus of Chalcedon (born 450s), Hippias of Elis ("much younger" than Protagoras, according to Plato, *Hippias Major* 282e), Antiphon of Rhamnous (a contemporary of Socrates), Critias of Athens (ca. 460–403), Antisthenes of Athens, Alcidamas of Elaea (a student of Gorgias), and perhaps a few others, including the unknown writers of the *Anonymous Iamblichi* and the *Dissoi Logoi*. This is a somewhat inclusive roster. Schiappa identifies a shorter "standard list" based on Diels and Kranz (which is Sprague's source) and notes that "the list is somewhat arbitrary and cannot be squared with the available ancient testimony" (1999, 50). He goes on (51–53) to describe various ways, both ancient and modern, of identifying persons as "Sophists."

11. Scott-Kilvert's translation of *deinotêta politikên* as "political acumen" may strike some readers as problematic (see Plutarch 1960). Guthrie (1971b, 36) translates the same expression as "political shrewdness." *Deinotês* derives from *deinos*, which in Homer means "fearful" or "terrible" (e.g., at *Iliad* 1.49), but in Herodotus (5.23) it means "clever" or "skillful," and not necessarily in a negative sense. In his translation of the Antiphon fragments in Sprague (1972, 123), Morrison renders the term as "cleverness" (DK 87 A 6, sec. 11), while Dillon and Gergel have it as "rhetorical power" (2003, 140). In his analysis of prudence (*phronêsis*) in book 6 of the *Nicomachean Ethics*, Aristotle describes *deinotês* ("cleverness," in Thomson's 1976 translation) as the capacity for "carrying out actions conducive to our proposed aim, and of achieving that aim" (1144a). The term is also translated as "cunning." Such words suggest astuteness in practical affairs, so the translation as "acumen," connoting a sharpness of mind, seems appropriate when it is linked to political activity.

12. Unless otherwise noted, quotations from the *Protagoras* are from Guthrie's translation in Plato 1961j. It will be assumed here that the speech Plato puts into the mouth of Protagoras substantially reproduces the latter's own views, if not his words. This is the opinion of a majority of scholars. See Guthrie 1971b, 63–64, 265–66; Kerferd 1981a, 167–68; Schiappa 1999, 180; Untersteiner 1954, 25, and 72n24. Also see Havelock 1957, 407–9, who summarizes objections to this view.

13. Thrasymachus, according to the Suda, collected or wrote about deliberative speeches and subjects for speeches (DK 85 A 1) but probably did not author a technical or theoretical treatise on rhetoric (Schiappa 1999, 45). Antiphon is credited with forming a school on politics and with teaching political and forensic speech, as well as with serving the Athenians as trierarch, general, and ambassador (DK 87 A 3). See Barker 1925; Untersteiner 1954; Kerferd 1956–57, 1964, 1981a; Gagarin 2002.

14. The first of these virtues, *aidôs*, according to Guthrie, is a "complicated quality combining roughly a sense of shame, modesty, and respect for others. It is not far from 'conscience'" (1971b, 66). Liddell and Scott (1996) characterize the term as "*reverence, awe, respect* for the feeling or opinion of others or for one's own conscience, and so *shame, self-respect, . . . sense of honour.*" The second, *dikaiosynê*, is a sense of right or fairness (from *dikê*, justice). For a helpful discussion of this term, see Schiappa 2003, 180–82. Atwill's discussion of Protagoras's "Prometheus Narrative" (1998, 149–55) is helpful in illuminating the distinctive features of his view of the *logon technê*.

15. Aristotle (*Nic. Ethics* 1180b) was skeptical about the Sophists' competence to teach politics, since "it is practiced not by any of them but by the politicians . . . ; for they are not found either writing or speaking about such matters." However, in 444 B.C.E. Pericles asked Protagoras to create a constitution and to write laws for the newly founded Athenian colony at Thurii (on the Italian peninsula), demonstrating the high regard in which this Sophist's political skills were held (Diogenes Laertius 9.50). Little is known about this constitution, but it was democratic, and the laws apparently included a provision, as Aristotle remarks, that "generals should only be re-elected after an interval of five years" (*Pol.* 1307b). Likewise Gorgias was selected by his fellow citizens in Leontini to represent their interests in Athens when he headed a diplomatic delegation to that city in 427 B.C.E. (see Diodorus 12.53, 1; DK 82 A 4). Philostratus (*Lives of the Sophists* 1.9; DK 82 A 1) comments that "his *Olympic Speech* dealt with political matters of the greatest importance, for seeing Greece involved in civil dissension, he became a counselor of concord to her inhabitants."

16. Guthrie 1971b, 68. Also see Havelock 1957, 88–94.

17. Also see Untersteiner 1954, 206–27; Guthrie 1971b, 274–80.

18. Heracles was revered from the earliest period in Greek history, both for his "labors" and as a benefactor of humankind. He was seen as a model of courage and endurance and was later credited with such virtues as wisdom and temperance. Prodicus delivered the tale in the form of an *epideixis*—in this case as "a speech composed for recital before a popular audience, conveying elementary moral commonplaces through the easily absorbed medium of a fable about one of the most popular figures of legend" (Guthrie 1971b, 277). Untersteiner's discussion of the Heracles myth casts the conflict as between *nomos* and *physis* rather than merely between virtue and vice (1954, 216–21). Quotations from the speech are taken from Xenophon 1990.

19. The identity of Antiphon of Rhamnous (ca. 480–411?), the Sophist, has been the subject of ongoing debate. Guthrie discusses the point at some length (1971b, 285–86, 292–94) and observes that "the question is of minor interest for the history of philosophy" (286). Morrison, in introducing his translation of the fragments in Sprague (1972), concludes that "there is nothing which rules out a single author" (111). Also see Untersteiner 1954, 228–29, 230n2; Gagarin 2002.

20. Of the fifth-century debates concerning the relationship between *nomos* and *physis*, Guthrie observes that "three positions may be distinguished: support of *nomos* against *physis*, support of *physis* against *nomos*, and an attitude of hard-headed realism or fact-facing which without passing judgment declares that the more powerful will always take advantage of the weaker, and will give the name of law and justice to whatever they lay down in their own interests. It will retain the name for as long as they keep their power" (1971b, 60). Also see Gagarin 2002, 65–73. Among the older Sophists adhering to the first position are Protagoras and Gorgias; to the second, Antiphon and Prodicus; and to the last, Thrasymachus.

21. DK 87 B 44, fr. B1, trans. Dillon and Gergel 2003. Quotations of Antiphon will be taken from this translation unless otherwise noted. Guthrie observes that "these fragments are invaluable as a source for contemporary moral views, though their incompleteness makes it difficult to say how far they represent the opinions of Antiphon himself" (1971b, 110).

22. Also see Guthrie 1971b, 108; de Romilly 1992, 123–24; Gagarin 2002, 73–78.

23. Antiphon's discussion of using justice "advantageously" (*xympheroniô*) is tantalizingly incomplete, but it is generally linked to preserving life (which is advantageous, while death is not, though both are "in accordance with nature"), the avoidance of harm, and securing pleasure while avoiding pain (DK 87 B 2–4). Gagarin concludes (rightly, in my view) that Antiphon did not conceive these to be objective values at which action should aim, but only as features of *nomos, physis,* and *dikaiosynê* (2002, 80).

24. The "concerning the gods" fragment (DK 80 B 4) is, after the "human-measure" fragment, Protagoras's best-known saying. It is quoted wholly or in part by Diogenes Laertius (9.51), Hesychius (DK 80 A 3), Sextus Empiricus (*Against the Schoolmasters* 9.55, 56), Cicero (*On the Nature of the Gods* 1.23, 63), and Eusebius (*Preparation of the Gospel* 14.3, 7). The translation used here is O'Brien's, in Sprague 1972, 20. Also see Untersteiner 1954, 26– 28; Schiappa 2003, 141ff. The "human-measure" fragment (DK 80 B 1) appears in Sextus (7, 60) and Plato (*Theaetetus* 151e). The Greek text of the fragment is: *Pantôn chrêmatôn metron estin anthrôpos, tôn men ontôn ôs estin, tôn de ouk ontôn ôs ouk estin.* The translation here is adapted from O'Brien's, in Sprague. Schiappa's careful reconsideration of "the standard translation" (2003, 118–21) is instructive. Also see Burrell 1932; Versenyi 1962; Cole 1972. Untersteiner (1954, 42) translates the fragment thus: "Man is the master of all experiences, in regard to the 'phenomenality' of what is real and the 'non-phenomenality' of what is not real."

25. Gorgias's "three theses": "nothing exists; . . . even if it exists it is inapprehensible to man; . . . even if it is apprehensible, still it is without a doubt incapable of being expressed or explained to the next man." The fragment, taken from Gorgias's work entitled *On the Nonexistent or On Nature,* appears in Sextus, *Against the Schoolmasters* VII, 65. I use Kennedy's translation in Sprague 1972, 42.

26. See, for example, Untersteiner 1954, 41–49, 77–91; Guthrie 1971a, 181–87; Schiappa 2003, 117–40; Versenyi 1962.

27. See Untersteiner 1954, 42–44; Guthrie 1971a, 183; Schiappa 2003, 119.

28. Translated by O'Brien, in Sprague 1972, 18. Also see Untersteiner 1954, 86–88; Schiappa 2003, 118–19. The epistemological, ethical, and ontological/metaphysical problems associated with what amounts to a solipsistic "black hole" are numerous and significant (see Aristotle, *Meta.,* 1063b), and the evidence of his own life suggests that Protagoras believed at least that intersubjectively legitimized perceptions and beliefs could be negotiated. After all, for a fee he taught arts of eloquence and of prudent household and political management.

29. The ambiguity of *anthrôpos* is echoed in Sextus's discussion of Protagoras's view. In his *Outlines of Pyrrhonism* (1.216–19), after quoting what are presumably Protagoras's own words, he says that "by 'measure' he means the criterion, . . . and consequently he posits only what appears to each individual, and thus he introduces relativity" (216). A few lines later, however, he says, "Thus, according to him, Man (*anthrôpos*) becomes the criterion of real existences; for all things that appear *to men* (*tois anthrôpois*) also exist, and things that appear to no man have no existence either" (219, my italics; Bury's translation in Sextus Empiricus 1967). The use of the plural here suggests that it is humans *collectively* who provide the criterion or measure by which the existent is distinguished from the nonexistent.

30. Seneca puts the matter thus: "Protagoras says that one can argue equally well on either side of any question, including the question itself whether both sides of any question can be argued" (*Letters* 88, 43, translated by O'Brien, in Sprague 1972, 13). Guthrie (1971b, 182n1) writes that "an equally possible translation would be: 'Of every thing two contrary accounts can be given.'" On Protagoras's doctrine concerning "two opposing arguments," see Untersteiner 1954, 19–26; Kerferd 1981a, 84–85; Schiappa 2003, 89–102; de Romilly 1992, 75–76. Schiappa points to Aristophanes' portrayal in the *Clouds* of sophistical teachings as important evidence for understanding the "two-*logoi*" and the "weaker/stronger *logoi*" doctrines in Protagoras (90, 106–7, 110–13). His discussion of these ideas is detailed and illuminating. The two-*logoi* doctrine apparently inspired the anonymous author of the *Dissoi Logoi* ("Double Arguments") to compose around 400 B.C.E. a guide for the study of argumentation and controversy. See Kerferd 1981a, 84–85; de Romilly, 76–78; Untersteiner, 304–10; Guthrie, 316–19.

31. Untersteiner, in elaborating this point, quotes Wilhelm Schmid (*Geshchichte der griechischen Literatur* III, 20n3): "for the sophist 'there does not in fact exist an absolute *orthotês* [correctness]; from the *logos orthos* [right account/reasoning/argument] there can always be subtracted the value, in the realm of opinion, of a *logos orthoteros* [more correct account]; *orthon* [the correct] is therefore that which at any time, by means of reason, can be rendered more probable than anything else, i.e. which works especially by way of persuasion in order that something more probable may appear'" (1954, 56). Also see 15–16, 64–70, 132–38, 141–42; Guthrie 1971a, 181–88; Schiappa 2003, 175–87; de Romilly 1992, 71–72, 80–81; Poulakos 1995, 23–25, 57–58; Hawhee 2004; Fredal 2006.

32. The phrases are taken from Kennedy's translation of Gorgias's *Encomium of Helen* in Sprague 1972, 50–54. Subsequent quotations from the *Helen* will be taken from this translation unless otherwise noted.

33. The treatise itself has not survived, but we possess two representations of its arguments, one in Sextus (*Ag. the Schoolmasters* 7.65–87, DK 82 B 3, sec. 65–87) and another in a work attributed (probably erroneously) to Aristotle (*Melissus, Xenophanes, and Gorgias* 5, 6, 979a–80b). According to Diogenes Laertius (5.25), Aristotle also wrote a monograph entitled *In Reply to the Opinions of Gorgias*, now lost. Kennedy's translation of Sextus's version appears in Sprague 1972, 42–46, and passages quoted here are taken from this unless otherwise noted. For interpretations of and commentaries on the treatise, see Untersteiner 1954, 143–63; Guthrie 1971b, 192–200; de Romilly 1992, 95–97; Consigny 2001, 35–59; McComiskey 2002, 34–38; Schiappa 1999, 133–52; Gargarin, 1997; Gaines, 1997; J. Poulakos, 1997.

34. Guthrie 1971b, 193–94. Also see Untersteiner, who sees Gorgias's aim as expressing "a sorrowful cry at the sorrowful discovery that ontology and epistemology are tragic" (1954, 143–45). Schiappa (1999) summarizes the "disciplinary presuppositions" underlying various approaches to interpreting the treatise (136–38) and examines several such approaches in detail (143–47).

35. Calogero 1957, 16n22. Guthrie contends that "the form of his arguments shows that their irony was aimed especially at Parmenides and his followers, to demonstrate that on their own reasoning it is as easy to prove the contrary of *x* as *x* itself" (1971b, 194). Consigny argues that *On Not-Being* is a serious philosophical inquiry into the

nature of being and knowledge (2001, 37–38), and Schiappa demonstrates convincingly that Gorgias's argument matches the logical structure of Parmenides' (1999, 148–52). Kerferd, however, argues that "Gorgias was concerned not merely to attack the Eleatics but . . . the pluralists among the Presocratics as well" (1981a, 96). Nonetheless, as Schiappa observes, "it is not necessary to ponder his intentions, fortunately, because the very ambiguity of Parmenides' subjectless *esti* required the hearers of *On Not Being* to supply parallel semantic content to make sense of his similarly subjectless *ouk esti*. In other words, despite the variety of interpretations possible, Gorgias could assume with confidence that *On Not Being* always would be read against Parmenides, Melissus, and Zeno" (147). Also see Untersteiner 1954, 143–44; Gagarin 1997.

36. Kerferd offers the following: "What is the *it* that is here being talked about? There seem to me clear indications that what Gorgias is concerned with is each and every thing no matter what, including above all phenomenal objects" (1981a, 96). Schiappa concludes that "Parmenides' and Melissus' 'is' is *pure* be-ing in the sense of being ungenerated and unperishing, unchanging, stable, and forever. And it is just this 'pure' sense of *esti* that Gorgias is attacking" (1999, 145). Also see Untersteiner 1954, 145–51.

37. McComiskey 2002, 37. The author argues for this interpretation, at least implicitly, when he writes that "the wording of *On Non-Existence* [DK] B3.85 is significant, for it shifts from using *to on* (a philosophical term) to signify external reality to using instead *to pragma*, signifying not only external reality, the term's most concrete sense, but also the deeds and circumstances of everyday communal life. . . . Gorgias' reference to external reality as *to pragma* ('deed' or 'act,' the concrete form of *praxis* that means 'action' and is often used in social contexts ranging from political to business to military to poetic), a force that generates sociolinguistic *logoi*, is perhaps an early Greek articulation of a nascent social constructionist view of language. Until this passage in *On Non-Existence*, Gorgias has referred to 'realities' only as *ta onta*, a philosophical term with a conceptual sense; however, when his discussion turns to the generation of *logoi*, Gorgias is no longer interested in conceptual realities. . . . [For] communal realities (*ta pragmata*, not *ta onta*) generate socially relevant discourse" (37). Also see Kerferd 1981a, 96; Consigny 2001, 60ff.

38. Schiappa (1999, 149–51) offers a technically detailed "intertextual analysis" of the passage that considers it in connection with and as a response to Parmenides' contention that what can be thought and said must exist (fr. 6, Simplicius *in Phys.* 86, 27). Also see Untersteiner 1954, 151–56; Kerferd 1981a, 96–97; de Romilly 1992, 96–97; McComiskey 2002, 35–36.

39. It is worth noting that Gorgias's argument was apparently put forth with enough sophistication to have helped inspire a philosophical tradition that persists into our own time. From such Academic skeptics as Arcesilas (ca. 315–241 B.C.E.) and Carneades (ca. 213–129 B.C.E.), and Pyrrhonists such as Pyrrho of Elis (ca. 360–275 B.C.E.) and Sextus Empiricus (fl. ca. 200 C.E.), to Reformation thinkers such as Erasmus (ca. 1466–1536) and Descartes (1596–1650), the very possibility of objective, certain knowledge has been challenged in ways that were foreshadowed in Gorgias's treatise. The views of the Hellenistic skeptics have come down to us principally through the writings of Cicero (for example, in his *Academica* and *De Natura Deorum*), Diogenes Laertius (in *Lives of Eminent Philosophers*), and St. Augustine (in his *Against the Academics*). Sextus presents his

own views as well as summarizing those of Pyrrho in *Outlines of Pyrrhonism*. See Guthrie 1971b, 200–203; Popkin 1964, ix–xiv, 17–43.

40. See *On Sophistical Refutations* 165b–66a. This fallacy is closely related to and indeed exploits the features of ambiguity (166a). As Aristotle says in opening this treatise, "some reasonings are really reasonings (*syllogismoi*), but . . . others seem to be, but are not really, reasonings" (164a). "Reasoning," he says (164a), "is based on certain statements made in such a way as necessarily to cause the assertion of things other than those statements and as a result of those statements." The problem with equivocal uses of terms is that, because the meanings of the terms change, no logically necessary implication can be drawn from the propositions in which the terms are used.

41. Poulakos argues that "the Sophists show no interest in a world of conceptual perfection or rational orderliness. Theirs is a constantly changing world, full of ambiguity and uncertainty, always lacking, never complete. Because it is ceaselessly unfolding, it is open to infinite possibilities which *logos*, its integrative force proper, can create. . . . The Sophists tend to look at the world not as it is but as it is not. Accordingly, they venture into the sphere of possibility searching for that which is not yet but which can be; therefore, we can say that their rhetoric aims at creating possibilities, opening what is closed, undoing what is done" (1984, 221).

42. For discussions of this argument, see Untersteiner 1954, 156–59; Guthrie 1971b, 198–99; Kerferd 1981a, 81, 97–98; McComiskey 2002, 36–38.

43. See, for example, Untersteiner 1954; Segal 1962; Kennedy 1963; Versenyi 1963; Guthrie 1971b; Poulakos 1983a; de Romilly 1992; Schiappa 1996, 1999; McComiskey, 2002. Valiavitcharska rejects this view, arguing instead that "in the *Encomium* Gorgias does not see his own art as deception, nor does he think that it necessarily rests on opinion (*doxa*), but he sees an intrinsic connection between truthful speech (*alêthês logos*) and correct speech (*orthos logos*)" (2006, 149). For reasons already given, it seems to me difficult to sustain this reading when the *Helen* is read holistically with *On Non-Being* and the *Palamedes*.

44. Schiappa argues for a "predisciplinary approach" to reading the *Helen* (and, it can be inferred, the *Palamedes*). Such an approach, he argues, "attempts to avoid vocabulary and assumptions about discursive theories and practices imported from the fourth century when analyzing fifth-century texts" (1996, 66–67). Also see Schiappa 1999, 114–20; de Romilly 1992, 61. My reading of both speeches proceeds in this spirit.

45. McComiskey notes that "we must keep in mind . . . that the term *alêtheia* did not develop its philosophical sense of The Truth until Plato. In most pre-Socratic and sophistical usages, *alêtheia* simply refers to sincerity of speech and is opposed to *pseudê* (lies). For Gorgias, then, *alêtheia* refers to a relative truth, which would in no way be a *pseudos* (lie), and as situations change, so, too, do the criteria for determining the truth of statements" (2002, 38–39).

46. De Romilly discusses Gorgias's argumentative strategy in the *Helen* and observes that "the impression given is that not a single possibility has been overlooked, and this makes the argument look like an impressive demonstration. The technique furthermore makes it possible to use general, theoretical arguments—definitely the hallmark of a philosopher. We are presented with a list of hypotheses rather than an analysis of the facts" (1992, 62).

47. On the importance of orality in Gorgias's teachings, see Johnstone 2001 (esp. 125–26), 2005, 2006. McComiskey appears to share this view when he explains the power of poetry: "[The] double sensory experience of both tragic sight and metrical sound moves the *psuchai* of the audience to *re*live (without having *first* lived through) the tragic experiences enacted on stage" (2002, 43; also see 44). Compare Segal, who contends that "the *metron*, the formal aspect of the *logos*, seems to play a significant part in causing the emotive reactions upon which persuasion rests; and it is, therefore, natural that conscious formalism is so important in the carefully balanced antitheses, rhyming coda, calculated sound-effects, and metrical patterns in Gorgias' own style" (1962, 127). Segal notes a possible link between Gorgias's understanding of how the sounds of speech can have an aesthetic impact on the hearer's *psychê* and the work of Damon (DK 37 B 6), who is reported to have perceived the psychological effects of the rhythm and harmony of music.

48. Gorgias's reputation for "extraordinary, dazzling oratory, . . . [and] poetic rhythms" is well documented (Barrett 1987, 14). Of his speaking, Philostratus comments that "he was an example of forcefulness . . . and of unexpected expression and of inspiration and of the grand style . . . and of detached phrases and transitions, by which speech becomes sweeter . . . and more impressive, and he also introduced poetic words for ornament" (*Lives of the Sophists* 1.9, 2; Kennedy's translation in Sprague 1972, 30). According to the Suda, "he was the first to give the rhetorical genre the verbal power and art of deliberate culture and employed tropes and metaphors and figurative language . . . and doublings of words and repetitions and apostrophes and clauses of equal length" (DK 82 A 2).

49. Segal, noting that "*peitho* 'forms' or 'molds' the psyche as it wishes" (1962, 106), writes that "the psyche itself responds to the physical structure of the word . . . with emotional impulses which, if strong enough, result in a total *ekplexis* [emotional disturbance] and a concrete action of an unexpected, nonrational type. The *logos*, therefore, if properly calculated, can through its 'impression' on the psyche lead the hearer into lines of action hitherto not considered. . . . The psyche thus stands in a middle position as the impressionable receiver of new emotions and the initiator of fresh actions resulting from these emotions; and *peitho*, as the art of awakening these emotions, is thus a powerful tool for directing and aiming human action" (107–8).

50. This sentiment is echoed by Antiphon in *On Truth*, where it is maintained that, because there is no permanent reality behind our words (DK 87 B 67), all words are deceptive (B 69). Also see Kerferd 1981a, 81; Untersteiner 1954, 106–14.

51. It is this feature of Gorgianic speech, in part, that leads Gagarin to argue that "pleasure," rather than "persuasion," is its primary aim (2001, 279–81, 287–89). He challenges the widely accepted idea that the Sophists were concerned chiefly with persuasion either in their own oratory or in their teaching. Rather, he argues, "in most cases persuasion is in the background and is less important than several other objectives, such as the serious exploration of issues and forms of argument, the display of ingenuity in thought, argument and style of expression, and the desire to dazzle, shock and please" (289). I find this argument interesting, but I do not find it persuasive, primarily because of the fact that many Sophists became quite wealthy from their teaching, and it seems unlikely that most people would have paid high fees merely to be

pleased and excited rather than to acquire a practical skill that would serve them in the assembly and in court.

52. Schiappa challenges the entire "traditional account" regarding Corax and Tisias, concluding that it is advisable to think of this version of rhetoric's origins as a "myth" (1999, 35–39). However, see Gagarin 1994, 50–51.

53. All quotations from the *Palamedes* are from Kennedy's translation in Sprague 1972, 54–63, unless otherwise noted. The *Tetralogies* (four-part speeches) of Antiphon are likewise translated by Morrison in Sprague, 136–63. Also see Gagarin 1994, 52ff.

54. Schiappa points out that, though the term *eikos* appears in fifth-century texts by Herodotus, Thucydides, Aeschylus, and Sophocles (used with such meanings as "likely," "fitting," "meet," "right," or "reasonable"), "the technical conceptualization of the term, signaled by the neuter singular paired with the definite article (*to eikos*), cannot be found prior to Plato's writings" (1999, 36). Thus, while we can certainly attribute the use of argument from probabilities to such Sophists as Gorgias, Antiphon, and Protagoras, we cannot impute to them the awareness of an abstract concept such as "the probable" or "probability."

55. Grimaldi, in summing up his discussion of the Sophists and their concentration on rhetoric, writes of the *technê logopoiikê*, the art of word-craft, as "a study of the ways in which to use both the spoken and written *logos* most efficiently for communication with others" (1996, 42). Both Philostratus (*Lives of the Sophists* 1.23.1) and Philo (1.526) use *logopôlês* (a "word-dealer") in their accounts of the Sophists. My coinage of *logosophia* is offered in a similar spirit. On sophistical teachings and the "logic of circumstances," see Poulakos 1995, esp. 57ff.

56. On sophistical teachings and eristic/counterargument, see Untersteiner 1954, 19–40; Kerferd 1981a, 61–67; Schiappa 2003, 164–66; de Romilly 1992, 76–77, 80–83; Poulakos 1995, 24–25.

57. Kerferd (1981a, 45) reports that Gorgias may have authored a technical treatise on rhetoric whose title was *On the Right Moment in Time* (*Peri Kairou*). Diogenes Laertius (9.52, DK 80 A 1) reports that "Protagoras was the first man . . . to expound the importance of the right moment" (trans. O'Brien, in Sprague 1972, 4). Schiappa, however, observes that "Protagoras, Gorgias and Critias may have discussed *kairos* in connection with public speaking, but there is no clear evidence that other Sophists did so" (2003, 79).

58. Elsewhere (1983b, 42), Poulakos describes *kairos* as one of the "artistic elements in rhetorical theory" that, unlike "rigid scientific principles," is a "matter of feeling." McComiskey observes that Gorgias's "rhetorical methodology works to seize the opportune moment (*kairos*) in which certain kinds of language can be used to unite subjective consciousnesses into a communal desire for action" (2002, 18). Hawhee contends that "In the realm of sophistic rhetoric, *kairos* emerges as a kind of immanent, rhythmic, embodied practice. . . . Gorgias hit on this kind of agonistic immanence when he took the stage in the theater at Athens and challenged the audience to 'suggest a subject,' a move which, according to Diogenes Laertius, showed that he 'would trust to the moment (*tôi kairôi*) to speak on any subject' (A1a). In other words, Gorgias would submit to immanence in a particular rhetorical moment—a *kairos*—for movement, to take discourse somewhere else" (2004, 76). Also see Hawhee, 76–85; Untersteiner 1954, 118–21, 195–99; Kerferd 1981a, 82; Schiappa 2003, 72–73; White 1987, 14–15.

59. *Lives of the Sophists* 1.11; DK 82 A 1a (trans. Kennedy, in Sprague 1972). Protagoras, Gorgias, Hippias, and other Sophists are characterized as being willing to speak extemporaneously on any matter put forward by those in attendance. See, for example, Plato, *Prot.* 329b; *Gorgias* 447a–d, 449c; *Meno* 70b–c; *Hippias Minor* 363c–d.

60. Schiappa (2003) challenges Poulakos's (1983b, 1984, 1995) claim that *to prepon* can be linked textually with sophistical teachings other than Gorgias's (71–77). Poulakos responds that "precisely where and how many times [this term appears in the fragments] are not interesting questions. . . . Rather, these terms are significant because they can help explain common features or tendencies of the available sophistical texts and because they can render the rhetorical practices of the sophists meaningful" (1995, 57).

61. See, for example, DK 84 A 9; Plato, *Cratylus* 384b, *Prot.* 337a, 340a, *Euthydemus* 277e, *Laches* 197d, *Charmides* 163b–d.

62. This translation is Robinson's (1979, 139). Compare Sprague's: "the man who knows the art of rhetoric will also know how to speak correctly on every subject" (1972, 292).

63. For discussion of contemporary scientific findings supporting the idea that the human brain is structured to respond emotionally to speech sounds, see Johnstone 2005, 10–12. Similarly, Schwartz describes "the resonance principle in communication" and examines its operation in the use of electronic media (1974, 1–40).

64. For useful discussions of the Sophists' approach to civic education, see Havelock 1957; Beck 1964; Jarrett 1969; Guthrie 1971b, 41–48; Simmons 1972; Kerferd 1981a, 28–41; de Romilly 1992, 196–203; Rapple 1993; Robb 1994; Grimaldi 1996, 27–31.

65. See Plato, *Prot.* 325d–26c. Kerferd writes that "in the primary school the standard system of education consisted of three parts, each with its own specialist teacher. The *paidotribês* was responsible for physical education and sporting activities, the *citharistês* for music. Thirdly, the *grammatistês* taught reading, writing, arithmetic, and his pupils were required to read and memorise writings of the great poets, Homer, Hesiod and others, chosen because of the moral wisdom they contained" (1981a, 37). In her description of the *citharistês*, de Romilly reports that "lessons devoted to the cithara and fine lyric works . . . teach the child harmony and rhythm, both of which are essential to human life" (1992, 197). Also see Hawhee 2004.

66. See Philostratus, *Lives of the Sophists* 1.2, DK 86 A 2. See also Plato, *Prot.* 318e; Cicero, *De Oratore* 3.32.127–28.

67. *De Oratore* 3.32.127–29. Protagoras is credited by Sextus (DK 80 A 14) with a doctrine that is similar to that of Empedocles and the atomists. Gorgias likewise was interested in Empedocles' theories (DK 82 B 31). Prodicus is said to have discussed the four elements (Epiphanius, *Adv. Haeres.* 3.21, a passage not in DK). See Plato's *Sophist* (232b–e) for an account of the range of topics with which Sophists are concerned. Also see DK 80 A 14, DK 31 A 92; DK 82 B 5 and B 31.

68. Among the works attributed to Protagoras are both an *Art of Debating* and *Contradictory Arguments in Two Books* (DK 80 A 1 55). Kerferd suggests that these two titles may have referred to the same work and contends that "there are good reasons for supposing that either or both of these contained 'commonplace' materials, in antithetical form . . . ready for use either by students or in real life" (1981a, 31).

69. Socrates lived through the rise, decline, and resurgence of democracy in Periclean and post-Periclean Athens. He represents a link between the old Athenians and the new. At his birth, Athens was still the city of those who had defeated the Persians at Marathon, Salamis, and Plataia. The prime of his life coincides with the period of Athenian supremacy under the leadership of Pericles and with the first years of the Peloponnesian War. The last decade of his life saw the defeat of Athens by Sparta and its allies, the brutal rule of the Thirty Tyrants, and restoration of a democracy that ultimately tried and executed him. See Brickhouse and Smith 2000, 18ff.

70. In the *Phaedo* (96a–97b) Plato seems to suggest that, when he was young, the historical Socrates took a serious interest in certain aspects of natural philosophy but that he abandoned these concerns when he became convinced that they could not explain the most important matters in life—ethical and moral matters. Diogenes Laertius (2.16, 2.19, and 2.23) says that Socrates was at one time the pupil of Archelaus, and he reports other testimony that Socrates had been a student of Anaxagoras, though the latter is doubted by modern scholars. Also see Scoon 1928, 155ff. One failure of Socrates was to appreciate the contributions that cosmology and cosmogony might have made to his inquiries. If one's own personal existence is viewed not as opposed to but as an expression of the processes of nature, then to "know thyself" in order to discover one's duties and obligations must include knowing the *Logos* of which one is an embodiment. Thus, natural philosophy and cosmology would be essential activities in the self-examined life to which Socrates was committed and to which he would have us commit ourselves. This conclusion was not altogether lost on Plato, his most illustrious student, as we shall see in chapter 5.

71. Elsewhere Cicero writes, "Socrates . . . was the first to divert philosophy from matters which nature herself has wrapped in obscurity, . . . and apply it to ordinary life. . . . Celestial phenomena he regarded as beyond our comprehension, or at any rate . . . as irrelevant to the good life" (*Acad.* 1.4.15). Also see Guthrie 1971a, 99ff.; Cornford 1950, 1–7, 27ff.

72. This does not necessarily mean that he never wrote anything at all. In the *Phaedo* (60c–d), set during the final hours of Socrates' life, Plato has one of the speakers inquire about the "lyrics which you [Socrates] have been composing lately by adapting Aesop's fables and 'The Prelude' to Apollo" (see D. L. 2.42 for his version of these lyrics). Since such a detail serves no philosophical aim that Plato might have had in writing the dialogue, there is no prima facie reason to reject its historical accuracy. Of course, neither is this necessarily evidence that Socrates *wrote* the lyrics out as he composed them.

73. Vlastos (1994, 135) includes in the earlier dialogues (listed in alphabetical order) the *Apology, Charmides, Crito, Euthydemus, Euthyphro, Gorgias, Hippias Major, Hippias Minor, Ion, Laches, Lysis, Menexenus, Protagoras,* and *Republic* Bk. 1. The *Meno* is described as marking "the point of transition from the earlier to the middle dialogues." The dialogues of the middle period are listed in probable chronological order as the *Cratylus, Phaedo, Symposium, Republic* bks. 2–10, *Phaedrus, Parmenides,* and *Theaetetus.* The later period includes (also listed in probable chronological order) the *Timaeus, Critias, Sophist, Politicus, Philebus,* and *Laws.* Also see Benson (2000, 9), where Vlastos's general schema is followed but the *Euthydemus, Hippias Major, Lysis, Menexenus,* and *Meno* are described as transitional. Gill's discussion of this matter in the introduction to his translation of

the *Symposium* is helpful (1999, xvi–xviii). For different approaches to assessing the historical veracity of Plato's dialogues, see Guthrie 1971a, 29–35; Brickhouse and Smith 2000, 44–49; Taylor 1953, 25–36.

74. Also see Gill, in Plato 1999, xvi–xx; Waterfield, in Xenophon 1990, 12–20.

75. Quotations from Xenophon's writings are taken from Treddenick's and Waterfield's translations in Xenophon 1990. On assessing Xenophon's portrait of Socrates, also see Rogers 1933, 165–80; Brickhouse and Smith 2000, 38–44; Taylor 1953, 22–25.

76. Guthrie notes that "he was not the only one to make fun of Socrates, who was evidently thought of as a peculiarly good subject. He was mentioned to our knowledge by four other writers of the Old Comedy, Callias, Ameipsias, Eupolis and Telecleides. . . . Ameipsias in the *Connus* says that along with being foolish, going hungry, having no decent coat and being 'born to spite the cobblers' (since he never wore shoes), he had great powers of endurance and never stooped to flattery. Eupolis spoke of him as not knowing or caring where his next meal was coming from. Apart from this he is represented as squalid (literally 'unwashed'), thievish, and as an endless talker indulging in time-wasting dialectical subtleties. . . . The *Connus* of Ameipsias called Sophists *phrontistai* (thinkers), and Socrates was nicknamed *phrontistes* and in Aristophanes presides over a private *phrontisterion* or thinking-shop" (1971a, 40–41).

77. Also see Brickhouse and Smith 2000, 33–38; Guthrie 1971a, 41–43.

78. Guthrie (1971a, 35–39) discusses in some detail the arguments for considering as reliable Aristotle's accounts of Socrates' thought. Also see Brickhouse and Smith 2000, 48.

79. Unless otherwise noted, quoted passages from the *Apology* are based on Treddennick's translation in Plato 1961a. Both Plato and Xenophon authored versions of Socrates' speech of self-defense. Though it is unlikely that either provides a word-for-word transcript of what Socrates actually said to the jurors, and scholars continue to debate whether either tells us much about his speech, most commentators think that, of the two, Plato's is more likely to be accurate. See Brickhouse and Smith 2000, 27–33.

80. Stone's view is that these events turned Socrates against the very idea of politics and the polis, and he argues that it was Socrates' antipolitical teachings that led to his indictment, trial, and conviction by his fellow Athenians (1989, 11–12, 174–96). Also see Ober 1998.

81. We possess the text of the actual indictment against Socrates from two sources, Xenophon and Diogenes Laertius. Drawing on both of these (Xenophon, *Memorabilia* 1.1.1; D. L. 2.40), Guthrie states the full version of the indictment thus: "This indictment is entered on affidavit by Meletus son of Meletus of the deme Pitthus against Socrates son of Sophroniscus of Alopeke. Socrates is guilty of refusing to recognize the gods recognized by the State and [of] introducing other, new divinities. He is also guilty of corrupting the youth. The penalty demanded is death" (1971a, 62). However, see Stone 1989, 5–6, 28–29, 154–55, 198–99.

82. For interesting discussions of this episode and its effects on Socrates, see Guthrie 1971a, 85–89; Taylor, 1953, 78ff.; Stone 1989, 78–82.

83. Also see 39–40, 55–58; Brickhouse and Smith 2000, 99–120; Vlastos 1985; Plato, *Theaetetus* 150b–d. On the sincerity of Socrates' profession of ignorance, see Guthrie 1971a, 122–29. "To be a Socratic," he concludes, "is not to follow any system

of philosophical doctrine. It implies first and foremost an attitude of mind, an intellectual humility easily mistaken for arrogance, since the true Socratic is convinced of the ignorance not only of himself but of all mankind" (129). Vlastos identifies several senses in which Socrates might be taken to have spoken about "knowing" and "knowledge." Stone acknowledges at several places that Socrates "had never been able to achieve the definitions he sought, as he himself admitted" (1989, 70; also see 82, 86–87). However, he concludes that Socrates was being disingenuous in his disavowal of knowledge (81–82).

84. On this matter, Guthrie notes that the search for general moral definitions distinguished Socratic from sophistical thought (1971a, 111). On the Socratic quest for definitions, see 105–22. Also see Brickhouse and Smith 2000, 113–20; and Stone 1989, 68–89, where this quest is described as a "wild goose chase."

85. Brickhouse and Smith observe that Socrates appears to be "deeply skeptical about our capacity to have such knowledge" (2000, 46). Also see Stone 1989, 70.

86. Guthrie observes that "the use of this word [*eidos*] as a technical term of logic is post-Socratic, for there was no science of logic before Plato, and it was only Aristotle who systematized it and gave it anything like a technical vocabulary. But *eidos* . . . was one of the names used by Socrates for the essential nature that he was seeking to define" (1971a, 110).

87. See also *Lysis* 222b and 223b, *Protagoras* 361c, *Laches* 190d, *Charmides* 159a, where the definitions sought are, respectively, of a *friend, virtue, courage*, and *temperance*. Scoon seems convinced that Socrates had a rather sophisticated theory of Forms (1928, 165–70). For myself, I find no evidence in the early dialogues that he had developed anything nearly as concrete and detailed as what Scoon outlines, and the evidence of the later dialogues is problematic in this regard.

88. For discussion of what he calls the "hedonic calculus," see Guthrie 1971a, 142–47. The idea that moral judgment and practical choice require the ability to estimate excess and defect anticipates, as we shall see, Aristotle's conception of how the soul's *logos* functions in determining the Mean in situations where a choice among possible actions is called for.

89. Xenophon, *Mem.* 4.5 6. Also see 4.5.11. In introducing his and Tredennick's translation of the *Oeconomicus* (*The Estate-Manager* in this edition), Waterfield observes, "For Xenophon's Socrates, to be a good estate-manager is part of what it is to be a 'truly good' person. . . . Estate-management is a good thing, and . . . good people are good at it, . . . [because] they can manage themselves—they have self-discipline" (Xenophon 1990, 277–78). This theme is developed most clearly in *Oeconomicus* 1.16–23; 9.11; 11.7–20; 12.11–14; 20.2–20.

90. Brickhouse and Smith conclude that, "because he thinks that virtue is a kind of wisdom that assures its possessor never to go wrong in choosing the best action to perform, those who do attain virtue will have good lives" (2000, 153). Herein lies a central tenet of Socratic teaching: the thesis that knowledge of the right and the just is a sufficient condition for choosing right and just actions, with its corollary that no one voluntarily acts wrongly or unjustly. On the former point, see, for example, Plato, *Prot.* 352b–e and 355a–57e; Xenophon, *Mem.* 3.9.5. On the latter, see *Prot.* 358c–d; *Mem.* 4.6.6. Useful discussions of these ideas can be found in Guthrie 1971a, 130–39;

NOTES TO PAGES 135–140

Brickhouse and Smith, 173–83. Aristotle objected to Socrates' view here on the grounds that it takes no account of "incontinence"—weakness of will or lack of self-control. Indeed, he devotes book 7 in the *Nicomachean Ethics* to consideration of continence or strength of will (*enkrateia*), incontinence or weakness of will (*akrasia*), and the nature of pleasure. Socrates does seem to recognize that the self-indulgent person will not choose wisely. However, he also apparently holds that once one has true knowledge of moral concepts, one must perforce be self-disciplined, for no one does wrong intentionally.

91. Socrates' own well-known disregard for his physical appearance appears to exemplify the latter issue. He was in the habit of going around barefoot, unwashed, wearing a worn cloak. See Xenophon, *Mem.* 1.6.2; Plato, *Symp.* 220b. Similarly, his personal poverty, lack of political ambition, and general unconcern about his reputation are revealed in his comments to the jurors after he had been convicted of the charges against him (*Apol.* 36b). Also see Guthrie 1971a, 89–96; and Stone 1989, 11–19, 81–86, for discussion of Socrates' political views.

92. Plato, *Theaetetus* 149a–50d (trans. Cornford, in Plato, 1961n). In Xenophon (*Oecononicus* 19.1ff.), Socrates is induced by Ischomachus's questions to articulate a sound understanding of agricultural principles and practices of which he thought himself to be ignorant, thus providing his own illustration of the general point being made here: knowledge lies within the soul and must be brought to birth through conversation.

93. As Brickhouse and Smith observe, in the middle and late dialogues the *elenchos* "virtually disappears. In the transition between the two periods [i.e., the early and middle], Plato seems to have come to the conclusion that knowledge can be achieved—though not easily—if we can gain a cognitive 'vision' of the transcendent realities he calls the 'Forms.' . . . Obviously, the philosophical method of the middle period is far more optimistic and ambitious in its scope than is the elenchos we find used [in the early dialogues] as Socrates' only approach to philosophical questions. What explains Plato's confidence that the philosopher can acquire knowledge is an elaborate metaphysics and epistemology that Plato seems to have developed some twenty years after Socrates' death, probably as the result of Plato's having met philosophers and mathematicians during travels in Italy. Whereas these doctrines are absolutely central to the philosophy of the middle dialogues, they are nowhere in evidence in the early period works" (2000, 47).

94. *Lives of the Philosophers* 2.13.122. These topics are included in a list of titles reportedly recorded by Simon the Cobbler: "Simon was a citizen of Athens and a cobbler. When Socrates came to his workshop and began to converse, he used to make notes of all that he could remember. And this is why people apply the term 'leathern' to his dialogues. These . . . are thirty-three in number, extant in a single volume: Of the Gods, Of the Good, On the Beautiful, What is the Beautiful, On the Just (two dialogues), Of Virtue, that it cannot be taught, Of Courage (three dialogues), On Law, On Guiding the People, Of Honor, Of Poetry, On Good Eating, On Love, On Philosophy, On Knowledge, On Music, On Teaching, On the Art of Conversation, Of Judging, Of Being, Of Number, On Diligence, On Efficiency, On Greed, On Pretentiousness, On Deliberation, On Reason, On Doing Ill." Socrates' habit of conversing in the shop is also attested by Xenophon (*Mem.* 4.2.1). As it happens, Simon's shop was identified

during the excavation of the Athenian agora, just outside the sacred precinct of the agora itself (a boundary stone was discovered in situ against its outside wall). In the courtyard of this small building were found a number of iron hobnails and bone eyelets (for laces), which would have been used in shoe and boot making, and in the drainage ditch outside the shop was found the base of a broken drinking cup inscribed "Simonôs" (Simon's). See Camp 1986, 145–47.

95. See Guthrie's explanation of the inductive process and the problems associated with it (1971a, 105–17). Also see Scoon 1928, 170–78; Ross 1924, 2:422.

96. Cf. *Gorgias* 491a and Xenophon, *Mem.* 1.2.37.

Chapter 5. Civic Wisdom, Divine Wisdom

1. Thucydides (1.89–117) examines the period between the end of the Persian wars and the years immediately preceding the outbreak of the conflict. He summarizes prewar developments in 1.18–19 and recounts in detail events leading up to the war's outbreak at 1.24–88 and 118–46. Plutarch provides additional insight in his "Life of Pericles" (esp. sec. 9–32). For useful contemporary accounts of the lead-up to the war, see Hammond 1959; Hooper 1978; Kagan 1969, 2003; Sealey 1976.

2. Thucydides describes the events connected with the plague in vivid detail at 2.47–55. Also see Plutarch's "Pericles" (1960, 34–38). Among recent accounts, Hooper's (1978, 286–88) and Hanson's (2005, chap. 3) are especially informative.

3. Cleon's influence on the assembly's decision making is demonstrated in the debates about how to deal with the revolt at Mytilene in 427 (Thucydides 3.36–50), the battle for Pylos in 425 (4.27–30, 36–39), and the battle of Amphipolis in 422 (5.1–12). Alcibiades, whom Hooper describes as "brilliant and daring, egocentric and amoral" (1978, 322), played prominent and problematic roles in the formulation of Athenian war policy until his defection to the Spartans during the ill-fated Sicilian campaign (6.61, 88–93). Munn contends that "there can be no doubt that Alcibiades had a greater impact on the fate of Athens and her empire in its final decade and a half than any other individual" (2000, 97; also see 71–76, chap. 4). Also see Plutarch's "Alcibiades" (1960).

4. See Thucydides 3.1–50, 4.130, 5.32, 5.84–116, 6–7. In the case of Mytilene, the Athenian Assembly—at the urging of Cleon—initially voted to sanction the execution of the adult males and the enslavement of the women and children who were left alive but reversed the decision the next day on the advice of Diodotus. At Mende, as Thucydides describes it, "the generals found it difficult to restrain their troops from massacring the inhabitants" (4.130). Scione and Melos suffered the fate originally decreed for Mytilene—for this time the *dêmos* would not be persuaded by appeals to compassion. The decision to launch the invasion of Sicily near Syracuse—which led ultimately to the death or enslavement of between forty thousand and fifty thousand Athenian troops and their allies and to the loss of over two hundred ships—was made after an appeal by Alcibiades to the Athenian Assembly that emphasized the promise of an expanded empire and greater glory for Athens (6.15). Munn writes of "the tyranny of the *demos*" during these years (2000, 76–77). Also see Kagan 1969, 2003; Hanson 2005.

5. The "Thirty Tyrants" referred to the members of the supreme council (Aristotle, *Athenian Constitution* 35.1), but the government also included overseers of the

Piraeus, prison guards, and three hundred lightly armed attendants. Critias was the leader of the thirty-member council, while Charmides was one of the ten overseers of the Piraeus. Plato titles two of his dialogues after these men.

6. An excellent account of the rise of Macedon, and particularly of Philip, can be found in Borza 1990, esp. chaps. 9 and 10.

7. Though he notes that it is a "vexed question," Jebb comments that "It can hardly be doubted that . . . Isocrates left Athens for Chios" in the autumn of 404 B.C.E., soon after the Athenians' capitulation to the Spartans and their allies and the installation of the pro-Spartan Thirty Tyrants. There "he opened a school of Rhetoric, and had some success. . . . He seems to have returned to Athens either just before or just after the Athenian democracy was formally restored in September 403" (1893, 6). It was following his return to Athens that Isocrates began writing forensic speeches for pay. See Jaeger 1944, 55, 65, 302n30, n32.

8. Jebb writes that, in his later writings, "Isocrates nowhere recognises this phase of his own activity . . . [and] speaks with contempt of those who write for the law-courts" (1893, 7). Indeed, Isocrates himself wrote, "I shall never be seen to have concerned myself with those [law-court] speeches" (*Antidosis* 36, in Isocrates 2000, trans. Mirhady and Too; also see 1–3), though this statement is refuted by the existence of six of his forensic speeches (Jebb, 7). Jebb reports that Isocrates taught his Athenian pupils free of charge and appears to have taken fees only from foreigners (28), suggesting that his career as a logographer had been a successful one. Translations of Isocrates are taken from the Loeb editions (1928, 1929, trans. Norlin); 2000, trans. Mirhady and Too; and 2004, trans. Papillon. Among these, I have selected the translations (as noted) that, in my judgment, express Isocrates' thinking most clearly and usefully.

9. See T. Poulakos 1997; J. Poulakos 2004.

10. See Jaeger 1944, 48; Berquist 1959, 252; Proussis 1965, 56; Jebb 1893, 2–5; Benoit 1984, 109–10. The latter notes that "it is not certain that Isocrates actually was a pupil of either Protagoras or Socrates . . . but plausible arguments can be advanced for the tutelage of Prodicus, Gorgias, Tisias, Theramenes, Protagoras, and Socrates, based on a combination of classical authorities and conceptual analysis" (110).

11. On Isocrates' educational program and its objectives, see Jaeger 1944; Berquist 1959; Proussis 1965; Jarrett 1969; Norlin 1972; T. Poulakos 2004; Timmerman 1998; Schiappa 1999; Garver 2004; Leff 2004. His political and social thought are discussed by Neserius 1933 and T. Poulakos 1997. Poulakos along with Wagner 1922, Benoit 1984, and Haskins 2004, among others, describe his implicit theory of rhetoric. Hawhee (2004) argues that Isocrates' pedagogical program aimed at "shaping a compounded self—body and mind—with training in gymnastics and discourse" (5) and that, consequently, he envisioned "deep relations between rhetoric and athletics" (6).

12. Norlin goes on (1972, 202–3) to enumerate certain characteristics of Isocrates' life and work that show Socrates' influence. Also see Ober 1998 (260–63), who compares Isocrates' *Antidosis* to Socrates' portrayal in Plato's *Apology*.

13. Isocrates 1929, 3. In the *Antidosis*, Isocrates says of his purpose in *On the Peace*, "After having . . . deplored the misfortunes of Hellas, and urged Athens not to allow herself to remain in her present state, finally I summon her to a career of justice, I condemn the mistakes she is now making, and I counsel her as to her future policy" (65;

trans. Norlin). On the *Areopagiticus*, see Jebb 1893, 202–3, 211–14; also Norlin's comments in Isocrates 1929, 100–103.

14. Wagner comments that Isocrates "may be regarded . . . , as he considers himself, a teacher of . . . a complete philosophy of life" (1922, 326). He continues, "Isocrates' school [was] characterized by thoroughness of methods, seriousness of purpose, largeness of views and permanent results. The keynote of the school was the practical application of the loftiest principles" (327). Also see Jaeger 1944, 148; Berquist 1959, 253; Timmerman 1998; Schiappa 1999, 168–74.

15. See Jaeger 1944, 112–23; T. Poulakos 1997, 105–6. The parallel of *Antidosis* 285 with the Protagorean account of sophistical pedagogy (Plato, *Prot.*, 318e–319a) is obvious, another clear indication that Isocrates carried on the *paideia* of the older Sophists, even as he condemned (*Ag. the Soph.*) what passed as "sophistical education" in his own time. It cannot be passed over without comment that in the very next paragraph Isocrates laments the current state of the student-class in Athens, who "spend their youth in drink, social gatherings, amusements, and games, while neglecting the serious business of self-improvement, and those with baser natures . . . pass the day in the sort of undisciplined behavior that no honest slave would have previously dared. Some of them chill wine in the Nine Fountains; others drink in the taverns, while others play dice in the gambling dens; and many hang out in the schools for flute girls" (*Antid.* 286–87, trans. Mirhady and Too). *Plus ça change, plus c'est la même chose.* Although he had been disillusioned by the failure of a "pure" democracy to manage the great military undertakings associated with the various wars in which Athens was engaged during his lifetime, Isocrates reaffirms his faith in a democratic ideal in his invocation of the "aristocratic" democracies of Solon and Cleisthenes (*Areopagiticus* 20–27). Ober remarks that "unlike Plato, Isocrates did not abandon hope for democratic amelioration; the question, Isocrates suggests, is how to improve *dêmokratia*, not how to replace it with *oligarchia*" (1998, 249). Also see Neserius 1933, 323.

16. See Wagner 1922; Jaeger 1944; Berquist 1959; Benoit 1984; J. Poulakos 1997, 2004; Schiappa 1999; Hawhee 2004. On the first appearance of *rhêtorikê*, see Schiappa 1990a, 1992; on Isocrates' use of *rhêtoreia* and his choice not to use *rhêtorikê* to describe his educational program, see Schiappa 1999, 156–60, 169–74.

17. On the place of historical studies in Isocrates' educational program, see Jaeger 1944, 100–103. On the aims of his *paideia*, see Wagner 1922, 328; Proussis 1965, 56; Timmerman 1998; Schiappa 1999; J. Poulakos 2004; T. Poulakos 2004; Leff 2004; Hawhee 2004.

18. Cf. Mirhady and Too's translation: "the wise (*sophoi*) are those who have the ability to reach the best opinions (*doxai*) most of the time." Also see Jaeger 1944, 148–49; Haskins 2004, 41.

19. See Ober 1998, 275–76, where it is argued that, for Isocrates, the Athenian *dêmos* was led to a false sense of its true interests as a result of the "corruption of language." Also see Haskins 2004, 43–44.

20. See *Panegyricus* 48ff. See also Proussis 1965, 60–63, 69–73; Jaeger 1944, 89–91, 309n36.

21. For useful comparisons between the views of Isocrates and those of Plato, see Jaeger 1944, esp. 46–48, 91–93; Perkins 1984; Konstan 2004; Morgan 2004.

22. Diogenes Laertius (3.2) quotes Apollodorus for Plato's birth but quotes Plato's pupil Hermippus for his death in the first year of the 108th Olympiad, 348–347. Modern accounts of Plato's life can be found in, among others, Field 1930; Woodbridge 1957; Randall 1970.

23. Svoboda comments on this feature of Plato's writings: "There is no note of wartime duress in . . . the entire body of Plato's work" (2002, 4). Nonetheless, in Svoboda's view, the war shaped Plato's philosophical outlook and activities for the rest of his life. See esp. 82–127, 222–75.

24. *Seventh Letter* 324b–25b; trans. Post, in Plato 1961l. Unless otherwise noted, all quotations of Plato are taken from translations published in *The Selected Dialogues of Plato* (1961), edited by Hamilton and Cairns. Munn notes that "although contemporary scholarship regards most of the letters attributed to Plato as spurious, the balance of opinion supports the authenticity of Plato's *Seventh Letter.* . . . [However,] even those who regard [it] as spurious treat it as a work of someone intimately familiar with Plato's thought and the details of his biography, post-dating his life by no more than a century. I prefer to regard it as a genuine work of Plato" (2000, 417n1). Also see Guthrie 1986a, 399.

25. The principal ancient source for these events is Diogenes Laertius, esp. 3.6, 2.106. Cicero (*De Republica* 1.10.16, *De Finibus* 5.29.87) provides a later account that is at times inconsistent with D. L.'s chronology. On such matters, see Woodbridge 1957, 17–20; Guthrie 1986a, 14–16.

26. Jaeger entitles his detailed account of Plato's relationship with Dionysius "The Tragedy of Paideia" (1944, 197–212). Later (213–14) he appears to suggest that Plato's experience with Dionysius was instrumental in turning his aim from the idealism expressed in the *Republic* to the realism—based on "his increasing tendency to appeal to experience"—of the *Laws*.

27. Guthrie also distinguishes among the dialogues on the basis of when they were written relative to Plato's trips to Syracuse (1986a, 53). Before the first Sicilian visit: *Ion, Hipp. Min., Prot., Apol., Crito, Laches, Lysis, Charm., Euthyphro, 'Thrasymachus' (Rep.* bk. 1), *Gorg.* In the next twenty years (between the first and second visits): *Menex., Euthydemus, Meno, Crat., Symp., Phaedo, Rep., Phaedrus, Parm., Theaet.* Between the second and third visits: *Soph., Politicus.* After the third visit: *Tim., Crit., Philebus, Laws.* This way of grouping the dialogues invites the reader to seek evidence for how the events at Syracuse might have influenced Plato's philosophical development, though it is beyond my present scope to pursue this; but see Guthrie 1986a, 45–48.

28. Also see Demos 1935; Cross 1954; Hamlyn 1955; Sallis 1986, 382–88.

29. Also see 506a, 508b–9a; Demos 1937. In an early reference to this idea, though not calling it the "Form of the Good," Plato writes (*Lysis* 220b) concerning such "useful" things as friendship, "do we not appear to be in reality (*tôi onti*) friendly only with that in which all these so-called friendships terminate? . . . With that, then, to which we are truly friendly, we are not friendly for the sake of any other thing to which we are friendly. . . . [A]re we friends [then] to good?" Guthrie (1986a, 151–53) summarizes the debate concerning whether or not we can trace Plato's intellectual development through how such ideas as the good are presented in his early, middle, and later dialogues.

30. Guthrie observes that "Plato did not think in an intellectual vacuum. Some of his profoundest and most original ideas resulted from the attempt to solve problems bequeathed by his predecessors, in whom he took the liveliest interest" (1986a, 32). On connections between Plato's thought and that of Heraclitus, see Guthrie, 33–38, 140n2; Kahn 1979, 222–27; Kirk, Raven, and Schofield 1983, 185–86; Turnbull 1983. Atwill writes that "Plato's social order is rooted in Pythagorean harmonics and geometry" (1998, 141). For Pythagorean influence on Plato, see Guthrie 1986a, 33–38, 251–52, 299–305; 1986b, 435–41; Cameron 1938. Plato himself refers to Heraclitus and his followers in several places, including *Theaet.* 159e, 156a, 161d, 179d; *Crat.* 401d, 411b, 416b, 436e; *Symp.* 187a; and to Pythagorean thought at, for example, *Rep.* 530d, 600b; *Phaedo* 86b.

31. Also see *Epinomis* 977c, 978a. On the idea that the Forms may be conceived as numbers, see Guthrie, who cites Aristotle (e.g., *Metaphysics* 988a10, *De anima* 404b24) in support of this view, as well as others who reject it (1986b, 435–42). Also see 521–26, where he writes that "mathematical order leads to the order of values, for order (*kosmos*) is itself good. The importance of mathematics to Plato [lies in] helping to answer the whole question whether there could be changeless forms at all, and so encouraging belief in the eternal order of Forms" (525).

32. On the epistemological uses of myth in Plato's writings, see Stewart's argument that "Platonic myths function first as the rudimentary beginnings of the epistemic process whereby one changes from thinking in purely 'physical' terms to 'conceptual' ones. Secondly, myth serves as the medium through which is made possible any discussion of the 'first principles' of philosophy" (1989, 260). Also see Edelstein 1949.

33. Also see *Phaedo* 75c–d: "Then if we obtained it before our birth, and possessed it when we were born, we had knowledge, both before and at the moment of birth, not only of equality and relative magnitudes, but of all absolute standards. Our present argument applies no more to equality than it does to absolute beauty, goodness, uprightness, holiness. . . . So we must have obtained knowledge of all these characteristics before our birth."

34. In the *Republic* (435ff.), Plato also divides the soul into three parts: the reflective or rational, the spirited or passionate, and the appetitive or acquisitive. The latter two appear to be analogous with the noble and ignoble passions portrayed in the myth of the chariot.

35. I have examined this dialogue in more detail in Johnstone 2008. For useful discussions of the dialogue and its philosophical significance, see Cornford 1967; Levy 1979; Guthrie 1986a, 365–96. Quotations from the *Symposium* are Joyce's translations in Plato 1961m unless otherwise noted.

36. In his translation of the *Symposium* for the Loeb edition, Lamb notes that "*Daimones* and *to daimonion* represent the mysterious agencies and influences by which the gods communicate with mortals" (Plato 1983, 179). Murray (1925, 175) holds that the term means the same thing as "Angel," from *angelos*, a "messenger" (especially from god). Burkert's discussion of the term and its role in Greek religion is particularly helpful (1985, 179–81).

37. The Greek terms are important here. "Begetting" is a translation of *tokos*, "a bringing forth, childbirth, procreation." It is the organic, natural process of "engendering" (*gennêsis*, at 206c) or "producing offspring," consistent with the use of *kuousi* (from

kuopsoreô, "to be with young," "to be pregnant") to describe the creative impulse in the human soul. All of these words and ideas represent the process of acquiring wisdom as natural, organic, and even mammalian.

38. Useful accounts of the "ascent passage" are to be found in Cornford 1967, 76–78; Moravcsik 1971; Guthrie 1986a, 387–95.

39. Also see Brockriede 1972, 5–8.

40. Fromm's conception of *erotic love* is clearly inspired by Plato's. In his account of "the theory of love," Fromm describes the nature of "erotic love" as "the craving for complete fusion, for union with another person" (1956, 52–53). A little later his explanation parallels my own interpretation of Plato's view of *eros* and the deepest nature of *psychê:* "Erotic love is exclusive, but it loves in the other person all of mankind, all that is alive. It is exclusive only in the sense that I can fuse myself fully and intensely with one person only. . . . Erotic love . . . has one premise: That I love from the essence of my being—and experience the other person in the essence of his or her being. In essence, all human beings are identical. We are all part of One; we are One" (55).

41. On Plato's possible concerns about the limitations and potential of writing, see Hyland 1968; Hikins 1981, 173–74; Guthrie 1986a, 56–64, 410–11; Sallis 1986, 19–21, 161–65. In the end, because he recorded his own thinking about all these matters in the form of written dialogues, it seems clear that Plato believed that writing per se does not preclude the possibility of moving souls to action and toward wisdom. At the same time, it is face-to-face interaction—in the processes of dialectic and erotic conversation—that are most efficacious in this regard. Plato's use of the dialogue form suggests, as Hyland argues, that Plato viewed it as a "visible if imperfect image" of the method of dialectic (41).

42. This interpretation of Plato's conception stands in stark contrast to that offered by Kauffman. While perceiving the same relationship between dialectic and rhetoric described here, he concludes from a consideration of Plato's rhetorical theory in the context of his political philosophy that "all [rhetoricians] will be members of the philosophic ruling class, dedicated to the propagation of doctrine," and that such a rhetoric "denies the values of freedom of speech, the marketplace of ideas, and reasoned discourse"; thus, it is "totalitarian" (1982, 363). This understanding of Plato as being anti-democratic resonates with Stone's (1989) account of Socrates.

Chapter 6. Speculative Wisdom, Practical Wisdom

1. The question of Aristotle's writings—how many, what kinds, by whom they were written, and for whom they were intended—is complicated. Guthrie lists thirty-two titles (1990, xiii–xiv), including one (the *Magna Moralia*) whose authenticity is disputed (as is the tenth book of the *Metaphysics*), and several (*De philosophia, Eudemus, Protepticus*) that are lost. Barnes lists forty-six titles (1995, xxiii–xxiv), including several that exist only in fragments (e.g., *On Length and Shortness of Life, On Youth, Old Age, Life and Death*); and sixteen (e.g., *On the Universe, On Breath, On Marvellous Things Heard, Rhetoric to Alexander*) that he describes as spurious. Even with the "authentic" works, there is disagreement as to whether what we have are the words of Aristotle himself, the notes of his students taken during lectures, or interpretations of his teachings written

by later editors and commentators (see Guthrie, 49–51; Barnes, 6–15). The poem, preserved by Diogenes Laertius, Athenaeus, and Stobaeus, took the form of a hymn to
Aretê and was written as an homage to Aristotle's friend and father-in-law Hermias,
tyrant of Atarneus in Asia Minor and benefactor of the Platonic circle of which Aristotle was a member when he lived there. Guthrie provides a translation (32–33). We also
have Aristotle's will, a translation of which appears in Barnes (2–3). It is a humane
document, and it gives some insight into his character.

   2. The principal ancient sources for biographical details of Aristotle's life are Philo-
chorus of Athens, preserved as *Die Fragmente der Griechischen Historiker* (ed. Felix
Jacoby).; Diogenes Laertius, *Lives and Opinions of the Eminent Philosophers* 5; and Dionysius of Halicarnassus, *De compositione verborum* (*On Arrangement of Words*) 24. Guthrie
also notes three biographies of neo-Platonic or Byzantine origin, as well as the Syriac
and Arabic tradition (1990, 18). These have been collected and edited in During 1957.
Useful modern summaries of these details are to be found in Guthrie, 18–45; Barnes
1995, 1–6.

   3. Guthrie, for example, maintains that "the *Eudemus*, though probably his own earliest dialogue, was written a good many years after his first entry into the Academy, yet
both it and the *Protrepticus* taught a purely Platonic doctrine, and the *Eudemus* was
closely modelled on the *Phaedo*" (1990, 21). He also observes (21n1) that Aristotle used
the *Phaedo* as his source when criticizing the theory of Forms. Barnes goes even further,
speculating that "no doubt he had learned some philosophy as a boy in Stagira; perhaps
he had read some of Plato's philosophical dialogues; and maybe he moved to Athens
precisely in order to study philosophy with Plato. But," he acknowledges, "there is no
positive evidence for these easy suppositions" (1995, 3–4).

   4. Guthrie notes later (1990, 31) that "Hermias not only welcomed the philosophers and gave them an honoured position, but accepted their instruction and shared
their studies. He even had the courage to put their ideas into practice, and found the
resulting conciliatory policy perfectly satisfactory from a practical point of view." Also
see During 1957, 273; Barnes 1995, 5.

   5. Pliny (*Naturelis historia* 8, 16.44) writes of various specialists whom Alexander
put at Aristotle's disposal during the Asian campaign: experts in hunting and fishing,
bird catching, herdsmen, and others. Also see During (1957, 288) for this and similar
accounts. Elsewhere he dismisses Pliny's account as a Hellenistic invention (523).
Jaeger contends that the *History of Animals* would not have been possible without a
knowledge of discoveries made by Alexander's expedition concerning elephants and
other species unknown in Greece (1934, 330).

   6. These issues, of course, point to the question of whose words we are actually
reading when we peruse "the writings of Aristotle." The surviving works may, indeed,
be Aristotle's actual "lecture notes," but they may just as easily be the notes of his students (Guthrie 1990; Barnes 1995, 10n20). Moreover, this difficulty is compounded by
the career of these writings after his death. Barnes provides an interesting rendition of
this: "Whence came our corpus? There was a story current in antiquity which told a
romantic tale about Aristotle's library: Theophrastus inherited it on Aristotle's death; it
then passed to Theophrastus's nephew Neleus, who took it to a city called Scepsis in
Asia Minor, where he hid it away in a cave. Two centuries later the manuscripts were

rediscovered, moulding and worm-eaten. They were transferred first to Athens and then to Rome, where the Peripatetic philosopher Andronicus eventually prepared an edition. . . . The ancient story may be true, in whole or in part. . . . The edition of Andronicus, however, was real enough; and it is also reasonable to think that our Aristotle derives ultimately from him. What did Andronicus do? . . . The answer, roughly put, is probably this: Andronicus himself composed the works which we now read" (1995, 10–11). Thus, the structure and unity of the Aristotelian corpus we must attribute to Andronicus, and we cannot be certain that these were what Aristotle himself had in mind when he wrote his notes/treatises originally. Barnes concludes that "you cannot read Aristotle in the way you might read Plato or Descartes or Kant. . . . It is proper to assume that you are picking up a set of papers united by a later editor; and it is proper to assume that you are reading a compilation of Aristotle's working drafts. In any case, you should surely read Aristotle's drafts in the manner in which you would read the notes which a philosopher had written for his own use. . . . The arguments are enthymematic—or mere hints: you must supply the missing premises. The transitions are sudden—and often implicit: you must articulate and smooth and explain" (14–15). Also see Kennedy's account in Aristotle 2007, 306–11. On the composition of the *Rhetoric*, see also McAdon 2001, 2004.

7. Quotations from the *Metaphysics* are taken from Tredennick's translation (Aristotle 1933) unless otherwise noted.

8. Quotations from the *Ethics* will be from Rackham's translation (Aristotle 1934) unless otherwise noted.

9. Aristotle's psychological model is somewhat more complex than is suggested by this preliminary analysis. The "sentient" or "appetitive" part of the soul, which humans share with all the other animals, "though irrational, yet in a manner participates in rational principle (*logos*)" (1102b) and is capable of being "amenable and obedient to it . . . as a child to its father" (1102b–3a). Aristotle thus suggests that either the irrational part of the soul is best conceived as having two parts—the vegetative, which has no part in *logos*, and the appetitive, which is capable of sharing in or obeying the soul's *logos*; or that the rational part be understood as having two parts—one "having rational principle in the proper sense and in itself" (1103a) and the other that "in a manner participates in rational principle" (1102b).

10. Quotations from the *Posterior Analytics* are from Mure's translation (Aristotle 1941a) unless otherwise noted.

11. On *nous* as grasping first principles, also see *Ethics* 1143a. Instructive discussions of Aristotle's doctrine of intuition can be found in Irwin 1990, 134–50; Guthrie 1990, 178–86, 192–94.

12. See, for instance, *gnôsis* at *Ethics* 1094a, *gnôseôs* at 1141b, *ginetai gnôrima* at 1142a, and *gnômên* at 1143a. Also see *gnôsis* at *Meta.* 981a.

13. Cf. *Post. An.* 81a–b. Quotations from the *Topics* are from Pickard-Cambridge's translation in Aristotle 1941m.

14. Also see Irwin 1990, 44, 490n13, 492n25; Guthrie 1990, 188–94; Block 1961. Hamlyn offers a pointed critique of Aristotle's view of induction, describing it variously as "crude," "incoherent," "not altogether perspicuous," and "not very plausible" (1976, 171ff.). However, see Guthrie 1990, 179n1, 182n1. Quotations from the *Prior*

Analytics are of Jenkinson's translation (Aristotle 1941b). Passages from *On the Heavens* are taken from Stocks's translation in the same work (1941e).

15. Principles of this science include the law of noncontradiction—that "it is impossible for the same attribute at once to belong and not to belong to the same thing and in the same relation"—which Aristotle terms "the most certain of all [logical] principles" (*Meta.* 1005b). Indeed, he says, "this [is] an ultimate belief; for it is by nature the starting-point of all the other axioms [of reasoning]." Other logical principles include the law of the excluded middle—"every predicate can be either truly affirmed or truly denied of any subject" (*Post. An.* 71a).

16. On Aristotle's theory of causation, see Lacey 1965; Guthrie 1990, 22–33; Irwin 1990, 94–116. In his physical and metaphysical inquiries Aristotle is clearly building on investigations and insights inherited from his philosophical forebears. His account of the science of *physis* is explicitly indebted to the speculations of such Presocratic "nature philosophers" as Thales, Anaximenes, Empedocles, and the Atomists, and it may fairly be said to represent some sort of fulfillment of those speculations. Likewise, his metaphysical investigations—looking into the nature of being as such—echo the quest of Anaximander, Heraclitus, Parmenides, and Plato for what is ultimately stable and enduring in a world beset by change. These features of Aristotle's work lead Guthrie to judge as "not inherently unreasonable" Aristotle's contention that he had expressed "the meaning of his predecessors better than they had expressed it themselves" (1990, 97).

17. As Guthrie notes, "the literature on Aristotle's ontology is vast" (1990, 203n1), but see especially, in addition to Guthrie, Owens 1963; Leszl 1970, 1975; Brentano 1975; Harter 1975; Reale 1980; Lloyd 1981; Irwin 1990.

18. Aristotle's conception of definition, essence, or form is not to be confused with Plato's. Plato, as we have seen, envisioned a "real" realm of transcendental Being beyond the world of appearances, whereas the realm of appearance or "seeming" was viewed as illusory. Aristotle's critique of Plato's theory of Forms (*Meta.* 990a–93a) notes that "wisdom is concerned with the cause of visible things" (992a). Also see Cherniss 1944; Annas 1974; Guthrie 1990, esp. 243–46.

19. On Aristotle's teleological inclinations, their relationship to Plato's teachings, and their implications for his metaphysical and ethical theories, see especially Guthrie 1990, 106–29, 243–67; Balme 1965; Blair 1967; Gotthelf 1976; Rist 1965.

20. It is here, as Guthrie observes (1990, 255–56n4), that Aristotle changes his language when referring to the final cause, from the neuter "mover" (*to kinoun*) to the masculine "God" (*o theos*). The latter term first appears at *Meta.* 1072b. Thus does the pronoun in translations change from "it" to "he." It is not clear why Aristotle thought it necessary to alter his terminology in this way, since the word *theos* has historical associations and creates certain expectations. "Aristotle with his respect for the widely held beliefs [of his contemporaries] was not indifferent to these expectations. Anthropomorphic and theriomorphic [beast-shaped] gods indeed he could not stomach. . . . Comment is sometimes evoked by the abrupt transition from the description of God as unmoved mover to the statement that his activity is thought, linking him at once to the highest faculty in man. He had of course Plato and Anaxagoras before him as models, but he could also have wished to grant as much to the religious instinct as was compatible with the preservation of his intellectual integrity" (259–60).

21. The remaining books of the *Metaphysics* are devoted to Aristotle's examinations and criticisms of the theories about "prime being" that were put forth by his predecessors, most conspicuously including Plato and his followers. So, alas, we will not find an answer there to the riddle with which we have been left in book 12.

22. Aristotle's term for "happiness" is *eudaimonia* (*Ethics* 1095a), which both "the multitude and persons of refinement . . . conceive [as] 'the good life' or 'doing well' (*to eu zên kai to eu prattein*)." The latter ideas might be understood both as "faring well" and "acting well." Thus does he offer a complex, even subtle, conception of the "proper life for a human being" (cf. Plato, *Apol.* 38a) incorporating elements of both chance and personal character. In any case, with the question of what constitutes a "good life," Aristotle takes up an inquiry that was pursued by thinkers ranging from Pythagoras and Democritus to Socrates—another instance of the continuity of his thought with that of his forebears. On Aristotle's conception of *eudaimonia*, see Atwill 1998, 176–85.

23. The passage quoted here is taken from book 5 of the *Ethics*, where Aristotle examines the nature of Justice (*dikaiosynê*), which he describes as "perfect [moral] virtue because it is the practice of perfect virtue" (1129b). He distinguishes two senses of the term "justice"—acting in accordance with law and acting fairly (1130a)—and considers two categories of the latter: distributive and corrective (1130b–31a). The former is a matter of "proportionate" distribution of honors, wealth, etc., and depends on an "equality of ratios" (the concept I have employed in my argument). The latter, which operates in private transactions, depends not on a "geometrical" but on an "arithmetical proportion" (1132a). In both senses of "fairness," then, Justice is a matter of proportionality (*analogia*) in how we treat others. In view of the centrality of Justice in the Greek value system (cf. Hesiod, *Theogony* and *Works and Days*, Anaximander's fragment, and Plato's discussion of Justice in the *Republic*), it seems fair to attribute to Aristotle the view that the idea of *analogia*—and thus of *logos*—is the central quality of natural law (cf. *Meta.* 993a, 1092b).

24. I invoke the words of Heraclitus here because his statement captures most succinctly the insight I attribute to Aristotle. I find no textual evidence that Aristotle himself understood this aspect of Heraclitus's doctrines; instead, he associated these doctrines with ideas such as that fire is the moving force in the universe (e.g., *Meta.* 984b, 1067a), that "the whole sensible world is always in a state of flux, and that there is no scientific knowledge of it" (987a, 1010a, 1078b), and that things are capable of both being and not being at the same time (1012a, 1062a). Nonetheless, Heraclitus's conception of the *Logos* is highly compatible with the idea I take Aristotle to have held about the object of God's thought.

25. Indeed, as he writes in *Post. An.* 71b, "the premises of demonstrated knowledge must be true, primary, immediate, better known than and prior to the conclusion, which is further related to them as effect to cause" (also see 71b–72a). Elsewhere (*Soph. Ref.* 183b), Aristotle observes that no one had previously sought to explain the rules governing logically valid inference, leading Smith to remark that "he was the first to conceive of a systematic treatment of correct inference itself. As such, Aristotle was the founder of logic" (1995, 27).

26. An example of a symbolic proof would be, "if A is necessarily predicated of B and B of C, then A is necessarily predicated of C" (*Post. An.* 75a). Much of Aristotle's

writing on the principles of logic, particularly in such works as the *Prior* and *Posterior Analytics* and the *Topics*, is devoted to explicating the structure and uses of the syllogism. See Smith on Aristotle's logic (1995, 27–65); Hankinson's discussion of Aristotle's philosophy of science (1995, 109–22); Shepherdson 1956; Lukasiewicz 1957; Patzig 1969; Lear 1980; Thom 1981.

27. See *Topics* 100a; *Rhetoric* 1358a. On the uses of dialectical argument to challenge the propositions derived from presumed principles of nature, see *Top.* 101a–b, 158a–b. Aristotle demonstrates this application of the dialectical method in his critical examinations of earlier theories in such works as the *Metaphysics* (988b–93a) and *On the Soul* (403b–5b). Also see Irwin 1990, 26–29, 36–72; Guthrie 1990, 150–55; Berlin 1993. Atwill (1998) examines the relationship among theoretical, practical, and productive knowledge (164–76), noting a "tendency throughout modern Aristotelian scholarship to make the theory/practice distinction override the theoretical/practical/productive triad" (165). She traces these divisions to the Pythagorean tradition (166–67).

28. On Aristotle's conception of practical reasoning and the practical syllogism, see Broadie 1968–69, 1974; Etheridge 1968; Martin 1977.

29. See particularly book 2, chaps. 22–23 (1395b–1400b). This is not the place to review the contents of these chapters, but it is worth noting that Aristotle's account of how deliberative enthymemes can be invented, and many of the examples he uses, can be readily applied to private deliberation and decision. The rhetorical dimensions of the latter are clear, given these connections. For elaboration of this argument, see Johnstone 1980.

Bibliography

Adkins, Arthur W. H. 1983. "Orality and Philosophy." In *Language and Thought in Early Greek Philosophy*, edited by Kevin Robb, 207–27. LaSalle, Ill.: Monist Library of Philosophy.

Andrewes, Antony. 1962. "The Mytilene Debate: Thucydides 3:36–39." *Phoenix* 16 (Summer): 64–85.

———. 1963. *The Greek Tyrants*. New York: Harper & Row.

Annas, Julia. 1974. "Forms and First Principles." *Phronesis* 19, no. 3: 257–83.

Aristotle. 1926. *"Art" of Rhetoric*. Translated by J. H. Freese. Cambridge, Mass.: Harvard University Press.

———. 1933, 1935. *Metaphysics*. Translated by Hugh Tredennick. 2 vols. Cambridge, Mass.: Harvard University Press.

———. 1934. *Nichomachean Ethics*. Translated by H. Rackham. Cambridge, Mass.: Harvard University Press.

———. 1941a. *Analytica Posteriora*. Translated by G. R. G. Mure. In *The Basic Works of Aristotle*, edited by Richard McKeon, 108–86. New York: Random House.

———. 1941b. *Analytica Priora*. Translated by A. J. Jenkinson. In *The Basic Works of Aristotle*, edited by Richard McKeon, 62–107. New York: Random House.

———. 1941c. *Catagoriae*. Translated by E. M. Edghill. In *The Basic Works of Aristotle*, edited by Richard McKeon, 3–37. New York: Random House.

———. 1941d. *De Anima*. Translated by J. A. Smith. In *The Basic Works of Aristotle*, edited by Richard McKeon, 535–603. New York: Random House.

———. 1941e. *De Caelo*. Translated by J. L. Stocks. In *The Basic Works of Aristotle*, edited by Richard McKeon, 396–466. New York: Random House.

———. 1941f. *De Interpretatione*. Translated by E. M. Edghill. In *The Basic Works of Aristotle*, edited by Richard McKeon, 38–61. New York: Random House.

———. 1941g. *De Partibus Animalium*. Translated by William Ogle. In *The Basic Works of Aristotle*, edited by Richard McKeon, 642–61. New York: Random House.

———. 1941h. *Ethica Nicomachea*. Translated by W. D. Ross. In *The Basic Works of Aristotle*, edited by Richard McKeon, 928–1112. New York: Random House.

———. 1941i. *Metaphysica*. Translated by W. D. Ross. In *The Basic Works of Aristotle*, edited by Richard McKeon, 682–926. New York: Random House.

———. 1941j. *Physica*. Translated by R. P. Hardie and R. K. Gaye. In *The Basic Works of Aristotle*, edited by Richard McKeon, 218–394. New York: Random House.

————. 1941k. *Politica*. Translated by Benjamin Jowett. In *The Basic Works of Aristotle*, edited by Richard McKeon, 1114–1316. New York: Random House.

————. 1941l. *Rhetorica*. Translated by W. Rhys Roberts. In *The Basic Works of Aristotle*, edited by Richard McKeon, 1318–1451. New York: Random House.

————. 1941m. *Topica*. Translated by W. A. Pickard-Cambridge. In *The Basic Works of Aristotle*, edited by Richard McKeon, 187–206. New York: Random House.

————. 1955. *On Sophistical Refutations*. Translated by E. S. Forster. Cambridge, Mass.: Harvard University Press.

————. 1976. *The Ethics of Aristotle*. Translated by J. A. K. Thomson. Middlesex, U.K.: Penguin.

————. 2007. *"On Rhetoric": A Theory of Civic Discourse*. 2nd ed. Translated by George A. Kennedy. New York: Oxford University Press.

Armstrong, Arthur H. 1949. *An Introduction to Ancient Philosophy*. Rev. ed. London: Methuen.

Atwill, Janet M. 1993. "Instituting the Art of Rhetoric: Theory, Practice, and Productive Knowledge in Interpretations of Aristotle's *Rhetoric*." In *Rethinking the History of Rhetoric: Multidisciplinary Essays on the Rhetorical Tradition*, edited by Takis Poulakos, 91–118. Boulder, Colo.: Westview Press.

————. 1998. *Rhetoric Reclaimed: Aristotle and the Liberal Arts Tradition*. Ithaca, N.Y.: Cornell University Press.

Ausband, Stephen C. 1983. *Myth and Meaning, Myth and Order*. Macon, Ga.: Mercer University Press.

Autenrieth, Georg. 1958. *A Homeric Dictionary*. Rev. ed. Translated by Robert P. Keep. Norman: University of Oklahoma Press.

Balme, D. M. 1965. *Aristotle's Use of the Teleological Explanation*. Inaugural Lecture, University of London.

Barker, Ernest. 1925. *Greek Political Theory: Plato and His Predecessors*. 2nd ed. Cambridge: Cambridge University Press.

Barnes, Jonathan. 1988. "The Presocratics in Context." *Phronesis* 33, no. 3: 327–44.

————, ed. 1995. *The Cambridge Companion to Aristotle*. Cambridge: Cambridge University Press.

Barrett, Harold. 1987. *The Sophists*. Novato, Calif.: Chandler & Sharp.

Barthell, Edward E., Jr. 1971. *Gods and Goddesses of Ancient Greece*. Coral Gables, Fla.: University of Miami Press.

Basin, S. L. 1963. "The Fibonacci Sequence Appears in Nature." *Fibonacci Quarterly* 1, no. 1: 53–56.

Beck, Frederick A. G. 1964. *Greek Education: 450–350 B.C.* London: Methuen.

Benoit, William L. 1984. "Isocrates on Rhetorical Education." *Communication Education* 33, no. 2: 109–19.

————. 1990. "Isocrates and Aristotle on Rhetoric." *Rhetoric Society Quarterly* 20 (Summer): 251–59.

Benson, Hugh H., ed. 1992. *Essays on the Philosophy of Socrates*. Oxford: Oxford University Press.

————. 2000. *Socratic Wisdom: The Model of Knowledge in Plato's Early Dialogues*. Oxford: Oxford University Press.

Berlin, James A. 1993. "Revisionary History: The Dialectical Method." In *Rethinking the History of Rhetoric: Multidisciplinary Essays on the Rhetorical Tradition*, edited by Takis Poulakos, 135–52. Boulder, Colo.: Westview Press.

Berquist, Goodwin F. Jr. 1959. "Isocrates of Athens: Foremost Speech Teacher of the Ancient World." *Speech Teacher* 8, no. 3: 251–55.

Biers, William R. 1987. *The Archaeology of Greece: An Introduction.* Rev. ed. Ithaca, N.Y.: Cornell University Press.

Black, Edwin. 1958. "Plato's View of Rhetoric." *Quarterly Journal of Speech* 44, no. 4: 361–74.

———. 1970. "The Second Persona." *Quarterly Journal of Speech* 56, no. 2: 109–19.

Blackson, Thomas A. 1995. *Inquiry, Forms, and Substances: A Study in Plato's Metaphysics and Epistemology.* Dordrecht & Boston: Kluwer Academic.

Blair, G. A. 1967. "The Meaning of *Energeia* and *Entelecheia* in Aristotle." *International Philosophical Quarterly* 7, no. 1: 101–17.

Blake, William T., and Frieda S. Brown. 1991. *Athenian Myths and Institutions: Words in Action.* New York: Oxford University Press.

Block, I. 1961. "Truth and Error in Aristotle's Theory of Sense Perception." *Philosophical Quarterly* 11, no. 42: 1–9.

Bluck, Richard S. 1949. *Plato's Life and Thought, with a Translation of the Seventh Letter.* London: Routledge & Kegan Paul.

———. 1954. "Logos and Forms in Plato: A Reply to Professor Cross." *Mind* 65, no. 260: 522–29.

Borza, Eugene N. 1990. *In the Shadow of Olympus: The Emergence of Macedon.* Princeton, N.J.: Princeton University Press.

Bowra, Cecil M. 1971. *Periclean Athens.* New York: Dial Press.

Bremmer, Jan, ed. 1987. *Interpretations of Greek Myths.* London & Sydney: Croom Helm.

Brentano, Franz C. 1975. *On the Several Senses of Being in Aristotle.* Translated and edited by R. George. Berkeley: University of California Press.

Brickhouse, Thomas C., and Nicholas D. Smith. 2000. *The Philosophy of Socrates.* Boulder, Colo.: Westview Press.

Broadie, A. 1968–69. "The Practical Syllogism." *Analysis* 29, no. 1: 26–28.

———. 1974. "Aristotle on Rational Action." *Phronesis* 19, no. 1: 70–80.

Brockriede, Wayne. 1972. "Arguers as Lovers." *Philosophy and Rhetoric* 5, no. 1: 1–11.

Brody, B. A. 1972. "Towards an Aristotelian Theory of Scientific Explanation." *Philosophy of Science* 39, no. 1: 20–31.

Bronowski, Jacob. 1973. *The Ascent of Man.* Boston: Little, Brown.

Brownstein, Oscar L. 1965. "Plato's *Phaedrus:* Dialectic as the Genuine Art of Speaking." *Quarterly Journal of Speech* 51, no. 4: 392–448.

Brumbaugh, Robert S. 1964. *The Philosophers of Greece.* New York: Thomas Crowell.

Bruno, Vincent J., ed. 1974. *The Parthenon.* New York: W. W. Norton.

Bryant, Joseph M. 1996. *Moral Codes and Social Structure in Ancient Greece: A Sociology of Greek Ethics from Homer to the Epicureans and Stoics.* Albany: State University of New York Press.

Burkert, Walter. 1979. *Structure and History in Greek Mythology and Ritual.* Berkeley: University of California Press.

————. 1985. *Greek Religion*. Cambridge, Mass.: Harvard University Press.

Burkhardt, Jacob. 1963. *History of Greek Culture*. New York: Frederick Ungar.

Burn, A. R. 1948. *Pericles and Athens*. New York: Macmillan.

Burnet, John. 1924. *Greek Philosophy: Part I, Thales to Plato*. London: Macmillan.

————. 1930. *Early Greek Philosophy*. 4th ed. Cleveland & New York: World.

Burrell, P. S. 1932. "Man the Measure of All Things." *Philosophy* 7, no. 25: 27–41; 7, no. 26: 168–84.

Bynner, Witter. 1962. *The Way of Life: According to Lao Tzu*. New York: Capricorn.

Calame, Claude. 1999. *The Poetics of Eros in Ancient Greece*. Translated by Janet Lloyd. Princeton, N.J.: Princeton University Press.

Caldwell, Richard. 1989. *The Origin of the Gods: A Psychoanalytic Study of Greek Theogonic Myth*. New York: Oxford University Press.

Calogero, Guido. 1957. "Gorgias and the Socratic Principle *Nemo sua sponte peccat.*" *Journal of Hellenic Studies* 77, no. 1: 12–17.

Cameron, Alister. 1938. *The Pythagorean Background to the Theory of Recollection*. Menasha, Wis.: Banta.

Camp, John M. 1986. *The Athenian Agora: Excavations in the Heart of Classical Athens*. London: Thames & Hudson.

————, ed. 1990. *The Athenian Agora: Guide*. 4th ed. Athens: American School of Classical Studies.

Campbell, Joseph. 1972. *Myths to Live By*. New York: Viking Press.

Carpenter, Rhys. 1933. "The Antiquity of the Greek Alphabet." *American Journal of Archaeology* 37, no. 1: 8–29.

Cassirer, Ernst. 1953. *Language and Myth*. Translated by Susanne K. Langer. New York: Dover.

Ceccarelli, Leah. 1998. "Polysemy: Multiple Meanings in Rhetorical Criticism." *Quarterly Journal of Speech* 84, no. 4: 395–415.

Cherniss, Harold F. 1935. *Aristotle's Criticism of Presocratic Philosophy*. Baltimore: Johns Hopkins University Press.

————. 1944. *Aristotle's Criticism of Plato and the Academy*. Baltimore: Johns Hopkins University Press.

————. 1970. "The Characteristics and Effects of Presocratic Philosophy." In *Studies in Presocratic Philosophy*, vol. 1, edited by David J. Furley and R. E. Allen, 1–28. London: Routledge & Kegan Paul.

Cherwitz, Richard A., and James W. Hikins. 1986. *Communication and Knowledge: An Investigation of Rhetorical Epistemology*. Columbia: University of South Carolina Press.

Chroust, Anton-Hermann. 1973. *Aristotle: New Light on His Life and on Some of His Lost Works*. Vol. 1. South Bend, Ind.: University of Notre Dame Press.

Chung-Hwan Chen. 1958. "The Relation between the Terms *Energeia* and *Entelecheia* in the Philosophy of Aristotle." *Classical Quarterly* 8, no. 3/4: 12–17.

Cicero. 1959. *De Oratore*. Translated by E. W. Sutton. 2 vols. Cambridge: Cambridge University Press.

————. 1970. *Brutus*. Translated and edited by J. S. Watson. In *Cicero on Oratory and Orators*, 262–367. Carbondale: Southern Illinois University Press.

Claus, David B. 1981. *Toward the Soul: An Inquiry into the Meaning of* Psychê *before Plato.* New Haven & London: Yale University Press.

Clay, Jenny Strauss. 2007. "Hesiod's Rhetorical Art." In *A Companion to Greek Rhetoric,* edited by Ian Worthington, 447–56. Oxford: Blackwell.

Cole, A. T. 1972. "The Relativism of Protagoras." *Yale Classical Studies* 22, no. 1: 19–45.

Cole, Thomas. 1991a. *The Origins of Rhetoric in Ancient Greece.* Baltimore: Johns Hopkins University Press.

———. 1991b. "Who Was Corax?" *Illinois Classical Studies* 16, no. 1–2: 65–84.

Consigny, Scott. 1992. "Gorgias's Use of the Epideictic." *Philosophy and Rhetoric* 25, no. 3: 281–97.

———. 2001. *Gorgias: Sophist and Artist.* Columbia: University of South Carolina Press.

Cook, R. M., and A. G. Woodhead. 1959. "The Diffusion of the Greek Alphabet." *American Journal of Archaeology* 63, no. 2: 175–78.

Cooper, John M. 1975. *Reason and Human Good in Aristotle.* Cambridge, Mass.: Harvard University Press.

Cornford, Francis M. 1927. "The Athenian Philosophical Schools." *Cambridge Ancient History* 6: 310–32.

———. 1930. "Anaxagoras' Theory of Matter." *Classical Quarterly* 24, no. 1: 14–30.

———. 1950. *Before and After Socrates.* Cambridge: Cambridge University Press.

———. 1952. *Principium Sapientiae: The Origins of Greek Philosophical Thought.* Cambridge: Cambridge University Press.

———. 1957. *From Religion to Philosophy: A Study in the Origins of Western Speculation.* New York: Harper.

———. 1967. "The Doctrine of Eros in Plato's *Symposium.*" In *The Unwritten Philosophy,* edited by F. M. Cornford, 68–80. Cambridge: Cambridge University Press.

Coulton, J. J. 1977. *Ancient Greek Architects at Work.* Ithaca, N.Y.: Cornell University Press.

Cross, R. C. 1954. "Logos and Forms in Plato." *Mind* 63, no. 252: 433–50.

Crowley, Sharon. 1979. "Of Gorgias and Grammatology." *College Composition and Communication* 30, no. 3: 279–84.

———. 1989. "A Plea for the Revival of Sophistry." *Rhetoric Review* 7, no. 2: 318–34.

Cunningham, Adrian, ed. 1973. *The Theory of Myth: Six Theories.* London: Sheed & Ward.

Curd, Patricia. 1998; reprint, 2004. *The Legacy of Parmenides: Eleatic Monism and Later Presocratic Thought.* Princeton, N.J.: Princeton University Press; Las Vegas: Parmenides.

Demos, Raphael. 1935. "The Fundamental Conceptions of Plato's Metaphysics." *Journal of Philosophy* 32, no. 21: 561–78.

———. 1937. "Plato's Idea of the Good." *Philosophical Review* 46, no. 3: 245–75.

———. 1961. "Some Remarks on Aristotle's Doctrine of Practical Reason." *Philosophy and Phenomenological Research* 22, no. 2: 153–62.

———. 1964. "Plato's Philosophy of Language." *Journal of Philosophy* 61, no. 20: 595–610.

De Rijk, Lambertius M. 1952. *The Place of the Categories of Being in Aristotle's Philosophy.* Assen: van Goreurn.

De Romilly, Jacqueline. 1992. *The Great Sophists in Periclean Athens*. Translated by Janet Lloyd. Oxford: Clarendon Press.

Devereax, D. T. 1986. "Particular and Universal in Aristotle's Conception of Practical Knowledge." *Review of Metaphysics* 39, no. 3: 483–504.

Dewey, John. 1922. *Human Nature and Conduct*. New York: Modern Library.

Dewey, John, and James Tufts. 1932. *Ethics*. New York: Henry Holt. Reprinted in *John Dewey: The Later Works* (1925–53), vol. 7 (1932), edited by Jo Ann Boydston. Carbondale: Southern Illinois University Press, 1985.

Dickinson, G. Lowes. 1958. *The Greek View of Life*. Ann Arbor: University of Michigan Press.

Diels, Herman, and Walther Kranz. 1951–54. *Die Fragmente der Vorsokratiker*. 7th ed. 3 vols. Berlin: Weidman.

Dillon, John, and Tania Gergel. 2003. *The Greek Sophists*. New York: Penguin.

Dillon, Matthew, and Lynda Garland. 1994. *Ancient Greece: Social and Historical Documents from Archaic Times to the Death of Socrates (c. 800–399 BC)*. London: Routledge.

Dinsmoor, William Bell. 1975. *The Architecture of Ancient Greece*. New York: W. W. Norton.

Dodds, Eric R. 1951. *The Greeks and the Irrational*. Berkeley: University of California Press.

Dorter, Kenneth. 1994. *Form and Good in Plato's Eleatic Dialogues: The* Parmenides, Theaetetus, Sophist, *and* Statesman. Berkeley: University of California Press.

Duerlinger, J. 1968. "Drawing Conclusions from Aristotelian Syllogisms." *Monist* 52 (April): 229–36.

Dupre, Wilhelm. 1975. *Religion in Primitive Cultures: A Study in Ethnophilosophy*. The Hague: Mouton.

During, Ingemar. 1950. *Notes on the History of the Transmission of Aristotle's Writings*. Goteborg: Steihm.

———. 1957. *Aristotle in the Ancient Biographical Tradition*. Stockholm: Almqvist & Miksell.

Edelstein, Ludwig. 1949. "The Function of Myth in Plato's Philosophy." *Journal of the History of Ideas* 10, no. 4: 463–81.

Edman, Irwin. 1936. "Poetry and Truth in Plato." *Journal of Philosophy* 33, no. 22: 605–9.

Edmunds, Lowell, ed. 1990. *Approaches to Greek Myth*. Baltimore: Johns Hopkins University Press.

Ehrenberg, Victor. 1964. *The Greek State*. New York: W. W. Norton.

———. 1968. *From Solon to Socrates: Greek History and Civilization during the Sixth and Fifth Centuries B.C.* London: Methuen.

Einstein, Albert. 1954. *Albert Einstein: The Human Side*. Edited by Helen Dukas and Banesh Hoffman. Princeton, N.J.: Princeton University Press.

Elder, George H. 1998. *The Scientific Foundations of Social Communication: From Neurons to Rhetoric*. Commack, N.Y.: Nova Science Publishers, Inc.

Eliade, Mircea. 1960. *Myths, Dreams and Mysteries*. London: Harvill.

———. 1961. *Images and Symbols: Studies in Religious Symbolism*. London: Harvill.

———. 1963. *Myth and Reality*. New York: Harper & Row.

———. 1977. *No Souvenirs*. New York: Harper & Row.

Engness, Richard A. 1973. "Implications for Communication of the Rhetorical Epistemology of Gorgias of Leontini." *Western Speech Journal* 37, no. 3: 175–84.

Enos, Richard Leo. 1976. "The Epistemology of Gorgias' Rhetoric: A Re-Examination." *Southern Speech Communication Journal* 42, no. 1: 35–51.

———. 1993. *Greek Rhetoric Before Aristotle.* Prospect Heights, Ill.: Waveland Press.

Ercolini, Gina L. 2000. "The Logos That Is Shared: The Proto-Rhetorical Dimension of Heraclitus's Fragments." M.A. thesis, Pennsylvania State University, 2000.

Etheridge, S. G. 1968. "Aristotle's Practical Syllogism and Necessity." *Philologus* 112, no. 1/2: 20–42.

Evans, John D. G. 1977. *Aristotle's Concept of Dialectic.* Cambridge: Cambridge University Press.

Ferris, Timothy. 1988. *Coming of Age in the Milky Way.* New York: William Morrow, 1988.

Field, Guy C. 1930. *Plato and His Contemporaries.* London: Methuen.

Fine, G. J. 1979. "Knowledge and *Logos* in the *Theaetetus*." *Philosophical Review* 88, no. 3: 366–97.

Finley, Moses I. 1979. *The World of Odysseus.* 2nd ed. New York: Penguin.

———. 1981. *Early Greece: The Bronze and Archaic Ages.* Rev. ed. New York: W. W. Norton.

———. 1985. *Democracy Ancient and Modern.* 2nd ed. London: Hogarth Press.

Fisher, Walter R. 1984. "Narration as a Human Communication Paradigm: The Case of Public Moral Argument." *Communication Monographs* 51, no. 1:1–22.

———. 1985. "The Narrative Paradigm: An Elaboration." *Communication Monographs* 52, no. 4: 347–67.

———. 1987. *Human Communication as Narration: Toward a Philosophy of Reason, Value, and Action.* Columbia: University of South Carolina Press.

Ford, Andrew. 1993. "The Price of Art in Isocrates: Formalism and the Escape from Politics." In *Rethinking the History of Rhetoric: Multidisciplinary Essays on the Rhetorical Tradition,* edited by Takis Poulakos, 31–52. Boulder, Colo.: Westview Press.

Forsdyke, John. 1957. *Greece Before Homer.* New York: W. W. Norton.

Foucault, Michel. 1965. *Madness and Civilization: A History of Insanity in the Age of Reason.* Translated by Richard Howard. New York: Pantheon.

———. 1970. *The Order of Things: An Archaeology of the Human Sciences.* New York: Pantheon.

———. 1972. *The Archaeology of Knowledge.* Translated by A. M. Sheridan Smith. New York: Pantheon.

———. 1977a. *Discipline and Punish: The Birth of the Prison.* Translated by Alan Sheridan. New York: Pantheon.

———. 1977b. *Language, Counter-Memory, Practice: Selected Essays and Interviews.* Translated by Donald F. Bouchard and Sherry Simon. Edited by Donald F. Bouchard. Ithaca, N.Y.: Cornell University Press.

Frankel, Hermann. 1993. "Xenophanes' Empiricism and His Critique of Knowledge (B34)." In *The Pre-Socratics,* edited by Alexander P. D. Mourelatos, 118–31. Princeton, N.J.: Princeton University Press.

Frankfort, Henri, and H. A. Frankfort. 1977. "Myth and Reality." In H. Frankfort, H. A. Frankfort, John A. Wilson, Thorkild Jacobsen, and William A. Irwin, *The*

Intellectual Adventure of Ancient Man: An Essay on Speculative Thought in the Ancient Near East, 3–27. Chicago: University of Chicago Press.

Frazer, James G. 1994. *The Golden Bough: A Study in Magic and Religion*. Abridged from the 2nd and 3rd eds. London: Oxford University Press.

Fredal, James. 2006. *Rhetorical Action in Ancient Athens: Persuasive Artistry from Solon to Demosthenes*. Carbondale: Southern Illinois University Press.

Freeland, Cynthia A. 1985. "Aristotelian Actions." *Nous* 19, no. 3: 397–414.

Freeman, Kathleen. 1950. *Greek City-States*. New York: W. W. Norton.

———. 1983. *Ancilla to the Pre-Socratic Philosophers*. Cambridge, Mass.: Harvard University Press.

Fromm, Erich. 1956. *The Art of Loving*. New York: Harper.

Furley, David J. 1967. *Two Studies in Greek Atomists*. Princeton, N.J.: Princeton University Press.

Furley, David J., and Robert E. Allen, eds. 1970. *Studies in Presocratic Philosophy*. Vol. 1. London: Routledge & Kegan Paul.

Furth, Montgomery. 1993. "Elements of Eleatic Ontology." In *The Pre-Socratics*, edited by Alexander P. D. Mourelatos, 241–70. Princeton, N.J.: Princeton University Press.

Gagarin, Michael. 1994. "Probability and Persuasion: Plato and Early Greek Rhetoric." In *Persuasion: Greek Rhetoric in Action*, edited by Ian Worthington, 46–68. London & New York: Routledge.

———. 1997. "On the Not-Being in Gorgias's *On Not-Being* (ONB)." *Philosophy and Rhetoric* 30, no. 1: 38–40.

———. 2001. "Did the Sophists Aim to Persuade?" *Rhetorica* 19, no. 3: 275–91.

———. 2002. *Antiphon the Athenian: Oratory, Law, and Justice in the Age of the Sophists*. Austin: University of Texas Press.

Gagarin, Michael, and Paul Woodruff, eds. 1995. *Early Greek Political Thought from Homer to the Sophists*. Cambridge: Cambridge University Press.

Gaines, Robert N. 1997. "Knowledge and Discourse in Gorgias' *On the Non-Existent or On Nature*." *Philosophy and Rhetoric* 30, no. 1: 1–12.

Galligan, Edward M. 1983. "Logos in the *Theaetetus* and the *Sophist*." In *Essays in Ancient Greek Philosophy*, vol. 2, edited by John P. Anton, 264–78. Albany: State University of New York Press.

Garver, Eugene. 2004. "Philosophy, Rhetoric, and Civic Education in Aristotle and Isocrates." In *Isocrates and Civic Education*, edited by Takis Poulakos and David Depew, 186–213. Austin: University of Texas Press.

Gentili, Bruno. 1988. *Poetry and Its Public in Ancient Greece: From Homer to the Fifth Century*. Baltimore: Johns Hopkins University Press.

Godley, Alfred D. 1896. *Socrates and Athenian Society in His Day*. London: Seeley.

Goldhill, Simon. 1991. *The Poet's Voice: Essays on Poetics and Greek Literature*. Cambridge: Cambridge University Press.

Gomperz, Heinrich. 1912. *Sophistik und Rhetorik*. Leipzig & Berlin: Teubner.

Gomperz, Theodor. 1901. *Greek Thinkers: A History of Ancient Philosophy*. Translated by Laurie Magnus (vol. 1) and C. G. Berry (vols. 2–4). 4 vols. London: John Murray.

Gotthelf, A. 1976. "Aristotle's Conception of Final Causality." *Review of Metaphysics* 30, no. 2: 226–54.

Gould, Thomas. 1963. *Platonic Love.* New York: Free Press of Glencoe.

Gower, Barry S., and Michael C. Stokes, eds. 1992. *Socratic Questions.* London: Routledge.

Graves, Robert. 1959. *Greek Myths.* New York: Braziller Press.

Greene, William C. 1951. "The Spoken and the Written Word." *Harvard Studies in Classical Philology* 60: 23–59.

Gregg, Richard B. 1984. *Symbolic Inducement and Knowing: A Study in the Foundations of Rhetoric.* Columbia: University of South Carolina Press.

Grimaldi, William M. A. 1996. "How Do We Get from Corax-Tisias to Plato-Aristotle in Greek Rhetorical Theory?" In *Theory, Text, Context: Issues in Greek Rhetoric and Oratory,* edited by Christopher Lyle Johnstone, 19–43. Albany: State University of New York Press.

Gronbeck, Bruce E. 1972. "Gorgias on Rhetoric and Poetic: A Rehabilitation." *Southern Speech Communication Journal* 38, no. 1: 27–38.

Grote, George. 1888. *A History of Greece from the Earliest Period to the Close of the Generation Contemporary with Alexander the Great.* 12 vols. London: John Murray.

Guthrie, W. K. C. 1950a. *The Greek Philosophers from Thales to Aristotle.* London: Methuen.

———. 1950b. *The Greeks and Their Gods.* London: Methuen.

———. 1952. "The Presocratic World-Picture." *Harvard Theological Review* 45, no. 2: 87–104.

———. 1953. *Myth and Reason.* London: London School of Economics and Political Science.

———. 1962. *A History of Greek Philosophy.* Vol 1, *The Earlier Presocratics and the Pythagoreans.* Cambridge: Cambridge University Press.

———. 1965. *A History of Greek Philosophy.* Vol. 2, *The Presocratic Tradition from Parmenides to Democritus.* Cambridge: Cambridge University Press.

———. 1968. *The First Humanists.* London: John Murray.

———. 1970. "Aristotle as Historian." In *Studies in Presocratic Philosophy,* vol. 1, edited by David J. Furley and R. E. Allen, 1–28. London: Routledge & Kegan Paul.

———. 1971a. *Socrates.* Cambridge: Cambridge University Press.

———. 1971b. *The Sophists.* Cambridge: Cambridge University Press.

———. 1986a. *A History of Greek Philosophy.* Vol. 4, *Plato: The Man and His Dialogues: Earlier Period.* Cambridge: Cambridge University Press.

———. 1986b. *A History of Greek Philosophy.* Vol. 5, *The Later Plato and the Academy.* Cambridge: Cambridge University Press.

———. 1990. *A History of Greek Philosophy.* Vol. 6, *Aristotle: An Encounter.* Cambridge: Cambridge University Press.

Halverson, John. 1992. "Havelock on Greek Orality and Literacy." *Journal of the History of Ideas* 53, no. 1:148–63.

Hamlyn, D. W. 1955. "The Communion of Forms and the Development of Plato's Logic." *Philosophical Quarterly* 5: 289–302.

———. 1976. "Aristotelian Epagoge." *Phronesis* 21, no. 2: 167–84.

Hammond, N. G. L. 1959. *A History of Greece to 322 B.C.* Oxford: Oxford University Press.

Hankinson, R. J. 1995. "Science." In *The Cambridge Companion to Aristotle*, edited by Jonathan Barnes, 140–94. Cambridge: Cambridge University Press.

Hanson, Victor. 2005. *A War Like No Other.* New York: Random House.

Hardie, William F. R. 1968. *Aristotle's Ethical Theory.* Oxford: Clarendon Press.

Harrison, E. L. 1964. "Was Gorgias a Sophist?" *Phoenix* 18 (Autumn): 183–92.

Harter, E. D. 1975. "Aristotle on Primary *Ousia.*" *Archiv für Geschichte der Philosophie* 57, no. 1: 1–20.

Haskins, Ekaterina V. 2004. *Logos and Power in Isocrates and Aristotle.* Columbia: University of South Carolina Press.

Hatab, Lawrence J. 1990. *Myth and Philosophy: A Contest of Truths.* LaSalle, Ill.: Open Court.

Havelock, Eric A. 1957. *The Liberal Temper in Greek Politics.* London: Jonathan Cape.

———. 1963. *Preface to Plato.* Cambridge, Mass.: Harvard University Press.

———. 1981. *The Literate Revolution in Greece and Its Cultural Consequences.* Princeton, N.J.: Princeton University Press.

———. 1983. "The Linguistic Task of the Presocratics." In *Language and Thought in Early Greek Philosophy*, edited by Kevin Robb, 7–82. LaSalle, Ill.: Monist Library of Philosophy.

———. 1986. *The Muse Learns to Write: Reflections on Orality and Literacy from Antiquity to the Present.* New Haven, Conn.: Yale University Press.

Hawhee, Debra. 2004. *Bodily Arts: Rhetoric and Athletics in Ancient Greece.* Austin: University of Texas Press.

Hawking, Stephen W. 1988. *A Brief History of Time: From the Big Bang to Black Holes.* New York: Bantam Books.

Heidegger, Martin. 1975. *Early Greek Thinking: The Dawn of Western Philosophy.* San Francisco: Harper & Row.

Heidel, W. A. 1910. "*Peri Phuseos:* A Study of the Conception of Nature among the Pre-Socratics." *Proceedings of the American Academy of Arts and Sciences* 45: 77–133.

Heidlebaugh, Nola J. 2002. *Judgment, Rhetoric, and the Problem of Incommensurability: Recalling Practical Wisdom.* Columbia: University of South Carolina Press.

Hendricks, Rhoda A., trans. 1974. *Classical Gods and Heroes: Myths as Told by the Ancient Authors.* New York: Morrow Quill Paperbacks.

Herodotus. 1947. *The Persian Wars.* Translated by George Rawlinson. New York: Modern Library.

———. 1954. *The Histories.* Translated, with an introduction, by Aubrey de Selincourt. Baltimore: Penguin.

Hesiod. 1966. *Works and Days.* Edited and translated by T. A. Sinclair. Hildesheim: Georg Olms Verlagsbuchhandlung.

———. 1978. *Works and Days.* Edited and translated, with prolegomena and commentary, by M. L. West. Oxford: Clarendon Press.

———. 1983. *Theogony, Works and Days, Shield.* Translated by Apostolos N. Athanassakis. Baltimore: Johns Hopkins University Press.

Hignett, Charles. 1952. *History of the Athenian Constitution to the End of the Fifth Century* B.C. Oxford: Oxford University Press.

Hikins, James W. 1981. "Plato's Rhetorical Theory: Old Perspectives on the Epistemology of the New Rhetoric." *Central States Speech Journal* 32, no. 3: 160–76.

Hoffer, William. 1975. "A Magic Ratio Occurs throughout Art and Nature." *Smithsonian* (December): 110–20.

Holland, R. F. 1956. "On Making Sense of a Philosophical Fragment." *Classical Quarterly* 6, no. 3/4: 215–20.

Holscher, Uvo. 1970. "Anaximander and the Beginnings of Greek Philosophy." In *Studies in Presocratic Philosophy*, vol. 1, edited by David J. Furley and R. E. Allen, 281–322. London: Routledge & Kegan Paul.

Homer. 1924. *The Iliad*. 2 vols. Translated by A. T. Murray. Cambridge: Harvard University Press.

———. 1965. *The Iliad of Homer*. Translated by Alexander Pope. New York: Macmillan.

———. 1990. *Homer: The Iliad*. Translated by Robert Fagles. New York: Penguin.

Hooper, Finley. 1978. *Greek Realities: Life and Thought in Ancient Greece*. Detroit: Wayne State University Press.

Hunt, Everett Lee. 1920. "Plato and Aristotle on Rhetoric and Rhetoricians." *Quarterly Journal of Speech Education* 6, no. 3: 33–53.

———. 1965. "On the Sophists." In *The Province of Rhetoric*, edited by Joseph Schwartz and John A. Rycenga, 69–84. New York: Ronald Press.

Huntley, H. E. 1970. *The Divine Proportion*. New York: Dover.

Hyland, Drew A. 1968. "Why Plato Wrote Dialogues." *Philosophy and Rhetoric* 1, no. 1: 38–50.

———. 1973. *The Origins of Philosophy*. New York: Capricorn Books.

Irwin, Terence H. 1975. "Aristotle on Reason, Desire, and Virtue." *Journal of Philosophy* 72, no. 17: 567–78.

———. 1990. *Aristotle's First Principles*. Oxford: Clarendon Press.

Isocrates. 1928, 1929, 1945. *Isocrates*. 3 vols. Vols. 1 and 2 translated by George Norlin; vol. 3 translated by La Rue Van Hook. Cambridge, Mass.: Harvard University Press.

———. 1990. *Panegyricus* and *To Nicocles*. In *Greek Orators*, vol. 3, translated by S. Usher. Warminster, U.K.: Aris & Phillips.

———. 2000, 2004. *Isocrates*. 2 vols. Vol. 1 translated by David Mirhady and Yun Lee Too; vol. 2 translated by Terry Papillon. Austin: University of Texas Press.

Jacobs, Melville, and John Greenway, eds. 1966. *The Anthropologist Looks at Myth*. Austin: University of Texas Press.

Jaeger, Werner. 1934. *Aristotle: Fundamentals of the History of His Development*. Translated by R. Robinson. Oxford: Clarendon Press.

———. 1944. *Paideia: The Ideals of Greek Culture*. Vol. 3. Translated by Gilbert Highet. New York: Oxford University Press.

———. 1947. *The Theology of the Early Greek Philosophers*. Oxford: Clarendon Press.

James, William. 1929. *The Varieties of Religious Experience*. New York: Modern Library / Random House.

Jarratt, Susan C. 1987a. "The First Sophists and the Uses of History." *Rhetoric Review* 6, no. 1: 67–77.

———. 1987b. "Toward a Sophistic Historiography." *Pre/Text* 8, no. 1: 9–26.

———. 1990. "The Role of the Sophists in Histories of Consciousness." *Philosophy and Rhetoric* 23, no. 2: 85–95.

———. 1991. *Rereading the Sophists: Classical Rhetoric Refigured.* Carbondale: Southern Illinois University Press.

Jarrett, James L. 1969. *The Educational Theory of the Sophists.* New York: Teachers College Press.

Jaynes, Julian. 1976. *The Origins of Consciousness in the Breakdown of the Bicameral Mind.* Boston: Houghton Mifflin.

Jebb, R. C. 1893. *The Attic Orators.* Vol. 2. London: Macmillan.

Jeffrey, L. H. 1976. *Archaic Greece.* New York: St. Martin's Press.

Johnstone, Christopher Lyle. 1980. "An Aristotelian Trilogy: Ethics, Rhetoric, Politics, and the Search for Moral Truth." *Philosophy and Rhetoric* 13, no. 1: 1–24.

———. 1981. "Ethics, Wisdom, and the Mission of Contemporary Rhetoric: The Realization of Human Being." *Central States Speech Journal* 32, no. 3: 177–88.

———. 1983. "Dewey, Ethics, and Rhetoric: Toward a Contemporary Conception of Practical Wisdom." *Philosophy and Rhetoric* 16, no. 3: 185–207.

———. 2001a. "Communicating in Classical Contexts: The Centrality of Delivery." *Quarterly Journal of Speech* 87, no. 2: 121–43.

———. 2001b. "Rhetoric, Civic Consciousness, and Civic Conscience: The Invention of Citizenship in Classical Greece." *Advances in the History of Rhetoric* 5: 1–9.

———. 2002. "Aristotle's Ethical Theory in the Contemporary World: *Logos, Phronêsis,* and the Moral Life." In *Moral Engagement in Public Life: Theorists for Contemporary Ethics,* edited by Clifford Christians and Sharon Bracci, 16–34. New York: Peter Lang.

———. 2005. "'Speech Is a Powerful Lord': Speech, Sound, and Enchantment in Greek Oratorical Performance." *Advances in the History of Rhetoric* 8: 1–20.

———. 2006. "Sophistical Wisdom: *Politikê Aretê* and '*Logosophia.*'" *Philosophy and Rhetoric* 39, no. 4: 265–89.

———. 2008. "Eros, Logos, and Sophia in Plato: Philosophical Conversation, Spiritual Lovemaking, and Dialogic Ethics." In *Communication Ethics: Between Cosmopolitanism and Provinciality,* edited by Kathleen Glenister Roberts and Ronald C. Arnett. New York: Peter Lang.

Johnstone, Henry W., Jr. 1981. "Toward an Ethics of Rhetoric." *Communication* 6, no. 2: 305–14.

Johnstone, William. 1978. "Cursive Phoenician and the Archaic Greek Alphabet." *Kadmos* 17, no. 2: 151–66.

Jones, A. H. M. 1958. *Athenian Democracy.* New York: Praeger.

Jordan, Robert W. 1983. *Plato's Arguments for Forms.* Cambridge: Cambridge Philological Society.

Jung, Carl G., and Carl Kerenyi. 1951. *Introduction to a Science of Mythology.* London: Routledge & Kegan Paul.

Kagan, Donald. 1969. *The Outbreak of the Peloponnesian War.* Ithaca, N.Y.: Cornell University Press.

———. 2003. *The Peloponnesian War.* New York: Viking Press.

Kahn, Charles H. 1960. *Anaximander and the Origins of Greek Cosmology.* New York: Columbia University Press.

———. 1966. "The Greek Verb 'To Be' and the Concept of Being." *Foundations of Language* 2, no. 3: 245–65.

———. 1969/70. "The Thesis of Parmenides." *Review of Metaphysics* 22, no. 4: 700–724.

———. 1979. *The Art and Thought of Heraclitus.* Cambridge: Cambridge University Press.

———. 1981. "The Role of *Nous* in the Cognition of First Principles." In *Aristotle on Science,* edited by E. Berti, 385–414. Padua: Editrice Antenore.

———. 1983. "Philosophy and the Written Word: Some Thoughts on Heraclitus and the Early Greek Uses of Prose." In *Language and Thought in Early Greek Philosophy,* edited by Kevin Robb, 110–24. LaSalle, Ill.: Monist Library of Philosophy.

———. 1993. "Pythagorean Philosophy Before Plato." In *The Pre-Socratics,* edited by Alexander P. D. Mourelatos, 161–85. Princeton, N.J.: Princeton University Press.

Kaufer, David S. 1978. "The Influence of Plato's Psychology on His Views of Rhetoric." *Quarterly Journal of Speech* 64, no. 1: 63–78.

Kauffman, Charles. 1982. "The Axiological Foundations of Plato's Theory of Rhetoric." *Central States Speech Journal* 33 (Summer): 353–66.

Kelley, William G., Jr. 1973. "Rhetoric as Seduction." *Philosophy and Rhetoric* 6, no. 2: 69–80.

Kennedy, George A. 1963. *The Art of Persuasion in Greece.* Princeton, N.J.: Princeton University Press.

———. 1994. *A New History of Classical Rhetoric.* Princeton, N.J.: Princeton University Press.

Kenny, Anthony. 1978. *The Aristotelian Ethics.* Oxford: Clarendon Press.

Kerferd, G. B. 1950. "The First Greek Sophists." *Classical Review* 64, no. 1: 8–10.

———. 1956–57. "The Moral and Political Doctrines of Antiphon the Sophist." *Proceedings of the Cambridge Philological Society* 5: 26–32.

———. 1964. "Thrasymachus and Justice: A Reply." *Phronesis* 9, no. 1: 12–16.

———. 1969. "Anaxagoras and the Concept of Matter Before Aristotle." *Bulletin of the John Rylands Library* 52: 129–43. Reprinted in *The Pre-Socratics,* edited by Alexander P. D. Mourelatos, 489–503. Princeton, N.J.: Princeton University Press, 1993.

———. 1981a. *The Sophistic Movement.* Cambridge: Cambridge University Press.

———, ed. 1981b. *The Sophists and Their Legacy.* Proceedings of the Fourth International Colloquium on Ancient Philosophy. Wiesbaden: Franz Steiner Verlag GmbH.

Kirby, John T. 1992. "Rhetoric and Poetics in Hesiod." *Ramus* 21, no. 1: 34–60.

Kirk, G. S. 1951. "Natural Change in Heraclitus." *Mind* 60, no. 237: 35–42.

———. 1954. *Heraclitus: The Cosmic Fragments.* Cambridge: Cambridge University Press.

———. 1962. *The Songs of Homer.* Cambridge: Cambridge University Press.

———. 1970a. *Myth: Its Meaning and Functions in Ancient and Other Cultures.* Berkeley & Los Angeles: University of California Press.

———. 1970b. "Popper on Science and the Presocratics." In *Studies in Presocratic Philosophy,* vol. 1, edited by David J. Furley and R. E. Allen, 154–77. London: Routledge & Kegan Paul.

————. 1983. "Orality and Sequence." In *Language and Thought in Early Greek Philosophy*, edited by Kevin Robb, 83–90. LaSalle, Ill.: Monist Library of Philosophy.

Kirk, G. S., J. E. Raven, and M. Schofield. 1983. *The Presocratic Philosophers*. 2nd ed. Cambridge: Cambridge University Press.

Kneupper, Charles W., and Floyd D. Anderson. 1980. "Uniting Wisdom and Eloquence: The Need for Rhetorical Invention." *Quarterly Journal of Speech* 66, no. 3: 313–26.

Konstan, David. 2004. "Isocrates' '*Republic*.'" In *Isocrates and Civic Education*, edited by Takis Poulakos and David Depew, 107–24. Austin: University of Texas Press.

Kramer, Hans J. 1990. *Plato and the Foundations of Metaphysics*. Albany: State University of New York Press.

Kuhn, Thomas S. 1970. *The Structure of Scientific Revolutions*. 2nd ed. Chicago: University of Chicago Press.

Lacey, A. R. 1965. "*Ousia* and Form in Aristotle." *Phronesis* 10, no. 1: 54–69.

Lao Tzu. 1944. *The Way of Life*. Translated by Witter Bynner. New York: Capricorn Books.

Larson, Gerald J., ed. 1974. *Myth in Indo-European Antiquity*. Berkeley: University of California Press.

Lawrence, Arnold W. 1957. *Greek Architecture*. Baltimore: Penguin.

Lawrence, Gavin. 1993. "Aristotle and the Ideal Life." *Philosophical Review* 102, no. 1: 1–34.

Leakey, Richard, and Roger Lewin. 1992. *Origins Reconsidered: In Search of What Makes Us Human*. New York: Doubleday / Anchor Books.

Lear, Jonathan. 1980. *Aristotle and Logical Theory*. Cambridge: Cambridge University Press.

Leff, Michael C. 1996. "Agency, Performance, and Interpretation in Thucydides' Account of the Mytilene Debate." In *Theory, Text, Context: Issues in Greek Rhetoric and Oratory*, edited by Christopher Lyle Johnstone, 89–96. Albany: State University of New York Press.

————. 2004. "Isocrates, Tradition, and the Rhetorical Version of Civic Education." In *Isocrates and Civic Education*, edited by Takis Poulakos and David Depew, 235–54. Austin: University of Texas Press.

Lentz, Tony M. 1989. *Orality and Literacy in Hellenic Greece*. Carbondale: Southern Illinois University Press.

Leszl, Walter. 1970. *Logic and Metaphysics in Aristotle*. Padua: Antenore.

————. 1975. *Aristotle's Conception of Ontology*. Padua: Antenore.

Levi, Albert William. 1984. "Love, Rhetoric, and the Aristocratic Way of Life." *Philosophy and Rhetoric* 17, no. 4: 189–208.

Levinson, Ronald B. 1953. *In Defense of Plato*. Cambridge, Mass.: Harvard University Press.

Levy, Donald. 1979. "The Definition of Love in Plato's *Symposium*." *Journal of the History of Ideas* 40, no. 2: 285–91.

Lewis, Naphtali. 1970. *Greek Historical Documents: The Fifth Century B.C.* Greek Historical Documents Series. Sarasota, Fla.: Samuel Stevens Hakkert.

Liddell, Henry George, and Robert Scott. 1996. *A Greek-English Lexicon*. 9th ed. (rev.). Oxford: Clarendon Press.

Livingstone, Niall. 2001. *A Commentary on Isocrates'* Busiris. Leiden: Brill.

Lloyd, A. C. 1981. *Form and Universal in Aristotle.* Liverpool: F. Cairns.

Lloyd, G. E. R. 1968. *Aristotle: The Growth and Structure of His Thought.* Cambridge: Cambridge University Press.

———. 1970. *Early Greek Science: Thales to Aristotle.* New York: W. W. Norton.

———. 1987. *The Revolutions of Wisdom.* Berkeley: University of California Press.

Lloyd, G. E. R., and G. E. L. Owen, eds. 1978. *Aristotle on Mind and the Senses.* Cambridge: Cambridge University Press.

Lord, Albert Bates. 1991. *Epic Singers and Oral Tradition.* Ithaca, N.Y.: Cornell University Press.

Loux, M. J. 1973. "Aristotle on the Transcendentals." *Phronesis* 18, no. 3: 225–39.

Lowman, Edward L. 1971a. "An Example of Fibonacci Numbers to Generate Rhythmic Values in Modern Music." *Fibonacci Quarterly* 9, no. 4: 423–36.

———. 1971b. "Some Striking Proportions in the Music of Bela Bartok." *Fibonacci Quarterly* 9, no. 5: 527–37.

Lukasiewicz, Jan. 1957. *Aristotle's Syllogistic from the Standpoint of Modern Formal Logic.* Oxford: Clarendon Press.

Lutz, Mark J. 1998. *Socrates' Education to Virtue.* Albany: State University of New York Press.

Mackintosh, Charles H. 1971. *Tao: A Poetic Version of the Tao The Ching of Lao Tsze.* Wheaton, Ill.: Theosophical Publishing House.

Makin, Stephen. 1988. "How Can We Find Out What Ancient Philosophers Said?" *Phronesis* 33, no. 2: 121–32.

Malinowski, Bronislaw. 1954. *Magic, Science and Religion.* Garden City, N.Y.: Doubleday.

Marcovich, Miroslav. 1967. *Heraclitus, editio maior.* Merida, Venezuela: Los Andes University Press.

Margolis, Joseph. 1983. "The Emergence of Philosophy." In *Language and Thought in Early Greek Philosophy,* edited by Kevin Robb, 228–43. LaSalle, Ill.: Monist Library of Philosophy.

Martin, R. 1977. "Intuitionism and the Practical Syllogism in Aristotle's *Ethics.*" *Apeiron* 11, no. 1: 12–19.

Matthews, Gareth B. 1999. *Socratic Perplexity and the Nature of Philosophy.* Oxford: Oxford University Press.

McAdon, Brad. 2001. "Rhetoric Is a Counterpart of Dialectic." *Philosophy and Rhetoric* 34, no. 2: 113–49.

———. 2004. "Two Irreconcilable Conceptions of Rhetorical Proofs in Aristotle's *Rhetoric.*" *Rhetorica* 22, no. 4: 307–25.

McCarter, P. Kyle. 1975. *The Antiquity of the Greek Alphabet and the Early Phoenician Scripts.* Missoula, Mont.: Scholars Press.

McComiskey, Bruce. 2002. *Gorgias and the New Sophistic Rhetoric.* Carbondale: Southern Illinois University Press.

McKendrick, Paul. 1981. *The Greek Stones Speak.* 2nd ed. New York: W. W. Norton.

McKeon, Richard. 1947. "Aristotle's Conception of the Development and the Nature of Scientific Method." *Journal of the History of Ideas* 8, no. 1: 3–44.

McPhee, John. 1998. *Annals of the Former World.* New York: Farrar, Straus & Giroux.

Meiggs, Russell. 1972. *The Athenian Empire.* New York: Oxford University Press.

Merlan, P. 1946. "Aristotle's Unmoved Movers." *Traditio* 4: 1–30.

Michalopoulos, Andre. 1966. *Homer.* New York: Twayne.

Michelakis, Emmanuel. 1961. *Aristotle's Theory of Practical Principles.* Athens: Cleisiounis Press.

Mifsud, Mari Lee. 1997. "The Rhetoric of Deliberation in Homer." Ph.D. diss., Pennsylvania State University.

Minar, Edwin L., Jr. 1939. "The Logos of Heraclitus." *Classical Philology* 34, no. 4: 323–41.

Mitchell, Stephen. 1988. *Tao Te Ching.* New York: HarperCollins.

Moravcsik, J. M. E. 1971. "Reason and Eros in the 'Ascent'-Passage of the *Symposium.*" In *Essays in Ancient Greek Philosophy,* edited by John P. Anton and Anthony Preus, 285–302. Albany: State University of New York Press.

———. 1983. "Heraclitean Concepts and Explanations." In *Language and Thought in Early Greek Philosophy,* edited by Kevin Robb, 134–52. LaSalle, Ill.: Monist Library of Philosophy.

Morgan, Kathryn. 2000. *Myth and Philosophy from the Presocratics to Plato.* Cambridge: Cambridge University Press.

———. 2004. "The Education of Athens: Politics and Rhetoric in Isocrates and Plato." In *Isocrates and Civic Education,* edited by Takis Poulakos and David Depew, 125–54. Austin: University of Texas Press.

Morrison, John S. 1961. "Antiphon." *Proceedings of the Cambridge Philological Society* n.s., 7: 49–58.

Mosshammer, Alden. 1981. "Thales's Eclipse." *Transactions of the American Philological Association* 111: 145–55.

Mourelatos, Alexander P. D. 1970. *The Route of Parmenides: A Study of Word, Image, and Argument in the Fragments.* New Haven, Conn.: Yale University Press.

———. 1973. "Heraclitus, Parmenides, and the Naïve Metaphysics of Things." In *Exegesis and Argument: Studies in Greek Philosophy Presented to Gregory Vlastos,* edited by E. N. Lee, A. P. D. Mourelatos, and R. Rorty, 16–48. Assen: Van Corcum.

———. 1976. "Determinacy and Indeterminacy, Being and Non-being in the Fragments of Parmenides." *Canadian Journal of Philosophy,* supplementary vol. 2: 45–60.

———. 1979. "Alternatives in Interpreting Parmenides." *Monist* 62, no. 2: 3–14.

Munn, Mark. 2000. *The School of History: Athens in the Age of Socrates.* Berkeley: University of California Press.

Mure, G. R. G. 1964. *Aristotle.* Oxford: Oxford University Press.

Murray, Gilbert. 1925. *Five Stages of Greek Religion.* New York: Columbia University Press.

Murray, James S. 1988. "Disputation, Deception, and Dialectic: Plato on the True Rhetoric (*Phaedrus* 261–266)." *Philosophy and Rhetoric* 21, no. 4: 279–89.

Natanson, Maurice. 1968. *Literature, Philosophy and the Social Sciences: Essays in Existentialism and Phenomenology.* The Hague: Martinus Nijhoff.

Navia, Luis E. 1993. *The Socratic Presence: A Study of the Sources.* New York: Garland.

Nehamas, Alexander. 1990. "Eristic, Antilogic, Sophistic, Dialectic: Plato's Demarcation of Philosophy from Sophistry." *History of Philosophy Quarterly* 7, no. 1: 3–16.

Neserius, Philip George. 1933. "Isocrates' Political and Social Ideas." *International Journal of Ethics* 43, no. 3: 307–28.

Neugebauer, O. 1951. *The Exact Sciences in Antiquity.* Princeton, N.J.: Princeton University Press.

Nicholson, Graeme. 1999. *Plato's* Phaedrus: *The Philosophy of Love.* West Lafayette, Ind.: Purdue University Press.

Norden, Hugo. 1964. "Proportions in Music." *Fibonacci Quarterly* 2, no. 3: 219–22.

Norlin, George. 1972. "That Old Man Eloquent." In *Integrity in Education and Other Papers*, 194–231. Freeport, N.Y.: Books for Libraries Press.

Nussbaum, Martha C. 1990. *Love's Knowledge: Essays on Philosophy and Literature.* New York & Oxford: Oxford University Press.

Ober, Josiah. 1989. *Mass and Elite in Democratic Athens: Rhetoric, Ideology, and the Power of the People.* Princeton, N.J.: Princeton University Press.

———. 1996. *The Athenian Revolution: Essays on Ancient Greek Democracy and Political Theory.* Princeton, N.J.: Princeton University Press.

———. 1998. *Political Dissent in Democratic Athens: Intellectual Critics of Popular Rule.* Princeton, N.J.: Princeton University Press.

Olson, Alan M., ed. 1980. *Myth, Symbol, and Reality.* Notre Dame, Ind.: University of Notre Dame Press.

Ong, Walter J., S. J. 1977. *Interfaces of the Word: Studies in the Evolution of Consciousness and Culture.* Ithaca, N.Y. & London: Cornell University Press.

———. 1982. *Orality and Literacy: The Technologizing of the Word.* London & New York: Methuen.

Overbye, Dennis. 1991. *Lonely Hearts of the Cosmos: The Story of the Scientific Quest for the Secret of the Universe.* New York: HarperCollins.

Owen, G. E. L. 1986. *Logic, Science, and Dialectic.* Ithaca, N.Y.: Cornell University Press.

———. 1993. "Plato and Parmenides on the Timeless Present." In *The Pre-Socratics*, edited by Alexander P. D. Mourelatos, 271–92. Princeton, N.J.: Princeton University Press.

Owens, Joseph. 1963. *The Doctrine of Being in the Aristotelian Metaphysics.* 2nd ed. Toronto: Pontifical Institute of Medieval Studies.

Patterson, Richard. 1985. *Image and Reality in Plato's Metaphysics.* Indianapolis: Hackett.

Patzig, Gunther. 1969. *Aristotle's Theory of the Syllogism.* Dordrecht: D. Reidel.

Perkins, Terry M. 1984. "Isocrates and Plato: Relativism and Idealism." *Southern Speech Journal* 50, no. 1: 49–66.

Philip, James A. 1966. *Pythagoras and Early Pythagoreanism.* Toronto: University of Toronto Press.

Plato. 1945. *The Republic of Plato.* Translated by Francis MacDonald Cornford. New York: Oxford University Press.

———. 1956. *Protagoras and Meno.* Translated by W. K. C. Guthrie. London & New York: Penguin.

———. 1961a. *Apology.* Translated by Hugh Tredennick. In *The Selected Dialogues of Plato*, edited by Edith Hamilton and Huntington Cairns, 3–26. New York: Pantheon Books.

———. 1961b. *Euthyphro.* Translated by Lane Cooper. In *The Selected Dialogues of Plato,* edited by Edith Hamilton and Huntington Cairns, 169–85. New York: Pantheon Books.

———. 1961c. *Gorgias.* Translated by W. D. Woodhead. In *The Selected Dialogues of Plato,* edited by Edith Hamilton and Huntington Cairns, 229–307. New York: Pantheon Books.

———. 1961d. *Greater Hippias (Hippias Major).* Translated by Benjamin Jowett. In *The Selected Dialogues of Plato,* edited by Edith Hamilton and Huntington Cairns, 1534–59. New York: Pantheon Books.

———. 1961e. *Laws.* Translated by A. E. Taylor. In *The Selected Dialogues of Plato,* edited by Edith Hamilton and Huntington Cairns, 1225–1513. New York: Pantheon Books.

———. 1961f. *Lysis.* Translated by J. Wright. In *The Selected Dialogues of Plato,* edited by Edith Hamilton and Huntington Cairns, 145–68. New York: Pantheon Books.

———. 1961g. *Meno.* Translated by W. K. C. Guthrie. In *The Selected Dialogues of Plato,* edited by Edith Hamilton and Huntington Cairns, 353–84. New York: Pantheon Books.

———. 1961h. *Phaedo.* Translated by Hugh Tredennick. In *The Selected Dialogues of Plato,* edited by Edith Hamilton and Huntington Cairns, 40–98. New York: Pantheon Books.

———. 1961i. *Phaedrus.* Translated by R. Hackforth. In *The Selected Dialogues of Plato,* edited by Edith Hamilton and Huntington Cairns, 475–525. New York: Pantheon Books.

———. 1961j. *Protagoras.* Translated by W. K. C. Guthrie. In *The Selected Dialogues of Plato,* edited by Edith Hamilton and Huntington Cairns, 308–52. New York: Pantheon Books.

———. 1961k. *Republic.* Translated by Paul Shorey. In *The Selected Dialogues of Plato,* edited by Edith Hamilton and Huntington Cairns, 575–844. New York: Pantheon Books.

———. 1961l. *Seventh Letter.* Translated by L. A. Post. In *The Selected Dialogues of Plato,* edited by Edith Hamilton and Huntington Cairns, 1574–98. New York: Pantheon Books.

———. 1961m. *Symposium.* Translated by Michael Joyce. In *The Selected Dialogues of Plato,* edited by Edith Hamilton and Huntington Cairns, 526–74. New York: Pantheon Books.

———. 1961n. *Theaetetus.* Translated by F. M. Cornford. In *The Selected Dialogues of Plato,* edited by Edith Hamilton and Huntington Cairns, 845–956. New York: Pantheon Books.

———. 1983. *Symposium.* Translated by W. R. M. Lamb. Cambridge, Mass.: Harvard University Press.

———. 1999. *Symposium.* Translated by Christopher Gill. London & New York: Penguin.

Plutarch. 1960. *The Rise and Fall of Athens: Nine Greek Lives.* Translated by Ian Scott-Kilvert. London: Penguin.

Pomeroy, Sarah B., Stanley M. Burstein, Walter Donlan, and Jennifer Tolbert Roberts.

1999. *Ancient Greece: A Political, Social, and Cultural History.* Oxford & New York: Oxford University Press.

Popkin, Richard H. 1964. *The History of Scepticism from Erasmus to Descartes.* Rev. ed. New York: Harper Torchbooks.

Popper, Sir Karl. 1970. "Back to the Presocratics." In *Studies in Presocratic Philosophy,* vol. 1, edited by David J. Furley and R. E. Allen, 130–53. London: Routledge & Kegan Paul. (First presented as the Presidential Address, Aristotelian Society, October 13, 1958).

Poster, Carol. 1996. "Being and Becoming: Rhetorical Ontology in Early Greek Thought." *Philosophy and Rhetoric* 29, no. 1: 1–14.

Poulakos, John. 1983a. "Gorgias' *Encomium of Helen* and the Defense of Rhetoric." *Rhetorica* 1, no. 2: 1–16.

———1983b. "Toward a Sophistic Definition of Rhetoric." *Philosophy and Rhetoric* 16, no. 1: 35–48.

———. 1984. "Rhetoric, the Sophists, and the Possible." *Communication Monographs* 51, no. 3: 215–26.

———. 1986. "Gorgias' and Isocrates' Use of the Encomium." *Southern Speech Communication Journal* 51, no. 4: 300–307.

———. 1990. "Interpreting Sophistical Rhetoric: A Response to Schiappa." *Philosophy and Rhetoric* 23, no. 3: 218–28.

———. 1993. "Terms for Sophistical Rhetoric." In *Rethinking the History of Rhetoric: Multidisciplinary Essays on the Rhetorical Tradition,* edited by Takis Poulakos, 53–74. Boulder, Colo.: Westview Press.

———. 1995. *Sophistical Rhetoric in Classical Greece.* Columbia: University of South Carolina Press.

———. 1997. "The Letter and the Spirit of the Text: Two Translations of Gorgias's *On Non-Being or On Nature.*" *Philosophy and Rhetoric* 30, no. 1: 41–44.

———. 2004. "Rhetoric and Civic Education: From the Sophists to Isocrates." In *Isocrates and Civic Education,* edited by Takis Poulakos and David Depew, 69–83. Austin: University of Texas Press.

Poulakos, Takis. 1989. "The Historical Intervention of Gorgias' *Epitaphios:* A Brief History of Classical Funeral Orations." *Pre/Text* 10, no. 1–2: 90–99.

———, ed. 1993. *Rethinking the History of Rhetoric: Multidisciplinary Essays on the Rhetorical Tradition.* Boulder, Colo.: Westview Press.

———. 1997. *Speaking for the Polis: Isocrates' Rhetorical Education.* Columbia: University of South Carolina Press.

———. 2004. "Isocrates' Civic Education and the Question of *Doxa.*" In *Isocrates and Civic Education,* edited by T. Poulakos and David Depew, 44–65. Austin: University of Texas Press.

Price, Anthony W. 1989. *Love and Friendship in Plato and Aristotle.* New York: Clarendon Press.

Proussis, Costas M. 1965. "The Orator: Isocrates." In *The Educated Man: Studies in the History of Educational Thought,* edited by Paul Nash, Andreas M. Kazamias, and Henry J. Perkinson, 55–76. Malabar, Fla.: Robert E. Krieger.

Putz, John F. 1995. "The Golden Section and the Piano Sonatas of Mozart." *Mathematics Magazine* 68: 275–82.

Quimby, R. W. 1974. "The Growth of Plato's Perception of Rhetoric." *Philosophy and Rhetoric* 7, no. 2: 71–79.

Ranasinghe, Nalin. 2000. *The Soul of Socrates.* Ithaca, N.Y.: Cornell University Press.

Randall, John H., Jr. 1970. *Plato, Dramatist of the Life of Reason.* New York: Columbia University Press.

Rankin, H. D. 1983. *Sophists, Socratics and Cynics.* Totowa, N.J.: Barnes & Noble.

Rapple, Brendan A. 1993. "The Early Greek Sophists: Creators of the Liberal Curriculum." *Journal of Thought* 28 (Fall/Winter): 61–76.

Raven, John E. 1948. *Pythagoreans and Eleatics.* Cambridge: Cambridge University Press.

———. 1965. *Plato's Thought in the Making.* Cambridge: Cambridge University Press.

Reale, Giovanni. 1980. *The Concept of First Philosophy and the Unity of Aristotle's Metaphysics.* Albany: State University of New York Press.

———. 1987. *A History of Greek Philosophy.* Vol. 1, *From the Origins to Socrates.* Albany: State University of New York Press.

Reinhardt, Karl. 1993. "The Relation between the Two Parts of Parmenides's Poem." In *The Pre-Socratics,* edited by Alexander P. D. Mourelatos, 293–311. Princeton, N.J.: Princeton University Press.

Rendall, Steven. 1977. "Dialogue, Philosophy, and Rhetoric: The Example of Plato's *Gorgias.*" *Philosophy and Rhetoric* 10, no. 3: 165–79.

Reyes, George Mitchell. 2000. "A Study of Discourse, Rhetoric, and Mathematics." M.A. thesis, Pennsylvania State University.

Ricoeur, Paul. 1977. *The Rule of Metaphor.* Toronto: University of Toronto Press.

Rist, J. M. 1965. "Some Aspects of Aristotelian Teleology." *Transactions of the American Philological Association* 96: 337–49.

Robb, Kevin. 1983. "Preliterate Ages and the Linguistic Art of Heraclitus." In *Language and Thought in Early Greek Philosophy,* edited by Kevin Robb, 153–206. LaSalle, Ill.: Monist Library of Philosophy.

———. 1994. *Literacy and Paideia in Ancient Greece.* New York: Oxford University Press.

Robinson, Thomas M. 1979. *Contrasting Arguments: An Edition of the Dissoi Logoi.* Salem, N.H.: Ayer.

———. 1987. *Heraclitus: Fragments.* Toronto: University of Toronto Press.

Rogers, Arthur Kenyon. 1933. *The Socratic Problem.* New Haven, Conn.: Yale University Press.

———. 1935. "Plato's Theory of Forms." *Philosophical Review* 44, no. 6: 515–33.

Roisman, Hanna M. 2007. "Right Rhetoric in Homer." In *A Companion to Greek Rhetoric,* edited by Ian Worthington, 429–46. Oxford: Blackwell.

Roochnik, David. 1996. *Of Art and Wisdom: Plato's Understanding of Techne.* University Park: Pennsylvania State University Press.

Rorty, Amelie Oksenberg. 1974. "The Place of Pleasure in Aristotle's Ethics." *Mind* 83, no. 332: 481–97.

———. 1978. "The Place of Contemplation in Aristotle's Nichomachean Ethics." *Mind* 87, no. 347: 343–58.

Rorty, Richard. 1984. "The Historiography of Philosophy: Four Genres." In *Philosophy in History: Essays on the Historiography of Philosophy*, edited by Richard Rorty, J. B. Schneewind, and Quentin Skinner, 49–89. Cambridge: Cambridge University Press.

Roseman, Norman. 1971. "Protagoras and the Foundations of His Educational Thought." *Paedagogica Historica* 11: 75–89.

Ross, William D. 1929. *Aristotle's Metaphysics*. Revised text with introduction and commentary. 2 vols. Oxford: Clarendon Press.

———. 1951. *Plato's Theory of Ideas*. Oxford: Oxford University Press.

———. 1995. *Aristotle*. 6th ed. London: Routledge.

Sacks, Richard. 1987. *The Traditional Phrase in Homer*. New York: Trustees of Columbia University.

Sagan, Carl. 1980. *Cosmos*. New York: Ballantine.

Saggs, H. W. F. 1989. *Civilization Before Greece and Rome*. New Haven, Conn.: Yale University Press.

Sallis, John. 1986. *Being and Logos: The Way of Platonic Dialogue*. 2nd ed. Atlantic Highlands, N. J.: Humanities Press International.

Santas, Gerasimos Xenophon. 1979. *Socrates: Philosophy in Plato's Early Dialogues*. London: Routledge & Kegan Paul.

———. 1980. "The Form of the Good in Plato's *Republic*." *Philosophical Inquiry* 2 (Winter): 374–403.

Sauvage, Micheline. 1960. *Socrates and the Human Conscience*. Translated by Patrick Hepburne-Scott. New York: Harper.

Schiappa, Edward. 1990a. "Did Plato Coin *Rhêtorikê?*" *American Journal of Philology* 111, no. 4: 457–70.

———. 1990b. "Neo-Sophistic Rhetorical Criticism or the Historical Reconstruction of Sophistic Doctrines?" *Philosophy and Rhetoric* 23, no. 3: 192–217.

———. 1992. "*Rhêtorikê*: What's in a Name? Toward a Revised History of Early Greek Rhetorical Theory." *Quarterly Journal of Speech* 78: 1–15.

———. 1995. "Gorgias's *Helen* Revisited." *Quarterly Journal of Speech* 81, no. 3: 310–24.

———. 1996. "Toward a Predisciplinary Analysis of Gorgias' *Helen*." In *Theory, Text, Context: Issues in Greek Rhetoric and Oratory*, edited by Christopher Lyle Johnstone, 65–86. Albany: State University of New York Press.

———. 1997. "Interpreting Gorgias's 'Being' in *On Not-Being or On Nature*." *Philosophy and Rhetoric* 30, no. 1: 13–30.

———. 1999. *The Beginnings of Rhetorical Theory in Classical Greece*. New Haven, Conn. & London: Yale University Press.

———. 2003. *Protagoras and Logos*. 2nd ed. Columbia: University of South Carolina Press.

Schipper, E. W. 1965. *Forms in Plato's Later Dialogues*. The Hague: M. Nijhoff.

Schwartz, Tony. 1974. *The Responsive Chord*. Garden City, N.Y.: Anchor Books.

Scoon, Robert. 1928. *Greek Philosophy Before Plato*. Princeton, N.J.: Princeton University Press.

Scott, Robert L. 1967. "On Viewing Rhetoric as Epistemic." *Central States Speech Journal* 18, no. 1: 9–16.

———. 1976. "On Viewing Rhetoric as Epistemic: Ten Years Later." *Central States Speech Journal* 27 (Winter): 258–66.

Sealey, Raphael. 1976. *A History of the Greek City States, ca. 700–338 B.C.* Berkeley: University of California Press.

Segal, Charles P. 1962. "Gorgias and the Psychology of the Logos." *Harvard Studies in Classical Philology* 66: 99–155.

———. 1984–85. "Literature and Interpretation: Conventions, History, and Universals." *Classical and Modern Literature* 5, no. 1: 71.

Sextus Empiricus. 1967. *Outlines of Pyrrhonism.* Vols. 1–3. Translated by R. G. Bury. Cambridge, Mass.: Harvard University Press.

Shepherdson, J. C. 1956. "On the Interpretation of Aristotelian Syllogistic." *Journal of Symbolic Logic* 21, no. 2: 137–47.

Sienkewicz, Thomas J. 1997. *Theories of Myth: An Annotated Bibliography.* Lanham, Md.: Scarecrow Press.

Simmons, George C. 1972. "Protagoras on Education and Society." *Paedagogica Historica* 12, no. 2: 518–37.

Sinaiko, Herman L. 1965. *Love, Knowledge, and Discourse in Plato.* Chicago: University of Chicago Press.

Slote, Michael A. 1970. *Reason and Scepticism.* London: Allen & Unwin.

Smith, Bromley. 1918. "The Father of Debate: Protagoras of Abdera." *Quarterly Journal of Speech Education* 4, no. 2: 196–215.

———. 1921. "Gorgias: A Study of Oratorical Style." *Quarterly Journal of Speech Education* 7, no. 4: 335–59.

———. 1927. "Thrasymachus: A Pioneer Rhetorician." *Quarterly Journal of Speech Education* 13, no. 3: 278–91.

Smith, Nicholas D., and Paul B. Woodruff, eds. 2000. *Reason and Religion in Socratic Philosophy.* Oxford: Oxford University Press.

Smith, Robin. 1995. "Logic." In *The Cambridge Companion to Aristotle,* edited by Jonathan Barnes, 27–65. Cambridge: Cambridge University Press.

Smolin, Lee. 1997. *The Life of the Cosmos.* New York: Oxford University Press.

Snell, Bruno. 1982. *The Discovery of the Mind in Greek Philosophy and Literature.* New York: Dover.

Solmsen, Friedrich. 1965. "Love and Strife in Empedocles's Cosmology." *Phronesis* 10, no. 2: 123–45.

———. 1975. *Intellectual Experiments of the Greek Enlightenment.* Princeton, N.J.: Princeton University Press.

———. 1983. "Plato and the Concept of the Soul (Psyche): Some Historical Perspectives." *Journal of the History of Ideas* 44, no. 3: 355–67.

Sprague, Rosamond Kent. 1972. *The Older Sophists.* Columbia: University of South Carolina Press.

Starr, Chester G. 1961. *The Origins of Greek Civilization, 1100–650 B.C.* New York: Knopf.

———. 1977. *The Economic and Social Growth of Early Greece, 800–500 B.C.* New York: Oxford University Press.

Stewart, John A. 1964. *Plato's Doctrine of Ideas.* New York: Russell & Russell.

Stewart, Robert S. 1989. "The Epistemological Function of Platonic Myth." *Philosophy and Rhetoric* 22, no. 4: 260–80.

Stone, I. F. 1989. *The Trial of Socrates*. New York: Anchor Books.

Strenski, Ivan. 1987. *Four Theories of Myth in Twentieth-Century History*. Iowa City: University of Iowa Press.

Sullivan, Dale L. 1992. "*Kairos* and the Rhetoric of Belief." *Quarterly Journal of Speech* 78, no. 3: 317–32.

Sutton, Christine. 1992. "Sunflower Spirals Obey Laws of Mathematics." *New Scientist* 134 (April): 16.

Sutton, Jane. 1993. "The Marginalization of Sophistical Rhetoric and the Loss of History." In *Rethinking the History of Rhetoric: Multidisciplinary Essays on the Rhetorical Tradition*, edited by Takis Poulakos, 75–90. Boulder, Colo.: Westview Press.

Svoboda, Michael G. 2002. "Plato and the Peloponnesian War." Ph.D. diss., Pennsylvania State University.

Sweet, Dennis. 1995. *Heraclitus: Translation and Analysis*. Lanham, Md.: University Press of America.

Taylor, A. E. 1911. *Varia Socratica, First Series*. Oxford: James Parker.

———. 1926. *Plato, the Man and His Work*. London: Methuen.

———. 1953. *Socrates: The Man and His Thought*. Garden City, N.Y.: Doubleday Anchor Books.

Taylor, C. C. W. 1983. "The Arguments in the *Phaedo* Concerning the Thesis That the Soul Is a *Harmonia*." In *Essays in Ancient Greek Philosophy*, vol. 2, edited by John P. Anton, 217–31. Albany: State University of New York Press.

Tejera, Victorino. 1984. *The City-State Foundations of Western Political Thought*. Lanham, Md.: University Press of America.

Thom, Paul. 1981. *The Syllogism*. Munich: Philosophia Verlag.

Thucydides. 1972. *History of the Peloponnesian War*. Translated by Rex Warner. London: Penguin.

Timmerman, David. 1998. "Isocrates' Competing Conceptualization of Philosophy." *Philosophy and Rhetoric* 31, no. 2: 145–59.

Toulmin, Stephen. 1982. *The Return to Cosmology: Postmodern Science and the Theology of Nature*. Berkeley: University of California Press.

Turnbull, Robert G. 1983. "*Episteme* and *Doxa*: Some Reflections on Eleatic and Heraclitean Themes in Plato." In *Essays in Ancient Greek Philosophy*, vol. 2, edited by John P. Anton, 279–300. Albany: State University of New York Press.

Untersteiner, Mario. 1954. *The Sophists*. Translated by K. Freeman. New York: Philosophical Library. Originally published as *I sophisti*. Torino: Einaudi, 1949.

Valiavitcharska, Vessela. 2006. "Correct *Logos* and Truth in Gorgias' *Encomium of Helen*." *Rhetorica* 24, no. 2: 147–61.

Verdenius, W. J. 1981. "Gorgias' Doctrine of Deception." In *The Sophists and Their Legacy*, edited by G. B. Kerferd, 116–28. Wiesbaden: Franz Steiner.

Verene, Donald P. 1981. *Vico's Science of Imagination*. Ithaca, N.Y.: Cornell University Press.

Vernant, Jean-Pierre. 1980. *Myth and Society in Ancient Greece*. New York: Zone Books.

———. 1982. *The Origins of Greek Thought*. Ithaca, N.Y.: Cornell University Press.

————. 1983. *Myth and Thought among the Greeks*. London: Routledge & Kegan Paul.

————. 1991. *Mortals and Immortals*. Princeton, N.J.: Princeton University Press.

Versenyi, Laszlo. 1962. "Protagoras' Man-Measure Fragment." *American Journal of Philology* 83, no. 2: 178–84.

————. 1963. *Socratic Humanism*. New Haven, Conn.: Yale University Press.

Veyne, Paul. 1971. *Writing History: Essay on Epistemology*. Translated by Mina Moore-Rinvolucri. Middletown, Conn.: Wesleyan University Press.

————. 1988. *Did the Greeks Believe in Their Myths? An Essay on the Constitutive Imagination*. Translated by Paula Wissing. Chicago: University of Chicago Press.

Vitanza, Victor J. 1991. "'Some More' Notes, toward a 'Third' Sophistic." *Argumentation* 5, no. 2: 117–39.

————. 1997. *Negation, Subjectivity, and the History of Rhetoric*. Albany: State University of New York Press.

Vivante, Paolo. 1970. *The Homeric Imagination: A Study of Homer's Poetic Perception of Reality*. Bloomington: Indiana University Press.

Vlastos, Gregory. 1950. "The Physical Theory of Anaxagoras." *Philosophical Review* 59, no. 1: 31–57.

————. 1970a. "Equality and Justice in Early Greek Cosmologies." In *Studies in Presocratic Philosophy*, vol 1, edited by David J. Furley and R. E. Allen, 56–91. London: Routledge & Kegan Paul.

————. 1970b. "On Heraclitus." In *Studies in Presocratic Philosophy*, vol. 1, edited by David J. Furley and R. E. Allen, 413–29. London: Routledge & Kegan Paul.

————. 1970c. "Theology and Philosophy in Early Greek Thought." In *Studies in Presocratic Philosophy*, vol. 1, edited by David J. Furley and R. E. Allen, 92–129. London: Routledge & Kegan Paul.

————, ed. 1980. *The Philosophy of Socrates: A Collection of Critical Essays*. Notre Dame, Ind.: University of Notre Dame Press.

————. 1985. "Socrates' Disavowal of Knowledge." *Philosophical Quarterly* 35, no. 138: 1–31.

————. 1991. *Socrates: Ironist and Moral Philosopher*. Ithaca, N.Y.: Cornell University Press.

————. 1994. *Socratic Studies*. Edited by Myles Burnyeat. Cambridge: Cambridge University Press.

von Fritz, Kurt. 1945; 1946. "*Nous, Noein*, and Their Derivatives in Pre-Socratic Philosophy." *Classical Philology* 40, no. 4: 223–42; 41, no. 1: 12–34.

Wagner, Russell H. 1922. "The Rhetorical Theory of Isocrates." *Quarterly Journal of Speech* 8, no. 3: 323–37.

Walker, Jeffrey. 2000. *Rhetoric and Poetics in Antiquity*. New York: Oxford University Press.

Walters, Frank D. 1994. "Gorgias as Philosopher of Being: Epistemic Foundationalism in Sophistic Thought." *Philosophy and Rhetoric* 27, no. 2: 143–55.

Warner, Martin. 1979. "Love, Self, and Plato's *Symposium*." *Philosophical Quarterly* 29, no. 117: 329–39.

Warren, Herbert Langford. 1919. *The Foundations of Classical Architecture*. New York: Macmillan.

Wheelwright, Philip. 1968. *Heraclitus.* New York: Atheneum Press.

White, Eric C. 1987. *Kaironomia: On the Will-to-Invent.* Ithaca, N.Y.: Cornell University Press.

White, Hayden V. 1966. "The Burden of History." *History and Theory* 5, no. 2: 111–34.

———. 1972–73. "Interpretation in History." *New Literary History* 4, no. 2: 281–314.

White, Nicholas P. 1976. *Plato on Knowledge and Reality.* Indianapolis: Hackett.

Wilcken, Ulrich. 1967. *Alexander the Great.* Translated by G. C. Richards. New York: W. W. Norton.

Wilkes, Kathleen V. 1978. "The Good Man and the Good for Man in Aristotle's Ethics." *Mind* 87, no. 348: 553–71.

Winspear, Alban D., and Tom Silverberg. 1960. *Who Was Socrates?* Rev. ed. New York: Russell & Russell.

Woodbridge, Frederick J. E. 1957. *The Son of Apollo: Themes of Plato.* Woodbridge, Conn.: Ox Bow Press.

Wright, M. R. 1981. *Empedocles: The Extant Fragments.* New Haven, Conn.: Yale University Press.

———. 1985. *The Presocratics.* Bristol: Bristol Classical Press.

Wycherley, Richard E. 1978. *The Stones of Athens.* Princeton, N.J.: Princeton University Press.

Xenophon. 1918, 1921. *Hellenica.* 2 vols. Translated by Carleton L. Brownson. Cambridge: Harvard University Press.

———. 1923a. *Apology.* Translated by O. J. Todd. Cambridge, Mass.: Harvard University Press.

———. 1923b. *Memorabilia.* Translated by E. C. Marchant. Cambridge, Mass.: Harvard University Press.

———. 1990. *Conversations with Socrates.* Translated by Hugh Tredennick and Robin Waterfield. Edited, with new material, by Robin Waterfield. London: Penguin.

Zielinski, Thaddeus. 1926. *The Religion of Ancient Greece.* Oxford: Oxford University Press.

Zimmern, Alfred. 1931. *Greek Commonwealth: Politics and Economics in Fifth-Century Athens.* 5th ed. Oxford: Oxford University Press

Index

Socrates, 121–24, 254n69, 254nn70–72, 255n76, 255nn80–81, 257n91; and *aretê*, 134–35; and Aristophanes, 125; and Aristotle, 125; early years, 127; and *elenchos*, 137–39, 145; and ignorance, 128–29, 255–56n83; and induction, 140–141; and *logos*, 130, 142; and Plato, 86, 124–25, 127–42; and reasoning by analogy, 141–42; and Socratic method, 120; and Socratic wisdom / *sophia*, 121–42, 144–45, 256–57n90; and soul, 135–36; and Xenophon, 125, 135, 256n89

Socratic wisdom. *See* Socrates

Solon, 89–90, 92, 244n9, 260n15

sophia, 29–30; and Aristotle, 193–97, 201, 205–7; and Democritus, 78; and Gorgias, 114–18; and Heraclitus, 54–55, 59, 61, 84; and Isocrates, 155–61; and mythopoetic worldview, 30–35, 53, 230n35; and naturalistic worldview, 82–84; and Parmenides, 69; and Plato, 161, 164–85; and Protagoras, 93, 97–99; and Pythagoras, 64–65; and Socrates, 121–42, 144–45, 256–57n90; and Sophists, 91–121

Sophists, 87, 91–94, 244n7, 244–45n10, 250n41; 251n52; context of, 87–91; and eristic, 115–16, 120; and *kairos*, 116; and *logos*, 92–93, 114–18, 144–45, 252n55; and Sophistical wisdom / *sophia*, 91–121; and teaching, 118–21; and *to prepon*, 117. *See also* Antiphon; Gorgias; Mnesiphilus; Prodicus; Protagoras; Socrates; Thrasymachus

Sophistical Refutations (Aristotle), 116, 208, 250n40

Sophistical wisdom. *See* Sophists

sophos, 14, 29, 92, 97, 244n9

sôphrosynê, 93, 134

speculative wisdom, 193, 196–97, 201, 205–7

stoicheion, 42, 47

Stone, I. F., 126, 255–56n83

Strabo, 191

Strife, 69–71, 241n75

Suda (Kirk, Raven, and Schofield, trans.), 94, 245n13, 251n48

Symposium (Plato), 130, 141–42, 166, 171, 173, 182–83, 262n36

Symposium (Xenophon), 125

Tao Te Ching (Mitchell), 48

Taylor, A. E., 124, 126

terpsis, 27, 109, 222

Tetralogies (Antiphon), 111, 116

Thales, 38–39, 42–46; 231n6, 232n14, 232–33n16; and Anaximander, 47–48

Theaetetus (Plato), 100, 136–37, 166, 181

Themistocles, 92–93

Theophrastus, 47, 190, 233n24, 234n27, 264–65n6

Theogony (Hesiod), 11, 13, 21–22, 27, 186, 228nn15–16

theos, 7, 37, 44–45, 174, 203–4, 230n34, 235n33, 266n20

Thirty Tyrants, 150, 254n69, 258–59n5

Thrasymachus, 93, 119, 131, and Plato, 133, 244–45n10, 245n13

"three theses" (Gorgias). *See* Gorgias

Thucydides, 148–49, 258n1, 258n4

To Demonicus (Isocrates), 160

To Nicocles (Isocrates), 157

to prepon, 116–17, 159–60, 253n60

to theion, 5, 45, 50, 70, 203, 235n32

Topics (Aristotle), 208

Toulmin, Stephen, 7

Tufts, James, 157

Untersteiner, Mario, 98, 246n18, 247n24, 248n31, 248n34

Vernant, Jean-Pierre, 26–28, 38–42, 229n29, 232n9

Vlastos, Gregory, 45, 49, 137, 139, 255–56n83

Wagner, Russell H., 155, 260n14

Walker, Jeffrey, 14, 26–27

Waterfield, Robin, 125–26, 256n89

wisdom. *See* civic wisdom; practical wisdom; *sophia;* speculative wisdom

Works and Days (Hesiod), 11, 21–22, 186

writing: invention of, 26–27, 37, 39–40, 226n13, 232n9; and Plato, 263n41

Xenophanes, 51–52, 72–73, 235n33

Xenophon, 34, 92, 94–95, 122, 125, 135, 255n79, 257n92

Zeus, 20–23, 29–31, 40–41, 50, 52, 95, 230–31n37; oracle of Zeus at Dodona, 230n33